Art's Undoing

Art's Undoing

In the Wake of a Radical Aestheticism

Forest Pyle

FORDHAM UNIVERSITY PRESS

NEW YORK 2014

Library of Congress Cataloging-in-Publication Data

Pyle, Forest, 1958–
    Art's undoing : in the wake of a radical aestheticism / Forest
    Pyle. — First edition.
        pages cm
    Includes bibliographical references and index.
    ISBN 978-0-8232-5111-7 (cloth : alk. paper) — ISBN 978-0-8232-
5112-4 (pbk. : alk. paper)   1. English literature—19th century—
History and criticism.   2. Aestheticism (Literature)   3. Art and
literature—Great Britain—History—19th century.   I. Title.
PR468.A33P95 2014
820.9′357—dc23   2013015249

Printed in the United States of America
16 15 14   5 4 3 2 1
First edition

To Susan, to Jack, to Kiko
from whom I learn that
"Love alone should one consider"

List of Illustrations　　　　　　　　　　　　　　　　　　　　　　　　ix

Preface　　　　　　　　　　　　　　　　　　　　　　　　　　　　　xi

Introduction: "From Which One Turns Away"　　　　　　　　　　1

Aestheticism and Its Radicality, 1　|　The Insistence of
the Aesthetic, 6　|　"Our Romantic Movement," 11
|　Scene of Shipwreck, 21

1.　"A Light More Dread Than Obscurity": Spelling and Kindling
　　in Percy Bysshe Shelley　　　　　　　　　　　　　　　　　29

"Frail Spells," 29　|　"Wholly Political," 35　|　Kindling
and Ash, 47　|　"A Shape All Light," 57

2.　"I Hold It Towards You": Keats's Weakness　　　　　　　　67

"Consumed in the Fire," 67　|　Weakness, 70　|　Threats, 81
|　"On He Flared," 92

3.　What the Zeros Taught: Emily Dickinson, Event-Machine　　105

"The Plunge from the Front," 105　|　"A Word Dropped":
The Dickinsonian Event-Machine, 111　|　"A System of
Aesthetics," 123　|　"Bright Impossibility," 132

4.　Hopkins's Sighs　　　　　　　　　　　　　　　　　　　145

"Let Him Oh! With His Air of Angels Then Lift Me, Lay Me!" 145
|　Hopkins's Breathturns, 149　|　"The Fire of Stress," 158
|　"The Fire That Breaks," 165

5. Superficiality: What Is Loving and What Is Dead in Dante
   Gabriel Rossetti   171

   On the Surface . . ., 171 | "One Face Looks Out," 176
   | "A Blunder of Taste"; or, What Would Clement Greenberg
   Say? 181 | "Love Is Addressed to the Semblance"; or, What
   Would Jacques Lacan Say? 187 | The Promises of Glass, 192

6. "Rings, Pearls, and All": Wilde's Extravagance   209

   The Soul of Man Under Aestheticism, 209 | Christ the
   Romantic, Christ the Dandy, 215 | The Cost of a Kiss, 223
   | Covered with Jewels, 241

Notes   245

Index   303

ILLUSTRATIONS

Géricault, *The Raft of the Medusa*   *facing page* 1
Cornell, *Toward the Blue Peninsula (for Emily Dickinson)*   27
Leonardo da Vinci (attributed), *The Medusa*   28
Joseph Severn, *Keats on His Deathbed*   66
Caravaggio, *David with the Head of Goliath*   103
Dickinson, Fascicle 32, "Like Eyes that looked on Wastes"   104
Dickinson, "Like Eyes that looked on Wastes" (detail)   143
Hopkins, Journal page, June 30   144
Rossetti, *Giotto Painting Dante*   170
Rossetti, *The Beloved*   207
Moreau, "Salomé dansant"   208

It is fitting that this book begins with Shelley, because it originated with Shelley. More precisely, my understanding of "art's undoing" arose from my repeated efforts to understand what was happening in certain crucial moments of Shelley's *The Triumph of Life*. More precisely still, this project began from what I felt to be the shortcomings of my previous book's attempt to come to terms with what happens when Shelley's last poem addresses the relationship between aesthetic and political judgment. Despite my attempts to use the most supple and nuanced notions of ideology at my disposal, I felt that *The Ideology of Imagination* came up short when trying to reckon with the poetics of aestheticization in *The Triumph*. That undoing led to *Art's Undoing*. By this title I mean to identify the capacity of certain literary representations of art and the aesthetic experiences they elicit to undo the projects (political, ethical, theological, and so on) to which they have been enlisted. For example, the poetic representation of art and aesthetics is often understood by Shelley as the "Power" that "wouldst free / This world from its dark slavery"; and yet at certain moments in certain texts—as in *The Triumph of Life*—the figuration of this same artistic "Power" *undoes* the prospect or "hope" of political liberation. At the same time, the affirmative values and humanizing roles traditionally assigned to art itself are also undone in this process: powerful though they are, the aesthetic experiences elicited in these examples get us nowhere. These instances of art's double or compound undoing are the results of what I call a "radical aestheticism." I am not using the term "radical" to mean something culturally advanced or politically avant-garde, though it is no coincidence that this derivation of "radical" begins to circulate in the period this book addresses. Instead, I am interested in how the literary representations of aestheticization can in certain circumstances result in an aestheticism powerful and extreme enough to deliver us to the roots of the aesthetic, its constitutive elements reduced to ashes or to sighs.

As for the images that accompany the beginning of chapters and, on occasion, their conclusions, sometimes I have chosen an image because it prompts one of the texts I am engaging. This is the case with my opening chapter's use of the painting of the "Medusa," long attributed to Leonardo da Vinci, about which Shelley wrote an ekphrastic poem after visiting the Uffizi. In other instances, these prefatory images function as illustrations and even provocations of the relationships between literary and visual art that the chapters address. For example, Dickinson's manuscript page becomes the visual evidence for the commitment to a poesis of an only imaginary ekphrasis. By contrast, Dante Gabriel Rossetti's poems are so saturated by the ekphrastic impulse that his paintings and poems become a strange Möbius strip of the chiasmic relationship between the two forms of art: the Pre-Raphaelite poet and painter Dante Gabriel Rossetti paints a picture of the "pre-Raphaelite" artist Giotto painting a picture of the poet Dante. I have chosen Moreau's watercolor version of "The Apparition" for the book's cover in part because of its depiction of Salomé and, by way of Huysmans's account of the painting in *À rebours*, its associations with Wilde's aestheticism. But I have also chosen this image because I think it is a painting that powerfully conveys the strange miraculating but undoing capacity of art that I am exploring throughout this book. Huysmans believed Moreau was representing a vision *after* the beheading had been performed; but the picture has always struck me as an astonishing compression of the biblical narrative into a lyric image of the fiat of art's glittering, if terrifying, "apparitions." With the disengaged Herod reduced to an oblique sculpted background, Salomé is no longer dancing for anyone; and, now artist herself, she points at the suspended head of John the Baptist within a luminous and radiating, if bloody aureole. In this version of Moreau's painterly obsession with Salomé, the princess conjures the Saint's head into appearance and, in the process, offers us a vision of art as beheading, as an act of severing that offers nothing in return but this glorious image.

Art's Undoing was a long time getting done, and I am grateful for the engagement, support, and provocation of many of my present and former colleagues: Lara Bovilsky, Ken Calhoon, Mai-Lin Cheng, Ian Duncan, Lisa Freinkel, Warren Ginsburg, Jeff Librett, Enrique Lima, John Lysacker, Dawn Marlan, John McCole, Randy McGowen, Alex Neel, Paul Peppis, Mark Quigley, Dan Rosenberg, Bill Rossi, George Rowe, Steve Shankman, and Irving Wohlfarth. I also want to acknowledge three colleagues whose contributions to my project—as readers, responders, mentors, cajolers—have been indispensible: without Karen Ford, Dick Stein, and Harry Wonham, I cannot imagine what—or when—this project would have been; and I am profoundly grateful to them that I don't have to imagine that any longer.

One of the real pleasures of the protracted gestation of this book has been its extensive and productive vetting in undergraduate classrooms as well as graduate seminars. Many of those moments are collective experiences, shared events in the development of an idea or the cultivation of a reading. I want to acknowledge a number of my present and former students for their invaluable contributions to this rewarding and exacting pedagogical engagement, the richly collaborative flip-side of the more solitary undertaking of scholarship: Bradley Butterfield, Anna Carroll, Erin Connor, Katherine Cook, Amanda Cornwall, Evan Dresman, Chris Hitt, Russell Durvenoy, Craig Franson, Jen Hammond, Alex Hunt, Kate Jenckes, Alison Lau, Jacob Leveton, Chet Liseicki, Mita Mahato, Mark Merrit, John Motley, Julia Mullen (who also worked to help me obtain permissions for the book's images), Kaila Fromdahl Nichols, Amy Novak, Virginia Piper, Stephanie Rowe, David Sandner, and Karen Shaup. And in the long course of this project there have been a few students whose thinking and engagement—whether by an elective affinity or the lucky alignment of stars—became a teaching all its own: I have learned so much from Ryan Dirks, Alastair Hunt, and Max Novick in the two-way street of intellectual exchange that the roles of student and teacher no longer apply.

The long and mostly solitary mode of composition of this book has been punctuated by sometimes brief and partial, but often decisive engagements with many members of the profession, whether as editors, readers, interlocutors, respondents, or inspirations. I'd like to acknowledge Marshall Brown, David Clark, Libby Fay, Neil Fraistat, Mike Goode, Jerry Hogle, Colin Jaeger, Jennifer Jones, Charles Mahoney, Mona Modiano, Jonathan Mulrooney, Thomas Pfau, Fred Pfeil, Marc Redfield, Dermot Ryan, Steve Shaviro, Michael Sprinker, Karen Swann, Mick Taussig, Rei Terada, David Wagenknecht, Orrin Wang, and Deborah Elise White. I doubt that my most influential teachers will recognize in what follows the form or content of their teaching; but this project is unthinkable without the intellectual examples and instruction of Ramon Saldìvar, Charles Sherry, and—above all—Gayatri Spivak.

I'd like to acknowledge another category of professional debt that spills over into something much more, something on the order of a deep intellectual friendship. The forms it takes are too various to enumerate here; but the support, engagement, and encouragement of Michael Clark, Sara Guyer, and Jacques Khalip have been indispensable. Ian Balfour and Anne-Lise Francois also belong in this category, not only because they read the manuscript for Fordham, but because their deeply insightful and beautifully written responses are the stuff of dreams. And, once again, I feel honored and privileged to call Helen Tartar my editor.

Pretty much everything I know about theatrical performance in general, and certainly everything I know about playing Salomé, I learned from Susan Tate. Beyond that, I wish I could say that my family helped me write this book; but in fact I hold Susan, Jack, and Kiko partially responsible for the length of time it took me to finish the project—which, in the end, at least as I see it, has been all to the good. One of the implicit arguments of the book revolves around the question of value, specifically the value of aesthetic experience and the value of the works of art that give rise to that experience. If my family did little to teach me about the worth of any poem's representation of art and aesthetics, they have taught me everything I know and feel about the meaning of value.

Early versions of some portions of the book were presented at annual meetings of the Marxist Literary Group's Institute for Culture and Society, the International Association for Philosophy and Literature, the Modern Language Association, and most often at the North American Society for the Study of Romanticism. And I am grateful for the invitations to present portions of this book as lectures at the University of Toronto, the University of Wisconsin, the University of Maryland, Willamette University, and Portland State University.

An earlier version of part 1 of the Introduction appeared in "Kindling and Ash: Radical Aestheticism in Keats and Shelley," *Studies in Romanticism* (Winter 2003): 427–59.

Portions of earlier versions of Chapter 1 appeared in "Kindling and Ash: Radical Aestheticism in Keats and Shelley," "'Frail Spells': Shelley and the Ironies of Exile," *Romantic Praxis*, special issue: "Irony and Clerisy" (Spring 1999): 1–17 (reprinted in *Shelley's Poetry and Prose*, ed. Donald Reiman and Neil Fraistat [New York: Norton, 2001], 663–69), and "Letter on an Aestheticist Education," *Romantic Praxis*, special issue: "The Sublime and Education" (Fall 2010): 1–25.

Earlier versions of parts 1 and 4 of Chapter 2 appeared in "Kindling and Ash: Radical Aestheticism in Keats and Shelley."

A much earlier version of part 3 of Chapter 6 appeared as "Extravagance; or, Salomé's Kiss," *The Journal of Pre-Raphaelite Studies* 7 (1998): 39–52.

Art's Undoing

Géricault, *The Raft of the Medusa* (© RMN–Grand Palais/Art Resource, NY)

Introduction: "From Which One Turns Away"

Aestheticism and Its Radicality

This book is about something I am calling a radical aestheticism, the term that I believe best describes a recurring event in some of the most powerful and resonating texts of the British Romantic literary tradition. A radical aestheticism offers us the best way to reckon with what takes place at certain moments in certain texts by P. B. Shelley, Keats, Dickinson, Hopkins, D. G. Rossetti, and Wilde when aestheticized representations reach their radicalization. I will go on to argue that this aesthetic radicalization, however isolated or rare, has profound consequences, not only for the specific texts in which it occurs, but for our understanding of the ambitious literary project undertaken by each of these writers and, finally, of our conception of the legacy of Romanticism.

We associate the term "aestheticism" with those nineteenth-century movements in England and in France that celebrated or promoted what Pater called "the love of art for art's sake," or what Cousin called *"l'art pour l'art."* The philosophical inspiration for this movement is often attributed to Schil-

ler or to Schelling; but it is invariably if unjustly Kant who offers the philosophical authorization. There is certainly no inherent reason that the *critique*
of a certain form of judgment—one that judges something made available to
the senses without the stability or ground of a law or concept—should result
in the *celebration* of the judgment or the sensation. And yet, in Marc Redfield's
elegant formulation, "through a sleight of hand that has always threatened to
make aesthetics as suspect as it is seductive, aesthetic judgment claims simultaneously to produce and to discover the essential harmony of the perceiv-
ing mind and the perceived world, sensation and idea, phenomenality and
cognition."[1] This "sleight of hand," this surreptitious metalepsis, this "sub-
reption" is not only *constitutive* of the aesthetic, but a boundless resource for
aestheticism. Moreover, it is certainly impossible to imagine the claims and
goals of any aestheticist tradition without the *Third Critique*'s delineations
of the specificities of an aesthetic judgment and its founding claim that "the
judgment of taste is not a cognitive judgment (either theoretical or practi-
cal)" and that the "satisfaction" derived from a judgment of beauty "is alone a
disinterested and *free* satisfaction; for no interest, either of sense or of reason,
here forces our assent."[2] And while the Kantian legacy of artistic autonomy
has been mobilized for any number of arguments and causes, from the most
conservative humanism to the most radical Marxism, it has never been invoked with more extravagance than by nineteenth-century aestheticism.

Throughout this book I will have occasion to examine in detail some of
the relevant and intricate relationships among eighteenth- and nineteenth-
century philosophical aesthetics, the various strains of nineteenth-century
aestheticism, and twentieth-century critical theory. These relationships have
been the topic of a rich and contentious critical literature, to which I will
turn both as resource and as object of study. But there remains one feature
of this relationship that, though obvious enough, tends to pass without commentary. I believe that without any exception of which I am aware, aestheticism is presented by its principal proponents—in the specific tradition I am
considering, Pater and Wilde—as something to be *espoused*. The forms of this
espousal are immediately recognizable and, given the considerable rhetorical
resources of its purveyors, remarkably limited. "Love art for its own sake,"
Wilde declares in his first New York lecture, "and then all things you need
will be added to you."[3] Thus is Kant's painstaking critical analysis of the nature of an aesthetic judgment transformed by way of a claim for the autonomy
of art into an extravagant creed, a dandy's refrain. Indeed, the tone and tenor
of Wilde's lecture makes the extent of aestheticism's ambitions clear: whether

as a collective mission or a personal disposition, aestheticism is offered as an *ethos*, one that can be professed, learned, cultivated, and lived.

What I am calling a *radical* aestheticism is not that which Pater or Wilde espoused. Nor is it the aestheticism that is often—and, I believe, mistakenly—attributed to the chiasmic intertwining of truth and beauty in Keats's "Ode on a Grecian Urn." Nor is it the *politically* radical declaration of a poetic "legislation" with which Shelley concludes his ambitious *Defense of Poetry*. We will examine the extent to which the poems of both Keats and Shelley consistently reflect upon—praise, mourn, describe, conjure, parry—aesthetic experience; but neither poet commits his project to a radical aestheticism. While there are many poetic images and prose statements in both Dickinson and Hopkins that demonstrate how deeply the problem of the aesthetic permeates their poetry and poetics, no responsible critic would suggest that either of these poets is undertaking an aestheticism, radical or otherwise. The examples of Rossetti and Wilde are at once more straightforward and more complicated. When Wilde celebrates the work of Rossetti and the Pre-Raphaelite Brotherhood in his New York lecture, for example, he does so on the basis of an aestheticism that Rossetti would not only resist, but treat as an incriminating "charge." In the case of Wilde, of course, aestheticism is explicitly identified as the foundation and the goal of his artistic undertaking. But, as we shall see in Chapter 6, the effect of this identification is a curious one: far from dispelling the crisis posed by the radicalization of that aestheticism, it only brings the crisis closer to home.

There are, as I see it, a number of conditions that must be met before a text can be said to arrive at what I am calling a radical aestheticism. In the first instance the text must *reflect* on art and its effects, either literature itself or its "sister arts" of music and painting or the relationships between them. Or, as is the case in many of the examples we will consider, the text aestheticizes the object of its reflection, makes it into a work of art (even if it isn't). Thus the prominence of ekphrasis in the tradition I will be considering; and thus the many poetic reflections on music and measure. Taking the aesthetic as its subject matter, the text must pose or present questions about art's relationship to history or to knowledge, and on the relationship between art's sensuous aspects and its ethical, political, or theological responsibilities. Of course, such questions do not of themselves constitute an aestheticism: one need only to think of "Ozymandias" to demonstrate that poetic reflection on art can produce unrelenting critical and demystifying effects. But such a poetic reflection on the workings and effects of the aesthetic is a necessary condition for a genuinely radical aestheticism. In the broadest sense an aestheticism can be attributed to a text when the *performance* of its aesthetic reflection (which is necessarily a self-reflection) effectively severs the relationships (whether analogous, homologous, preparatory, supplementary, or complementary) between art and knowledge by subsuming the latter into the former. And finally, a text can be understood as *succumbing* to a *radical* aestheticism the moment it finds itself and its representations of the aesthetic at its vacating radical. Paradoxically, this is also the moment that the text registers—and we might even say *experiences*—"aestheticization" as the undoing of any claim to an aesthetic autonomy or self-reflexive totality. What I am describing as the radical aestheticism encountered in these writers is that which in the course of its very extremity takes us to the constitutive elements—the figures, the images, semblances—that are at the root of any aestheticism, an encounter registered as undoing, as evaporation, as combustion.[4]

A *radical aestheticism* offers no positive claims for art (either those based on ethical or political grounds or on aesthetic grounds, as in "art for art's sake"): it provides no "transcendent or underlying ground" for their validation. In this sense a radical aestheticism is the experience of a *poesis* that exerts such a pressure on the claims and workings of the aesthetic that it becomes (or reveals itself to be) a kind of black hole from which no illumination is possible.[5] The analogy of the black hole is relevant in another sense: like the black hole that bends and warps any body that enters into its dark gravitational pull, the sites of a radical aestheticism in these texts absorb all the elements of the text into its sphere and, consequently, engulfs the trajectory of the text's "desires." But the analogy of the black hole only serves us so far. In a sense it is what a radical aestheticism looks like from the outside, how it appears from the perspective of a text's or an author's "project," from the perspective of its ethical charge in Keats, its political ambitions in Shelley, or its theological mission in Hopkins. On its "inside," a radical aestheticism does not appear as a black hole of imagelessness, but, in Shelley's version, as "a shape all light" or "a light more dread than obscurity," light without illumination, a preponderance of untethered images, the concatenations of figures so "overwrought" that there no longer appears to be any "outside" and nothing "real" or reliable on the inside.

Each of these authors represents this experience of radical aestheticism and the crisis it manifests in forms and figures that are specific to his or her poetic idiom. In Shelley, for instance, radical aestheticism is registered as something on the order of self-immolation, as when the very "kindling" that serves as a figure for poetic agency results in a fire that leaves as its residue nothing but ashes and a light that is to be feared "more than obscurity." In Hopkins it transpires through the poetic oscillations between inspiration and aspiration. But in each case a *radical* aestheticism delivers us not to an autonomous domain of pure sensuous perception, but to the effects of an interference—what Keats calls a "barren noise"—that voids all that we habitually claim in the name of the aesthetic. To say that it delivers us to its radical is thus much like saying that we are given over to the ashes that are the constitutive mineral matter of the burnt substance and to the remains of an event that has erased itself. Thus, to the extent that we follow those Victorian aesthetes who in one form or another attribute the birth of aestheticism to the poems of Keats, this birth bears with it a simultaneous radicalization of its issue in the ashes of its kindling. If a radical aestheticism undoes the crucial role of the aesthetic necessary for the full flowering of the literary project envisioned by these authors, it also fails to get us *outside* aesthetics. And I should stress at the outset that my own attempt to engage the radical aestheticism of these texts offers none of the "reassuring" knowledge Bourdieu promises with his sociology of the aesthetic. The most we may be able to say is that a radical aestheticism might leave us with what Celan would call the *singbarer Rest*, the "singable residue." At certain moments in certain texts by each of these writers we encounter a radical aestheticism, one that undoes the claims made in the name of the aesthetic—as redemptive, restorative, liberating, compensatory, humanizing, healing—claims that are not only an irreducible aspect of the legacy of Romanticism, but are often spelled out in their most compelling forms by the writers themselves.

By asserting that certain of these texts produce at certain moments a radical aestheticism, I am not suggesting that they are radical works of art, which would be a judgment of a rather different order, one that would entail considerations of literary history, social history, and the dialectical relationship between the two. By saying that they arrive at a radical *aestheticism*, I am arguing that these texts produce a radical engagement with the very processes by which we conceive of the aesthetic, those processes by which the world is not merely known, but felt—and felt as an effect of representation. A radical aestheticism returns us to the aporias between perception and sensation, on the one hand, and cognition and conceptualization, on the other; and it forces us to behold the insuperable nature of these aporias, the aporias out of which the aesthetic as a "domain" is constituted in the first place.

The Insistence of the Aesthetic

For Paul de Man, the conventional strain of aestheticism that culminates with Wilde finds its origins in Schiller's fundamental misreading and misappropriation of Kant: "the idealism of Schiller contrasts with the transcendental-critical language of Kant. Schiller," asserts de Man bluntly, "appears as the ideology of Kant's critical philosophy."[6] One structural as well as symptomatic version of this misreading arises from the difficulty that Kant encounters and acknowledges in the *Third Critique* regarding the role of figuration—what he calls *hypotyposis*—or, as de Man puts it, "the difficulty of rendering, by means of sensory elements, purely intellectual concepts": "hypotyposis for Kant is certainly a problem for understanding, and a very difficult problem that again threatens philosophical discourse; whereas . . . it is offered by Schiller as a solution" and, ultimately, as "the aim of an ideological desire" (*Aesthetic Ideology*, 153, 147).[7] Perhaps the most straightforward expression of the transformation and transvaluation of the *critique of aesthetics* into an *aesthetic solution* is Schiller's second letter on *Aesthetic Education*: "If man is ever to solve the problem of politics in practice he will have to approach it through the problem of the aesthetic, because it is only through Beauty that man makes his way to Freedom."[8]

It is certainly the case in the British tradition with which I am concerned that those who espouse aestheticism make the claim that art offers the solution to the many ethical, epistemological, and political problems generated by aesthetic judgment in the first place: "Love art for its own sake and then, etcetera, etcetera." At the same time—and this basic observation is fundamental to the book's argument—if the aesthetic can be imagined, projected, incorporated as a "bridge" or vehicle or medium toward something else—political liberation, erotic love, ethical regard, God's grace—*aestheticism* always poses the risk of disrupting that articulation or foreclosing that trajectory. And thus an espousal of aestheticism cannot be "radical" in the mode I am proposing unless it creates a crisis not only for the espouser, but for the very act of espousing.

These days nothing is less likely to be espoused by critics or artists than an aestheticism of any sort. In fact, if there is one thing in the fractured field of what used to be called literary studies that a conservative humanist, a critical Marxist, a rhetorically oriented deconstructive critic, a Levinasian ethicist, and a practitioner of cultural studies can actually agree on, it is likely to be a *rejection* of aestheticism. It is certainly ironic—perhaps even symptomatically so—that the major critical currents of late twentieth- and early twenty-first century literary and critical theory can find agreement in an *aversion* to aestheticism, even as they often ascribe an aestheticism to their various opponents. Critical approaches as divergent and even as irreconcilable as structuralist poetics and hermeneutics, feminism and the New Criticism, ethico-poetics and the New Historicism can all be said to share this aversion. Each of these fundamentally disparate critical orientations would be likely to endorse the Swiss theologian Emil Brunner's characterization of aestheticism as "being satisfied with the freedom of an illusion": it adopts the "attitude of a spectator," flees "responsible decision," and destroys "that community which is based on responsibility."[9] Conservative critics continue to oppose aestheticism on the basis of many of the same moral objections raised against it at the end of the nineteenth century. To the critics on what might best be described as the "institutional left"—a critical orientation deeply influenced by Pierre Bourdieu's sociology of "the rules of art" within "the field of cultural production"—aestheticism appears as the thoroughly mystified celebration of the logic of aesthetic autonomization.[10] Nothing could be more antithetical to Emmanuel Levinas's philosophy of ethical regard than an espousal of art for its own sake.[11] Hans Urs von Balthasar's magisterial work of Christian aesthetics may have renewed theological interest in the insistence of the aesthetic, but its dismissal of *aestheticism* is as definitive as it is orthodox.[12] For Alain Badiou, whose undertaking to return "philosophy to itself" is as ambitious as it is provocative, the romanticism from which contemporary thought has yet to be delivered is simply a displaced name for "aesthetic religion."[13]

If my account of a radical aestheticism does not take its cue from Badiou or von Balthasar or Levinas or Bourdieu, it is not because I am invested in what the latter decries in *The Rules of Art* as "the angelic belief in a pure interest in pure form," but because I believe that none of these otherwise vital critical projects opens a reckoning with the radical aestheticism at work in the texts I am examining. A radical aestheticism is not the "aestheticism unbound" that John Guillory famously proposed as a solution to our critical dilemmas.[14] Rather, I believe that by engaging fully the trajectory of an immersion in the aesthetic—at the far end of reading—we might encounter the scene and the effects of aesthetic radicalization. This results in a crisis from which we may turn away, but that may well have significant repercussions for the conceptions of culture and the aesthetic that remain the legacy of Romanticism.

I owe my deepest methodological debts to the practices of interpretation and rhetorical analysis designated by the rubrics of Marxism and deconstruction, because I believe that in their most advanced or refined versions these critical projects deliver us to the constitutive elements of the literary text and to the aporias of the aesthetic. Nevertheless, neither tradition can exactly be called a friend to aestheticism. From the perspective of a Marxist critical theory, in which Theodor Adorno's *Aesthetic Theory* stands as an unsurpassed achievement, as magisterial as it is austere, aestheticism is understood dialectically as a critique of the commodification of culture and, simultaneously, as the withdrawal into a reified and ultimately fetishistic conception of an autonomous and pseudo-sacred art. If, on the one hand, Adorno believes that the most profound human hopes are those that have by necessity acquired aesthetic form, nothing degrades those hopes more than what he denounces as "aesthetic hedonism." When, for instance, Adorno undertakes his critical reading of "committed" literature, he invokes aestheticism as the dialectical flip-side of commitment, the hedonistic twin, so to speak, of the zealot.[15] Adorno's denunciation of what he calls "aesthetic hedonism" echoes Marx's own distaste for an aestheticism that leads to vulgarity [*Gemeinheit*] and perversion: "those who seek in every subject an occasion for stylistic exercises in public will be led, by this purely formal activity, to a perverted content; and such perverted content, in its turn, will impress the stamp of vulgarity on this form."[16] Even Walter Benjamin, whose account of the "withering" of the "aura" of the work of art "in the era of its technological reproducibility" can feel as elegiac as celebratory, declares that "art" "*reacted*" to the "advent of the first truly revolutionary means of reproduction" with "the doctrine of *l'art pour l'art*—that is, with a theology of art."[17]

From the perspective of deconstruction, in which de Man's last essays still constitute the last word, the sensory "seductions" of the aesthetic conceal a more originary violence that can only be confronted in the textual disarticulations disclosed through the experience of reading. It is impossible to work through the essays collected in *The Resistance to Theory* or *Aesthetic Ideology* without regarding them in an important sense as the extended dismantling of the premises and promises of the aesthetic—this "seductive notion" full of "strong temptations"—even as they demonstrate the unavoidability, the insistence of the aesthetic.[18] I know of no instance in de Man's work where the terms "aestheticist" or "aestheticism" possess anything other than pejorative connotations. In "Kant's Materialism," for instance, de Man summarily dismisses as illegitimate any "lineage that is supposed to lead from Kant, by ways of Schiller and Coleridge, to decadent formalism and aestheticism," declaring that "the juxtaposition of Kant and Oscar Wilde" "borders on caricature" (*Aesthetic Ideology*, 119).

If, for de Man, the danger of the aesthetic—its "Pandora's box"—derives from the fundamental "instability" of a category that is "by definition a seductive notion," the recent historicizing strains in literary and cultural studies tend to rely not only on a stable relationship between text and context, but also, ironically, on the presumption of the aesthetic as a stable realm in which more properly and literally historical, social, or sexual agendas and dramas are played out, most often according to a plot of displacement. No *genuinely* dialectical criticism—and Adorno remains its unsurpassed exemplar—regards the "disinterestedness" of aesthetic judgment or the autonomy of the aesthetic simply as the retreat of art into its own domain; but the characterization of the aesthetic as a *space* or *domain* often underwrites the now familiar political criticism of aesthetic autonomy.[19] Terry Eagleton's tidy summary of the left-wing position demonstrates the pervasive purchase of this spatial logic: "art is . . . conveniently sequestered from all other social practice, to become an isolated enclave within which the dominant social order can find an idealized refuge from its own actual values."[20]

When we understand the aesthetic as a state or domain, one that possesses—or claims to possess—autonomy (whether relative or absolute) from the pressures of politics or the workings of history, aestheticism can indeed be construed as the efforts to protect or shield that domain from the various forces and materialities of social existence. One traditional "leftist" interpretation of this condition merely reproduces the claims of the aesthetic: namely, that the aesthetic recaptures through art the freedom that is denied it by the social world—that it is the utopian game of a reified world in which play has no purchase. Ultimately, most contemporary "leftist" accounts reiterate the genuinely dialectical version of this relationship in Hegel's *Aesthetics*, which begins by ascribing to art a special and refining liberating capacity: "Art liberates the true content of phenomena from the pure appearance and deception of this bad, transitory world, and gives them a higher actuality, born of the spirit."[21]

My own emphasis in this book arises from a less trodden and perhaps illegitimate account of the Kantian legacy, an account that opens up one crucial element of a *radical* aestheticism. If we regard the aesthetic as the *imposition* of a sensuous apprehension, if we understand an aesthetic judgment to be something that forces or insists itself upon us without the grounding of concepts, and if we conceive of aesthetic "experience" as something that does not deliver knowledge, but that plays against the claims of knowledge, something quite unexpected and unsettling may result from an aestheticism that is radicalized. I believe, for instance, that this is what Keats meant by "the obtrusive and unmanageable claims of literature and philosophy." When we approach the aesthetic not as a state or domain, but as an "obtrusive and unmanageable claim"—what Shelley in "Hymn to Intellectual Beauty" calls an "unseen Power"—we find ourselves in a keener if more vulnerable position to engage the combustible, eruptive, mercurial textual performances that open a hole at the very heart of what we traditionally understand as aesthetic experience.[22] I think that Peter de Bolla gets to the heart of the antimony posed by aesthetic experience for the relationship between epistemology and phenomenology when he says that "intense moments of *aesthetic* experience feel as if they are in the orbit of knowing."[23] Thus, if an aesthetic experience makes us feel *as if* we are gaining knowledge, then when the experience of a radical aestheticism "bursts" upon us, it makes us feel as if we never knew anything or, perhaps, *anything else but this*: in the words of the disfigured Rousseau in Shelley's *The Triumph of Life*, our "brain" becomes "as sand."

To approach aesthetic experience in general and a radical aestheticism in particular as something that imposes itself upon us rather than a state or a domain we might freely enter is the only way to allow for the possibility of an aesthetic experience as something *involuntary*, as something that approaches the status of an *event*. It would be more accurate to characterize it as the imposition of the peculiar *pseudo-event* of aesthetic experience. This possibility is, as many have noted in one form or another, at the heart of Romanticism. De Man's early account of this "prevailing" Romantic "concern" is particularly pertinent:

> Imaginative literature of the Romantic period is distinguished by its prevailing concern of recreating, or constructing, or inventing, aesthetic experience. Aesthetic experience . . . , rooted in the senses, requires a confrontation with the apparent division between spirit and matter. An object, usually visual, arrests the senses and becomes the occasion for an expression of feeling, a "spontaneous overflow of powerful feelings," in Wordsworth's version. Materiality is essential to aesthetic experience because it makes viable the notion of involuntary aesthetic response.[24]

I am interested in what happens when "imaginative literature" of the Romantic tradition presents us at certain moments in certain texts with an aesthetic experience of art in which the object, "usually" but not necessarily visual, "arrests the senses" and "becomes the occasion for an expression of feeling" that not only happens "involuntarily," but that overwhelms the other "prevailing concerns"—whether this be politics, ethics, poetics, theology, love, even aesthetics itself—of these Romantic writers. Those events I call radical aestheticism.

"Our Romantic Movement"

The phrase is Oscar Wilde's. It appears in the inaugural lecture of Wilde's North American tour, a lecture he delivered at New York's Chickering Hall on January 9, 1882, called "The English Renaissance of Art." The phrase "our romantic movement" identifies the historical contours of the literary trajectory—from Percy Shelley and John Keats to Dante Rossetti and Oscar Wilde—that is the focus of this book. The slightly conspiratorial and possessive, even *possessed*, sense of "our romantic movement" is the "insider's" name for the aestheticist strain of the Romantic tradition that I am addressing here. When, moreover, Wilde invokes "our Romantic movement," he declares the open-ended nature of the literary inheritance of this romantic problematic, one that could also go by the name "aesthetics." "I call it our English Renaissance," declares Wilde, "because it is indeed a new birth of man, like the great Italian Renaissance of the fifteenth century, in its desire for a more gracious and comely way of life, its passion for beauty, new forms of art, new intellectual and imaginative enjoyments" ("English Ren of Art," 243).[25] If Wilde believes this new English Renaissance to be "indeed a new birth of man," it is not what we would identify these days as the "dominant" or "hegemonic" cultural tradition; it is, rather, the persistence of a "romantic movement" not only that Wilde has joined, but that claims him as one of its own. This "romantic movement" belongs to those conspirators who find themselves hailed as one of "ours."

With this lecture Wilde identifies (without effectively *instituting*) the historical contours of the strain of Romanticism with which I am concerned. Wilde judges "our romantic movement" to be that which is worthy of the "great Italian Renaissance of the fifteenth century" in part "because it is our most recent expression of beauty" ("English Ren of Art," 243)—the site of beauty's own contemporary manifestation—and in part because it is the source for what he characterizes as "the two most vital tendencies of the nineteenth century":

> The two most vital tendencies of the nineteenth century—the democratic and pantheistic tendency and the tendency to value life for the sake of art—found their most complete and perfect utterance in the poetry of Shelley and Keats who, to the blind eyes of their own time, seemed to be as wanderers in the wilderness, preachers of vague or unreal things. ("English Ren of Art," 259)[26]

Not only does Wilde identify the poetry of Shelley and Keats as the site of the "most complete and perfect utterance" of these "vital tendencies"; more crucially, he recognizes these tendencies to be the poetic *projects* of Shelley and of Keats, these animating but "unapprehended" "spirits" of their age, "wanderers" to whom the "eyes of their own time" remained "blind." In other words, the "most vital tendencies" are by no means the *dominant* ones. It is certainly the case that Shelley also understood it in this way. As Jerrold Hogle puts it, "too many of us have forgotten that Shelley himself saw what he called 'The Spirit of [his] Age' less as the dominant mind-set of his time, of which he sometimes despaired, than as the oft-hidden but emergent force of an 'electric life' of subversive counter-poetry prompting social change."[27] To this I would add that what we conventionally understand to be aestheticism is by no means a dominant mode of literary or artistic representation in the period but, at least from Shelley and Keats onward and *for the first time*, always a *potentiality*.[28]

If Wilde's lecture locates Shelley and Keats as the advent of "our romantic movement" and Wilde himself as its apex, the art of Dante Gabriel Rossetti and the Pre-Raphaelite Brotherhood is given a prominent place in this company precisely on the basis of its aestheticism, its devotion to "beautifully colored surfaces, nothing more" ("English Ren of Art," 261). Wilde was unaware of the poetry of Hopkins or Dickinson, but his inclusion of Poe in this company will have signaled to his New York audience that what he calls "our romantic movement" is not restricted to Great Britain. If Poe's obsessive reflection on beauty often produces an aestheticism that is tortured and even creepy, it is not *radical* in the sense I am proposing. But, as I hope to demonstrate in Chapter 3, I do believe such a genuinely radical aestheticism to be discernible in one of Poe's compatriots and in the stitched intervals and "bright impossibilities" of some of Emily Dickinson's most compressed and crisis-ridden lyrics. Nonetheless, I suspect the inclusions of both Hopkins and Dickinson require further justification.

A radical aestheticism is the last thing that Hopkins intends to achieve through his poetry. For if Hopkins's speculations on aesthetics and poetics are as singular and adventurous as anything produced in the century, everything in those speculations—and everything in the *conceptions* of his poems—labors to resist the temptations of an aestheticism, whether radically or conventionally conceived. Hopkins certainly resists the aestheticism that he would have associated with his Oxford years and with the figure of Pater in particular. Nevertheless, I believe that at certain moments of certain poems, Hopkins arrives at what is best described as a radical aestheticism that demonstrates, among other things, that the atheism of Shelley or the agnosticism of Keats is not its precondition.

Wilde's inclusion of Poe notwithstanding, my claim that Dickinson belongs to a British Romantic tradition may well be the most debatable, especially given the case often made for her as distinctively "New Englandly." But, as I will demonstrate in Chapter 3, such prominent and diverse Dickinson scholars as Gary Lee Stonum, Sharon Cameron, Judith Farr, and Anne-Lise Francois have demonstrated that Dickinson was deeply—and perhaps even primarily—engaged with "our romantic movement." "There is reason to believe," writes Stonum, "that Dickinson sometimes saw herself . . . as heir to a recognizable wing of nineteenth-century English poetry [one that includes Keats, Shelley, and the young Tennyson] and that her style was designed to carry out the aims generally ascribed to that wing."[29] And, of course, Higginson's own efforts to introduce Dickinson famously invoked Blake, a comparison that is often singled out for its justness by many of her earliest reviewers.[30] My own claim is a more modest one: however much the poetic thinking and practice of Emily Dickinson are formed and cultivated in her New England *habitus*, the poems themselves—their concerns, their workings, their outcomes—claim a significant place in "our romantic movement."[31]

"At certain moments in certain texts": by this refrain I mean that a radical aestheticism is not a constitutive feature of textuality as such, not another name for the "materiality of the signifier" or a "permanent parabasis" or a constitutive "disequlibrium." Nor is it a generic feature of Romanticism, canonical or otherwise. Despite the thematic, rhetorical, and formal adventurousness—indeed, *radicality*—of many of Wordsworth's poems, I am not convinced that one encounters in them a radical *aestheticism*. This is not to say, of course, that Wordsworth's poetry does not reflect long and hard on the nature of aesthetic experience and its aftermath. Indeed, de Man's account of the significance of aesthetic experience for Romanticism invokes the most canonical of phrases—the "spontaneous overflow of powerful feelings"—to epitomize this "prevailing concern." But a powerful and sustained poetic reflection on and engagement with aesthetic experience does not necessarily result in a radical aestheticism. In the case of Wordsworth, these reflections and engagements are effectively contained, or, as I have argued elsewhere, "enshrined" in forms that prevent them from succumbing to the aesthetic experiences they explore.[32] The puritanical strain in Wordsworth seems to serve as prophylactic to aestheticism, a deep aversion to the "soulless" or "waxen" "image" that protects the poetry from the seductions of sheer aesthetic immersion, surely another reason for its appeal to de Man's critical interests and dispositions.

In the case of Coleridge, the *threat* of a radicalized aestheticism is everywhere present, from the "Eolian Harp" through "Constancy to an Ideal Object," and articulated most spectacularly in "Kubla Khan," which we might regard as radical aestheticism's great cautionary tale. The poem offers a Pandora's box of the temptations and seductions that attend to aestheticism's radicalization. "Kubla Khan" is a poem of absolute beginnings and apocalyptic ends, a poem of temporal looping and an auratic music, a poem that among its "pleasure domes" and "mingled measures" offers us the *image* of a radical aestheticism that is as seductive to its speaker as it is terrifying; and this is why it is conjured in the form of a parade of conditionals: the "ifs" and "woulds" of those famous closing lines. To this image of a "deep delight" conjured by the "revival" of that "symphony and song" we are given the gesture that becomes emblematic of the response to a radical aestheticism: "close your eyes with holy dread," the kind of "holy dread" about which "all *should* cry, Beware! Beware!" In the terms of my argument, Coleridge *knows* what a radical aestheticism is before it arrives: it is something "from which he turns away" before it can be made present.

Nor is this merely a generational matter: Byron's feverish poetics of subjectivity, for instance, never culminates in anything that resembles a radical aestheticism. And I would argue that the radicality of *Frankenstein* involves its exploration of the relationship between ethics and aesthetics in its treatments of sympathy and monstrosity, but that its own narrative performance does not arrive at a radical aestheticism. *Wuthering Heights* may well be the most adventurous narrative undertaking in the Romantic tradition; but its performance of what I would call a radical identification, one that is distilled by and in Catherine's utterance—"I *am* Heathcliff"—abstracts that experience, shears it entirely away from the aesthetic dimension, and leaves us with a convulsive whirlwind of pronouns and pure affect. In this sense *Wuthering Heights* achieves the inverse of what I am calling a radical aestheticism.

The references to *Wuthering Heights* and *Frankenstein* beg the question of genre. When I have presented or published earlier versions of this material, some members of my audiences and some of my readers have speculated that the condition I am describing is unique to the *poetry* of the Romantic tradition. My contention that Wilde's radical aestheticism is encountered in his "verse" drama *Salomé* rather than his comedies, dialogues, or *Dorian Grey* tends only to confirm those speculations. It is true that I do not find a *radical* aestheticism at work in the novels, stories, or essays of that other principal theorist of aestheticism, Walter Pater. In order to encounter what I am describing as a radical aestheticism in a novel, one would have to look outside the tradition I *am* considering here; but I predict a reading of Proust or *Moby Dick* or *The Temptation of Saint Anthony*—or, closer to us, *The Sheltering Sky* or *Blood Meridian*—would reveal its presence and effects.

But even as we accept Shelley's declaration that "the distinction between poets and prose writers is a vulgar error" and acknowledge that in principle a radical aestheticism may be experienced in any literary form, we must also recognize that the writers of this tradition regarded the classical genres more seriously. Thus what Shelley calls the "determinate forms" of epic, drama, and lyric have more relevance to this study than the distinction between poetry and prose. We encounter aestheticization and the potential of its radicalization not only in the lyric forms of Dickinson's compressed verses or Rossetti's sonnet sequence, but, as the examples of the *Hyperion* poems or *The Wreck of the Deutschland* demonstrate, in its epic or quasi-epic versions. And as remote from each other as *Salomé* and *This Living Hand* may be in every other aspect, they present us with a radical aestheticism in the dramatic mode. Still, the lyric does indeed hold a special place for the experience I am describing, for every case of a radical aestheticism of which I am aware is marked by what one could call *lyricization*. There is no single or master trope that produces, represents, or epitomizes a radical aestheticism; but *lyricization* is the most precise way to describe its formal, rhetorical, and generic dimensions. By lyricization I mean the pressure or force exerted by the lyric upon other "determinate forms" (as well as the radicalization of the lyric itself). How better, for instance, to account for the generic uncertainty with which critics have responded to a poem such as *The Triumph of Life*? When de Man describes

Shelley's last text as that "for which we have no name readily available among the familiar props of literary history," he is identifying, among other things, the disruption the poem poses to our understanding of its generic classification (*Rhetoric of Romanticism*, 99).

If we follow Shelley and understand lyric, drama, and epic as determinate and not determined or fixed forms, we are in a better position to understand and assess the effects of this lyricization and its relationship to a radical aestheticism. And though Northrop Frye's own "Theory of Genres"—the fourth essay of his *Anatomy of Criticism*—might seem to reinforce the "diagrammatic framework" of the classical triad, the precision of his analyses and the care of his distinctions are illuminating and entirely relevant in this context. For Frye the lyric is the genre in which the pressures of music (*melos*) or painting (*opsis*) are experienced to such a degree that their "radicals" are reached. "The radical of *melos* is *charm*," says Frye, "the hypnotic incantation that, through its pulsing dance rhythm, appeals to involuntary physical response, and is hence not far from the sense of magic, or physically compelling power" (*Anatomy*, 278). This is precisely how Shelley describes the seductive and deluding force of "uttered charms" or "frail spells" in "Hymn to Intellectual Beauty" or how Keats opens "The Fall of Hyperion" by asking how poetry might "save" the imagination from "the sable charm/And dumb enchantment" (ll. 10–11).

Frye locates a lyric "enchantment" of another sort in the "close relation between the visual and the conceptual": "the radical of *opsis* in the lyric is *riddle*, which is characteristically a fusion of sensation and reflection. . . . [A]nd the riddle seems intimately involved with the whole process of reducing language to visible form" (*Anatomy*, 280). For Frye the manifestation of this optical radicalization of the lyric is "the curiously wrought object" that—as the lyrics of both Hopkins and Rossetti demonstrate—"is not far from a sense of enchantment or magical imprisonment" (280). In other words, *melos* and *opsis* are the two "vital tendencies" of the lyric, the formal manifestations of the aesthetic experiences associated with music and painting. Both of these tendencies or forces are fully operative in *Salomé*; and the experience of that play can perhaps best be characterized as the fusion of *opsis* and *melos*. This helps us understand what it means *formally* when Wilde in *De Profundis* claims that he "took the drama, the most objective form known to art, and" with *Salomé* "made it as personal a mode of expression as the lyric or the sonnet."[33] I can think of no better test case than *Salomé* to begin addressing a fascinating question Frye poses about the immersions of poetry in these other modes: "a question on which little has yet been said is the extent to which poetry may, so to speak, disappear into painting or music and come back with a different rhythm" (275).

I have chosen these particular authors from British Romanticism and its aftermath because I have found at certain moments in certain of their texts acute instances of a radical aestheticism. But the selection of these authors is important for another reason. I believe that it is possible to identify for each of them a defining element to their poetic undertaking: what Wilde called their "vital tendency" and what I more mundanely call their project. The notion of an author's project is sufficiently broad and old-fashioned enough to require some refining. By "project" I mean not the sense of a plan or scheme in the most restricted sense—an author's specific or immediate "intentions"—but the sense of an *animating* principle that is "thrown forth" with and through the works themselves, a kind of fundamental task that the works assign themselves. One might describe the project as a kind of "vocational agency" insofar as it comes to define and direct the undertaking we will come to know as "Keatsian" or "Dickinsonian." This notion of a project is thus quite different from our conventional accounts of a poet's "calling" insofar as it designates *what* the poet is called upon to say or do or make. When, for instance, in *Wordsworth's Profession* Thomas Pfau describes "the extraordinarily elusive and flexible cultural agency known as Wordsworth," "driven more by a prospect than by a debt," he elaborates in the broadest sense the notion of a poetic project that interests me here. Pfau's meticulous study specifies the poetic strategies by which that "flexible cultural agency known as Wordsworth" undertakes his specific project: "It involves a professional poet continually developing new hermeneutic scenarios to help his envisioned audience reconfigure its political, economic, and cultural anxieties and hopes" (*Wordsworth's Profession*, 10). In each of the following chapters I hope to outline the animating project or "vital tendency" of these poets, projects that—in spite of the accidental or elective affinities of the poets themselves—are genuinely diverse. So, for instance, in Chapter 1 I spell out Shelley's poetic project or "vital tendency," what Wilde calls his "democratic and pantheistic tendency" and what I refer to simply as "politics;" and in Chapter 4 I discuss Hopkins's poetics of divine "inspiration" and "aspiration," a project I classify under the rubric of "theology." But my ultimate interest here is not solely to discern and develop the literary forms and modes of interpretation—what Pfau calls the "hermeneutic scenarios"—by which these writers would "help his [or her] audience envision" and in one form or another confirm the significance of those projects. I am interested, rather, in what happens when the project an author "envisions" encounters and is undone by the radicalized aestheticism that it has itself generated.

As for my choice of texts, I realize that I have, for the most part, selected those that are well known and widely discussed. These selections are not intended to reinforce or reassert canonical judgments of the texts; and some of the poems under consideration are relatively obscure. The historical, institutional, and sociopolitical issues surrounding canon formation are not the focus of this book. But it does seem to be the case that, within the discourse of British Romanticism, texts become canonical not merely on the basis of their literary merit (however we evaluate that), but often because they thematize the project of their author's undertaking. It should go without saying that not each and every text an author writes carries with equal weight the author's project. There are countless occasional, generic, personal, formal motivations for the production of literature; and I am not arguing, for instance, that each of Dickinson's almost 1,800 poems is explicitly *about* the project of a "poetics" or that Keats's "Give me women wine and snuff" reflects in any way on poetry's ethical mission. Thus, if I read and discuss "Hymn to Intellectual Beauty" or "England in 1819" and not such a delicate late lyric as "The Serpent Is Shut Out from Paradise," it is because the former and not the latter engage the question of the aesthetic in the development of Shelley's project of a political poetics.

Each of these authors is keenly aware that his or her project must pass through the aesthetic, and not only in the sense that, as a literary artist, each is self-conscious about the inherited forms of literary representation or the pressures of composition. More importantly, each of these authors implicitly and explicitly reflects upon the workings of the aesthetic and the nature of aesthetic experience, not only by their thematization in essays or letters, but, most crucially, by making the issues attendant to the aesthetic dimension that is made manifest in the performance of the literary texts themselves. And on some occasions, the performances of these texts—their *aestheticizing* representation of the nature of aesthetic experience—delivers the author's project to a fundamental crisis: it is the point at which that aestheticized representation of aesthetics can no longer accommodate the poetic project it is meant to serve. I am interested in what happens when these writers, deeply committed to certain versions of ethics or politics or theology, nonetheless *produce* the encounter with a radical aestheticism in their own work. To the degree that no one in this tradition espouses a radical aestheticism, its occurrence will have the appearance of singularities. But if these instances of a genuinely radical aestheticism are not the aims of these authors, neither can they be explained away as mere accidents. They are, rather, the sites and occasions at which those projects are subjected to a fundamental crisis. It is the event and consequence of this critical encounter "from which one turns away."

The word "crisis" carries such weight that, in the context of literature, especially in the context of a literature produced by authors relatively unknown to their contemporaries, it can scarcely avoid the whiff of melodrama. *Crisis for whom?*

And it is certainly not self-evident that the rhetoric of crisis is ever really appropriate for, of all things, *aestheticism*. I would never argue that the fate of the nation or the course of its empire—or even the principal forms of their cultural self-representation—were in play at these moments of radical aestheticism. The "crises" are both more local and more mediated. It is certainly the case that each of these writers took his or her literary project quite seriously: none could be characterized as serene about the nature of his or her vocation as writer. In fact, the relative obscurity and isolation in which most of the writers discussed here labored liberated them in a sense to pursue these undertakings fully, to explore in a sustained form the nature of the relationships between aesthetics and politics in the case of Shelley, or aesthetics and ethics in the case of Keats. Thus, when the latter undertakes the *Hyperion* poems, the collapse of those poems is indeed a crisis for Keats's conception and practice of poetry's "humanizing" ethos. And since I believe that Keats took that ethical project seriously, that it guided the way of his poetic adventures "round many goodly state and kingdom," the crisis is a serious one for any critical efforts to conceive of humanist poetics in the name of Keats.

There is another *critical* dimension to the crisis of this encounter, "from which one turns away": the phrase implies that every "one," writer as well as reader, has turned away from this radical aestheticism—until now. I recognize that I have placed myself in the unique and heroic position of being the one who did not turn away, the one who looked, at least long enough to point at it and give it a name. About this one can never say enough, so that anything said likely seems to be both too little and too much. I will venture only that I hope to be clear enough about what I believe to be happening in those "certain moments in certain texts" to demonstrate throughout my engagements with them that they *remain* a genuine crisis for me and for my understanding of the theories and practices of reading that have prepared me to come to terms with this "radical aestheticism." It is for this reason that I turn to Walter Benjamin's notion of the aura (Shelley, Hopkins), Roland Barthes's accounts in his late work of "the third meaning" and the indolence of aesthetics (Keats), Jacques Derrida's notion of the "event-machine" and Giorgio Agamben's account of an originary *poesis* (Dickinson), Hans Urs von Balthasar's theological aesthetics (Hopkins), absorption and theatricality according to Michael Fried (Rossetti), Jacques Lacan and Slavoj Žižek on the ethics of desire (Rossetti), and Georges Bataille's notions of expenditure and sacrifice (Wilde). These diverse theoretical projects are not marshaled as authorities that might demystify the relationships between poetry and aesthetics in this tradition or reveal their ideological impulses. While I do indeed turn to these now canonical figures in twentieth- and twenty-first-century intellectual history as sources of conceptual illumination, they become in the course of my readings something of a parallel text, one that reveals through a mutual illumination the reach and purchase of this problem of aesthetics and aestheticism in new historical contexts and in new critical idioms.

A crisis is always a "turning point"; once upon a time, the word "crisis" designated a "point by which to judge, a criterion, token, sign." This latter meaning may indeed be obsolete, but it remains implicit in de Man's declaration that "all true criticism occurs in the mode of crisis."[34] I must leave it for others to decide whether the crisis of *this* critic will result in a "true criticism" and indicate a deeper crisis or "turning point" in the texts themselves, one that prompts us to turn away on the basis of so many different critical judgments, which are themselves constituted as tokens and signs. In an important sense the most prominent traditions of Anglo-American criticism have always been constituted by the "turning away" from aestheticism's most radical implications. That "turning away" is their turning point, their constitutive relation to crisis. This extends, ironically enough, to the proponents of aestheticism itself who identify and name it as such, understand its eruptive force in the psycho-sensual "impressions" it leaves, and then "turn away" from the radical dimensions of this experience as they tell us to turn toward art, "for its own sake."

Thus "from which one turns away" refers us not only to the act of aversion that takes place in response to a textual event, the critical *disregard* of a radical aestheticism, but more crucially to the more subtle forms of an interpretive "turning" that take place at the point of crisis and that are mobilized to rescue or redeem the text, even if only for the sake of understanding. This is what I take de Man to mean when he refers to the "defensive motion of understanding" (*Rhetoric*, 261). But the phrase is also meant to point us to the tropological turning that is present at the very origins of *poesis*, as Timothy Bahti has stressed, a "sense of 'turning' that has much to do with the inconceivability of lyric poetry without tropes."[35]

This attention to the work and effects of tropes should signal, if the repeated references to de Man had not, that my own critical practice derives from a recognizable version of close reading. I am scarcely the first to note the tensions between the gerund and its adjective. One must get close enough to the text, as we say, to permit its operations to come into focus and for reading to commence, a process by which the elements of a constitutive infratext can be discerned and identified. But one of the questions that will concern us throughout this study is whether at certain moments in certain texts we find ourselves *too close* to the text, rendered incapable of reading and stuck in a kind of auratic fascination that we dispel only by turning away, what Barthes called becoming "unglued."[36] What I hope to perform in the chapters that follow is a practice that is reflective and careful enough to identify the rhetorical processes at work in these texts (and thereby contribute local insights into our understanding of them) while simultaneously venturing an intimacy with the text and its radiances that might at times appear to be reading's opposite.[37]

Scene of Shipwreck

Though this is a book about the forms and effects of a radical aestheticism in British Romantic literary discourse, the title of my introduction identifies a version of the critical response of aversion—a crisis or "turning point"—that is not only a response of their contemporaries or of us, but an irreducible formal, rhetorical, and thematic element of the texts themselves. But I take this title neither from the literature nor from the critical responses it elicited, but from a phrase found in a review of Theodor Géricault's *The Raft of the Medusa* (1819), the painting that is reproduced in this chapter's frontispiece. The history of the painting's critical reception is, characteristically enough for such an audacious work of art, full of fascinating and symptomatic responses. But there is one eloquent response to this picture that struck me powerfully the first time I came across it and from which I have found it impossible to extricate myself. It is the judgment of a reviewer identified as "P.A." in the *Revue*

Encyclopedique (1819). Invoking Horace, "P.A." affirms that "the aim of paint-ing is to speak to the soul and to the eyes, and not to repel. . . . M. Géricault would always have overshot the mark. . . . This picture is a heap of corpses from which one turns away" (329). I believe this final phrase—"from which one turns away"—most directly identifies the sensation-reaction that repeat-edly occurs when a radical aestheticism is encountered.

Though there are plenty enough of corpses to be found in "our romantic movement," it should be clear by this point that what causes the gesture of aversion that I am examining is by no means restricted to the representation of the "corpse" or to the thematics of death. Rather, what interests me are the ethico-aesthetic premises—in this case neo-Horatian decorum—that prompt a beholder to "turn away" from a work of art that radicalizes its own relation to the aesthetic experience. What is objectionable to "P.A." is not the fact that dead bodies are depicted on the canvas; it is, rather, that "M. Géricault" has done both too much and too little with his depiction. He has neglected the true "aim of painting"—"to speak to the soul and to the eyes"—and "overshot the mark." What makes Géricault's painting demand this act of aversion on the part of "P.A." can be attributed to the *absence* of aesthetics: it is a mere and artless "*heap* of corpses from which one turns away." This "heap" is, to use another relevant term, deprived of *spirit*, of the aesthetic form that might ani-mate or redeem it.[38] From this heap one must turn away: the canvas remains an *it*, its thingliness the cause for repulsion. From this perspective it is not yet art—not sufficiently aestheticized.

Or perhaps Géricault is guilty of "too much" aestheticizing: the paint-ing, according to "P.A." "overshoots the mark," exceeding the proper "aim of painting" and in the process failing to "speak to the soul and to the eyes" of the beholder. Indeed, for Michael Fried, Géricault is "the first painter who found himself compelled to assume the burden" of the problem of "the pres-ence of the beholder" as "*insuperable*"; and *The Raft of the Medusa* is "the prin-cipal monument to that compulsion."[39] For Fried the painting itself is aware that it is a work of art; and the gestures and responses of the men depicted on the raft may well be understood as a response to their own aestheticization: "The strivings of the men on the raft to be beheld by the tiny ship on the ho-rizon . . . may be viewed as motivated not simply by a desire for rescue from the appalling circumstances depicted in the painting but also by the need to escape our gaze, to put an end to being beheld by us," as if, says Fried, "our presence before the painting were the ultimate cause of their plight." If "P.A."

"turns away" from the "heap of corpses" presented to us on the canvas, that turn mirrors the one already made by the figures in the painting itself, "turning away" from their beholders in this crisis of theatricalization, which is also a crisis of aestheticization. Versions of this scene are repeated in a variety of permutations throughout the Romantic literary discourse I am examining.

If I introduce this study of a radical aestheticism with the title of an exemplary critical response, it is not because I am principally interested in examining the full range of responses and reactions to such texts. But, as the example of *The Raft of the Medusa* should illustrate, works of art and aesthetic judgments have a way of becoming inextricably intertwined, sometimes at the very level of their conception and production. It is certainly the case that a notion of aesthetics is always already in place, awaiting the occurrence of that which will confirm, refuse, or exceed it, "overshoot the mark," as "P.A." puts it. Though this is a work of British Romantic and post-Romantic literary criticism and not French art history, Géricault's *The Raft of the Medusa* and the responses it prompts present us with the problem of seeing and beholding that is at the heart of this literary tradition. Indeed, "P.A.'s" invocation of the Horatian dictum—*"ut pictura poesis"*—may well serve as but another neo-classical misrepresentation of Horace's argument, but stripped of its didacticism, the famous passage in *Ars Poetica* identifies a technical problem that is as important to this literary tradition as it is to Géricault's painting. "As with the painter's work, so with the poet's: one piece will take you more if you stand close to it, another at a greater distance." This is reflected in Delacroix's remark in a journal entry about the exhibition of *The Raft* in the Louvre: "one has to see it close enough," writes Delacroix, who posed for one of the prominent corpses, "to appreciate its worth." It is certainly the case that the force of *ut pictura poesis* represents something more than the weight of neo-classical convention: however much that tradition may attempt to resolve the problem, it cannot help but remind us of the perpetual braiding of painting and poetry, an often chiasmic intertwining between the literary and the visual arts that is a recurrent topic of the Romantic literary tradition with which I am concerned here. It is at least one way to indicate the power of the ekphrastic impulse in each of these authors.[40] Thus is my title drawn from a turning that is provoked by a certain deployment of images that are felt to be an affront to vision. Is it, in other words, merely a coincidence that the controversial painting that prompts this aversion is *Medusa's* raft, the residue of Medusa's demise? How can we *not* regard *The Raft of the Medusa* as a consequence of the "Medusa effect," something that links my first and final chapters, Shelley's poem "On the Medusa of Leonardo da Vinci in the Florentine Gallery" to the "Medusan" effects of Wilde's *Salomé*?

Géricault's painting has achieved the status of an emblem of a thought or representation confronting its limit, nearing its own radicality. Originally titled "Scene of Shipwreck" (*Scene de Naufrage*), the painting can be understood to allegorize the relationship between catastrophe and art, or catastrophe as aesthetic possibility. That is the question that Julian Barnes raises at the beginning of Chapter 5½ of his novel *A History of the World in 10½ Chapters*: "How do you turn catastrophe into art?"[41] In the case of Géricault, Barnes answers this question by demonstrating, carefully and eloquently, how the painting refuses the various aims to which it could be enlisted: "(1) political; (2) symbolic; (3) theatrical; (4) shocking; (5) thrilling; (6) sentimental; (7) documentational; or (8) unambiguous." The list of projects Géricault does *not* undertake sounds like an alternate version of the rubrics I am proposing; but for Barnes these refusals are registered not as crises, but as the elements in the "process"—"freeing, enlarging, explaining"—by which "catastrophe has become art" (137). "This is no reducing process," no radicalization of the elements. Barnes is describing in the context of this "masterpiece" not only the history of its production, but the process of its aestheticization. The catastrophe is not, in other words, merely the calamitous fate that befell those upon the raft; it is not, in other words, a catastrophe as disastrous *end*, but as a sudden and violent overturning that may yet be overturned again, "turned to art," finally redeemed.

Barnes offers a compelling account, as illuminating as it is reflective. But this account opens a possibility from which it also turns away: what if art itself in the production of its own self-reflection, at certain moments in certain places, is itself this catastrophe, a sudden and radical *overturning*, a final "subversion," calamitous on its own to the hopes and projects to which we would assign it? We are close here to Bataille; and it is certainly no accident that one of Bataille's most brilliant critics, Denis Hollier, would invoke *The Raft of the Medusa* to epitomize Bataille's thought in general and his notion of expenditure in particular. Hollier turns to the painting in order to come to terms with Bataille's "Corps celeste," an essay on the blinding of the "ex-beholder," his implication in the visual event, and his destruction by proximity. For Hollier, Bataille's theory of expenditure opens itself to the possibilities of the unredeemed, "a thought which sustains itself beyond the loss of the subject,

when thought keeps going even after its subject has been spent": "this philosophical raft of the Medusa is the allegory of a thought that has left behind
the world we live in."[42] "In the final analysis," suggests Hollier, "the major
interest of Bataille's theory of expenditure might not be of an economic or
anthropological order but, rather, of an epistemological one" ("Dualist Materialism," 138). I don't know whether the lonely moment of the final analysis
of Bataille has yet arrived or if more turning points—more "catastrophes"—
await us upon the horizon. But I suspect few who know his work would deny
that another "major interest" in the theory of expenditure is of an aesthetic
order; and I do believe that it offers us one of the most compelling formulations of what happens epistemologically in the wake of a radical aestheticism.
And formally, when the work of these authors approaches or encounters a
radical aestheticism, their language begins to sever its relationship to referen-
tiality and—as in the case of *The Triumph of Life* or the *Hyperions* or "To pile
like thunder"—to drift into the horizon of abstraction.[43]

Crises, catastrophes, turning points, both to and from: if it is impossible to avoid these tropes and figures—indeed, necessary, to move through
them—in order to approach the nature and consequences of a radical aestheticism, it may be possible to change their scale and thereby modify the
way we think about them. There is, in conclusion, another visual artist whose
work belongs to the legacy of this tradition to whom we might turn. In one
of Joseph Cornell's exquisite "boxes," the late piece called *Toward the Blue
Peninsula (For Emily Dickinson)* (c. 1953), we encounter a construction that
opens a space beyond the limit, beyond containment, beyond the place from
which the bird—if we must believe this to be the absent referent—has, apparently, "flown away" toward "the blue peninsula," a figure no less delusive
than the point on the horizon at which Géricault's imperiled Medusans wave.
In this particular box—one of Cornell's many "curiously wrought" objects,
lyric riddles of delicate visual compression—the "open" window at the back,
which still bears the shadows of the cage, may appear to reveal a piece of the
sky or an image of the sea. But more precisely, it is merely a rectangular swath
of white that emanates from the blue. The wire mesh in the front of the box is
opened—"cut away," it seems—such that it frames the "window." It conjures
"a thought which sustains itself beyond the loss of the subject" *and* the loss of
the object, for nothing more than two tiny snippets of paper remain. The best
way into the box that I know of is the final stanza of the poem from which the
title of the box is derived and to which it is dedicated, "It might be lonelier,"

by Emily Dickinson: "It might be easier/To fail—/With land in sight/Than gain my blue peninsula/To perish of delight." I hope to embark on a project that hails or points to such moments as they occur on the far horizons of Romanticism and to do so by taking the risk of proximity, to get as close to those "blue peninsulas" as possible "from which one turns away" and to understand who or what might "perish" in the process.

Cornell, *Toward the Blue Peninsula (for Emily Dickinson)*

"Leonardo da Vinci," *The Medusa* (Gianni Dagli Orti / The Art Archive at Art Resource, NY)

ONE

"A Light More Dread Than Obscurity":
Spelling and Kindling in Percy Bysshe Shelley

> Ordinary harps play under any fingers, Aeolian harps only when struck by
> the storm.
>
> — KARL MARX, "Notebooks on Epicurean Philosophy"

"Frail Spells"

Wilde characterized the "vital tendency" of Shelley's poetry as "the democratic and pantheistic tendency." I call it "politics." This is the project that
animates Shelley's poetry; and politics is the term the poet would have been
likely to use and that is inseparable from his legacy. I will examine several poems that are explicitly political in their subject matter, poems Shelley would
have described as "wholly political." But my principal focus in this chapter is
the nature of Shelley's political investment in the aesthetic. I am interested
in Shelley's representations of aesthetic experiences, effects, and judgments;
and I want to examine how these representations function as constitutive elements in his political poetics. And I hope to demonstrate how at some crucial
instances this singularly powerful project of a political poetics is subjected
to the "storm" of an aestheticism. In Shelley's poetic idiom, the two terms
through which aesthetics and politics repeatedly converge are spelling and
kindling.

I start with spelling. The "frail spells" I refer to above appear in the third stanza of Shelley's "Hymn to Intellectual Beauty" (1816), where they follow the series of questions addressed to the "Spirit of BEAUTY."[1] The celebrated questions that constitute the hymn's second stanza are elaborations of the first question posed to the spirit: "where art thou gone?" (l.15). "Why," asks the speaker, "dost thou pass away and leave our state,/This dim vast vale of tears, vacant and desolate?" (ll.16–17). "Intellectual Beauty," that which unlike church or state most deserves our "vows" of worship and celebration, has "pass[ed] away" without explanation; and the poem announces the withdrawal of the spirit of beauty in the form of a hymn to its absence or, more precisely, to the "path of its departure." The spirit of this beauty is nothing if not divine, for it is a spirit that "consecrates" with its own "hues" all "it dost shine upon/Of human thought or form" (ll.13–15). Why, asks the poem's speaker, has this divine spirit of beauty been exiled from us, an exile that, whether self-imposed or enforced by worldly powers, leaves our state, our worldly actuality, a place of desolation?

Far from proposing an answer to this question—which would require the poem to speak in the name of the spirit—the subsequent stanza serves instead to nullify the entire history of proposed answers, to demystify the claims of all those "sage[s] or poet[s]" who may fancy that they have heard a response:

> No voice from some sublimer world hath ever
>> To sage or poet these responses given—
>> Therefore the name of God and ghosts and Heaven,
> Remain the records of their vain endeavour,
> Frail spells—whose uttered charm might not avail to sever,
>> From all we hear and all we see,
>> Doubt, chance, and mutability.
>
> (ll.25–31)

Placing God and Heaven in the company of ghosts, the lines appear to be a straightforward declaration of Shelley's radical philosophical skepticism. The passage spells out his critique of the "uttered charms" of the various religious and philosophical ideologies that, try as they might to seduce us into belief, cannot "avail to sever" the irreducible condition of "doubt, chance, and mutability" from the sensual world. But the critique is not as straightforward as it first appears, for Shelley qualifies his refusal of the power of these "frail spells": their "uttered charm *might not* avail to sever" "doubt, chance, and mutability" from our worldly perception. If this qualification does not diminish the force of the poem's repudiations, it does nonetheless demonstrate the *necessity* of countering the "uttered charm" of onto-theology with the act of a demystification: a spell can be rendered "frail" only when the "charm" of its utterance is revealed.

Shelley's demystification of the "frail spells" of poetry, theology, and philosophy should be extended to his political critique of what we call the nation-state and the nationalisms that institute and preserve it. From Shelley's effort to vacate all false groundings comes a poetics of the idea that conducts a politics of love and liberty beyond the "frail spells" of national character or identity. In the idiom of Shelley's critical neo-Platonism, there can be no *idea* of the nation: the idea is always in exile and the nation always the scene of the actuality of power. Thus the idea is in a permanently ironic relation to the nation and to its worldly legislative powers. This is why, according to Shelley, the poet must in an entirely positive sense remain an "unacknowledged legislator of the World." If "all authors of revolutions are poets," as Shelley declares in the *Defence*, it is because as "hierophants of an unapprehended inspiration" they liberate us from what in *The Triumph of Life* he calls "thought's empire over thought." The moment poetic legislation is *acknowledged* is the moment that poets begin laying down the law, the moment they cease their service to the idea and enlist themselves in the actualities of institution. In other words, were the "awful shadow of some unseen Power" to be construed as official authorization, we would call it the "ideological" moment.

From the perspective of beauty—the only legitimate authority recognized by the poem—"our state," our originary condition, is one of "statelessness": beauty only "lends" "for some uncertain moments" (l.37) its "glorious train" (l.41). Beauty's perpetual disappearance leaves a "vacancy" in "our state"; but this "vacancy" is the prerequisite for Shelley's politics. It is by virtue of that very vacancy that the "voices" that sage and poet alike call truth—the "voices" of God and ghost and Heaven—can be recognized as echoes of their own "uttered charms." Shelley would voice his commitment to the power of "vacancy" in his 1819 prose fragment "On Life," where it is quite explicitly the "duty" of critical philosophy not to "establish" or institute truth, but "to destroy error, and the roots of error" (*Shelley's Poetry and Prose*, 477). The destruction of error, an interminable critique, results in the "leaving" of a vacancy: "It leaves, what is too often the duty of the reformer in political and ethical questions to leave, a vacancy" (*SPP*, 477). This is, moreover, not merely the "duty of the reformer in political and ethical questions," but the role of the poetic imagination as Shelley conceives it in a poem as late as

Epipsychidion: it is an illuminating negation, a "reverberated lightning" that "As from a thousand prisms and mirrors, fills / The Universe with glorious beams and kills / Error" (ll.166–69).

To sing a hymn to intellectual beauty is to invoke the incantatory "charm" of the hymn form and defiantly sing in praise of vacancy, the vacancy left by this aesthetic spirit's exile from our state. To sing a hymn to intellectual beauty is thus to be both perverse and reverent and to join one's voice to a non-priestly, non-nationalist chorus that, like the silent voice of the mountain in "Mont Blanc," has the capacity to "repeal large codes of fraud and woe," such as those "sealed" in English statutes. To sing this resplendent hymn is to keep the "vow" to the "awful LOVELINESS" that offers the best hope to "free / This world from its dark slavery" (ll.69–70). To sing this godless, but still sacred hymn is to give worship to the absent spirit of beauty and every form and thought it consecrates. If the proper worship of the spirit of beauty demands an initial demystification of the "frail spells" of God and ghosts and heaven, this worship nonetheless makes good on its vows only through the conjuring, the "calling" of phantoms: in the sixth stanza, the poet, asking the silent spirit to confirm that he has indeed "kept his vows," declares that "even now / I call the phantoms of a thousand hours / Each from his voiceless grave" (ll.63–65).

Ghosts, gods, spirits, phantoms: if each of these figures by turns haunts or inspires Shelley's poem, its success as a *"hymn* to intellectual beauty" depends upon a rigorous distinction between them. It is not, in other words, a matter of opposing actual reality or the living present to the spectral properties of the ghost; it is, rather, a question of distinguishing the differences between God and Spirit, between ghosts and phantoms. While the phantom, for instance, may suggest the spectral qualities of the ghost, Shelley's phantom is not mere ideological delusion, but the shadowing forth of something ideal, such as the appearance of the Spirit of "Intellectual Beauty" addressed by the poem. But since no one can *see* this Spirit, the distinctions the poem insists upon between spirit and ghost or phantom and God depend on measuring and evaluating their various effects, which might be characterized as the difference between the theological and the aesthetic. It amounts to measuring the differences between the "frail spells" of "God and ghosts and Heaven" on the one hand and the "hues and harmonies of evening" or the "memory of music fled" (ll.8, 10) on the other. "Hymn to Intellectual Beauty" not only speaks of and to the aesthetic, it recounts its deep commitment, and in the process recommits itself, to the "binding" spirit of beauty.

As much elegy as hymn, the poem mourns the absence of that "awful LOVE-LINESS" (l.71) to whom the poet "vowed" to "dedicate" his personal "powers" (l.61). But it would be more accurate to describe the spirit as transient, fugitive, perpetually impermanent rather than simply absent. After all, the poem identifies "Intellectual Beauty" as the primary and even prime "Power" that, though unavailable to the sense of sight, casts an "awful shadow" that "Floats though unseen amongst us" (l.2). While it is forever elusive as presence—it is nothing that we could point at—Shelley's "spirit of Beauty" is nonetheless a "Power," a force that *insists*. And it is the insistence of this force and the magnitude of this "Power" that make the distinctions between theology and aesthetics difficult to maintain, as the poem's early praise of the "grace" and "mystery" of the spirit of beauty demonstrates. It may well appear that the poem has challenged the "frail spells" of theology only to succumb to the theologizing charms of the aesthetic. Thus the speaker declares to the spirit of beauty that its "light alone" "gives grace and truth to life's unquiet dream" (ll.32, 35).[2] If the mediations and complexities of these lines are not unusual for Shelley, the extent of their disarticulations is unexpected in a poem that sounds so lovely. If "beauty's light alone" "Gives grace and truth to life's unquiet dream"—grace and truth as gifts bestowed upon the world by beauty—this happens "like" "music by the night wind sent / Through strings of some still instrument" (ll.32, 36, 33–34). This is the poem's aesthetics and its poetics: indeed, it is its *aestheticist* poetics. The poem teaches us the charms and seductions of an aesthetic experience that, through the manifold instances of its appearance, it tries to name and deliver.

And yet, as many readers have stressed, intellectual beauty is not to be confused with sensuous beauty; and thus the hymn is addressed not to the aesthetic as such—not to the sensory manifestation of the spirit—but to the spirit of beauty itself. This means that the aesthetic exists only in the realm of likeness and that its figural model is that of the simile. But if the "visitations" of the "awful shadow of some unseen Power" leave us with a string of similes; they are similes that, as Carol Jacobs has rightly noted, do not operate in the service of similarity: "The first stanza of the 'Hymn to Intellectual Beauty' . . . is an attempt to define that elusive poetic force through a long series of similes whose terms of comparison seem peculiarly at odds with one another."[3] Our "state" is thus one of failed likenesses, a potentially interminable series of figures that, in Jacobs's words, "mark the refusal of language to define by affirming an identity" (203). No linguistic system based upon a principle of identity could "define" a spirit that not only remains unseen, but whose own "seeing" is nothing more than an "inconstant glance" (1.6).[4]

If such a "spirit fair" does not preside over the idea or form of any national community, it does nonetheless exert supreme "binding" powers of its own. In the poem's last lines, where this hymn becomes supplication, the poet-suppliant beseeches the spirit of beauty to lend him its power as "one who worships thee,/And every form containing thee,/Whom, SPIRIT fair, thy spells did bind/To fear himself, and love all human kind" (ll.81–84). No one is likely to confuse this with the *International*, but it is a hymn that, after sounding the emptiness of the "frail spells" of "God and ghosts and heaven," turns its praise to an exiled spirit whose genuinely binding spells are those solely of universal love. Drawing on the democratic and ecstatic energies of the English hymn, Shelley's secular version of this genre is not merely a song of praise or adoration, but also a form of spell; and one of the intended effects of this hymn to intellectual beauty is to extend its sacred powers to its readers and, most importantly, make them sing: it is intended to place those who give voice to it under the spell of love. This is its effect on the poem's own hymn-singer who feels the "shadow" of Beauty's spirit fall upon him as a kind of counter-charm, an antidote to the "poisonous names with which our youth is fed" (1.53). The result is something like a conversion experience in which the eruption of an ecstatic "shriek"—"I shrieked, and clasped my hands in extasy" (1.60)—prompts the declaration of his poetic vows: "I vowed that I would dedicate my powers/To thee and thine" (ll.61–62). And as the poem reestablishes itself in the present tense, it performs in the middle of its sixth stanza a passionate and tearful renewal of that vow, echoing while displacing the earlier "call" "on poisonous names":

> With beating heart and streaming eyes, even now
> I call the phantoms of a thousand hours
> Each from his voiceless grave: they have in visioned bowers
>   Of studious zeal or love's delight
>   Outwatched with me the envious night—
> They know that never joy illumed my brow
>   Unlinked with hope that thou wouldst free
>   This world from its dark slavery,
>   That thou—O awful LOVELINESS,
> Wouldst give what'er these words cannot express.
>
>   (ll.64–72)

These are phantoms—not unlike those "glorious phantoms" promised by "England in 1819"—whose knowledge points the way not only to beauty, but to its inherent "link" or "bond" with the hope of freedom from "dark slavery." To those who join Shelley in opposing what in another context he identified as "the advocates of injustice and superstition," the "worship" of the spirit of beauty and its sensory manifestations ("every form containing thee") spells for "all human kind" the binding hope of universal love.

Thus the comings and goings of the spirit of beauty, a power both unseen and unheard as such, are according to Shelley figured through its phantoms and known only through its effects, like the blind falling of a shadow.[5] And yet it is by its very inconstancy that the spirit of beauty generates the binding force of love, which the poem's last line identifies as the "love of all human kind." If this resembles the "spectropoetics" that Derrida unearths in his reading of Marx, perhaps this likeness accounts more than a little for Marx's famously sympathetic assessment of the poet. And perhaps it is because Marx and Shelley, both illegitimate heirs of the Platonic tradition, recognize in this cluster of specters—ghosts, gods, spirits, phantoms—the elements of a theory of ideology and commit themselves to the project of its *dispelling*.[6]

"Wholly Political"

The characterization—"wholly political"—is Shelley's own, a definition of the "political" that is itself a feature of Romantic discourse. Shelley participates in the development of the term "political" as something more directed and more partisan than "the science and art of government" or even "the administration of the state or polity." In a letter to Leigh Hunt on May Day, 1820, Shelley writes, "I wish to ask you if you know of any bookseller who would like to publish a little volume of *popular songs* wholly political, and destined to awaken and direct the imagination of the reformers." He was likely to suspect that Hunt did not know of such a bookseller; but Shelley's commitment to such a political poetics is unwavering. Indeed, in the "Preface" he composes for *Prometheus Unbound* (1819), Shelley spells out the nature of his political project, one in which he proposes not only to compose "popular songs" that would "awaken and direct the imaginations of reformers," but to produce a treatise that would constitute "genuine" political inquiry: "Should I live to accomplish what I purpose, that is, produce a systematical history of what appear to me to be the genuine elements of human society, let not the advocates of injustice and superstition flatter themselves that I should take Aeschylus rather than Plato as a model" (*SPP*, 209).[7]

Shelley's political project is present and legible in those "popular songs," poems such as "To Sidmouth and Castlereagh," "Song to the Men of England," and "The Mask of Anarchy." But this "vital tendency" is also at work in poems with greater formal and philosophical ambitions, such as "Hymn to Intellectual Beauty"; and it is also legible in the other great poem Shelley wrote on the workings of the aesthetic during that decisive summer of 1816. The most explicitly political moment in "Mont Blanc" occurs at the end of Part III, the famously tricky lines in which the poem spells out the lessons to be learned from the "mysterious tongue" of "wilderness" and then directly addresses the mountain and its capacity to effect profound ethico-political change. Here the critical activity shifts from "dispelling" to a cognate form of undoing, the "repeal":

> The wilderness has a mysterious tongue
> Which teaches awful doubt, or faith so mild,
> So solemn, so serene, that man may be
> But for such faith with nature reconciled;
> Thou hast a voice, great Mountain, to repeal
> Large codes of fraud and woe; not understood
> By all, but which the wise, and great, and good
> Interpret, or make felt, or deeply feel.
>
> (ll.76–83)

In Earl Wasserman's unsurpassed reading of the poem, there is no essential difference between the "mysterious tongue" of "the wilderness" and the "voice" possessed by the "great Mountain": both teach us the truth of Power, that it is "an inexorable force man cannot command or control" and that it "has no human concerns."[8] The lesson to be learned from the tongue and voice of Power is the lesson of a relentless skepticism: "The skeptical doubt and the submission to the Power lead to no further truth, but merely destroy man's false conceptions of Power, expressed in the institutions man has constructed and called ultimate and compelling truths" (229). This is as compelling an account of the "dispelling" or "repealing" power of Shelley's skepticism as we have; and it is fully consistent with the poet's own accounts in "On Life" of the task of the "Intellectual Philosophy."

But Wasserman's interpretation does not account for the shift in tone and figure as the lines move from the trope of "wilderness" as such to the address to *this* particular mountain, a shift that can be understood to indicate a meaningful disjunction between the Wordsworthian reverence offered by the former and the revolutionary political force of the latter. Indeed, if we imagine Shelley to be ignoring his poem's sustained dismantling of the effects of prosopopoeia, we might read the final lines of this passage as an exhortation to the mountain itself: *Find your voice, Great Mountain!* Or, more to the point of the prospective and instructive form of the infinitive: *Use your voice, Great Mountain, to annul once and for all those fraudulent statutes that cause our world nothing but misery!* Of course, to suggest this is to imply that the speaker, if not the poem, has succumbed to the spell of anthropomorphism. We might ignore the lessons that "Mont Blanc" teaches us about workings of tropes in general, and specifically about the epistemological and even ethical inability of any trope of comprehension to account for the apprehension of the sublime: they are, says the poem, "not understood / By all." After all, the knowledge to be gleaned from the rhetorical lesson of the "great Mountain's" "voice" is as unrelentingly ironic as it is vacating: the poem points explicitly at the failure of the trope its speaker deploys. What the "wise" "interpret," the "great" "make felt," and the "good" "deeply feel" is the obdurate refusal of the mute mountain to accommodate the voices that will inevitably be ascribed to it. If the Shelley of the "Hymn to Intellectual Beauty" can be construed to endorse the trajectory that leads from beauty to freedom, the Shelley of "Mont Blanc" spells out the problem of an aesthetic experience that cancels every proposed solution and leaves it an open question.

These are, as I see it, two of the aesthetic manifestations of the "vital tendency" of Shelley's political poetics. If *identifying* politics as the "vital tendency" of Shelley's project has never been controversial, *evaluating* its nature and its effects has long been one of the defining controversies of Romanticism and its legacy. Among Shelley's detractors as well as his admirers, the efforts to determine the meaning, function, and effects of Shelley's politics have resulted in the most contrasting set of interpretations and judgments among any of the prominent writers of the Romantic tradition. The persistence of this contestation is in itself noteworthy, given that the terms and parameters of those interpretations and judgments have remained remarkably stable for over one hundred and fifty years. Over the past few generations, as interest in Shelley has waned and waxed, there are but a few recognizable Shelleys, each quite at odds with the other. When in 1993, with great economy and precision, Jerrold Hogle reviewed "60–70 years of interpretive criticism directed at Shelley's texts," he revealed a pattern of revolutions that—though this is *not* the point of his essay—hinge on the figure of politics.[9] Thus Eliot's denunciation of Shelley's radical political views ("his ideas are repellant") is replaced by what Hogle describes as the Leavisite "devaluation" that is itself political in nature, predicated as it is on the perception of the poet's "weak grasp upon the actual," a weakness that makes his "surrendering to inspiration" nearly indistinguishable "from surrendering to temptation" (69). Analogously, the recuperations of Shelley over the past fifty years fall into two opposing camps, on the one hand the "philosophical" Shelley epitomized most influentially by Wasserman's *Shelley*, and on the other what Michael Davidson identifies as the visionary political poetics celebrated by the Beats, the Black Mountain poets, and the San Francisco renaissance.[10]

This pattern of reception has, in fact, been in effect for much longer than seventy-five years. If we know anything of Arnold's opinions of Shelley, it is likely to be that the Victorian critic regarded the Romantic poet as an "ineffectual angel, beating his luminous wings in vain." If Wilde's celebration of Shelley is recited less frequently, the terms he uses are not far removed from those that Arnold invokes to denigrate him: a "wanderer in the wilderness, preacher of unreal things." With a critical gesture that Wilde might well have learned from Shelley, Wilde's formulation hinges on its own political turn, an indictment of the very spirit of Shelley's age: "to the blind eyes" of his "own time," the "vital tendency" of Shelley's politics "seems" "vague or unreal," rootless transience and not nomadic subversion.[11]

Still, the influence of Shelley on British radical and working class movements in the nineteenth and twentieth centuries is both continuous and unrivaled by any of his contemporaries or heirs.[12] The fact that Shelley's poetry—its lyric adventurousness as well as its radical commitments—would be championed by Marx and Engels, by DuBois and Brecht only hints at the range and depth of its political purchase. In 1888, seven years after Wilde's New York lecture on "our romantic movement," Marx's daughter, Eleanor, co-authored a fascinating lecture with her companion, Edward Aveling, called "Shelley's Socialism."[13] The lecture offers a glimpse of the extent to which Shelley's political writings, in both poetry and prose, were being read and debated by English radicals during the late decades of the nineteenth century: it demonstrates an engagement that runs deeper than what Marx Aveling calls "the Shelley-worship of the Chartists." Indeed, Marx Aveling claims that Engels once declared to her that "we all knew Shelley by heart."[14] The lecture spells out just how much was at stake *politically* in the legacy of Shelley, the poet who "flung himself into politics and yet . . . never ceased singing" (11). The authors take as their point of departure the elder Marx's famous—if apocryphal—distinction between Shelley and Byron:

> The real difference between Byron and Shelley is this; those who understand them and love them rejoice that Byron died at thirty-six, because if he had lived he would have become a reactionary bourgeois; they grieve that Shelley died at twenty-nine, because he was essentially a revolutionist and he would always have been one of the advanced guard of socialism. (16)[15]

For Aveling and the daughter of Karl Marx the nature of Shelley's revolutionary commitment is confirmed explicitly by a declaration the poet makes in his May Day letter to Hunt: "the system as it exists at present must be overthrown from the foundations" (14–15).

But the authors "claim" Shelley "for socialism" (38) not merely because he is a poet with radical political convictions—his "advocacy" of a "political creed" (19)—but because he is a political thinker whose writings are characterized by "extraordinary political insight" (19). The acuity of Shelley's political analysis is present not only "in the abstract," but in what the authors regard as the unprecedented attention by a poet to "tyranny in the concrete form" (27) and the precision of Shelley's "perception of the class struggle" (29). Shelley is credited with being "the first, . . . indeed the only man of his time to see through Napoleon," to understand him as something other than "a hero or monster" (19).[16] Most pertinently, they argue that the power of Shelley's demystification extends to "the ideas that exercise a malevolent despotism over men's minds" (27), the *spells* of "superstition and empire in all their forms" (27).

To measure the consistency with which politics asserts itself in the reception of Shelley, we can compare "Shelley's Socialism" with another meditation "on the necessity of Shelley" presented, initially also in the form of a lecture, a little over one hundred years later by the poet Michael Palmer. Regarded by many as one of the "advanced guard" of North American letters, Palmer tends to be grouped or anthologized with the L-A-N-G-U-A-G-E poets; but his own self-characterization in the published version of his lecture is more illuminating, and is as apt a description of Shelley as it is for himself: "a poet committed to an exploratory prosody, an assertion of resistance to 'meaning' and 'expression' as givens, and a radical questioning of our means of representation."[17] Not unlike Oscar Wilde a hundred years earlier, Michael Palmer enlists himself in "our romantic movement," in part by claiming Shelley as *our* contemporary, by "reread[ing] and in some sense rediscover[ing] Shelley for contemporary poetics" (197). According to Palmer, Shelley "is a poet of his present moment who invokes alternative social orders through an evocation of the specific injustices of the present and a highly abstract vision of future redress" (197). At times, as Palmer puts it, Shelley "speaks to contemporary injustice . . . with an almost agit-prop directness," and "even his most 'displaced' and idealized poetry has a proto-dialectical character to it" (197). And yet Palmer alerts us to the irony that what Shelley called his *"popular songs wholly political"* are "impossible," their "suppression preordained" (197).

This "suppression preordained" is one feature of a more pervasive erasure of the poet's legacy, one that seems inextricable from the cultural and political significations of "Shelley." For the poets of my generation," writes Palmer, who was born in 1943, "Shelley was a poet under several erasures": Shelley's "often baroque syntax" and his "difficult and audacious juxtaposing of (at his best) precise physical detail with philosophical rumination ran counter to the entire economy of modernism" (201). Pound and Eliot are modernism's exemplars here; and Palmer quotes at length from the famous and famously "condescending" dismissal of Shelley in "The Use of Poetry and the Use of Criticism," where Eliot not only declares Shelley's "ideas" "repellant," but suggests that they cannot be "separated" from the poetry. To which Palmer asks, "Why must a poet be separable from his ideas? To free him for pure, ahistorical readerly delectation? To isolate him definitively in aesthetic space?" (203). Palmer values Shelley precisely for those features Eliot deplores: if for Eliot "we are struck from the beginning by the number of things poetry is expected to do" such that "we shall not know what to expect," Palmer ascribes Shelley's inexhaustible power to his marshaling of poetry's resources "beyond the self and *beyond aesthesis* to engage with contradiction and paradox" (197, emphasis added). Shelley's is a poetry "of critique and renewal" that remains as much with us as behind us (197).

However removed this late twentieth-, early twenty-first-century avantgarde poet might be from the socialist activism of the youngest daughter of Marxism and her companion, they arrive at what is fundamentally the same assessment of Shelley's political poetics. For Palmer, Shelley "more clearly than any of the other English Romantics, represents a radical alterity, an alternative to the habitual discourses of power and mystification by which we are bombarded" (204). It is, in other words, the rhetorical power of Shelley's poetry that achieves this demystification, the same rhetorical capacity Aveling and Marx Aveling invoke in the final section of their lecture, "His Understanding of the Real Meaning of Words" (*Shelley's Socialism*, 33). What these Victorian radicals value above all about Shelley is what we would now call his critical-linguistic analysis, a rhetorical practice that makes possible the critique of ideology as it coheres in those "phrases that are to most of us either formulae or cant" (33). The Shelley pictured in both lectures offers "an alternative to the habitual discourses of power and mystification" by moving "*beyond aesthesis*" (Palmer), by "fling[ing] himself into politics" without ceasing to sing (Aveling and Marx Aveling). In both assessments it is in the final analysis the critical force of Shelley's spelling that breaks the spells of mystification.

Aveling and Marx Aveling could only dream of a Walter Benjamin (though they would never conjure someone with so many theological impulses); but Palmer recognizes that Shelley's own conception of history, his poetics of "futurist vision and address," finds its most compelling crystallization in Benjamin's theses "On the Concept of History." Palmer frames his own lecture on Shelley with invocations of the ninth thesis, the ekphrastic thesis prompted by Klee's *Angelus Novus* that has come to be known as "the angel of history." For Palmer "the visual meaning of this image . . . is anything but stable": what Benjamin calls "the angel of history" might be "refigured" as "the Angel of Poetry whose many faces are like the multiple Shelleys which, since his death, have been imagined or posited and projected toward our time" (*Active Boundaries*, 196).

What Palmer calls Shelley's "multiplicity" certainly applies to Benjamin as well and is the source for much of the vitality, difficulty, and disagreement that accompany his work. Palmer characterizes this as "the various contradictory threads that are responsible for the complex and compelling fabric of his social and aesthetic thought" (196). The "various contradictory threads" have made it possible over the years for Benjamin to mean so many things to so many people and practices, not unlike the case of Benjamin during his *own* lifetime, who might best be described by his own notion of "a constellation saturated with tensions."[18] To speak, then, of a "Benjaminian" Shelley is "anachronistic" only from the perspective of the historicism that is the object of Benjamin's critique. It is far more illuminating for us to grasp the relationship between poet and critic as what Benjamin famously, if enigmatically, calls the "constellation," a historical concept based on a decontextualization that liberates the objects of the past into a reconfigured relationship with those of the present and those yet to come. The notion of the "constellation" allows us to break with the accidental connection of temporal contiguity and to establish a necessary, even "allegorical," if temporally disjunctive, relationship between cultural phenomena. It is a historical understanding that is *kairological* (in the rhetorical as well as theological sense), as opposed to *chronological*.[19] If, invoking Benjamin's second thesis, "On the Concept of History," I suggest that there is a "secret agreement" between Benjamin and Shelley, it is in part because the German critic and the English poet are committed to the engagement between radical political transformation and philosophical aesthetics or, more precisely, because for both to be "wholly political" means to reckon in the deepest sense with the nature of aesthetic experience.[20] I think it is possible to read *The Triumph of Life* as an extended poetic "demonstration" of Benjamin's famous declaration in the seventh thesis that "there is no document of culture which is not at the same time a document of barbarism" (Benjamin, *Selected Writings* [hereafter *SW*], IV, 392). And Shelley's radical revaluation of Milton in the *Defence*—"nothing can exceed the energy and magnificence of Satan as expressed in *Paradise Lost*"—serves as an exemplary version of what Benjamin calls critical "redemption."

The facets of Benjamin's work that are most important to my understanding of Shelley's political poetics are the highly contested notions of the "aura" and the "flash" [*aufblitz*]. The first of these, the Benjaminian aura, we might describe in a preliminary way as the problem posed by aesthetic experience for ethico-political judgments and for historical understanding. The aura is certainly a pivotal term in Benjamin's work, his "attempt," as John McCole puts it, "to bundle [the] diverse elements" of history, politics, and art "into a single concept."[21] If, as McCole argues, "Benjamin's theory of the aura was first and foremost an aesthetic theory" (3), it is a theory that comes with a full historical and political "index." There are about as many explanations and evaluations of Benjamin's "aura" as there are commentators; but Robert Kaufman's version offers one particularly relevant point of departure. Kaufman describes the Benjaminian notion of the aura as a product of Romanticism: the aura is that which is "created through the artist's imaginative labor, the trace presence of something no longer literally, physically present but nonetheless still shimmering."[22] Kaufman's emphasis is the *origin* of the work of art—the aura of *poesis*—and its relationship to "the contiguous concept of *aesthetic autonomy*": "the two (*aura* and *aesthetic autonomy*) had been brought together in the theory and practice of the romantic work of art, whose aura and autonomy were not only simultaneous but synonymous" (122).

Benjamin opens "The Work of Art in the Age of Its Reproducibility" by implicating the aura with those "traditional concepts—such as creativity and genius, eternal value and mystery"—that he hopes his essay will "neutralize" (*SW*, IV, 252). But the essay's most famous explanatory passage on the aura is the one that emphasizes not its poetic origins, but its phenomenological effects. In the third thesis Benjamin turns to the example of "natural objects" in order to "illustrate" the aura surrounding works of art: "We define the aura . . . as the unique apparition of a distance, however near it may be" (255). Benjamin offers this definition of the aura, which derives from "the here and now of the artwork," its "authenticity" (254), to explain its disappearance in "the age of its technological reproducibility": "what withers in the age of the technological reproducibility of the work of art is the latter's aura" (254). If from a genuinely historical perspective the aura of the work of art decays (*Verkummerung*), from the perspective of the auratic experience itself, its vanishing is registered with the shock of something shattered. There can be little disagreement that in *this* essay, written near the end of his life and devoted to the "formulation of revolutionary demands in the politics of art" [*Kunstpolitik*]" (252), Benjamin is committed to the "rupture" [*Bruch*] that would shatter the auratic experience: his project is to *dispel* the aura. In the accompanying footnote, Benjamin writes that the aura "represents nothing more than a formulation of the cult value of the work of art in categories of spatiotemporal perception" (272).[23] In Mc-Cole's account, "the auratically perceived object seems to cast a spell that binds and absorbs the observer"; and it is "this spell [that] lends the cultic object its authority" (5). In the next year, as Benjamin revised his reflections on Baudelaire into a form Adorno might find acceptable, he would characterize "the experience of the aura" according to Marx's logic of commodity fetishism:

> Experience of the aura . . . arises from the fact that a response characteristic of human relationships is transposed to the relationship between human and inanimate or natural objects. The person we look at, who feels he is being looked at, looks at us in turn. To experience the aura of an object we look at means to invest it with the ability to look back at us. (*SW*, IV, 338)

The mystified "experience of the aura" makes us believe that an object, namely the work of art, can return the gaze of the beholder. There is a cluster of Shelleyan figures that convey this "experience of the aura," each of which cast one form or another of a spell, from the "frail spells" of the "Hymn" to the deeper and more intractable form of the "oblivious spell" of *The Triumph of Life*.

However ambivalent Benjamin may have been about the historical disappearance of the aura in modernity, his writings insist that the experience of the aura always bears within itself the potential for the kinds of aesthetic spells that must be countered by the jolt of politics. But this does not place aesthetics and politics in opposition. Benjamin's figure of the "flash" [*aufblitzt*], for example, is to the best of my knowledge exclusively "redemptive" in his work, the sole and fragile medium for critical illumination. The "flash" is the means by which constellations are grasped; it is the form taken by the genuine images of history. For Benjamin—as for Shelley in a related idiom—history famously appears in the *aesthetic* form of an *image*: "The true image of the past [*Das wahre Bild der Vergangenheit*] flits by. The past can be seized only as an image that flashes up [*aufblitzt*] at the moment of its recognizability, and is never seen again. . . . For it is an irretrievable image of the past which threatens to disappear in any present that does not recognize itself as intended in that image" (*SW*, IV, 390). The genuine mode of historical comprehension, according to Benjamin, occurs by way of the apprehension of images sent like "ashes and sparks" from the past. It is the structure of history itself that offers up these images; and these images *intend* us, single us out "momently" with the great gift of their revival: they flash up for us to behold. But this process is both precious and urgent: the image of the past "appears unexpectedly" "at a moment of danger" (392); and if the opportunity to "seize" it is missed, it "threatens to disappear" *at once and ever* into oblivion. The "past" is a nonhuman image that flashes up, solicits the gaze, asks to be seen, "seized," recognized. The "auratic" features of this experience, and thus its aesthetic dimension, are unmistakable and inextricable from Benjamin's concept of historical understanding. While none of this may *explain* Shelley's own difficult conception of historical agency, I believe Benjamin's theory of history *illuminates* it. In its grappling with the spellbinding nature of an auratic aesthetic experience and its account of the "flashing" of an image from the past, Benjamin's work offers the most cognate examples of which I am aware regarding the effects of Shelley's figure of "spelling" in its mystifying and even "oblivious" forms and the "kindling" images sent from the past that open onto futurity. The ashes and cinders of the poetic word, remainders of a previous burning, await futurity's rekindling, where "for some uncertain moments" they might "flash up" at "the moment" of their "recognizability."

Shelley's "wholly political" poems, such as those provoked by the Peterloo massacre, feature both dimensions of this activity: a rhetorical demystification or dispelling (England itself is a "veil" or "mask of anarchy") that is accompanied by the image of an incalculable opening, the "flash" of possibility.[24] "England in 1819," for example, a sonnet that Shelley sent to Hunt with no illusions that it would be published, identifies the institutions of the English state as a series of graves:

> An old, mad, blind, despised, and dying King;
> Princes, the dregs of their dull race, who flow
> Through public scorn,—mud from a muddy spring;
> Rulers who neither see nor fell nor know,
> But leechlike to their fainting country cling
> Till they drop, blind in blood, without a blow.
> A people starved and stabbed in th'untilled field;
> An army, whom liberticide and prey
> Makes as a two-edged sword to all who wield;
> Golden and sanguine laws which tempt and slay;
> Religion Christless, Godless—a book sealed;
> A senate, Time's worst statute, unrepealed—
> Are graves from which a glorious Phantom may
> Burst, to illumine our tempestuous day.

The dating in the title (Mary's addition) is significant not because things might be better in 1820 or, say, 1832, but because the phrase "England in 1819" demonstrates that the nation and the poem are bound to this date: the nation itself is now "Time's worst statute," imprisoned to actuality. Indeed, the form itself of this sonnet seems to be oppressed by the actualities of the nation it describes: this strange sonnet is a static catalogue of phrases and clauses, an enumeration of the ills that characterize the English state in 1819: "An old, mad, despised, and dying King"; "Princes, the dregs of their dull race"; "Rulers who neither see nor feel nor know"; "A people starved and stabbed"; "Religion Christless, Godless"; "A senate, Time's worst statute, unrepealed." The litany extends for twelve lines without hint of turn or, in Shelley's words, "repeal." It is not until the closing couplet that this poem finds its verb, its agreement secured in the static form of the copula: the institutions of the state "are graves." Significantly, the poem turns after this agreement has been reached or, as Adorno might have put it, after the identity between subject and copula has been "extorted" [*erpresste*].[25] The poem's final prepositional phrases herald, through the explosive enjambment of the last lines, the disruptive force of the "glorious phantom." These English institutions "are graves from which a glorious phantom may / Burst, to illumine our tempestuous day": these "graves" are empty places—vacancies or "dead zones"—from which the phantom (called) possibility *may* erupt with the force of illumination.[26]

If Shelley's poetry is, as he says in his preface to *Hellas*, often "written at the suggestion of the events of the moment" (*SPP* 407), its call is to and from the future: poets are, after all, the "hierophants of an unapprehended inspiration, the mirrors of the gigantic shadows which futurity casts upon the present" (*SPP* 508). Without this poetic mirroring of futurity's shadows, England in 1819 would remain a "book sealed." But if poetry opens the book of the future, it does not spell out its contents in advance. "England in 1819" calls upon the phantom as the redemptive force of history, but the power of this resurrected phantom is qualified by the subjunctive mode and figured as potentiality. And yet it is also the turn from the indicative to the subjunctive that opens this redemptive potential: one might call it the grammatical vehicle of the phantom's liberation from the "graves" of the nation-state.

The England in 1819 that is represented to us in Shelley's "England in 1819" thus qualifies as what Benjamin in the eighth thesis "On the Concept of History" calls a "state of emergency" (*SW*, IV, 392) from which the messianic phantoms of the poem "may/Burst, to illumine our tempestuous day." That the sonnet—its method and its effects—should be illuminated by Benjamin's theses on history demonstrates Shelley's incompatibility with historicism: genuine history for Shelley, as for Benjamin, is not composed of events unfolding through "homogenous, empty time" (395). And like Benjamin's "historical materialist," Shelley "cannot do without the notion of a present which is not a transition, but in which time takes a stand [*einsteht*] and has come to a stop" (396). *This* is "England in 1819": the poetic "sign of a messianic arrest of happening, . . . a revolutionary chance in the fight for the oppressed past" (396). As with Benjamin's sense of a "*weak* messianic power (*eine* schwache *messianische Kraft*), a power on which the past has a claim" (390), a messianism without the messiah, Shelley's phantoms would "blast" the state out of "the continuum of history," a revolutionary break with its historical conditions (396).[27]

One might assert that Shelley's manipulation of the sonnet form, the sudden force of the enjambment in the closing couplet, expresses his sense of the disruptive power of revolutionary illumination; but it would be more to the point of Shelley's own "Benjaminian" poetics and politics to say that the poem is less an *expression* of his historico-political understanding than that the poem itself—the poetic resources that are conjured in and by the sonnet—*produces* this sense of historical and political possibility. Much of the power of the "Hymn to Intellectual Beauty" derives from a similar poetic act, its performance of the call to "the phantoms of a thousand hours / Each from his voiceless grave," a call intended to invoke the spell of redeeming love in the phantom conjuring of futurity. In the later sonnet the subjunctive agency of the phantom is conjured to "repeal" not the spell of "God and ghosts and heaven," but the *spell of the actual*. Thus what we might call the critical redemption value of Shelley's poetry, including the sonnet "written at the suggestion of the events of the moment," resides not in its reference to the present or the empirical, but in its blank opening onto futurity.

Kindling and Ash

Kindling is scattered throughout Shelley's poetry; and by the time of *Adonais*, it has become one of the primary figures for an aesthetic illumination that bears a political force in the poet's mature conception of history.[28] In the metaleptic account of history often featured in Shelley's poems, we arrive at this agency of kindling through the figure of ash. Perhaps the most famous version of the kindling of ash appears in the fifth stanza of "Ode to the West Wind." It follows the speaker's imploring of the wind's "Spirit fierce" to *be* his spirit and, in one of Romanticism's most extravagant and defining apostrophes, to *be him*. Nothing can guarantee that such an impetuous spirit would accommodate a demand for identification; and thus, without marking the shift in requests, the speaker settles for something else:

> Drive my dead thoughts over the universe
> Like withered leaves to quicken a new birth!
> And, by the incantation of this verse,
> Scatter, as from an unextinguished hearth
> Ashes and sparks, my words among mankind!
> (ll.64–68)

Singled out by history, the speaker seizes upon this moment to make good on the promise of this great gift: "by the incantation of *this* verse," *this* poetic utterance calls upon the wind to regard it as nothing more, but nothing less, than "ashes," but the very ashes that might "spark" future re-ignition. The ashes of the poetic word are traces not only of a *past* burning but, unextinguished and called upon by the *present* incantation of verse, offer the kindling of a *future* birth—should the wind oblige. In Shelley's ode the residue of fire requires the agency of the wind—indeed, the *aura* as a messianic "breath of air"—to fulfill its revolutionary historical potential. In Shelley's poetics of the trace structure of history, ashes await the rekindling of futurity, ashes that, to invoke once again Benjamin's theses on history, "flash up" again at a moment of danger.

But the power of this apostrophic poetics of history is also a measure of its fragility. For nothing *guarantees* its future re-ignition; and everything depends on the willingness of the "Wild Spirit," an "uncontrollable" spirit of the wind, to hear the incantation of the poet's letters *and* respond to it. It's the wind's decision or, as we might say, the wind's "call"; and only the wind can decide the status of the famous question with which the poem closes. For if the poetic word is an ash or a spark, there is no promise that it won't simply burn out and deliver us not to the hope of spring, but to nothing more than the ashes of time. "Ode to the West Wind," in other words, spells out a model of history and poetry that is not itself what I am calling a radical aestheticism, but that leaves such a radical consequence suspended as the obverse of its apostrophic and revolutionary desires.[29] There are, however, poetic sites in Shelley's work where one may confront and even experience the radical aestheticism that haunts the Ode. These sites are marked by a different sense of kindling. And it is by the light of this kindling that I want to read in some detail Shelley's poem "On the Medusa of Leonardo da Vinci in the Florentine Gallery."

I

It lieth, gazing on the midnight sky,
    Upon the cloudy mountain-peak supine
Below, far lands are seen tremblingly;
    Its horror and its beauty are divine.
Upon its lips and eyelids seems to lie
    Loveliness like a shadow, from which shine,
Fiery and lurid, struggling underneath,
The agonies of anguish and of death.

II

Yet it is less the horror than the grace
    Which turns the gazer's spirit into stone,
Whereon the lineaments of that dead face
    Are graven, till the characters be grown
Into itself, and thought no more can trace;
    'Tis the melodious hue of beauty thrown

Athwart the darkness and the glare of pain,
Which humanize and harmonize the strain.

III

And from its head as from one body grow,
  As [   ] grass out of a watery rock,
Hairs which are vipers, and they curl and flow
  And their long tangles in each other lock,
And with unending involutions show
  Their mailed radiance, as it were to mock
The torture and the death within, and saw
The solid air with many a ragged jaw.

IV

And, from a stone beside, a poisonous eft
  Peeps idly into those Gorgon eyes;
Whilst in the air a ghastly bat, bereft
  Of sense, has flitted with a mad surprise
Out of the cave this hideous light had cleft,
  And he comes hastening like moth that hies
After a taper; and the midnight sky
Flares, a light more dread than obscurity.

V

'Tis the tempestuous loveliness of terror;
  For from the serpents gleams a brazen glare
Kindled by that inextricable error,
  Which makes a thrilling vapour of the air
Become a [   ] and ever-shifting mirror
  Of all the beauty and the terror there—
A woman's countenance, with serpent-locks,
Gazing in death on Heaven from those wet rocks.

[Additional Stanza]
It is a woman's countenance divine
  With everlasting beauty breathing there
Which from a stormy mountain's peak, supine
  Gazes into the [   ] night's trembling air.
It is a trunkless head, and on its feature
  Death has met life, but there is life in death,
The blood is frozen—but unconquered Nature
  Seems struggling to the last, without a breath—
The fragment of an uncreated creature.[30]

The poem would certainly seem an unlikely candidate for any sort of aestheticism, radical or otherwise. It exhibits none of the formal elegance we often find on display in Shelley's poetry, such as the spectacular *terza rima* of the "Ode to the West Wind." And despite the attention in "On the Medusa" to the *painting's* "grace" and "melodious hue of beauty," there is little "grace" to be found in its own tortured lines, and the hues of its melody are strained and discordant. The irregularities of its meter, the contortions of many of its rhymes, the enjambments that are more entangling than unfolding, the repeated awkwardness of its syntax, its unfinished state: one could with good cause regard the poem as a handbook of aesthetic infelicities. The formal straining extends to the persistent doublings in the poem's catalogue of the painting's properties, doublings that seem to alternate between oppositions and similarities. One finds "horror and beauty" (l.4), "horror and grace" (l.9), "darkness and glare" (l.15), "beauty and terror" (l.38), as well as the more parallel or equivalent relationships: "anguish and death" (l.8), "fiery and lurid" (l.7), "torture and death" (l.23). Perhaps the best articulation of the rhetorical, formal, and thematic condition of the poem is to be found in the accumulation of clauses and conjunctions, phrases and prepositions that conclude the second stanza: "'Tis the melodious hue of beauty thrown/Athwart the darkness and the glare of pain,/Which humanize and harmonize the strain" (ll.14–16). In almost every line, one encounters clauses and phrases that seem gathered and "thrown/Athwart" one other; and in almost every line one encounters a persistent "straining" in the poem's attempts at conjunction, most dramatically in the very process of "humanizing and harmonizing" that might constitute a "hue of beauty." Put simply, "On the Medusa of Leonardo da Vinci in the Florentine Gallery" is in every way a very hard read.

One might get around the many difficulties of this hard poem by turning to the context of post-revolutionary Europe to consider how the apotropaic image and blazon of the Gorgon had become associated in both France and England with fantasies of Jacobin terror. One might explore how "Medusa's head" reappeared time and again in conservative accounts of the Revolution as a symptomatic emblem of what Neil Hertz has analyzed as "male hysteria under political pressure."[31] One might consider how Shelley's poem addresses the figure and fantasy of the Medusa that is brandished at the very moment that fear overwhelms political analysis. Or one might take up the psychoanalytic discourses that, beginning with Freud's account, have regarded the myth of the Medusa as an emblem of male fear and desire. But as much as the political context or the psychoanalytic model of the Medusa may resonate in the poem, Shelley is trying to come to terms with a *particular* Medusa found in a painting long and incorrectly attributed to Leonardo that hung in the Uffizi where Shelley often visited during his Italian exile.[32] For if there is one thing that Shelley's title insists upon with its string of prepositional phrases, it is that the poem is about *one thing*. Never wavering from this singularity of focus, the poem is itself an uncompromising engagement with that other aesthetic object. All of which suggests that to be a very hard read is perhaps precisely what the poem *wants* to be. It is certainly the quality that would attract Adorno, for instance, who might well read the poem as a refusal to "humanize and harmonize the strain," as a formal act of poetic resistance to the very "grace" that might turn the poem's *readers'* "spirit into stone." To the degree that Adorno would regard the poem as fulfilling the task of a great work of art—"the greatness of works of art . . . consists solely in the fact that they give voice to what ideology hides"[33]—it is because the poem "gives voice" to the true machinations of an aesthetic ideology and performs this truth-telling by its own formal and rhetorical resistances to the false reconciliations performed in the name of a spurious "humanizing and harmonizing."

How better to undertake a poetic critique of the aesthetic than by way of an ekphrastic poem? Unlike "Ozymandias," Shelley's most famous ekphrastic effort, "On the Medusa" does not perform the kind of multiply historicizing and contextualizing gestures that give the former poem its stark, critical power. When looking at this Medusa, Shelley looks directly into the picture without asking any questions of its maker: he does not, in other words, reframe the object with the same critical irony that makes "Ozymandias" into a genuine poetic critique of the relationship between power, history, and the aesthetic. Indeed, the poem's title is the only indication that we are reading a poem about a painting. Which is to say that the gaze of the poem never ventures beyond the frame of the painting, never addresses the picture's context. But without the historicizing move and without any of the interpretive strategies that would break the frame, Shelley's "Medusa" poem immediately raises important questions about the aesthetic hopes and desires that inform the ekphrastic mode, its hopes and desires to "make us see." And in a larger sense, by maintaining the framing of the aesthetic, by keeping the frame intact, Shelley's poem immerses us into the aesthetic and into the kindling and ash at work there.

Surely to write a poem on, of all things, a painting of the head of the Medusa immediately announces a complication of—if not downright provocation to—the ekphrastic mode. In a chapter called "Ekphrasis and the Other" in his book *Picture Theory*, W. J. T. Mitchell discusses Shelley's poem in terms of the anxieties that always haunt the ekphrastic impulse.[34] According to Mitchell, ekphrasis provokes the "fear" that the "reciprocity or free exchange and transference between visual and verbal art" will result in a "dangerous promiscuity" that must be "regulated" (155). Emphasizing the triangulated structure of an ekphrastic poem—the triangulation of seeing poet, seen object, and reader—Mitchell describes the crisis that Shelley's "Medusa" poses for ekphrasis by demonstrating what one could describe as the poem's ethical refusal to speak for the object. Any serious reading of the poem must heed Mitchell's example and address a series of vexing questions involving the ekphrastic impulse. What does it mean for a poet to try to make us see something that would turn "our spirit" as "gazers" into stone? Is the poem, in other words, less an instance of what Mitchell describes as Shelley's responsible restraint than an example of Shelley's perverse confrontation with the reader and an instance of Shelley's perversion of the ekphrastic mode? Does Shelley occupy the role of the triumphant Perseus here by brandishing the head of Leonardo's Medusa to those of us who read the poem while he prudently looks away? Or, as Carol Jacobs muses at the beginning of what is to my mind the finest essay written on the poem, does its ekphrastic framing "function like the shield of Perseus, mirroring the Gorgon's head and protecting us from its effects?"[35] In other words, does the prosaic title "On the Medusa of Leonardo da Vinci in the Florentine Gallery" serve as a double frame that permits us to look and master the image, situating the viewer as a kind of proxy Perseus that allows us to occupy the role of the hero?

But if we look still closer, we begin to realize that no act of seeing is free and clear in a poem that incessantly bends the lines of sight and complicates at every turn the relationship between seeing subject, seen object, and reader, a poem in which the most apparently straightforward acts of description become entangled in their own figures. This is the picture of the poem that emerges from Jacobs's painstaking reading. Beginning with problems of gazing and viewing, Jacobs "traces" the poem's involutions and demonstrates the oscillations that occur that make it difficult, even impossible, to distinguish between a beholding subject and the object that is beheld. These involutions extend, as Jacobs demonstrates, to all readers of the poem, herself included, and makes it impossible to "extricate our gaze from this scene" in order to "contemplate its critical implications" (8).

We thus have the "lineaments" of two readings of the poem that are attentive to its relationship to the aesthetic: (1) Mitchell's account of Shelley's poem as a critique of ekphrasis, an account that resonates with Adorno's understanding of the dissonant power of poetic demystification; and (2) Jacobs's deconstructive reading of the "inextricable error" revealed by the poem's "involuted" figurations. What I want to propose in what follows is a kind of supplementary reading, one that accounts for the force of both readings, but in so doing retraces the work of "kindling" in the poem's figurations of light and sight and then reckons with their consequences for the aesthetic.

If the poem refuses the role of the Persean hero, what is its relationship to the figure of the Medusa? The poem appears to identify not with Perseus, but with the Gorgon. But *identification* isn't quite right: rather, the poem refuses the ekphrastic tendency to speak for the Medusa, and instead displays the political and aesthetic machinery that reifies her. The poem thus resists the dubious position of identification while simultaneously undermining the mythological and conservative gestures of making the Gorgon into the abject figure of terror. Regarded from this perspective, "On the Medusa of Leonardo da Vinci in the Florentine Gallery" undertakes a bold demystification of the ekphrastic desires announced in its title: not speaking for the figure, the poem reveals instead the apparatus that makes "it" threatening, the aestheticizing that does so. If "Its horror and its beauty are divine," it is this very beauty that deceives: "Upon its lips and eyelids seems to lie/Loveliness like a shadow" (ll.4–6). "Loveliness" veils or covers the authentic and human "agonies of life and death" that, "fiery and lurid," struggle underneath. Loveliness lies, and as we might say colloquially, it lies like a shadow—as does "the melodious hue of beauty thrown/Athwart the darkness and the glare of pain,/Which humanize and harmonize the strain" (ll.14–16). If we read this "strain" as much as a poetic or artistic strain as a physical strain, the lines cue us to Adorno's critique and prompt us to question the status of this humanizing and harmonizing cast by the "melodious hue of beauty." In other words, the poem says that we are enticed by the painting's humanizing and harmonizing to ignore the more dissonant strains that play beneath its "melodious hue." What, then, are humanizing and harmonizing other than an aesthetic cover-up, a refusal to look more closely upon the agonies that reside there, in the head of the Medusa?

Medusa remains an "it" until the last official stanza restores her as "A woman's countenance . . . /Gazing in death on Heaven from those wet rocks" (ll.39–40). Thus what we really and truly see there is "a *woman's* countenance," whose face and therefore humanity we deny in order to aestheticize *it* into a thing of terror: the poem seems to assert that the violence of this aestheticization is the "terror of the beauty there." Moreover, the lines demonstrate what has been at work throughout the poem's torqued accumulation of conjunctions—namely, the twists and turns of the relationship between death and the aesthetic that are now revealed to be two intimately linked forms of transformation. The aesthetic transformation of "face" to "head," "countenance" to "it" is bound to the very transformation of death itself that is caught in a kind of "freeze-frame," still "gazing in death on Heaven." In other words, the processes of aesthetic transformation mystify the painful truths of death that the "woman's countenance" *sees all too well*. Thus would the poem reveal the veneer of the aesthetic as well as the social and sexual politics that lie underneath. In this reading the poem reveals the machinery, the apparatus and consequences of that aestheticization. As such the poem brings to light what the shields of our mythologies, aesthetics, and politics have prevented us from seeing: a woman. This, then, is the ethical power of the poem: to give a face to a figure.[36]

But if beneath the "beauty and terror" of the aesthetic ideology lies a "woman's countenance," *countenance* is still nothing but a figure, a trope for the face and the expressions of the face. Thus Shelley's poetically bold and ethically compelling move—to rewrite the Medusa's head as a woman's countenance—does not free us from the unending involutions or ever-shifting mirrors of figuration. Moreover, to interpret the poem as an ethical demystification of the aesthetic would seem, in an irony that would not be lost on Shelley, to reconfirm the success of the ekphrastic impulse that the poem seems at every point to complicate. In such a demystifying interpretation the poem would seem to have unveiled the aesthetic ideology that has by turns demonized, slain, and frozen the Medusa and, by virtue of this unveiling, delivered us into the light and made us see. But certainly the prospects of any such clarity of vision are unlikely in a poem that seems to complicate every act of seeing it describes or invites.

The complications begin with the opening words. "It lieth, gazing": all reference to Leonardo or its status as painting vanishes after the title; and this forces the reader to confront at the outset the interpretive difficulty of an uncertain reference. The poem's opening word should refer to the painting and not to the head of the Medusa. But the lines read not "it hangeth," but "it lieth"; and they effect at one turn the transfer from frame to picture: "it" is the head lying and gazing. The opening lines thus introduce an instability of beholder and beheld that the poem, a series of oscillations and their consequences, never resolves. There is at the outset, for instance, the "cloudy mountain-peak" that itself seems by virtue of the syntax "supine": "below, far lands are seen tremblingly" (l.3). Such a strange adverbial attribution poses still another question: lands are seen tremblingly, but by whom and from where? The lines would seem to position a viewer where only Perseus could stand, but in only the most precarious and "trembling" position.

The consequences that the viewer "faces" come soon enough. The second stanza begins by describing what occurs when the "gazer's spirit is turned to stone": "the lineaments of that dead face/Are graven, till the characters be grown/Into itself, and thought no more can trace" (ll.11–13). "That dead face" would be inscribed with the figures or characters until they are grown into itself and thus inseparable from the characters. But the Medusa effect makes the poem's reference into an uncertain one, for, does the "dead face" belong to the Gorgon or to the one who "gazes" at her? The involuted syntax of the sentence that traces out this process does not much clarify matters: here, "thought no more can trace." As Jacobs is "tempted to ask," "Can no longer trace what?" (9). We expect an object for the verb "trace" and are confronted instead with an end, a limit: no object appears to complete the tracings of thought. By making "trace" into an intransitive verb, the lines demonstrate or perform the dead end of this process. "Thought" stops with the end of the line, but the sentence and signifying do not, just as the third and fourth stanzas begin as if they were paratactic additions that then complicate and entangle everything that has preceded them.

The complications are due in part to the shift in the poem's "gaze" from face to hair. After considering the status of the head and its relation to beauty, the poem turns to the "hairs which are vipers and they curl and flow/And their long tangles in each other lock,/And with unending involutions show/Their mailed radiance" (ll.19–22). Certainly by this point in this difficult poem, we will interpret the "mailed radiance" of these "unending involutions" not only as poetic descriptions of Medusa's serpent-hair, but as a reflection—and perhaps even a judgment of sorts—on the poem's own tangled and "involuted" signifying. The poem's syntactical, formal, and rhetorical "involutions" complicate the work of the poem's demystification. For if the "involutions" that the poem addresses and that we experience are indeed "unending," it becomes harder to imagine a place from which the demystification of the aesthetic could take place. We find ourselves getting tangled in its syntax and diction, propelled by enveloping adverbial clauses that seem to acquire a life of their own, caught in the spell of the poem's elaborate figurations, such as the spell of a "midnight sky"/[which] flares, a light more dread than obscurity" (ll.31–32). This light is more dread than obscurity because, unlike the obscurity that awaits its illumination, only darkness could spell us from the effects of the flaring of this light. Nothing is more dread for Shelley, whose poetics is, at least at this point in his career, organized on the work of the sun, the true sun, which, announced by daybreak, banishes error and reveals truth in its radiant multiplicity. But there is no sun in this painting or this poem, not even the excess of sun that might blind at the point of illumination. Here we gaze upon a light that is "dread more than obscurity" precisely if paradoxically because it *isn't* blinding. The poem produces a light that no longer conforms to the dialectic of blindness and illumination. And thus the only light to be seen in or gleaned from this poem is that which flares from a midnight sky or gleams from serpents, a light that offers no knowledge, no illumination, no prospect of futurity dawning or spring following.

It is the "gleaming" in Shelley's poem that is the key. "For from the serpents gleams a brazen glare /Kindled by that inextricable error, /Which makes a thrilling vapour of the air/Become a [   ] and ever-shifting mirror/Of all the beauty and the terror there—" (ll.34–38). We are directed by these lines to search for the source of the "inextricable error" that does all this kindling. But everything we have encountered in the poem insists this error is *irreducibly* inextricable, particularly since the poem offers no source of illumination that might deliver us from the serpent's own gleaming. The lines imply that once we look into the painting, once we engage in the act of looking that is made possible by the "brazen glare/Kindled by that inextricable error," we are caught in the play of an ever-shifting mirror that transforms what is "there" into something insubstantial and that aestheticizes "it" into a "thrilling vapour." This is what awaits the reader "singled out" to confront Shelley's non-ekphrastic poem about the act of looking at a painting and about the looking that occurs within that painting: he or she will encounter the event of the poem's own "kindling" of the "inextricable error" that is experienced *at* and *as* aestheticism's radical.

If a radical aestheticism creates a crisis of sorts for the rhetorical reading in pursuit of Shelley's deconstruction of the aesthetic as well as for the ethico-political reading intent upon revealing Shelley's demystification of the aesthetic, it also creates a crisis for Shelley's own skepticism, or at least for our ways of understanding it.[37] In the opening paragraphs of his *Memoirs of the Blind*, Derrida notes that skepticism resides in "the difference between believing and seeing": "Before doubt ever becomes a system, *skepsis* has to do with the eyes."[38] Shelley's poem poses to its own poet the difficulty of maintaining a genuine skepticism in the face of the aesthetic "kindling" of "*inextricable error*" that undoes the basis upon which one can be "skeptical," for one must be able to trust both the eyes and the light to practice a skepticism. Shelley's poem vacates the grounds of such skepticism without substituting anything like belief, and certainly not any belief in the aesthetic itself, for how could one *believe* in what can only appear to be the "frail spell" of the "thrilling vapour" of "an ever-shifting mirror"?[39]

Heidegger famously concludes "The Origin of the Work of Art" by declaring that Hölderlin is "the poet—whose work still confronts the Germans as a test to be stood."[40] If, as I believe, Shelley is the poet whose work still confronts the Anglophone poetic tradition as a "test to be stood," it is precisely for the "confrontation" of his most radical aestheticism.

"A Shape All Light"

I want to conclude this chapter as I began, with a *spelling*. Until the mini-renaissance initiated by Carol Jacobs, "On the Medusa of Leonardo da Vinci in the Florentine Gallery" remained little read and less studied: it was not, to be sure, a poem that critics had placed at the forefront of Shelley's poetic project. *The Triumph of Life*, on the other hand, has long occupied a principal place in that project, and certainly not exclusively because it was the final entry in a foreshortened trajectory. *The Triumph of Life* is one of the few Shelley poems to win Eliot's approval; and, as arguably Shelley's most ambitious undertaking, it is a poem that critics from Wasserman and Bloom to Hogle and de Man have regarded as necessary to confront in detail. If the question of politics frames "On the Medusa" both in terms of the context of French Revolutionary terror and in light of the gendered representation of its principal image, *The Triumph of Life* explicitly addresses the intertwining of politics and history. The poem's sustained representation of the "triumphal pageant" of history can be read as an allegory of Benjamin's account of the inextricability of culture and history, of aesthetics and politics, fully anticipating and confirming the famous declaration in the seventh thesis, "On the Concept of History," that "there is no document of culture which is not at the same time a document of barbarism" (*SW*, IV, 392).

If "On the Medusa" confronts the reader with the prospect of "a light more dread than obscurity"—an image in which the sun and its powers of illumination have been banished—*The Triumph* famously opens with daybreak:

> Swift as a spirit hastening to his task
>> Of glory and of good, the Sun sprang forth
> Rejoicing in his splendour, and the mask
>> Of darkness fell from the awakened Earth.
>
> (ll. 1–4)

Readers have long noted the eruptive force and brisk economy of these enjambed opening lines; and once we behold that "the mask / Of darkness" has
fallen "from the awakened Earth," we recognize that the poem has begun with
an "awakening" that Shelley would regard as "wholly political." Thus whatever
else might transpire in the "triumphal pageant" that constitutes the body of
the poem, those grim and sordid events are set in motion by a political image
that seems to offer the source and force of an illumination, "a spirit hastening to his / Task of glory and of good" (ll. 1–2). The politics of daybreak and
daybreak *as* politics: in the idiom of Shelley's political poetics, the lines register
the force and hope of a "phantom bursting to illumine our tempestuous day."

This glorious beginning of glory's beginning inaugurates a procession of
images of nature's own form of worship. Following the almost instantaneous
combustion of the forceful beginning, the subsequent lines unfold in the
stately and ceremonial manner of a processional:

> The smokeless altars of the mountain snows
>> Flamed above crimson clouds, and at the birth
> Of light, the Ocean's orison arose
>> To which the birds tempered their matin lay.
> All flowers in field or forest which unclose
>> Their trembling eyelids to the kiss of day,
> Swinging their censers in the element,
>> With orient incense lit by the new ray
> Burned slow and inconsumably, and sent
>> Their odorous sighs up to the smiling air . . .
>
> (ll. 5–14)

Maybe we are meant to understand these lines as presenting and celebrating
a natural mode of worship; but the images of religious pageantry inject a note
of ambivalence that deepens as the earth's "orisons" give way to the institutions of ceremony and reverence. It is at this point that the poem unmistakably introduces its own political self-critique that, in turn, complicates the
ostensibly liberating force of the image with which it begins:

And in succession due, did Continent,

> Isle, Ocean, and all things that in them wear
> The form and character of mortal mould
>> Rise as the Sun their father rose, to bear

Their portion of the toil which he of old imposed on them . . .

(ll.15–20)

With the "imposition" of his "portion of toil" upon "all things that in them wear / The form and character of mortal mould," the politics of the Sun shifts registers. The combustive force of the beginning is drawn into the slow, laborious movement of the morning's pageantry as all things are obligated to rejoice in the Sun's "splendour." Thus is the topic of politics injected into these opening lines with the full range of Shelleyan torsion: the origins of illumination—and, indeed, the very possibility of an originary "awakening," one repeated often enough that we assure ourselves that if darkness is here, dawn cannot be far behind—are suddenly and inextricably bound up with the imposition of power.

"But I," says the speaker, I missed all that. On account of "thoughts which must remain untold," the speaker declares his obliviousness to this dawn processional in the glorious cathedral of the Apennines. Indeed, it is the ceremony of daybreak from which the speaker has turned away. In his recumbent position, "a strange trance" over his

> fancy grew
>> Which was not slumber, for the shape it spread
>
> Was so transparent that the scene came through
>> As clear as when a veil of light is drawn
> O'er evening hills they glimmer . . .

(ll.29–33)

The "strange trance" spreads a "shade" "so transparent" that it resembles a glimmering "veil of light" over "evening hills." I can think of no better name for this illusory phenomenon than Benjamin's "aura"; and it is in this state that the triumphal "Vision" unfolds for the speaker. The auratic state or "spell," quite distinctly described as a veil produced from a trance, gives rise in the poem to a historical pageant that is, ironically, *the true image of history* as Benjamin calls it, "*das wahre Bild der Vergangeheit*," flashing up at this "moment of danger," a "Vision" that this speaker is singled out to behold.

One of the pressing questions posed by *The Triumph of Life* is one that is equally urgent for Benjamin and indeed for anyone concerned with how history is witnessed: who are the privileged spectators of this pageant of history—who are those who have been addressed or "singled out"—and who are its participants? This question is addressed most explicitly in the scene in which the poet-narrator encounters the "triumphal pageant" that accompanies the conquering chariot's advance: "where'er / The chariot rolled a captive multitude / Was driven" (ll.119–20). The list of those imprisoned to this "triumphal pageant" is an extensive one:

> all those who had grown old in power
> Or misery,—all who have their age subdued,
>> By action or by suffering. . . .
> All those whose fame or infamy must grow
>> Till the great winter lay the form and name
> Of their green earth with them forever low—
>>> (ll.121–27)

The scope of ideological enslavement is such that only the "sacred few" can be said to escape it; and the poet's account of the "sacred few" is worth noting:

> All but the sacred few who could not tame
> Their spirits to the Conqueror, but as soon
>> As they had touched the world with living flame
> Fled back like eagles to their native noon . . .
>>> (ll.128–31)

The lines rearticulate a structure we have identified in Shelley's earlier poems: all those touched by the worldly actuality of power, whether philosopher or statesman or theologian, are enslaved to the "Conqueror." Only those who managed to flee the world and to place their thought in exile, namely Christ and Socrates, have successfully avoided this defeat. Christ and Socrates belong to this sacred group of exiles because, as de Man puts it, "they are mere fictions in the writings of others."[41] In the poem, moreover, they are not named as such: Socrates and Christ, who left no written traces of their existence, are referred to as "they of Athens and Jerusalem," metonymic identifications that figure them in terms of their displacement from all worldly power.

This sense of irreducible implication—of spectator and victim, of aesthetic and politics—is only deepened during the sequences of the "Vision" in which the speaker's guide and interlocutor, namely Rousseau or "what was once Rousseau," recounts the story of his own entrancement (ll.305–525). With these lines we find the poem spiraling into perhaps the most extended and extravagant aesthetic figurations and experiences in this extravagant poet's brief career. These figures and experiences participate in a sensual engagement of such intensity that they broach the threshold of synesthesia and with "savage music, stunning music" "spell" out nothing less than the repeated "Visions" of a radical aestheticism (ll.434–35).

The figure of Rousseau beholds an image that "flashes up" and threatens everything in the poem with oblivion. Rousseau, or "what was once Rousseau," recounts to the speaker of Shelley's poem the origin of his implication in the "parade of wickedness" that has unfolded before the speaker (and the reader) and that the poem offers as the structure of history. Rousseau poses the story explicitly as a cautionary tale: he succumbed as a result of the spells and enchantments of aesthetic incantation. Rousseau didn't intend to be there; but he found himself in a "place/. . . filled with many sounds woven into one/Oblivious melody, confusing sense" (ll.339–41). If *you* were to hear this music, he tells his interlocutor, *you*, too, would be seduced: "so sweet and deep is the oblivious spell," cast by this music that "thou wouldst forget" all ethical obligations, commitments, and intentions should "thou" hear it (ll.331, 327).

How else are we to read this "spell," now twice "oblivious," than as an aesthetic entrancement, the complete and "deplorable" succumbing to what Keats calls "sable charms and dumb enchantments"? "Oblivious" works as adjectives often do in Shelley's poetry: the spell manufactures forgetfulness because, *as a spell*, it is itself "oblivious." This obliviousness extends to Rousseau's distinction between past and present and, at the very moment of its recalling, returns the poem to the present tense: "Whether my life had been before that sleep/The Heaven which I imagine, or a Hell/Like this harsh world in which I wake to weep/I know not" (ll.332–35). The effect of this spell is thus deep enough to "confuse sense" and to remove the grounds of knowledge. "Spelling" is in this sense far from frail: it implies a condition, a "turn" or "fit" for which there is no outside, no recovery. To call this poetry radical is to suggest that it delivers poetry itself to its radical, to its own vacancy, where the phantoms that may burst from their graves do so not in order to "illumine our tempestuous day," but, by the "kindling of inextricable error," cast a spell of "light more dread than obscurity." The effect of this dread bright light may well be the voiding of the "frail spells" of "God and ghosts and heaven"; but the obliterating aesthetic trance it casts is represented by the poem as insurmountable. And it is to this spell that our narrator—"what was once Rousseau"—traces the origins of his own implication in the "wretchedness" of world history.

But the scene is also the site of his encounter with a figure that erupts from the fire and the Sun and that yet belongs to no natural or sensory optical system: "A shape all light." If the cascading of Shelley's *terza rima*, a seemingly self-generating single sentence that unfolds over more than twenty wildly enjambed lines, makes it difficult to cite the instance of the shape's appearance, that seems precisely the point. We take up the sentence at the point of Rousseau's encounter with the shape:

"And as I looked the bright omnipresence
    Of morning through the orient cave flowed,
And the Sun's image radiantly intense

"Burned on the waters of the well that glowed
Like gold, and threaded all the forest maze
    With winding paths of emerald fire—there stood

"Amid the sun, as he amid the blaze
    Of his own glory, on the vibrating
Floor of the fountain, paved with flashing rays,

"A shape all light . . ."

(ll. 343–52)

As the "Sun's image radiantly intense / Burned on the waters," there appears, "standing," "*amid*" that very sun, a sensory impossibility, a non-natural and non-theological "shape all light" that can exist only as an aesthetic effect. Unlike the sun or God, however, this "shape all light" that is in reality *nothing at all* offers no genuine illumination or truth. By definition, "a shape all light" is not representable as such; and, in fact, it "stands there" before Rousseau as a sensory impossibility. But *as poetry*, the effects the shape has on the senses and on cognition are extensive and obliterating. In the first instance it effaces the reflection of that most "radiantly intense" and illuminating of images, the "Sun's image," what one might have called the image of images before the appearance of "a shape all light" rendered it irrelevant.

The effects and implications of this encounter with a "shape all light," which is but another name for the encounter with the vacating radical of the aesthetic itself, are played out in the final passage narrated by this post-Rousseau:

"And still her feet, no less than the sweet tune
To which they moved, seemed as they moved, to blot
    The thoughts of him who gazed on them, and soon

"All that was seemed as if it had been not,

As if the gazer's mind was strewn beneath
Her feet like embers, and she thought by thought,

"Trampled its fires into the dust of death . . .
(ll.382–88)

The lines both name and perform the consequences of the radical aestheticism I have been describing. The lines address both the aesthetic movement—its poetic feet as well as its tune—and the consequences for those who, in a compounding if not confusing of the senses, "gaze" on it. Of the many indispensable lessons of de Man's reading of this poem, none is more to the point of our discussion than his awareness that the "sweet tune" is a lure, a tease that hides the violence of the act of obliteration that it performs, an obliteration moreover of all sense of history and of any meaningful context: "all that was seemed as if it had been not." As de Man phrases it, "the trampling gesture enacts the necessary recurrence of the initial violence: a figure of thought, the very light of cognition, obliterates thought" (119).

And yet de Man's own most rigorous efforts to resist the aesthetic ideology he names and reads leads him, in the case of Shelley, to turn away from "light's severe excess" (l.424), from the *aestheticism* that burns a hole in the heart of this poem and, one might say, in the very heart of Shelley's poetic project. The radical aestheticism encountered in this poem leaves us with no prospect that its "ashes and sparks" might be kindled into anything like illumination or liberation, no means by which the scattering of these "oblivious" embers of might be transformed into the instrument of prophecy or awakening. To declare that there are genuine matters at stake in the fleeting appearance of a poetic image in an unfinished text of a poet long dead runs the risk of hyperbole to the point of caricature. But to the degree that we take Shelley's poetry and poetics seriously—to the degree that we believe his *project* continues to pose a set of possibilities for the relationship between poetry and history—the stakes of this image are indeed considerable, for the poem's representations of Rousseau's story, of course, but also for the poem's critique of history as triumphal pageant. For if *The Triumph of Life* reads history by "brushing it against the grain" in a genuine Benjaminian fashion, the poetic (which is to say non-phenomenal) occurrence of "a shape all light" turns the poem into Benjamin's catastrophe: the appearance of "a shape all light" that offers no historical illumination. Indeed, one can say it appears *in order* to "blot the thoughts of him who gazed" on it. When this "shape all light" "flashed up" to Rousseau at his own "moment of danger," it produced no "index" of "redemption" (*SW*, IV, 390). We might call it an *event*, but only if we understand by "event" that that undoes the possibility of historical reckoning. If this is a visual image, there is nothing "pictorial" about it, since its appearance supersaturates the visual field to the point of white-out.[42]

If my readings of Shelley have been persuasive, one will have found in these extraordinary poems a simultaneous reflection on and *experience* of the aesthetic that leaves the minds of poets, readers, and all varieties of "gazers" "strewn beneath / Her feet like embers." If Shelley's last poem makes it clear that this radical aestheticism is nothing to be espoused, it is also clear that the poem cannot avoid its incendiary effects. The poem and those who read it are confronted by this condition and thus assigned the same experience the poem recounts: "the thoughts of him who gazed on them" are, as in Shelley's poem, blotted by this uncontrolled aestheticizing, and the mind itself is burned up as the shape all light "tramples its fires"—the fires of the mind—"into the dust of death." Ashes, cinders, embers: these are the poetic traces of an aesthetic "enkindling" that can be called radical.

The radical aestheticism I have been working to read and describe in "On the Medusa of Leonardo" and *The Triumph of Life* makes no claim for the autonomy of art—which would be the most predictable recuperative gesture—but delivers us instead to the very root of the aesthestic, undoing all the comforts and compensations of aestheticization. Of course, there are times when we desperately want the aesthetic to heal and to comfort, times when no other function of art seems more urgent or necessary. It is a longing that Shelley deeply understood. At such times—which Benjamin described as "states of emergency"—the very last thing we may want is to be delivered to aestheticism's radical; the very last thing we may believe that we need is a confrontation with, of all things, kindling and ash. At such times even the poetic exploration of cinders and embers may strike us as perverse and horrific. But it is precisely during such a "state of emergency" that Benjamin in his ninth thesis, "On the Concept of History," taught us to reckon with what an angel saw. To Benjamin's eyes, the "angel of history" he saw in Klee's "Angelus Novus" confronts "one single catastrophe, which keeps piling wreckage upon wreckage and hurls it at his feet. The angel would like to stay, awaken the dead, and make whole what has been smashed" (*SW*, IV, 392). But for Benjamin the angel brings no redemption: he cannot "awaken the dead, and make whole what has been smashed." "A storm is blowing from Paradise" that "drives him irresistibly into the future, to which his back is turned, while the pile of debris grows toward the sky" (392). If a radical aestheticism *teaches* us anything, perhaps it teaches us to read the figures of Medusa and "what was once Rousseau" as Benjaminian angels of a sort, not as *redemptive* "angels of history," but as the allegorical markings of art's undoing. This is the angel as Adorno came to read it, the angel as the "inhuman" figure that makes no promise of redemption. "It takes and gives nothing back," said Adorno. If this is the case, then Shelley's embers and cinders, their flaring and burning, their kindling and ash may in our own state of emergency offer a "light more dread" but more necessary "than obscurity."

Joseph Severn, *Keats on His Deathbed* (Eileen Tweedy / The Art Archive at Art Resource, NY)

TWO

"I Hold It Towards You": Keats's Weakness

"Consumed in the Fire"

The title of this opening section on Keats's weakness comes from a poem
that by some conventional reckonings inaugurates Keats's strengths as a poet.
The phrase "consumed in the fire" belongs to "On Sitting Down to Read
King Lear Once Again," a sonnet Keats wrote in 1818 on a page inside his
folio Shakespeare, a sonnet that both anticipates and recalls the experience
of reading. The poem opens with a closing and a leave-taking: an address to
the "Romance," to the "serene lute," to what we could call the poet's own
aestheticizing:

> O golden-tongued Romance, with serene Lute!
> Fair plumed syren, queen of far-away!
> Leave melodizing on this wintry day,
> Shut up thine olden pages, and be mute.
> Adieu! for, once again, the fierce dispute
> Betwixt damnation and impassion'd clay
> Must I burn through; once more humbly assay

The bitter-sweet of this Shakspearean fruit.
Chief Poet! And ye clouds of Albion,
Begetters of our deep eternal theme!
When through the old oak forest I am gone,
Let me not wander in a barren dream:
But, when I am consumed in the fire,
Give me new Phoenix wings to fly at my desire.[1]

The poem's opening lines are a preparation for a fundamentally different experience: "sitting down to read *King Lear* once again" entails a silencing of all the seductive enticements associated with the sensuous dimension of sound—the "golden-tongued Romance," the "serene lute," the "fair plumed syren." The prologue to reading, completed by the opening lines, says goodbye to all forms of "melodizing." Indeed, the first quatrain seems addressed to the lure of the aesthetic that our speaker seems to know all too well, a temptation that must be repelled repeatedly: Shut up! Be mute! Adieu!

The opening quatrain closes the book on aestheticizing, because the speaker has been summoned by an ethical "dispute." The summons is in part a generic one: the "Romance" of the first quatrain gives way to the tragedy of the second. In the course of this displacement, the poem change registers entirely: we move from the "fair plumed syren" to the "fierce dispute / Betwixt damnation and impassion'd clay," from the seductions of the aesthetic to the rigors of the ethical. Keats's interpreters have been correct to conclude that the poem marks this shift formally and thematically as a deepened understanding on the part of the poet as well as that of the speaker. The completion of the octave coincides with the supremacy of tragedy and the provocation of its ethical *necessity*, the "bitter-sweet of this Shakespearean fruit."

Keats never relinquishes the prospect of poetry as an ethical project, of art itself as a "friend to man." But this aesthetic friendship—"To sooth the cares, and lift the thoughts of man"—is most often posited as a goal, "the end and aim of Poesy," as Keats spells it out in *Sleep and Poetry* (ll.245–47). The contrast with what I have described as Shelley's project is illuminating: if Shelley doubts everything *but* the effective coordination between politics and aesthetics, Keats *never presumes* that an aesthetic orientation leads to an ethical conclusion. Many of his best poems begin with aesthetics and ethics in a disjunctive relationship, a "fierce dispute" that must be overcome; and the poems are compelled to revisit this disjunction over and over again.

To be sure, the "fierce dispute" at the core of *King Lear* makes it not just a tragedy, but for Keats *the* tragedy, the one in which he encounters the all-consuming conflict between irreconcilables. If some readers or spectators have discovered a way to understand how the play manages to "lift the thoughts of man," it is fair to say that it has never been known to "sooth the cares": the intense crucible of its ethical dilemma is a far cry from the comforting vision of literature and ethics pronounced in *Sleep and Poetry*. Keats's only allusion to the play's action is of Lear wandering "through the old oak forest," his power reduced to naught. And of course the sonnet figures this condition as one that befalls the play's reader, who knows in advance the experience he will undergo and its potential for utter disorientation: "When through the old oak forest I am gone, / Let me not wander in a barren dream." The act of reading *King Lear* is thus an act of inevitable misidentification with the one whose might is made into absolute nothing.

"Sitting Down to Read *King Lear* Once Again" is exemplary in Keats's strongest poetry, not only for its torqued confrontation between aesthetics and ethics, but also for the complicated outcome of that relationship. The disjunction between aesthetics and ethics is not resolved or superseded in or by the sonnet. Here as elsewhere in Keats's most distinctive poetry, the turn to the ethical does not in fact leave the aesthetic behind. In this sonnet the engagement between ethics and aesthetics hinges on the figure of reading. The advent of the ethical orientation—the "fierce dispute" through which the genuine reading will occur—is described in performative terms, the risky repetition of a self-immolation, an event the speaker "must" "burn through." To subject oneself to reading is to subject oneself to the play's disorienting might and in the process to submit oneself to the fire; and the result of burning with *this* "hard gem-like flame" is to be reduced to ashes. The speaker must implore his "Chief Poet" in advance to give him the necessary "Phoenix wings" "to fly at his desire"; but there is no promise that a resurrection will occur from the incendiary act of reading. If there was a prior burning, moreover, there is no suggestion of a *first* burning: the "Chief poet" and the "clouds of Albion" are the "begetters" of an "eternal theme," a perpetual burning. And thus the turn to the ethical is not represented as an overcoming of the seductions of the aesthetic, but as a succumbing to a radically aestheticized version of the ethical.

But, crucially, the poem's account of reading is described in prospective terms. Compelled to return to the pages of *Lear*, poised before an act of reading that must be repeated, the poet writes his sonnet as a prologue to rereading, one that recalls the fate of an earlier burning and might thus prepare the reader, "sitting down," for its consequences. The sonnet is thus best understood as the *description* of a radical aestheticism: "On Sitting Down to Read *King Lear* Once Again" announces a burning that, if undertaken, might well consume the sonnet itself. But poised between a past and future burning, the formal qualities and properties of the sonnet are preserved. Fire is only the medium that delivers us here and in some other vital poems to a more decisive opposition between strength and weakness, one that makes Keats's poetry the most "vital" place to reckon with the aesthetics of weakness and its consequences for a poetry of ethical regard.

Weakness

We recall that in his New York lecture on "The English Renaissance in Art," Wilde identifies Keats alongside Shelley as inaugurating the strain or "tendency" of poetry and aesthetics that would establish what Wilde called "our romantic movement." Moreover, he stresses the "*vitality*" of this tendency. But in the case of Keats this vitality derives in the poet's complete devotion to art, "the tendency to value life for the sake of art." Wilde's elegiac sonnet "On the Grave of Keats" reaches into the catalogue to find yet another figure by which to eroticize and mythologize an aesthetic "sacrifice" that, even before the poet's death, had been both variously eroticized and mythologized. "Fair as Sebastian, and as early slain," writes Wilde, "O poet-painter of our English land" (ll.5, 11).[2] From the moment that Keats's poems were first read and discussed, it is the "vitality" of this "tendency," this capacity to sacrifice life for art, this "painterly-poetry"—indeed, this "aestheticism"—that establishes an index of Keats's *ethical* "weakness," one delineated in the most precise terms by Hopkins in a letter to Patmore:

> It is impossible not to feel with weariness how his verse is at every turn abandoning itself to an unmanly and enervating luxury. It appears that he said something like "O for a life of impressions instead of thoughts." It was, I suppose, the life he tried to lead. The impressions are not likely to have been all innocent and they soon ceased in death. His contemporaries, as Wordsworth, Byron, Shelley, and even Leigh Hunt, right or wrong, still concerned themselves with great causes, as liberty and religion; but he lived in mythology and fairyland the life of a dreamer.[3]

"Unmanly and enervating luxury": Hopkins makes it clear that this is not merely the feature of an indolent and langorous poetry, but an *ethos*, "the life he tried to lead." The identification of Keats with weakness itself has been one of the most persistent legacies of Romanticism. Indeed, Keats's archive constitutes a dictionary of weaknesses. There is, for instance, the poet's "deficiency in physical strength," the sort of weakness that either made him susceptible to consumption or that was made manifest by the sickness that took his life. Once he had succumbed, we know that Fanny Brawne was keen to dispel the charge that Keats had displayed "weakness of character."[4] And then there is the equally notorious emotional weakness that has long been attributed to the poet who composed the great ode on melancholy, an inability to "control emotions"; and the poetry itself has often been regarded as "unduly swayed by grief, compassion, or affection." These "unmanly" modes of weakness converge in the pathos of his death, the tremulous and fragile beauty of the poet who was always about to leave us. It may very well be this fragility that prompts our often outsized allegiance to Keats and delivers us repeatedly and vicariously, perhaps even pathologically, into a state of mourning, at least those of us weak enough to be seduced by the aura of transient beauty in a minor key that hovers about this iconic poet. The topos of this pathos is enshrined in *Adonais*, Shelley's elegiac hymn to Keats's weakness, which, interestingly enough, stresses the weakness of Keats's "hands": "Why did thou with weak hands though mighty heart / Dare the unpastured dragon in his den? / Defenceless as thou wert, oh where was then / Wisdom the mirrored shield?" (ll.237–40). Far from being "warm and capable of earnest grasping," Keats's "living hands" are, in Shelley's poem, weak: without Perseus's "mirrored shield" the poet's "mighty heart" is open and "defenceless" when confronted by the Gorgon of criticism. And thus does Keats's mortal weakness prompt Shelley's own extravagant poetics of mourning, a flood of tears so deep and relentless that it drowns every English elegy written in its wake.[5]

But I am interested here less in Keats as a figure *for* weakness than in Keats's own figures *of* weakness and their significance for his poetic project. There are many poignant letters that chronicle Keats's acute awareness of the want of strength precipitated by his infirmity; and many of those letters offer a keen sense of the doubts and insecurities Keats felt about his poetic skills. Even in 1819, at what we typically regard as the height of his powers, Keats fears his poetry is weak to the point of being "smokeable," an expression that, as James Chandler has noted, is best understood as "an act of *comprehension* that implies an act of *condescension*" (*England in 1819*, 399): "I smoke more and more my own insufficiency," Keats writes to George and Georgiana. And the

self-deprecating account of a poet's weakness in Book III of *Endymion* is sufficiently definitive to have earned an entry in the *OED*: "O 'tis a very sin for
one so weak to venture his poor verse in such a place as this" (III, l.933).

The opposition between strength and weakness has from the very beginning framed our understanding and evaluation of Keats; and it is an opposition that has governed every effort to fashion a narrative of the poet's career.
And it is also the case that Keats's own sense of his poetic project, which de
Man rightly characterizes as "prospective rather than retrospective," is organized by this opposition and consists of "anticipations of future power."[6] The
most formative version of this opposition can be found in *Sleep and Poetry*,
where the speaker, "holding" and "grasping" his pen, twice pleads in an "ardent prayer" to the figure of Poesy to be admitted as "a glorious denizen/Of
thy wide heaven" (ll.47–49). It is, of course, a central element of the poem's
conceit that the speaker knows he is not "yet" strong enough: better then
to "kneel/Upon some mountain-top" in complete submission until he can
"feel/A glowing splendour round about me hung/And echo back the voice"
of Poesy's "own tongue" (ll.49–52). Hanging hung at the end of the line to
rhyme with tongue as a means of playing at strength and weakness: we recognize this as a characteristic note in Keats's poetry, sounded again most exquisitely at the end of the "Ode on Melancholy."

The closing image in this prayer for poetic power, a prayer delivered with
the force of a refrain, is not merely an image of poetic power, but a vision of
a fundamentally ethical project to be accomplished through that poetry: to
"write on my tablets all that was permitted" and "then the events of this wide
world I'd seize/Like a strong giant" (ll.80–82). Even Hopkins discerned the
glimmers of this "powerful" ethical project in Keats. In the very letter to Patmore in which he would stress Keats's "unmanly and enervating luxury," he
alludes to the nature of this project: "I feel and see in him the beginnings of
something opposite to this [abandonment to unmanly and enervating luxury],
of an interest in higher things and of powerful and active thought" (Hopkins,
Letters, 272). The *Hyperion* poems demonstrate that the topic of poetry's relationship to ethics retains its force and its significance throughout Keats's brief
career; and they serve as the occasion for two of the "strongest" poems in the
Romantic tradition. But in *Sleep and Poetry* figures of strength are projections,
something to be imagined only by way of a thoroughly aestheticized self-
immersion, an absolute submission of the self to the "great Apollo," "a fresh
sacrifice" that is experienced as a kind of death. "To die a death/Of luxury"

is how Keats describes this self-indulgent undoing, a necessary turn in the trajectory of this fantasy of poetic achievement. It is a moment that we may want to ascribe to "negative capability," but only if we understand that Keats is imagining that to get strong he must first get completely weak.

This trajectory is registered in the disproportionate relationship between the titular figures of sleep and poetry that is belied by the conjunction that binds them: in the poem itself, sleep certainly gets short shrift, only eighteen lines, against the almost four hundred lines devoted to poetry. But the opening ode to sleep—"light hoverer around our happy pillows/Wreather of poppy buds, and weeping willows" (ll.13–14)—provides the portal through which the sources and effects of poetry can be discerned and measured. These intricate relationships between strength and weakness in this early poem arrive at their most posed version in the account of poetry's illuminating might: "A drainless shower/Of light is poesy; 'tis the supreme of power;/'Tis might slumb'ring on its own right arm" (ll.235–37). "'Tis might" *posed*, indolent, langorous, sleepy.[7]

The figure of poetry's "wakened" might appears as the speaker assesses Lord Byron's strength, the "supreme poetic power" of his own age, which the speaker describes as "Strange thunders from the potency of song/Mingled indeed with what is sweet and strong/From majesty" (ll.229–31). But for Keats's speaker this potency is both too much and too little: "strength alone though of the muses born/Is like a fallen angel" (ll.240–41). "Strength alone" annihilates what Keats's speaker identifies as "the great end/Of poesy": to "be a friend/To sooth the cares, and lift the thoughts of man" (ll.245–47).

This is not merely an assessment of the power of Byron's poetic achievement: Keats discerns in Byron's poetry itself the presence of "strength alone," a sheer and unrelated power that, while it may have been issued by the muses, is in its non-relative form not only an ethical failing, but that which *produces* an aesthetic experience that is unredeemable. "Strength alone" disfigures poetry's ethical mission.

The opposition between strength and weakness is pervasive for Keats; and the extent and effects of Keatsian oxymorons are an index of the rhetorical experimentation undertaken in the poet's complicated engagements with oppositions.[8] But the degree to which Keats puts the terms of this opposition into play tends to obscure what I believe to be a fundamental question of Keats's poetry: how to figure absolute weakness—as well as absolute strength—atheologically.

In the long journal-letter to George and Georgiana in that "miraculous" spring of 1819, Keats sketched out another kind of weakness, one that compelled him into the mode of confession. This is a form of weakness that we admit, always with a measure of guilt, as when we confess to a weakness for some form of indulgence. It is, by dictionary definition, a "self-indulgent inclination" that often indicates "an infirmity of character." The weakness to which Keats confesses in this letter is indolence. "My passions are all asleep," Keats writes, "from having slumbered till nearly eleven and weakened the animal fibre all over me to a delightful sensation about three degrees on this side of faintness.—If I had teeth of pearl and the breath of lilies I should call it languor—but as I am + I must call it laziness." We are less than "three degrees" removed from the condition Roland Barthes describes as the "glorious and philosophical form of laziness": "In a situation of idleness the subject is almost dispossessed of his consistency as a subject. He is decentered, unable even to say 'I.' That would be true idleness. To be able, at certain moments, to no longer have to say 'I.'"[9] It is at this point—where the weakness of an aestheticized indolence assumes an ethical charge—that the affinities between Keats and Barthes are most productive and, however unlikely, most mutually illuminating.

"*La paresse*": in his later work Barthes was drawn to this condition of laziness, idleness, indolence as an aesthetic disposition. Barthes's radiant essays—sketches, really—on the "extreme delicacy" of the art of Cy Twombly return time and again to this experience of indolence. In Twombly indolence is the effect of the hand, of a script that is "far away" from the "formed, drawn, deliberate, shapely writing which in the eighteenth century was called *a fine hand*."[10] This lazy hand, weak and incapable of anything but "negligent" "gestures": Twombly's drawings, which Barthes pointedly refers to as "writings," are "the scraps of an indolence (*les bribes d'une paresse*), hence of extreme elegance" (158). Given the insouciant coupling of indolence and elegance, it is striking that Barthes concludes his reflections on Twombly's works on paper with a section devoted to the "morality" of the artist. "The artist has no morals," he insists, "but he has a *morality*" (173). This "morality"—what I have been describing in the case of Keats as ethical impulses—comprises a series of questions posed by the works themselves: "*What are others for me? How am I to desire them? How do I lend myself to their desire? How am I to behave among them?*" (173). And it turns out that Twombly's "morality" is in fact achieved by the indolence "which constitutes his entire art":

What *seems* to intervene in TW's line and to conduct it to the verge of that very mysterious *dysgraphia* which constitutes his entire art is a certain indolence (which is one of the purest of the body's signs). Indolence: this is precisely what enables "drawing," ... TW's art—this is its morality, and also its greatest historical singularity—*does not want to take anything*; it hangs together, it floats, it drifts between desire, which subtly animates the hand, and politeness, which dismisses it. (173, 175)

Twombly's "On Mists of Idleness" (ultimately retitled, "Say Goodbye, Catullus, to the Shores of Asia Minor") is an evanescent manifestation of this indolent disposition, the same disposition evident in Keats's "The Human Seasons," the sonnet from which Twombly takes his (modified) title and, ostensibly, his inspiration. In the poem Keats describes how the autumnal soul is "contented so to look/On mists *in* idleness—to let fair things/Pass by unheeded" (ll.10−12): he is, in other words, by the time of autumn, sufficiently contented in his idleness that he would look at mists and allow "fair things" to pass by "unheeded."

As in the case of the "Benjaminian" Shelley I developed in Chapter 1, the relationship I am proposing here between Barthes and Keats is less on the order of a hermeneutic than an "affinity," in this case a shared aesthetic disposition. But the fulcrum of Cy Twombly should demonstrate that the ascription of this affinity is not capricious. Twombly is the artist whose paintings and drawings solicited two of Barthes's most exquisite essays; and the figures, titles, obsessions of Keats are scrawled across many of Twombly's paintings and drawings. Twombly's Keats is Barthes's Twombly, "nurtured by Antiquity" (186); it is the Keats of the Hyperions, Psyche, Apollo, the Keats who is by turns fragmented and belated, indolent and elegant. Thus the constellation Keats-Barthes-Twombly suggests not the methodological model of a hermeneutic circle, but rather what Barthes calls "a kind of golden triangle," the illumination generated by bringing poetry, painting, and criticism to bear upon these aesthetic effects.[11]

In his letter to George and Georgiana, Keats describes his immersion in the "mists of idleness" as approaching a "state of effeminacy": "neither poetry, nor ambition, nor love have any alertness or countenance as they pass by me: they seem rather like three figures on a Greek vase . . ." (*KL*, II, 122). In such a weakened condition of indolence, the passions and projects of Keats's life are aestheticized, transformed into allegorical figures that pass before him, "masque-like figures on the dreamy urn." This "state of effeminacy," this "weakening" of the "animal fibre," this sybaritic repose, this indolence: these are the affective features of a discourse of aesthetic experience that, however embarrassed or embarrassing, is far from exhausted. If we are "about three degrees on this side of faintness," we cannot be far from heaven, from "dying the death of luxury."

"In love with death?" writes Barthes of *s'abimer* in the first entry of *A Lover's Discourse*. "*S'abimer,*" or the "crisis of engulfment," delivers Barthes to the second of only two references to Keats in Barthes's work, a reference that leaves its mark as an "exaggeration": "In love with death? An exaggeration (*c'est trop dire*) to say, with Keats, *half in love with easeful death*. Death liberated from dying."[12] If this is something too much for Barthes to say or claim, nothing better describes the state of indolence to which Keats confesses his own love. And Barthes's fleeting reference to those lines from the "Ode to a Nightingale" prompts the admission of a fantasy that should earn him honorary membership to the Keats Circle:

> Then I have this fantasy: a gentle hemorrhage which flows from no specific point in my body, an almost immediate consumption (*consumption*), calculated so that I might have the time to abate my suffering without yet having died. . . . I conceive of death *beside me*: I conceive of it according to an unthought logic, I drift outside of the fatal couple which links life and death by opposing them to each other. (*Lover's Discourse*, 12)

However slight Barthes's knowledge of Keats's life or reading of his poems may have been, he has effectively absorbed the English poet's discourse of love into his own. Almost any reference to Keats's love letters will bear this out, such as the celebrated—or infamous—declaration to Fanny: "You have absorbed me. I have a sensation at the present moment as though I was dissolving. . . . You have ravish'd me away by a Power I cannot resist" (*KL*, II, 223–24).

In the ode Keats wrote on the topic, not even the ravishments of love have a purchase on the "benumbing" effects of the "blissful cloud of summer-indolence" (l.16). Keats's account of an aestheticized indolence in the letter to George and Georgiana serves as a kind of epistolary draft of the figures that would appear in the ode that is often regarded as the weakest of the group. "A disappointment," claims Stuart Sperry, and following as it does the odes to the Nightingale, Urn, and Melancholy, "an anti-climax."[13] But I regard it to be among Keats's most exquisite poems, sustaining its sense of fragile repose over six delicate stanzas in which nothing really happens save for the fleeting appearance of shadows that haven't the might to "raise" the speaker's "head cool-bedded in the flowery grass." Here the Greek figures are transferred from Keats's letter on indolence to the ode in the form of ghostly "shadows" that have scarcely "pass'd by" before they disappear. It is a poem in which "appearance" is always experienced in its flickering transience: "they pass'd, like figures on a marble urn" (l.5). Indeed, the poem is a meditation of sorts on the various forms and conditions of "passing" as it lingers over and through the actions of melting, vanishing, and fading. The poem's only figures of stress or strain arise from fading: the speaker's temporary "burning" and "aching" "for poetry's wings" in the third stanza, to which he says "farewell" and, weakness restored, leaves us with this trembling glissade of an ode.

The ode is not only a meditation on the experience of indolence, but an exploration of the ways in which the dissipating effects of this condition extend to the most assertive forms of language, the speech act of the command. When the poem bids its final "adieu" to the "three ghosts," it commands them to "fade" and "vanish": "Fade softly from my eyes, and be once more / In masque-like figures on the dreamy urn" (ll.55–56); "Vanish, ye phantoms, from my idle spright, / Into the clouds, and never more return" (ll.59–60). The "fading" and "vanishing" to which the poem refers diminish the power of its linguistic imperatives: the force of those orders fades and vanishes in turn. "Fade *softly* from my eyes" (l.55) and be the figures that you *seemed* to be ("They pass'd, *like* figures on a marble urn" [l.5]); or "vanish" "Into the clouds, and never more return." Indeed, the urn on which these masque-like figures are projected is drained of its own materiality by the end of the ode: the "marble urn" in the first stanza becomes "the dreamy urn" of the final lines.

"Leaving the British Museum": this is the rubric for a crucial strain of Keats's reckonings with his aesthetic experience of the Elgin Marbles that, according to Severn, Keats went to see "again and again," sitting before them "for an hour or more" "rapt in revery."[14] Weakness is the point of departure for two sonnets composed March 1, 1817 on the topic of *seeing* the Elgin Marbles. Unlike the ode that Keats would later write on another Grecian object, in which the speaker undertakes an urgent, feverish reading of the imaginary urn he projects to view, neither of these early sonnets ventures anything as rigorous as a reading of the objects. Indeed, they scarcely qualify as ekphrastic poems, so little do the qualities or features of the seen marbles seem to matter. It is only in the sestet of the first of the sonnets that Keats makes reference to the objects named in the title; and even this reference is scarcely more than a gesture, a mere pointing at "these wonders."

Sperry stresses the immaturity of "On Seeing the Elgin Marbles" and "To Haydon," describing their failure "to elaborate [the] deeper value and significance [of seeing the marbles] through a meaningful play of images rather than permitting it to evaporate in blank amazement" (75). His evaluation is, of course, an ethical one based on the assumption that sonnets *should* do something more "meaningful" than "evaporate in blank amazement," that the poet is under an ethical obligation to "elaborate the value and significance" of aesthetic experience.[15] For Sperry it is an index of the poet's early weakness—and a measure of his subsequent strength—that these two sonnets simply languor in the scented vapors of this experience. But this misses the most important feature of the sonnets: that they point to the event of an aesthetic encounter of such magnitude that Keats must twice devote the form of a sonnet to this engagement with the "blank amazement" of aesthetic experience, what Peter de Bolla has called the "mutism" of aesthetic surprise, the effect of being struck dumb or, as another early sonnet has it, blanked with "wild surmise," reduced to "silence, upon a peak in Darien" (*Art Matters*, 3–4).[16] Whether we understand it as a "state of inarticulacy" or as what Keats in "To Haydon" calls "staring with browless idiotism"—aphasiac tongue or feeble mind—these two sonnets on the power of Greek art are *about* being undone in the wake of an aesthetic experience.

Barthes concludes his late essay on "Leaving the Movie-Theatre" by acknowledging that he is also leaving behind the Brechtian relationship to the image that had informed much of his demythologizing criticism: "armed by the discourse of counter-ideology," such spectatorial "critical vision" labors to break "ideological hypnosis." Giving up this ideological struggle, Barthes elaborates a new orientation to the image and its effects: to "let oneself be fascinated *twice over*." How better to describe Keats's own poetic account of the aesthetic experience of seeing the marbles than letting himself be fascinated *twice over*? Twice in fast succession Keats writes sonnets on the "same" experience as if to luxuriate yet again in the "dizzy pain" of the experience. "To Haydon" opens with a confession of weakness that is developed throughout the octave in a series of relatively stable oppositions between "these mighty things"—presumably the marbles—and the poet's abject sense of his inabilities. If this pattern of oppositions also characterizes the second sonnet, "On Seeing the Elgin Marbles" does nothing to break the auratic spell conjured by "To Haydon." Here, however, the poem opens with a declaration—"My spirit is too weak"—that is never qualified or overturned: no Pauline reversal ("my strength is accomplished in weakness" [II Corinthians 12:9]) is forthcoming; rather, the declared weakness is "accomplished" with the poem's final dissipation.

> My spirit is too weak—mortality
> Weighs heavily on me like unwilling sleep,
> And each imagined pinnacle and steep
> Of godlike hardship, tells me I must die
> Like a sick eagle looking at the sky.
> Yet 'tis a gentle luxury to weep
> That I have not the cloudy winds to keep,
> Fresh for the opening of the morning's eye.
> Such dim-conceived glories of the brain
> Bring round the heart an undescribable feud;
> So do these wonders a most dizzy pain,
> That mingles Grecian grandeur with the rude
> Wasting of old time—with a billowy main—
> A sun—a shadow of a magnitude.

The "undescribable feud" that is at the heart of the poem is not the conventional "feud" between poetry and sculpture: as I see it the "object of this poem is" *not*, as Marjorie Levinson has asserted, "to turn sculpture into writing."[17] There is no contest here: the "feud" generated by the "dim-conceived glories of the brain"—a meditation on poetic ambitions and the voice of mortality—is decided in advance. Description itself is surrendered: not only is this "feud" "undescribable," the sculpted features of the marbles themselves remain entirely undescribed. In this sonnet the act of seeing or looking is an index of weakness, "like a sick eagle looking at the sky." "These wonders," the properties of which the poem ignores, "bring round the heart" "a most dizzy pain," a kind of vertiginous unease "that mingles Grecian grandeur with the rude wasting of old time." Like so many readers, I am moved by what happens in the final three lines of the sonnet, this strange prepositional phrase bereft of subordination, this disarticulation that leaves us with a sonnet in ruins. However much the lines may summon us to manufacture a narrative or supply the comparison, their very disconnection demands that we linger among these images of the exquisite syntactical breakdown that comes of an aesthetic experience of this "magnitude."

"My spirit is too weak": *for what?* we might ask, especially if we are indolent enough as readers to be arrested by that statement, forgetting that the dash might be read as some form of subordinating conjunction or disjunction.

If we allow that opening statement, which is also a confession of sorts, the autonomy of its position, the declaration can be understood as giving rise to the lines that follow. "My spirit is too weak," in other words, to write an ekphrastic poem that would describe "these wonders," so here instead is a sonnet on the weakness they have induced. Thus it is only on the condition that the spirit is "too weak" that this second sonnet about the "weakness" induced by the aesthetic experience can appear.[18]

This is not merely a feature of Keats's early "weak" poetry, one that is overcome by the strong works of 1819, where weakness is no longer conveyed through "blank amazement" and broken syntax, but through some of Keats's strongest lines of poetry. Keats never takes leave of the figures of weakness. Its presence is unmistakable in both versions of the *Hyperion* experiment and evident in the swirling last lines of another of the great odes, the one on melancholy, where the "falling" of a "melancholy fit" delivers the speaker, the subject, and the reader to "the very temple of delight" where "Veil'd melancholy has her sovran shrine," oblivious to all "save him whose strenuous tongue / Can burst joy's grape against his palate fine." No muteness here, no "browless idiotism": the sight of "veil'd melancholy" is reserved for the poet who is not only immersed in this aestheticized condition, but whose special gift, that "strenuous tongue," leaves him in the last stunning line of this poem reduced to "a cloudy trophy hung." It is a poetic strength that results in the absolute weakness that the speaker seeks.

Where does this dispossessing weakness of aesthetic experience get us, those of us willing to linger longer with Keats over this spell, to succumb to its "sable charms and dumb enchantments"? Another late essay by Barthes, his Cerisy essay on "The Image," offers one destination, the aesthetic not as an autonomous domain or as purity of judgment, but precisely as "the field of corruption." This is the figure he proposes as he acknowledges the potential apostasy of the turn to aesthetics in his own thought: "In the case of semiology, which I helped constitute, I have been my own corrupter, I have gone over to the side of the corrupters. It could be said that the field of this corruption is aesthetics" (*RL*, 352). This acknowledgment could not sound more removed from Barthes's exhortations, only five years earlier, that "the *text* is the methodological field" (*RL*, 56). But I suspect that most of us who read Barthes then—and those of us who still read him now—believe that he always harbored a weakness for the aesthetic and that, in every sense of the word, a certain aestheticism was Barthes's "weak point."[19]

It was also his *last* point, the point or *punctum* to which he turned more overtly in those luminous essays that appeared in the last years of his life. The final essays seek neither to demystify nor to disarticulate. If they do not seek to establish a grammar, neither do they follow the path of deconstruction. Indeed, to follow Barthes in this, "the third way," is *not to read*. His late essays can be understood as the obverse of deconstruction: their attention is directed not at the textual mechanisms and rhetorical operations of the text, but at its surface, at the *effects* they generate. "The 'effect' is a general impression suggested by the poem—an eminently sensuous and generally visual impression. . . . But the effect's characteristic is that its generality cannot really be decomposed: . . . Hence, the effect is not a rhetorical 'device': the generality is not mysterious . . . yet it is *irreducible*" (*RF*, 185). Situated before the "effects" given off by Twombly's canvases—in the jubilation of their discovery—Barthes admits that he is rendered "mute": "he can only exclaim: 'How beautiful this is!' over and over: that is one of language's minor torments: we can never explain why we find something beautiful; pleasure engenders a certain indolence of speech (*paresse de parole*)" (191). "On leaving the canvas," the image "returns, becomes a memory, a tenacious memory": "The spectator of the canvas will then be exploring his own impotence (*impuissance*)—and at the same time, of course, as though by contrast, the artist's power" (192).

What Barthes's work still has to offer is the understanding that an aestheticism such as that we experience in John Keats—weak, indolent, elegant—is also exploring its own *impuissance* and in the process presenting its readers with an *ethos*. It is an *ethos* that takes shape from the aesthetic experiences that leave *us* pointing in uncertain amazement and reduced to such "indolent" utterances as "these mighty things," "my spirit is too weak," one in which we give way and surrender to the experience of our own weakness.

Threats

Keats is prone to poetic utterances that demonstrate the deictic aspect of aesthetic experience, linguistic acts of pointing in which the speaker declares his weakness by resorting to the necessity of the gesture, as if nothing more than mere indication could be achieved in the face of such aesthetic might. At such moments his "living hand," however warm, is capable only of pointing. But what happens when the living hand warm and capable of such pointing becomes "This living hand," a fragment that addresses its status as aesthetic object and ethical imperative?

"Finger pointing" is, of course, not merely that which is performed in the mute here and now of a powerful aesthetic experience. It can often imply some form of intersubjective relationship, the acknowledgment or indication by the pointer of the presence or proximity of another being. A pointed finger can also be intended or construed as an act of accusation and even as a threat.[20] What is "This living hand" if not, at least in effect, a threat?

> This living hand, now warm and capable
> Of earnest grasping, would, if it were cold
> And in the icy silence of the tomb,
> So haunt thy days and chill thy dreaming nights
> That thou wouldst wish thine own heart dry of blood
> So in my veins red life might stream again,
> And thou be conscience-calm'd—see here it is—
> I hold it towards you.

Insomuch as the fragment attempts to influence its addressee by the prospect of menace or to the extent that this utterance "gives ominous indication of impending" harm (*OED*), it satisfies the definition of a threat.[21] And insofar as it is a threat, to whom is it addressed? Biographical conjecture invariably points us to Fanny Brawne; and we will return to the implications of the fragment's status as a love letter straight from the hand. But however much this metered utterance may have been intended for Keats's intended, it fails to account for the effects the fragment has upon any of its *actual* addressees.[22] Much of the power of "This living hand" derives from the immediacy of its address as it implicates me in the here and now of reading: I am hailed by "This living hand," and I must reckon with the threat it poses, insisting itself upon me.

But if "This living hand" threatens its readers, what are the contents of that threat? What does it presage or portend? Every night it promises to "haunt" and "chill." Not only would it cause us to shudder through our nights, it would present itself recurrently or habitually as a persistent waking cause of distress. One is haunted, after all, not only by spirits and phantoms, but by memories, thoughts, and, in this case, by the image of "this living hand" *presently* "warm and capable." Like all threats it assumes a position of strength and identifies a point of weakness. But unlike the refrain of British Romanticism's most famous threat—"*I'll be with you on your wedding night*"—"This living hand" threatens indefinitely. If the threat issued by the fragment is a species of blackmail, it takes hold once the poem is read, once I "see" "it," held toward me. In other words, if the threat posed by "This living hand" is issued in the present, its terms cannot be met in empirical time, and it thus stands without end.

A threat is something that need not be issued by an individual or entity, but may be implied or construed. Threats can come from nonhuman as well as human sources. We may be "threatened" by an individual, whether with raised voice or pointed finger, or by such nonhuman forces as an asteroid or volcano, or by such non-intentional human manifestations as consumption. In fact, threats that do not appear to have readily identifiable human origins are often felt to be the most unnerving, which is doubtless why we are often so desperate to ascribe a face to a generalized threat, to give an identity to an unnamed entity, something that can be pointed at. This is, of course, catachresis by prosopopoeia.[23]

The language of the *threat* is a recognizable feature of the literary and cultural criticism of an entire generation. It is audible in the perpetually alarmed, if now somewhat diverted, responses of cultural conservatives who, despite empirical evidence to the contrary, continue to regard such unlikely comrades as deconstruction, feminism, cultural studies, and Roland Barthes as "threats" to literary canons and cultural legacies. In the case of Barthes, any of his guises could be invoked to pose such a threat, demystifier of mythologies, peddler of *jouissance*, lover of signs. But nothing in Barthes's collected works prompted a more hysterical response than what remains his most anthologized essay, "The Death of the Author." The essay, which bears all the political enthusiasm of its date of composition, lacks the thrill of discovery discernible in Barthes's earliest forays into semiotics and the nuance of his most rigorous textual readings. The essay does not tell any reader familiar with Benveniste or Jakobson anything new about the linguistic displacement of the author function; and its historicization of this event seems very crude when it is situated alongside "Structure, Sign, and Play in the Discourse of the Human Sciences," the lecture Derrida delivered in Baltimore two years prior. But "The Death of the Author" endures; and it remains a source of fascination in part for its awkwardness and inelegance. Not only does Barthes marshal the scientific research of structuralist linguistics into something on the order of a "properly revolutionary" break, but he claims that in the process we witness the literary and linguistic "subversion" of the "Author's empire" and the event of the "birth" of the "modern *scriptor*" (*RL*, 50, 52).[24]

Susan Wolfson is, to my knowledge, the first to write about the uncanny relationship between Keats's final fragment and Barthes's essay, an uncanniness that I imagine anyone familiar with both must have felt the very instant they were both read, particularly given Barthes's insistence that his "modern *scriptor*" gives us a "hand, detached from any voice, borne by a pure gesture of inscription" (*RL*, 52). In Wolfson's account, what Barthes "states as 'fact' Romantic poets sense as threat: namely, that the written text represents the author by substitution rather than expression; that the 'future' of writing is reading, which comes into being 'at the cost of the death of the Author.'"[25] In a romantic pathos as iconic as it is apparently inexhaustible, Keats's final fragment cannot help but conjure the prospect of the death of its author. Though it is an effect prompted more by the "old biography" than the "new linguistics," the threat of the poem's "chill" produces more shudders when we know that "this living hand" belongs to such a famously failing "lunger." The irony is, of course, that perhaps no author's death in the Anglo-American tradition has done more to secure what Barthes calls the "empire" of the author than that of John Keats. The writer who gives us this bold speaker who holds his hand before us and demands we behold it is, as he writes, declining, wasting. At the same time the power of the lines themselves is such that they achieve what Wolfson calls "a peculiarly revivifying effect against the death so reported" (189).

But it is important to recall that what Wolfson calls Barthes's "post-formalist manifesto" is declared in the name of an explicitly ethico-political position:

> Literature (it would be better, from now on, to say *writing*) by refusing to assign to the text (and to the world-as-text) a "secret," i.e. an ultimate meaning, liberates an activity we may call countertheological, properly revolutionary, for to refuse to halt meaning is finally to refuse God and his hypostases, reason, science, the law. (*RL*, 54)[26]

Barthes's celebratory assertion of a critical "liberation"—at least at the level of ideology—is as familiar as it is unwarranted. But what is most fascinating now about Barthes's gestures is how they make the terms of the structuralist threat explicit, nowhere more so than in the essay's final sentence: "the birth of the reader must be requited by the death of the Author" (*la naissance du lecteur doit se payer de la mort de l'Auteur*) (*RL*, 55). I might have been tempted to translate "*se payer*" in this context somewhat more colloquially, as "payback"; but Richard Howard's more formal choice of "must be requited" conveys the element of threat that permeates the essay; for to requite is not merely to repay, but to retaliate, to avenge.

Cultural conservatives are not alone in employing the language of the "threat." It is something asserted time and again in the most rigorous version of deconstruction. If, for instance, in "The Resistance to Theory," de Man acknowledges "the threat inherent in rhetorical analysis" (*Resistance*, 17), this is merely a variant of the threat posed by reading as such, "mere reading," as de Man would put it in "The Return to Philology." For de Man, of course, such threats are resisted, by readers and writers alike—Keats's extensive ethical investments can be understood as one form of this resistance— and yet no ethics or hermeneutics is strong enough to overcome the threat posed by reading. Readers and writers alike will invariably succumb, by way of reading itself, to the experience of this threat at its most acute, because the threat is inherent in language, in what de Man calls "the sheer strength of figuration."[27]

It is for this reason that the "threat" posed by Barthes was rightly regarded by those critics most invested in the practices of deconstruction as "weak." If Barthes proudly announces the "birth of the reader," de Man's own readings not only insist that the reader was never *not* there, but that such a reader is scarcely something to celebrate. De Man delivered us to the terms and conditions of the threat of reading in forms so deep and pervasive that it can make Barthes's celebrations of the reader seem not only unfounded or premature, but a little silly. Indeed, throughout his career de Man's admiration for Barthes's work is leavened with considerable suspicion. In "The Resistance to Theory," for example, Barthes is accused, along with Jakobson, of something like aestheticism: they "often seem to invite a purely aesthetic reading" (*Resistance*, 10); they often seem, in every sense of the word, to be *superficial*.

There is nothing superficial, delicate, or indolent about "This living hand." It is difficult to imagine "a purely aesthetic reading" of this confrontational fragment: the powerful ethical burden it imposes upon the reader can force the aesthetic experience of the poem to recede entirely. The speaker not only makes the fate of "this living hand" a matter of conscience for the reader, but spells out precisely what it would take to be "conscience-calm'd." Conscience here is not merely the "consciousness of right and wrong as regards things for which one is responsible" (*OED*): the poem does not so much *appeal* to our ethical sense as it imposes such a responsibility upon us. It conjures a responsibility that did not exist prior to the poem, a responsibility that did not exist—given the temporality of the poem's address—prior to this present moment. Once we are addressed by "This living hand," once it points at us, extending itself "warm and capable of earnest grasping," we are made party to its terms: when we read this poem, we take this strong hand and are thereby obligated to the most extravagant terms of exchange. The only way to avoid this sacrificial ethics is to turn away from its offering before it is made, to refuse a reading in advance.[28]

Where does this threat originate? Beneath the reverberating pathos of the poem's address and inextricable from its production, the poem points, metonymically, to the source of poetry in the hand of the scribe. The poem's opening line is cut and refigured from the famous opening passage of another fragment Keats wrote in 1819: *The Fall of Hyperion.* The opening paragraph of this great failed epic begins by addressing the difficulty of discerning the *speech* of a poet from that of a "fanatic"—"the fine spell of words" that "alone can save / Imagination from sable charm and dumb enchantment" (ll.9–11)— and closes by linking poetic language not with the voice, but with the hand: "Whether the dream now purposed to rehearse / Be poet's or fanatic's will be known / When this warm scribe my hand is in the grave" (ll.16–18). Here the prospect of the "grave" does not "haunt" or "chill"; rather, it distinguishes genuine poetry from the enthusiast's visions. If the speaker of *The Fall of Hyperion* looks at "this warm scribe my hand" as the potential source of a "fine spell of words," "This living hand" makes this source of poetry an object to behold. Not only does it point at itself, but it demands that we look at this object it points to. And it is the force of the threat that prevents this from degenerating into just another game of Escher's hands.[29]

If the implied metonymic relationship between poetry and the hand tells us where this came from, it is the explicit power of the apostrophe that hails us in the present and holds us interminably. No one has written more lucidly about the apostrophic power of "This living hand," its capacity to bring the entire might of this figure to bear upon the reader, than Jonathan Culler. "This living hand" becomes, in Culler's investigation of apostrophe, the epitome of the figure. According to Culler, "This living hand" is a "daring and successful example" of the apostrophic mode, a poem "that exploit[s] this sinister reciprocity [between trope and reader]," a poem "which capture[s] the time of the apostrophic *now* and thrust[s] it provocatively at the reader."[30] Of course, what gives the poem its "sinister" quality is not the apostrophe itself, but the terms and conditions that precede it. But if the subjunctive tense of lines 2–7 should serve to moderate its effects—"it would if it were" is, after all, only a warning—the extravagance of the outcome, however contingent, seems to efface its conditions all at once. In the brief time it takes the poem to arrive at its direct address to the reader, the hand seems no longer to be the "warm and capable" scribe, but the other one, "cold/And in the icy silence of the tomb," a hand severed from its body and presented before us. Far from recounting an act or representing an object, "This living hand" takes place in a doubly apostrophic mode, as an address to the hand itself and then to the reader. As Culler puts it, "the very brazenness with which apostrophe declares its strangeness is crucial, as indication that what is at issue is not a predictable relation between signifier and signified, a form and its meaning, but the incalculable force of an event" (*Pursuit*, 152). What makes this apostrophic fragment such a threat to our own predictable habits of interpretation is not that it meditates on the relationship between life and death, but is itself an event of increasing intensity in which, our "conscience" implicated, we are made to believe we are witnessing the very sacrifice it demands, that we are beholding an act of dismemberment. "See," says the poet whom we believe to have become an automutilator in the most confrontational use of this address, "here it is/I hold it towards you." The poem "predicts this mystification," says Culler, "dares us to resist it, and shows that its power is irresistible" (154): its power, in other words, is to make weak readers of us all.

Culler concludes with a fascinating and enigmatic declaration: "This is the kind of effect which the lyric seeks, one whose successes should be celebrated and explained" (154). If no one has done more than Culler to explain the successes of the apostrophe, I have never understood why these are successes to be "celebrated," especially in such a poem as this; for to "celebrate" these successes is to disregard how they occurred, to overlook the force of their "happening" and the threat they pose. Culler's conclusion asks us to regard the poem not exclusively as a threat, but, simultaneously, as a gift we can celebrate. *But what a gift!* We are extended the hand that has produced the object before us as a sort of offering. Indeed, the terms of the sacrifice it presents us with make this poetic fragment an "offertory" in the full—if perverted—ecclesiastical sense of that term. "This living hand" is not merely a prayer said or song sung by the poet-priest at the time of the offering; it *is* the symbolic body and blood offered prior to consecration.[31] This is the kind of offering, the kind of gift that takes us from the realm of the ethical to the erotic. After all, the body part threatened by this fragment is the heart, that ultimate gift-object that Barthes calls "the organ of desire." In his lover's dictionary,

Barthes says that while *Coeur* is that which "refers to all kinds of movements and desires," its "constant" is that it is "constituted into a gift-object whether ignored or rejected" (*Lover's Discourse*, 52), or, we might say, requited or unrequited. Thus does Keats invoke the heart—the source of love and life—as that which is dispensable and offer "this living hand" as the unsurpassable "gift-object." "Thy would wish thine own heart drained of blood" and thus incapable of the diastolic swelling and slackening that constitutes the heart as desire's organ.

By most accounts "This living hand" was written sometime in the fall of 1819, when the signs of Keats's consumption were unmistakable—his life becoming increasingly "posthumous"—but the tone and terms of his letters to Fanny Brawne remain optimistic, permeated with his dazzled declarations of love: "My Creed is Love and you are its only tenet" (*KL*, II, 224). By the spring of 1820 Keats's letters to his intended begin to display the tone and terms of the fragment he had written and, apparently, abandoned. A remarkable letter from May of that year, filled with finger-pointing, not only makes its appeals to the conscience, but speaks the language of sacrifice. The letter makes it clear that Keats's turn to the erotic does not constitute a relinquishing of the ethical; on the contrary, it demonstrates that at moments of erotic crisis, the platitudes of love are quickly dispensed with, and we are made aware that the ethical is always present as a substrate to Keats's erotic discourse. If this letter is a confession, it is one coerced by the conditions of his weakness. "Ask yourself," writes Keats to his lover,

> how many unhappy hours Keats has caused you in Loneliness. For myself I have been a Martyr the whole time, and for this reason I speak: the confession is forc'd from me by the torture. I appeal to you by the blood of that Christ you believe in. . . . Be serious! Love is not a plaything—and again do not write unless you can do it with a crystal conscience. I would sooner die for want of you than—
> (*KL*, II, 304)

Fanny could not have read this other than as a threat, an act of emotional blackmail. But in the next letter Keats wrote her, he asserts that the threat is not addressed to Fanny, but to himself: "How threaten to leave you? Not in the spirit of a Threat to you—no—but in the spirit of wretchedness in myself" (*KL*, II, 312). "Such is love's wound," as Barthes would describe it, "a radical chasm (at the 'roots' of being), which cannot be closed, and out of which the subject drains, constituting himself as a subject in this very draining" (*Lover's Discourse*, 189). "This living hand" produces just such a lover's discourse: this *fragment* is the site of "love's wound," the "radical chasm," to which the movement of Keats's life and love would tend.

Any genuine reckoning of "This living hand" must engage with the ethical, erotic, and rhetorical features that make it not only such a powerful poem, but something on the order of an "incalculable event." But there is something more at stake in this poem, something inherent in the tense of that dramatic opening sentence. When that breathtaking seven-line sentence assumes the subjunctive, it is not only making use of some fundamental resources of language, but simultaneously conjuring what we might term the aesthetic conditional: "it would if it were." This is the capacity of art to make what is not seem as if it were, to make the non-event of the imagined seem to happen. In an important sense art has always belonged to the world of "would-be" and, as that old proverb has it, artists are nothing but "woulders." That the threat posed by the lines makes use of the same grammatical resources should alert us to the possibility that the poem is showing just how this threat, however ethical and erotic in its themes, is one posed formally and rhetorically by and for the work of art. It is here that we might best address something in the poem that many readers have noted: its theatricality, what Wolfson calls the "stagey eloquence" of its opening lines (*Formal Charge*, 189).

The poem's formal and rhetorical power has elicited strong and memorable readings from such rigorous critics as Wolfson, Bahti, and Culler; but the very rigor of their formal and rhetorical analyses makes them overlook something that is present on the surface of the poem: *it wants to be a painting*. These are readers who are not, in other words, "weak" enough to believe that the poem makes us see. But it is precisely the poem's "staginess" that activates another critical tradition, one that extends from Diderot to Fried and addresses the relationship between beholder and beheld in terms of the opposing poles of "absorption" and "theatricality."[32] This visual tradition helps us see the poem not only as a work of art, but as a reflection on and engagement with the very question of art and aesthetic experience. The poem begins in the mode of contemplation, taking "this living hand" as an object of reflection, pointing at it in a form that recalls other instances of Keats's reflections on the aesthetic, such as the opening phrase of "On Seeing the Elgin Marbles": "this living hand," "these mighty things."[33]

We have seen how Keats's poems often *indicate* the aesthetic objects that demand their existence, calling them into being. The sonnets on the Elgin

Marbles, for instance, offer us the "mutism" of the pointed finger—what Sperry designates as the "blank amazement" of Keats's poetics of wonderment. The power of such aesthetic experiences often leaves Keats's speakers blank, weakened, undone. It is, therefore, a reversal of sorts when the speaker of this fragment presents "this living hand" to the reader-beholder who is threatened with a similar undoing. The hand in Keats is frequently figured as a metonym for poetry: recall the "ardent prayer" uttered by the speaker of *Sleep and Poetry* who, "holding" and "grasping" his pen, prays to be admitted "as a glorious denizen" of poetry's "wide heaven." Here and now, "This living hand" "warm and capable of earnest grasping" offers itself and then demands of us that we behold it. The crux of the poem's difference from our earlier examples is not only the shift from aesthetics to ethics, but the deictic distinction between "look at that" and "see, here." A far cry from the indolent forms of weakness characterized by Keats's earlier aestheticist mode, this strange little poetic fragment suddenly hurls us into a "poetic strength alone" of the "muses born" that forgets that poetry's ethical charge is to "sooth the cares and lift the thoughts of man." Far from offering a "system of salvation," the poetic "strength alone" of "This living hand" posits a conception of the aesthetic that is itself a threat to the very forms and figures out of which an ethics might be articulated with aesthetics.

The apostrophic eruption of the closing line and a half—"see, here it is / I hold it towards you"—may be anchored in the ethics of sacrifice embedded in those opening lines, but it demands to be beheld: *I hold it towards you and you must behold it.* The additional foot in the seventh line, the emphatically stressed "see," marks this apostrophic break and demands that we hear it the very instant we see it. How can one not *see* the hand if one *hears* the foot that says "sees"? The poem's ekphrastic features invite us to consider this "break" in terms derived from the discourses of painting; with this gesture the poem has broken perspective and broken with the aesthetic values that underwrite the notion of perspective. The gesture is registered with a physicality that makes it seem "as if it were" literal. Barthes's notion of the *punctum* in *Camera Lucida* might tell us something about the phenomenon that occurs here: the *punctum* "is that accident that pricks me, points me (but also bruises me, is poignant to me."[34]

These visual metaphors drawn from the discourses of painting and photography show us how the poetic fragment held before us is not only a reflection, but a pun on the very nature of beholding. If the poem opens with the ekphrastic directive, pointing the reader at "this living hand," line seven implores us to see it with our own eyes, to behold it. And by giving us this seeing and holding, it reasserts the ethical, the ethics inscribed in the word *behold*: not only does *behold* mean to look at and consider or contemplate with an aesthetic regard, the word also retains the ethical sense of *holding* "by some tie of duty or obligation," as in "beholden" (*OED*). Thus this brief fragment begins by beholding, makes that beheld object—one that "grasps" or holds"—into that which obligates the reader and "would" commit us to a sacrificial response, before demanding that we behold that held hand. In other words, we are made to behold that which makes us beholden. At that instant the poem reasserts the ethical only to aestheticize it, radically.

There is, of course, another ethically oriented interpretation of the poem, namely that a "living hand" need not necessarily be a "warm scribe" holding a pen to write, but may merely be extended to another living hand to be grasped in friendship. But not only is the image of this warm ethical act undone by the "haunting" and "chilling" conditions that follow, the hand itself is withheld, and when it is extended again, it is no longer presented for us to take and hold in the mutual reciprocity of a handshake, but to see and behold as an aesthetic object that confronts every reader-beholder with his or her own weakness. In the face of such presentation, we may behold or turn away.

The most instructive visual analogue for "This living hand" is Caravaggio rather than Twombly, specifically the Caravaggio of "David with the Head of Goliath." One can only wonder what Keats thought of the painting when Severn accompanied him to the Galleria Borghese during those last months in Rome, before he became altogether too feeble to leave his room. "David with the Head of Goliath" is, of course, an allegory of the overturning of strength and weakness in which a "living hand, warm and capable of earnest grasping" manages to slay—and display—strength itself. In Caravaggio's three-quarter-length composition, the distortion of perspective, the contortions of David's body and the light that is cast from beneath the painter contribute to the effect of a gesture that seems to have broken the frame: with his left hand, David, with a look that is more resigned than triumphant, thrusts the recently decapitated head of Goliath toward the viewer. "See here it is," says the painting, "I hold it towards you." Moreover, what the young shepherd holds toward us to behold is the head of Caravaggio, who has painted the slain Philistine as a self-portrait. Most of Caravaggio's commentators have noted this representation of the painter's self-representation. To my mind, none have touched its implications more precisely than Leo Bersani and Ulysse Dutoit, who say that it is the painter himself whom . . . Caravaggio represents as having made that ultimate sacrifice. In drawing his own features on the decapitated head of Goliath, Caravaggio could be thought of as saying to us: In this painting I offer you my head. Or perhaps: In painting (not just this painting) I lose my head. Painting, he might claim, is the decapitation of the artist.[35]

Similarly, Keats could be thought of as saying to us: in this poem I offer you my hand. Or perhaps: in poetry I lose my hand. Poetry, Keats "might claim," is the dismemberment of the poet. But what is perhaps more important is that Keats—our "poet-painter," "fair as Sebastian"—can not only be thought of as saying these things, but of *showing* them. What precipitates the gesture that breaks the frame of the poem is the urgent demand to see. It is at this point that Keats is addressing a reader who does not yet see and must be shown. It is at this moment, in other words, that "this living hand," this "it" is shown and held "towards you" in a breaking of the frame that is also a show of strength: at this instant the reader is constituted as beholder. And thus does the poem turn us into something both more and less than a reader: more, because we must read the poem, and read it closely, to recognize what it does to us; and less, in that it makes us at this moment into something weaker than a reader: a mere looker, a mute beholder. This is the poem's radical aestheticism, encountered beyond and beneath reading.

"On He Flared"

It is one thing to locate a radical aestheticism in a discarded text, however central it may have become to our understanding of the poet. It is another thing entirely to discern this radical aestheticism in two of the poems that Keats and generations of his readers have regarded as central to the project: the *Hyperion* experiment, where the topic of strength and weakness returns us to the experience of being "consumed in the fire," not only as a *description* of reading and its undoing, but as the *production* of poetry. I want to begin with the figure of Apollo and his encounter in Book III with the goddess Mnemosyne. The encounter is an explicit, if "perplexing" scene of reading: when "with solemn step an awful Goddess came, / And there was purport in her looks for him" (III ll.46–47), Apollo "with eager guess began to read / Perplex'd" (ll.48–49), as if it is not merely Apollo who is "perplex'd," but the very object of his reading, for the line break and object position contribute to this blurred sense of the subject and object. At the very same time that he is engaged in this act of reading, Apollo is responding "melodiously": "the while melodiously he said:/How cam'st thou over the unfooted sea?" (III ll.49–50). Apollo is already an aesthetic and aestheticized figure in the poem: though Apollo may *possess* a "melodious" voice, he *is* the "golden theme" (l.28). Moreover, Mnemosyne tells Apollo that his "waking" announces to "the whole universe" the "birth" of a "new tuneful wonder":

> "Thou hast dream'd of me; and awaking up
> Didst find a lyre all golden by thy side,
> Whose strings touch'd by thy fingers, all the vast
> Unwearied ear of the whole universe
> Listen'd in pain and pleasure at the birth
> Of such new tuneful wonder."
>
> (III ll.61–67)

Apollo is thus presented not merely as a new god in a new order of divinity, but as the birth of the aesthetic itself: "the father of all verse" (l.13), Apollo *is* "loveliness new born" (l.79). In Heidegger's concise gloss, Mnemosyne is "the mother of the nine Muses. Drama and music, dance and poetry are of the womb of Mnemosyne, Memory" (352).[36] In Keats's poem we are also likely to read Mnemosyne's account of Apollo's birth as an allegory of the aesthetic, the "syllables" that "throb" from "his white melodious throat" (ll.82, 81) articulate difficult epistemological questions: "Are there not other regions than this isle?/What are the stars?" (ll.96–97). Apollo's questions give voice to the tension between aesthetics and knowledge; but he also responds with the promise of a song and thus announces the prospect of reconciling the two, as if his lyre might in every sense of the word accompany knowledge: "Point me out the way/To any one particular beauteous star," asks Apollo, "And I will flit into it with my lyre,/And make its silvery splendour pant with bliss" (ll.99–102).[37]

The prospect of a complementary relationship between knowledge and the aesthetic in the poem is short-lived, however, for Apollo's stunning next question—"Where is power?"—undoes the harmonious vision of song and star. And by placing the question of the location of power into the equation, Apollo shifts both the question and the poem from a mapping of the heavens to a reflection on aesthetics, politics, and history. Heidegger calls Mnemosyne "the source and ground of poesy" (352), and Keats's version of her "remains" "mute" to Apollo's urgent question about the location of power and to the increasingly desperate questions that follow, as if the mutism prompted by aesthetic experience issued from its poetic source.[38] But if Apollo hears nothing at this point from the goddess, he can *read* everything; and in the "knowledge enormous" that he gains from this reading, Apollo is "deified":

> Mute thou remainest—Mute! yet I can read
> A wondrous lesson in thy silent face:
> Knowledge enormous makes a God of me.
> Names, deeds, gray legends, dire events, rebellions,
> Majesties, sovran voices, agonies,
> Creations and destroying, all at once
> Pour into the wide hollows of my brain
> And deify me, as if some blithe wine
> Or bright elixir I had drunk,
> And so become immortal.
>
> (III ll.111–20)

I am interested in the effects of this "wondrous lesson" and in the component elements of this "knowledge enormous," which offers itself both as narrative and as catalogue. The "lesson" progresses from the most prosaic accountings of the past, the "names, deeds, gray legends," through the historical reckoning of "dire events, rebellions" and, in an increasingly feverish register, to a mytho-poetic understanding of the cause and consequences of history, "sovran voices, agonies,/creations and destroyings": all of this the god receives "at once." Thus Apollo's reading lesson is an experience of history—or, more precisely, an incorporation of history—*without context*. Indeed, it is difficult to tell in the accumulated force of this enumeration whether the last items, the "creations and destroyings," constitute additions to the encyclopedia of historical knowledge or whether they are simply the phantasmagoric form history takes when it is ingested whole. Or perhaps this is what history looks like to a god.

It would seem that a knowledge of such magnitude will necessarily be aestheticized, figured here in recognizably sublime terms. But the effects of this sublime aestheticization are worth noting. "Knowledge enormous" is knowledge sheerly enormous and not cognition of any thing; but neither does it offer anything like a free realm of aesthetic pleasure. It remains the kind of knowledge that not even a god, not even *Apollo*, can do anything with. Even from the standpoint of divinity, this "knowledge enormous" offers no illumination or redemption; rather, the magnitude of such knowledge results in nothing but a noisy crisis, a "commotion" from which neither the god nor the poem can recover. Deified by his reading lesson, "the God,/While his enkindled eyes, with level glance/Beneath his white soft temples, stedfast kept/Trembling with light upon Mnemosyne" (ll.120–23). "Enkindled" with the kindling of his reading, Apollo continues to look—as if with Dusketha's "bare unlidded eyes"—upon Mnemosyne and the results of this enkindled looking are the "wild commotions" that follow: "Soon wild commotions shook him, and made flush/All the immortal fairness of his limbs" (III ll.124–25).[39] Apollo begins to convulse with strange and violent death throes. Yet it turns out it is not death that is taking place here, but some other thing that twists the boundaries between death and life: as his "very hair, his golden tresses famed/Kept undulation round his eager neck," the new god "dies into life" (ll.131–32,130). If both the state (between death and life) and the image (the "famed tresses") call to mind the frozen gaze of Shelley's Medusa, Keats's Apollo does not look on in silence: he "shrieks" and "from all his limbs/Celestial . . ." (ll.135–36). A disarticulate cry, a vocal shriek, announces the disarticulation of Apollo's limbs, a disarticulation that extends to the poem itself, for it is at this point of a "celestial" dismemberment that the poem comes suddenly to a halt. "I have not gone on with Hyperion," is Keats's terse comment to his brother and sister (*KL*, II, 214). Still, if the poem cannot "go on" past this point, there insists a residue: present on the page of the earliest extant versions of Keats's poem are the asterisks that we tend to reproduce in each printed version of the poem, asterisks that ask to be read as the ashes of a fire that has burned the page, the cinders of Apollo's burning. They are the material remains of reading the history inscribed in Mnemosyne's face with the trembling light of those "enkindled eyes." What does it mean to read the asterisks of a poem's incompletion as ash, the signs of poetic flame-out? In part it means that whatever actually caused John Keats to stop writing his epic poem called *Hyperion*, he stopped writing it at the moment the poem had reached the radical of the aesthetic.[40]

When Keats returns to Hyperion, as if by the same compulsion that forces him into his rereading of Lear, he raises the aesthetic stakes still higher. Indeed, *The Fall of Hyperion* is perhaps Keats's most sustained late reflection on the aesthetic and its relation to poetry. In *Hyperion* Keats approaches the gap between knowledge and aesthetics as something to be overcome; and the poem's failed attempt to accomplish that task kindles an aestheticism. In the *Fall*, by contrast, the relationship between aesthetics and ethics is negotiated by way of the sacred in a shift that appears to constitute a turn away from the aesthetic itself. I want to conclude this account of Keats's radical aestheticism by examining the workings and turnings of those poetic reflections.

The opening lines of the poem address the status of the aesthetic and its relationship to the very nature of the poetic undertaking. Poetry's aesthetic dilemma is presented in the form of the famous questions that hang over the body of the poem:

> Fanatics have their dream, wherewith they weave
> A paradise for a sect; the savage too
> From forth the loftiest fashion of his sleep
> Guesses at Heaven: pity these have not
> Trac'd upon vellum or wild Indian leaf
> The shadows of melodious utterance.
> But bare of laurel they live, dream and die;
> For Poesy alone can tell her dreams,
> With the fine spell of words alone can save
> Imagination from the sable charm
> And dumb enchantment.
>
> (I ll.1–11)

Does the "fine spell of words" save imagination from the perpetual threat of "sable charm and dumb enchantment"? At stake here in one of Keats's most explicit formulations is the problem of the aesthetic, both what "Poesy" can achieve by its "fine spell of words" and the threat that hangs over the imagination, its potential to succumb to the "sable charm/And dumb enchantment" of what we would call aestheticism. The threat of this aestheticism—what Barthes would call its "hypnotic" capacity to "glue" us to the image—is only deepened by the fact that the only thing that can prevent aestheticism is the aesthetic itself: in a formulation that recalls Shelley, it is poetry's "fine spell" that dispels "sable charm/And dumb enchantment." Thus the poem asks about itself: is *this* poetic saying? And if so, is this a humanizing poetry? In other words, what is the relationship between the aesthetic and the human? This is what accounts for the tone of urgency in the questions the poet asks of the goddess Moneta about poetry's relationship to the aesthetic: "If it please,/Majestic shadow tell me: sure not all/Those melodies sung into the world's ear/Are useless: sure a poet is a sage;/A humanist, physician to all men" (I ll.186–90). We have seen how this is a question variously posed by and in much of Keats's poetry; and it is a question that the *poetry* if not the poet resists answering in the affirmative.[41]

It is also a question that it is difficult for the poet-speaker of *The Fall of Hyperion* simply to *ask*, perhaps in part because he drinks the "full draught" of that "cool vessel of transparent juice" for which he thirsts (ll.46, 42). When the "cloudy swoon" is lifted and the poet comes to his senses, he finds himself outside an unearthly and sublime sanctuary. As the poet approaches that "eternal domed monument" (l.70), he finds a "store of strange vessels, and large draperies" (l.73). The accumulation of sacred objects continues, though in a "confus'd" and meaningless fashion: "All in a mingled heap confus'd there lay / Robes, golden tongs, censer, and charing dish, / Girdles, and chains, and holy jewelries—" (ll.78–80). "Turning from these with awe" (l.81), the poet encounters an "Image" (l.88) and proceeds to the "altar" of this image with pious slow movement, "repressing haste, as too unholy there" (l.94). If we are tempted to read the poet's pious turn as a turning away from an aestheticized sacred, the subsequent scene demonstrates that the aesthetic is far from discarded, for when the poet approaches that sacred altar he sees "beside the shrine / One minist'ring; and there arose a flame" (ll.95–96). Far from marking a deaestheticized relationship with the sacred, the effects of this "lofty sacrificial fire" merely intensify the hypnotic experience of the aesthetic:

> that lofty sacrificial fire,
> Sending forth Maian incense, spread around
> Forgetfulness of every thing but bliss,
> And clouded all the altar with soft smoke,
> From whose white fragrant curtains thus I heard
> Language pronounc'd.
>
> (ll.102–7)

The "language" "pronounced" may be spoken by Moneta; but it issues from the folds—the "white fragrant curtains"—of the aesthetic. And certainly the *effect* is a thoroughly aestheticized confusion, a pervasive blurring of language and the "Maian bliss" spread by the fire. Moneta's speech is a provocation to the poet and, ostensibly, to any member of his indolent tribe: demonstrate your strength, "ascend / These steps" or "die on that marble where thou art" (ll.107–8).

What results is the displacement of the presumed split between the sacred and the aesthetic onto two instances of aestheticization. For the poet's ostensible turn away from the aesthetic does not result in the *poem's* turn from the aesthetic. Rather, it results in a deepening and extension of aestheticization at the very expense of an "autonomous" aesthetic realm: aestheticization as what Barthes calls the "field of corruption" and to which he ascribes a "catastrophe." If the poet purports to turn away from the aesthetic, but then undergoes an experience that we can only describe as aetheticized, the aesthetic must then be understood in the poem not as a space or realm, but as a force that corrupts and "confuses" the boundaries that would separate the aesthetic from the sacred. This aestheticization continues through Moneta's speech, for in spite of her austere tone and severe demand, the effect of her lines on the poet is a heightening of the primary aesthetic senses (hearing, sight) in response to the "fierce threat" of the "hard task proposed." At the moment that "prodigious seem'd the toil" (l.121), there occurs a scene of kindling—"the leaves were yet/Burning" (ll.121–22)—and the poet is struck with a sudden chill that delivers him to the point of death. Through this kindling the poet reaches the limit of the human. In terms of the poem's unfolding, however, this is the also limit of the sacred, for when the poet asks Moneta why he is alone there at that altar, why he does not see others there who "labour for mortal good" (l.159), the poem and the Goddess have shifted their focus to the relationship between the aesthetic and the ethical. Moneta answers the poet with an extended figuring of the distinctions between the two:

> They are no dreamers weak,
> They seek no wonder but the human face;
> No music but a happy-noted voice—
> They come not here, they have no thought to come—
> And thou art here, for thou art less than they—
> What benefit canst thou do, or all thy tribe
> To the great World? Thou art a dreaming thing:
> A fever of thyself—think of the earth;
> What bliss even in hope is there for thee?
> What haven?
>
> (ll.162–71)

The relationship is figured as an opposition between an aesthetic realm of the dream and the ethical realm of the "human face." According to Moneta, this "dreaming thing," this aesthetic "fever" remains thoughtless of "the Earth" and therefore entirely hopeless of "bliss." And yet, as was the case in the earlier *Hyperion*, the aesthetic has not been purged altogether, for even in Keats's poetic representation of the ethical one finds the insistence of an aesthetic moment inscribed in the grammatical ambivalence of the disjunctions. For instance, one could read line 163 with an implied ellipsis: "They seek no wonder but *the wonder of* the human face." The following line enforces such an interpretation: "No music but a happy-noted voice" places harmony as well as the "voice" on the side of the ethical.

And yet, however porous the boundary between the aesthetic and the ethical, there is no happy reconciliation between the two; instead, the aesthetic and the ethical remain at odds if not wholly distinct, divided along the fissure that runs like a fault-line throughout Keats's poetry. Thus the urgency behind the poet's entreaties regarding the ethical possibilities of poetic song: "sure not all / Those melodies sung into the world's ear / Are useless: sure a poet is a sage; / A humanist, Physician to all Men" (ll.187–90). If these are questions that Keats asks in and of his poetry from *Sleep and Poetry* onward, it is in this poem that these questions are given their most elaborate preparation, having moved through what we might call the moment of the sacred in order to reach the proposition of an explicitly humanist ethics. But the poem does not carry through with this humanism, nor has the sacred been surpassed; instead, we must with the poet "look upon" the blaze of a sacrificial fire and the ashes it scatters: "I look'd upon the altar and its horns / Whiten'd with ashes, and its lang'rous flame, / And then upon the offerings again" (ll.237–39). The persistence of the sacred is registered here by the figures of ashes and flames that, in a movement that recalls Keats's "*King Lear*," must be entirely "consumed" to complete the passage to the human.

Once "the sacrifice is done" (l.241), the Goddess informs the poet that he will be recipient of her power: "my power," she says "which to me is still a curse, / Shall be to thee a wonder" (ll.242–44). When the poet parts the veil and looks upon the face that to this point has been but a voice, it is not a human face that he beholds, but a "wan face, / Not pin'd by human sorrows . . . but bright blanch'd / By an immortal sickness which kills not" (ll.256–58). "But for her eyes," says the poet, "I should have fled away" (l.264): the face itself, this nonhuman immortal face, is like the head of the Gorgon, a cause for aversion, "but for the eyes." These are eyes that "with a benignant light, / Soft mitigated by divinest lids / Half closed" (ll.265–67) can be perceived, but that perceive not: "Visionless entire they seem'd / Of all external things—they saw me not, / But in blank splendour beam'd like the mild moon" (ll.267–69). Incapable of the physical sense of sight, these are eyes that have severed any relationship to the sensual world: it's as if they have blinded themselves to the aesthetic. But by not turning away from the face of the Goddess, the poet "sees"—by witnessing "in blank splendour"—a vision not available to the senses. The subsequent lines chronicle the poet's desire to "see" this non-phenomenal vision: "At the view of sad Moneta's brow,/I ached to see what things the hollow brain/Behind enwombed" (ll.275–77). And the poet is granted this power, a "power of enormous ken,/To see as a God sees, and take the depth/Of things as nimbly as the outward eye/Can size and shape pervade" (ll.303–6). This seeing that is not a seeing, this vision that is "vision-less entire of all external things" is thus a vision—perhaps it can be called an "insight"—that would seem to be of a wholly different order from aesthetic vision or seeing. Or perhaps we might, with that famous line in Keats's most famous poem in mind, regard this as "unseen visions," or what Marshall Brown has aptly described as a spiritual rather than sensational aesthetics.[42] At any rate, when the poet is given access to this vision of history—the fall of a house, the collapse of a deity—he is bereft of the aesthetic senses he had before felt so keenly: "Nor could my eyes/And ears act with that pleasant unison of sense/Which marries sweet sound with the grace of form" (ll.441–43). It would seem that "To see as a God sees" means to lose "that pleasant unison of sense" that can be said to define the aesthetic itself. It is as if the very capacity for aesthetic judgment is no longer available to a poet granted knowledge, at least the "enormous ken" of a god.

The turn to the truncated second canto appears to confirm the cancellation of the aesthetic. When Moneta renews her story in the canto's opening lines, she asserts that for the poet to understand her, she must "humanize" her "sayings" to his ear:

> Mortal, that thou may'st understand aright,
> I humanize my sayings to thine ear,
> Making comparisons of earthly things;
> Or thou might'st better listen to the wind,
> Whose language is to thee a barren noise,
> Though it blows legend-laden through the trees—
>
> (ll.1–6)

The language of the gods is thus "barren noise" unless it is "humanized" with the measure of metaphor, with "comparisons of earthly things." But if the gods speak of things "too huge for mortal tongue" (l.9), it is more than a question of scale: "barren noise" occurs in the very absence of the aesthetic, in the voiding of the aesthetic form that "marries" sight and sound with "the grace of form." But Moneta is in fact making an aesthetic judgment in these lines; for even without "humanization" hers is a language, one "that blows legend-laden through the trees." In other words, "barren noise" is itself an aesthetic form. Thus the aesthetic is not superseded; rather, a gap is opened between this nonhuman "barren noise" and the humanizing aesthetic that with a "pleasant unison of sense" "marries sweet sound with the grace of form." And, as the subsequent lines demonstrate, Keats's poem is itself immersed in this gap, an immersion for which there is no extraction.

The poem's last lines demonstrate that this aesthetic immersion offers no hope for the humanizing that would restore "the grace of form" to the poet's senses or to the poem itself. The vision of the poet's "quick eyes" "runs" from "stately nave to nave, from vault to vault, / Through bowers of fragrant and enwreathed light, / And diamond paved lustrous long arcades" (ll. 53–56). We can certainly characterize this language as the aesthetics of the sublime: the poet apprehends that which exceeds the scale of human comparison, a "stately nave" that exceeds the comprehension of the poet's "quick eyes." But however much we may want to read the scene according to the conventions of the sublime, the lines achieve their sublime effects by culminating in another "kindling," the flaming and flaring of "bright Hyperion":

> Anon rush'd by the bright Hyperion;
> His flaming robes stream'd out beyond his heels,
> And gave a roar, as if of earthly fire,
> That scar'd away the meek ethereal hours
> And made their dove-wings tremble: on he flared—
> (ll. 57–61)

Thus ends the poem, burnt out as it has reached aestheticism's radical once again. The prospect of "humanizing" the "saying" has collapsed without "understanding aright." The effort to establish human comparisons—Hyperion roars "as if of earthly fire"—actually undoes the very measure of human time: it has "scar'd away the meek ethereal hours." The fire of the gods cannot be compared to "earthly fires." Hyperion is thus born out of aestheticism's own "flaring"—the point of the poem's deepest immersion in the experience and predicament of the aesthetic—and short-lived Hyperion and this short-lived poem are "consumed in the fire" yet again, leaving us with nothing but the ashes of its burning.

From the perspective of this glorious burn-out, the fault-line between ethics and aesthetics in Keats's poetic project looks profoundly different from the way in which it is conventionally drawn. Keats's poetry of luxuriating indolence and blank amazement—Keats's weakness—makes no ethical claims and yet offers a kind of *ethos* that Barthes would call a "morality." But when that fault-line is breached, when Keats makes his "ethical turn," the results are not the accommodation of the ethical with the aesthetic or the superseding of the latter by the former. Rather, this is the place we encounter Keats's radicalized aestheticism, the gift of an all-consuming poetry that bestows us nothing at all. See, here it is, Keats's weakness held before us.

Caravaggio, *David with the Head of Goliath* (Alinari / Art Resource, NY)

Like Eyes that looked on Wastes—
Incredulous of Ought—
But Blank—and steady Wilderness—
Diversified by Night—

Just Infinites of Nought—
As far as it could see—
So looked the face I looked opon—
So looked itself—on Me—

I offered it no Help—
Because the Cause was Mine—
The Misery a Compact—
As hopeless—as divine—

Neither—would be absolved—
Neither would be a Queen
Without the Other—Therefore—
We perish—tho' We reign—

Dickinson Fascicle 32, "Like Eyes that looked on Wastes"

THREE

What the Zeros Taught: Emily Dickinson, Event-Machine

> Did you ever read one of her Poems backwards, because the plunge from
> the front overturned you? I sometimes . . . have—a something overtakes
> the mind.
>
> —DICKINSON, *Prose Fragment*

for KJF

"The Plunge from the Front"

What the zeros taught in the forceful opening line of one especially enigmatic Dickinson poem was "Phosphorus": "The Zeros taught Us - Phosphorus -/We learned to like the Fire" (284).[1] Something comes from nothing,
and that incendiary teaching leaves us with the lessons of fire. And as in so
many Dickinson poems, the eruptive force that goes from the zeros to the
fire subsequently asserts its opposite, nullifying the initiating event, making a something—even the originating "something" of our source of light
and warmth—into a nothing, the blockage of an eclipse: "Of Opposite - to
equal Ought -/Eclipses - Suns - imply -" (ll.5–6). Thus does eruption prompt
or "imply" extinction, the event implying the machinery of its own eclipse.
More acutely still, given the poem's astonishing compression, the "Opposite"
is immediately "implied," an event eclipsed in the spacing of a dash. Perhaps
this sounds far too abstracted: Dickinson may simply have had in mind how
the "zeros" of a New England winter taught her how to use fire. But one need
not have a mind of winter to recognize how Dickinson's poetics is formally,

rhetorically, and thematically animated by the discourse of the zero: the combustible force that can take her poems from nought to one and then, just as quickly, the absolute divestment of the one to the nought. And if we're likely to know of any of Dickinson's pronouncements on the nature of aesthetic experience, it is likely her famous poetic "thermometer": "If I read a book [and] it makes my whole body so cold no fire ever can warm me I know *that* is poetry." This is the poetry that the zeros teach.[2]

I have added a subtitle to this chapter that might appear as inappropriate as it is certainly inelegant. If the chapter's title on the teaching of zeros is taken from one of Dickinson's most arresting and aesthetically powerful opening lines, "event-machine" implies something blank and repetitive, at such a remove from the aesthetic as to appear nonhuman. But I borrow this term from the work of Jacques Derrida because I believe it offers us the best way to address the *manufacture* of a poetry that repeatedly moves from nought to one and back again, a poetry that seems to come full-force from nothing and then to recede or dissipate.[3] In poem after poem Dickinson's work demonstrates an intense compression in which meaningful dramatic contexts are sheared away by what Anne-Lise Francois calls "a negative harvesting" that ultimately leaves us to confront the radicalization of art produced by the poems. The "zeroing" built into the "event-machinery" of her poetics is manifested in the singular and sustained capacity of the poetry's beginnings to "clear out," to produce a depopulated and decontextualized space. When this zeroing fixes upon and dwells in the peculiar nature of the aesthetic experience, the conditions are created for Dickinson's version of radical aestheticism.

The "event-machine" also offers a means by which we might revisit in a new light David Porter's condescending characterization of Dickinson as the "poet without a project."[4] If Dickinson is indeed a poet without Shelley's political mission, for instance, or Keats's ethical concerns, the absence of a distinctive program only makes it more evident that *poetics* itself is Dickinson's project. For Dickinson the stakes of *poesis* manifest themselves from the start and *in the starting*: they are apparent in the status of her poetic career and in the devising of a new poetic idiom, in the repeated thematizing and abstracting of this *poesis*. It is here that we find Dickinson's poems confronting the problem of the aesthetic and encountering the radicality of aestheticism. To be sure, Dickinson's version of this radical aestheticism does not look or sound like Shelley's: there is nothing like the eruption of "a shape all light" that supersaturates the senses in the cascading *terza rima* of *The Triumph of Life*. And Dickinson's radical aestheticism is not accompanied or signaled by the formal fragmentation or syntactic breakdown we witness in Keats, since these are defining features of her poetics. Dickinson's version of this thing I am calling a radical aestheticism is as about as far as possible from the "over-wrought" aestheticism of baroque adornment that we encounter in Dante Rossetti's sonnet sequence. Dickinson is the lyric poet who delivers us repeatedly to encounters with aesthetic experience that derive from the aporetic and poetic relationship between event and machine, occurrence and structure. That is where her radical aestheticism resides.

My reading of Dickinson is predicated on two initial observations: (1) Emily Dickinson produced an extraordinary number of poems during her career; and (2) in an inordinate number of those poems the first line is inordinately strong. The first of these observations is straightforwardly objective: the labors of scholars in the Dickinson archives have unearthed almost 1,800 of her poetic objects. My second observation involves an evaluation of the effects of her opening lines and, as such, constitutes an aesthetic judgment. More precisely, it is the reiteration of an aesthetic judgment expressed time and again by critics both hostile and sympathetic, from R. P. Blackmur to Sharon Cameron, who puts it most succinctly: "many poems contain lines that are memorable in contexts that are not, and the memorable lines are frequently the first lines."[5] Porter describes this pattern as a "slackening" that follows an eruptive, forceful beginning, a slackening experienced as an aftermath (*Modern Idiom*, 89, 92). Charles Anderson's version of this observation is rendered into the most disparaging assessment: "Not one in ten [poems] fulfills the brilliant promise of the opening words."[6] Thus, to consider the event-like status of these opening lines requires us to address the experience of their aftermath: the deflation or diffusion that characterizes so many of the poems. Karen Jackson Ford characterizes this pattern as Dickinson's "poetics of enactment," which can be "abbreviated" by the poet's "confession" to Higginson: "when I try to organize - my little Force explodes."[7] My epigraph demonstrates that Dickinson was acutely aware of and sensitive to the "explosive" effects of powerful opening lines. In this prose fragment Dickinson is referring to another unidentified poet, but "the plunge from the front" that "overturns" the reader with a "something" that "overtakes the mind" also serves as the best description of the sudden, disorienting, "overturning" and "overtaking" power of so many of her own initial lines.

I want to consider the poetic mechanisms of the "plunge from the front" that cause this initial "overturning" and "overtaking," poetic mechanisms that manufacture what feels like an event; and I want to examine the apparatuses by which those quasi-events are swallowed by noughts. For as much as we may work to reconstitute a meaningful context to many of Dickinson's poems, I suspect that no serious reader has avoided, at least initially, the experience of her poems as a form of "zeroing out" or zeroing in. Many of the important developments in recent Dickinson scholarship have been dedicated to reconstructing the meaningful and meaning-making contexts of her poetry, from cultural and personal history to the fascicles on which the poetry was composed. Much of this work has opposed itself to the "de-contextualizing" and de-empiricizing practices of previous generation of Dickinson scholars; and it has produced a much more complete and complex picture of Dickinson's world and materials.[8] But it is my premise that the *abstracting* and *evacuating* force *in* Dickinson's poetry is of such magnitude that the poems themselves often produce this eradication of context, scene, or setting. I am interested in the poetics of eruption and negation that must be accounted for (even if only to be overcome) by any reader of Dickinson. Perhaps this is Romanticism's Dickinson, the one who dwells in the *mis-en-abyme* of those "Infinites of Nought" ("Like Eyes that looked on Wastes," 693); but this picture also resonates with what Porter identifies as those "strangely abstracted images" that deliver the reader to the destitution of sense experience. The route to Dickinson's radical aestheticism is the path of her own lyric radicalization, which is the path of abstraction, negation, "zeroing." The best way I know to start us on that path is by the effects of her first lines.

There are many metrical, rhetorical, syntactic, and thematic factors that, singularly or in combination, contribute to the formal power of the first line in a Dickinson poem. Though her metrical irregularities are famous, Dickinson's *opening* lines are often assertive in their regularity. And the rhetorical complexities that are consistent features of her poems become all the more acute in their effects when they *initiate* the poem. The deleted references also contribute to this effect, particularly when an absence of reference inaugurates an especially forceful metrical line. More than one hundred fifty poems open with the pronoun "I" or one of its contractions: these poems establish a speaker with the first word who, in whatever ultimately complicated or compromised or even overturned form, posits an initial context and identifies responsibility for the poetic utterance. These opening lines are often among the most forceful and memorable: "I started Early - Took my Dog -" (656); "I like a look of Agony" (339); "I felt a Funeral, in my Brain" (340); "I reckon - When I count at all" (533); "I dwell in Possibility" (466); "I felt a cleaving in my mind" (867); "I heard a fly buzz when I died" (591); "I took my power in my hand" (660); "I'm ceded - I've stopped being theirs" (353). There are in addition almost thirty poems that open with a possessive first pronoun, "my" or "myself," such as "My Life had stood - a Loaded Gun" (764) or "My Wars are laid away in Books" (1579). Much of the power of these opening lines derives from their first-person authorization and from the iambic pulse they generate.

But almost fifty of Dickinson's poems exhibit a different pronominal beginning: these poems begin with an "it" that is often, in Cameron's words, "deliberately unspecified" (15).⁹ And yet many of these same opening lines also possess a strange declarative force, an impersonal power that summons us to what Cameron calls the "the imperative world of Dickinson's poems" (*Lyric Time*, 2). These lines exhibit the full force of the capacity of the impersonal pronoun to state what Benveniste describes as "a pure *phenomenon* whose occurrence is not connected with an agent."¹⁰ As instantiated in the sentence, the "it" has the ability, in other words, to *declare* the occurrence it indicates and thus to generate the effect of an event. And when "it" *opens* the opening sentence of a poem as it does in so many memorable Dickinson poems, it makes that "it" into an enigmatic, despecifying initiator (e.g., "It dropped so low - in my Regard" [785]; "It is dead - Find it" [434]; "It knew no Medicine" [567]; "It knew no lapse - nor Diminution" [568]; "It was given to me by the Gods" [455]).

The sense of this "imperative world" extends to another class of impersonal opening lines: these are the poems whose inaugurating power derives from their pseudo-definitional status as an adage or aphorism. "The Brain - is wider than the Sky" (598); "Tell the truth but tell it slant" (1263); "A Charm invests a face" (430); "Kill your Balm and it's Odors bless you" (309); "Each Life converges to some Centre" (724); "'Faith' is a fine invention" (202); "It is easy to work when the soul is at play" (242); "The Zeros taught us - Phosphorus -" (284); "Love reckons by itself - alone" (812); "Nature - Sometimes sears a Sapling" (457); "No Man can compass a Despair" (714). As with the other classes of opening lines we have identified, the values or positions established by these aphoristic beginnings are often reversed or annulled or overturned or even abandoned in the course of the poem, and their currency as adage is likewise undone or ironized. And yet never entirely, for in the untitled universe of Dickinson's poems, the opening lines have served for the generations of her readers as the principal points of access and—together with the (shifting) numerical references—indicators of the poem. In other words, Dickinson's poems may have no titles; but they have come to acquire names and numbers.

If the numbers have not proven to be stable over time, the names have. Indeed, many of Dickinson's powerful and memorable opening lines have all the force and effect of an *event*, often and importantly an event of language. Giorgio Agamben's "theo-poetical" reflections on the relationship of poetry to the event of language are particularly pertinent here, despite the fact that Agamben's topic is the "*end* of the poem" as "a point of crisis that is in every sense fundamental to the structure of poetry."[11] Nonetheless, the terms and ramifications of Agamben's exploration of language as an event offer a point of entry—which is also "a point of crisis," a turning point—onto the *beginnings* of Emily Dickinson's poems, beginnings that are certainly "fundamental to the structure" and the effects of *her* poetry.

"Modern lyric poetry has its origin," says Agamben, in the Augustinian "reinterpretation" of *ratio inveniendi* as *raza de trobar*, "and it is from this expression that they [the troubadors] drew their name (*troubador* and *trobaritz*). . . . The troubadors want not to recall arguments consigned to a *topos* but instead to experience the very event of language as original *topos*" (79). Emily Dickinson, troubadour: to regard the "event of language as original *topos*" helps us explain what Robert Weisbuch calls the singular "scenelessness" of so many Dickinson poems. How better to stage the event of language as original *topos* than to eliminate from the poem any stabilizing representation of *topos* as scene or place?[12] And when a critic such as Stonum asks, "Why did Dickinson invent such an unusual manner of writing?" he is making an implicit claim that the appearance of her poetic idiom both marks an event and belongs to this troubadorian tradition.[13] Whether we regard Romanticism as the fulfillment, the extension, or the revisitation of this troubadorian desire, it is certainly a defining feature of the Romantic tradition we are considering in this study. This is how Shelley understands this legacy in the *Defence* when he describes the "spells" cast by the verses of the "Provencal Trouveurs, or inventors": "a paradise was created as out of the wrecks of Eden; and as this creation itself is poetry, so its creators were poets; and language was the instrument of their art" (*SPP*, 497). It is just this troubadorian impulse that delivers each of the poets in our study to the brink of what Agamben calls "a purely theological presupposition: the dwelling of the word in the beginning, of *logos* in *arche*, that is, the absolutely primordial status of language," "the word made flesh" (77).

"A Word Dropped": The Dickinsonian Event-Machine

When Dickinson writes of "the plunge from the front," she is describing the event or the occurrence of language and its disorienting effects: no topic in particular, but solely the powerful and initial plunge or drop that "overturns" and "overtakes" us. The often "overturning" power of Dickinson's own opening lines compels us to consider the something that takes place, the event of language and its effects and implications. Nowhere is this more apparent thematically than in the late poem "A word made Flesh is seldom" (1715), which takes its beginning and its cue from the linguistic event announced by John 1:14: "The word made flesh and dwelt among us." Dickinson's poetic rendering of that theological and linguistic event is both a citation of the "original" and an immediate rarification of it: "A word made Flesh is seldom / And tremblingly partook / Nor then perhaps reported" (ll.1–3). We have become more aware of Dickinson's distinctive skepticism: her resistance to acute evangelical pressure is well documented. Dickinson's dedication to—as well as deviance from—the conventional hymn form has been widely discussed.[14] And we also know from reading her poems that scriptural themes and topics frequently appear, sometimes ironized, sometimes not. A poem such as "A word made Flesh is seldom" addresses that topic of origination and demonstrates the convergence of the theological and the linguistic in its accounting or "reporting" of the event, the "word made flesh" that is also "this loved Philology" (l.16). For Dickinson this is the most fragile of events, an occurrence only "tremblingly" "partook" and even then perhaps not "reported" or recounted, a lyric event resistant to narration. But such an event is not resistant to *repetition*, as in the repetition of the communion by which the "word made flesh" is given to our mouths: [if] "I have not mistook / Each one of us has tasted / With ecstasies of stealth / The very food debated / To our specific strength" (ll.4–8). Christ is the definition of "condescension": the singular event of a coming down from spirit into the world; and his subsequent worldly "expiration" establishes the source of a genuinely "loved Philology" (l.16). Dickinson returns to the topic of Christ's condescension and ascension in "The event was directly behind Him" (1724), reporting both the event's occurrence—its ability to fit "itself to Himself like a Robe" (l.3)—and "His ignorance" of it, an ignorance that he "relished." However we reckon the theological implications of these and other poems that represent Christ's passion and resurrection, they belong to a strain of poems, some religious and some not, that can be said to *seek events*.

The question of the event is always present, for instance, in the "volcano" poems that directly thematize the event as "eruption." And though the figure of lightning may well be a poetic commonplace, it is often invoked in Dickinson to mark an event's suddenness and unforeseeability.

Sometimes, however, an event in Dickinson is nothing but an accident, as in "A Word dropped careless on a Page" (1268):

> A Word dropped careless on a Page
> May stimulate an Eye
> When folded in perpetual seam
> The Wrinkled Maker lie
>
> Infection in the sentence breeds
> And we inhale Despair
> At distances of Centuries
> From the Malaria -

Even in this unplanned form, the merely "careless" dropping of a word on a page, the event of language still possesses the power to "stimulate an Eye/When folded in perpetual seam" (ll.2–3), when the word is folded in the "perpetual seam" of the bifurcated page. Here the "stimulation"—or, as in 1268B, the "consecration"—of the reader's eye is prompted without any design or intention, a "word careless dropped" and "folded" in "perpetual seam," the infinite machinery of the book or the stitching of the fascicles. There is, moreover, another "perpetual seam" to this—indeed to any—poem: namely, the folding of the line break. Thus when the reader's "Eye" sees the enjambment, she may take the first line of the poem to mean "A Word [which is] dropped careless . . ./May [nonetheless] stimulate an Eye"; but the *sound* of the end-stop after "Page" authorizes us to hear the first line as the *account* of an occurrence: "A Word [has] dropped careless on a page."

Josef Raab argues that the poem exemplifies Dickinson's "fascination" with the "concept of uncontrollable language": "the word—as well as the poem that employs it—can animate or 'stimulate,'" but, asserts Raab, it can also be a contagion that imperils. Once uttered or written, the word assumes a dynamic of its own; it can never be recalled by its "'Wrinkled Maker'[v. Author] since at the moment of its use the word acquires its independence."[15] Raab is right to attend to the problem of linguistic agency and effects in the poem; but I believe that there is more at stake in Dickinson's poem than an expression of her "fascination" with the "concept of uncontrollable language." Taking 1268B as the basis of his interpretation, Raab reads "the Wrinkled Maker" as the source or origin of a word that, "once uttered . . . assumes a dynamic of its own." But the diction and figures in the stanza suggest another, more radical possibility: namely, that "the *wrinkled* author" is the *page* itself, the machinery of the book that "lies" there. An event occurs, a word is dropped, and the simple convergence of dropped word and open book has the power to "consecrate," an effect deepened by the sense of divinity that resonates through the "author/maker" variants. Theologically speaking, it is only through God that an object, including the human eye, can be rendered holy or "consecrated." "A Word dropped careless on a Page" conjures what Agamben calls the troubadorian desire and its "purely theological presupposition" of the poetic advent of the "word." But the poem's account of the word's "careless" occurrence— its sheerly accidental status—*de-theologizes* the event as it aestheticizes it by the "consecration" of the "folds" of the "perpetual seam."[16]

What Dickinson called "the plunge from the front" occurs throughout the poems and, in a certainly banal, but necessary sense, marks almost every poem of the *oeuvre*, insofar as they are left untitled. Cameron's parenthetic remarks on this topic are thus very much to the point: "Dickinson . . . produc[es] utterances that are extrageneric, even unclassifiable, and (for that reason, in a way that it seems to me no one yet has quite explained) untitled" (*Choosing*, 46). I cannot explain Dickinson's decision to leave nearly all of her poems untitled, but the fact that she did contributes to what I am calling the "event-effect" of the opening lines. However we regard the conventional status of the title—is it inside or outside the text? a frame? an occasion? a topic?—it is almost invariably the first thing encountered in the course of reading. The title always serves, at least in part, to announce and situate the text that follows, however much that text may ironize, qualify, or simply ignore the topic or situation posed by the title. The absence of the title in Dickinson clears the space for the event of language. Put more forcefully and more to the point of the force of the poems in question, Dickinson's language events leave no space for the stabilizing framework of a title. When Dickinson *does* provide titles for her work, says Judith Farr, "they are afterthoughts, and primitive. . . . They were obviously selected because she knew titles were customary, not because she conceived of them as improving the coherence of her work."[17] In Heideggerian terms the absence of titles provides the "clearing" through which the event of language is made possible. In Dickinsonian terms, the absence of titles forces us to experience the poetic "plunge from the front" or the inaugurating "drop of a word" as an "overtaking" and "overturning" event. And in the terms of my own thesis, this absenting participates in the lyric radicalization I am pointing to in her work, another form of her zeroing.

If most readers of Dickinson have in one way or another wrestled with what I am describing as the "event-status" of her opening lines for as long as they have been reading the poems, the second of my guiding terms—the machine—may seem entirely counterintuitive, if not perversely reductive: it is as if I were regarding the poems or even Emily Dickinson herself as something crudely mechanical. Indeed, one of the most insistent legacies of a certain interpretation of Romanticism is the organicism that perceives the "system" or the "apparatus" as a threat that resists, to the point of phobic reaction, anything mechanical, nonhuman. But for William Carlos Williams—certainly as "humanist" a modern poet as the American tradition would produce—the alliance of poetics and mechanics, far from threatening, was regarded as demystifying and even liberating: "A poem is a small (or large) machine made of words," declares Williams in his 1944 preface to *The Wedge*. In a letter to Higginson in 1874, Dickinson expressed her own understanding of the relationships between the organic and the mechanical, between the work of the "wrinkled maker" and the material workings of the thing made: "I thought being a Poem one's self precluded the writing Poems, but perceive the Mistake." It is mistaken, in other words, to assume that human beings are the only "makers" of poetry: those "makers" can be poems themselves, and those poems can, it seems, write more poems. Dickinson's rhetorical awareness of the metalepsis also demonstrates her understanding of the intertwining of the origin and apparatus of poetry.

Dickinson's poetics activate other senses of the machine, including that most general definition offered by the *OED* as "a structure of any kind." But even more relevant to Dickinson's project is the now archaic definition of "machine" as a "material construction or erection, the handiwork of a divine or supernatural power." Dickinson would also have understood "machine" to mean "fabric" as well as an "appliance, instrument, or apparatus." Textile or instrument, divine power or material construction, each of these meanings resonates with the conception of language itself as a form of machine, as in Coleridge's definition of language as a "blessed machine." *Webster's* offers another relevant secondary definition of the machine in the context of theater: a theatrical "machine" is "an apparatus for the production of stage effects," mechanisms that manufacture dramatic effects, *art-effects*. Metaphors of machinery are present throughout Dickinson's poems and letters. She notes the mechanical movements of the "wheel" and the "loom" in "My wheel is in the dark!" (61); and then there are inoperative systems or structures, such as the "broken mathematics" of "As by the dead we love to sit" (78). In "The Lightning is a yellow Fork" (1140), "The Apparatus of the Dark" is revealed through the non-concealing flash of lightning. Of course, many of Dickinson's poems address and reflect on the machinery of their own poetic structure, most often by referring to the functioning of poetic feet and measure. And in their most self-reflexive moments, the poems confront the poetic instruments and rhetorical devices they employ.

Figures of machinery offer the best way to approach the contested nature of Dickinson's *oeuvre*, specifically the issue of her poetic development or trajectory. When Porter characterized Dickinson as a "poet without a project," he was identifying what appears to be the absence of organic form, growth, or evolution to the course of her poetic production. While the *absence* of a "project" may be deemed to diminish our critical estimation of a poet's career, to deprive it of the self-conscious poetic design we esteem in the great poets, the opposing interpretation also asserts itself: this ostensible lack of a project may well *distinguish* the very nature of Dickinson's poetics. To put this in other words, the "absent" project of Dickinson's poetry is not only poetics itself, but a poetics of *absenting*.[18] This is precisely the connection Cameron makes in *Lyric Time* between the absence of Dickinson's development and the refusal of narrative progression in many of the poems themselves: "The absence of development within the 1775 poems is reflected in the resistance of many individual poems to the rigors and exactions of sequence and progression" (14). In other words, the force of compression that characterizes Dickinsonian poesis produces that oxymoronic effect of "lyric time" that Cameron explores in her painstaking (and often breathtaking) analysis. Cameron's understanding of the "non-shape" of Dickinson's career, the absence in the *oeuvre* of an organic form of growth and development (a model that includes periods of late "withering" and diminution), suggests that we look elsewhere for metaphors that might account more adequately for her poetic production, such as the metaphor of the machine. When Cameron revisits Dickinson by way of the fascicles, her account of Dickinson's "poetic structures" demonstrates the poet's unlikely affinity with the mechanical, particularly "the way in which [she] derive[s] [her] elements simultaneously from variation and repetition, subordination and autonomy" (*Choosing*, 60). The justness of these metaphors is confirmed by Dickinson's style, which, as Stonum puts it, "is remarkably consistent from beginning to end. . . . From about 1858, when she first began making and preserving fair copies, until her death in 1886, the same distinctive features appear over and over again" (*Dickinson Sublime*, 23). From the instance of its first appearance, in other words, the machinery of Dickinson's poetic idiom is evident and remains in operation throughout the course of her poetic production. In fact, the rhetoric of the machine might well be the best means to an understanding of the role of the fascicles. The fascicles constitute the apparatus—special, hand-designed machines—for which Dickinson manufactured so many of her poems.

My "mechanistic" reading allows us to undo the opposition between the archivally based approaches that attempt to secure what the poems said and the hermeneutic interpretations that attempt to uncover what the poems mean or to chronicle their unintelligibility. A reading attentive to Dickinson's poetic mechanisms permits us to think of the variants in Dickinson as "replacement parts." For instance, as Cameron points out, "the metric of the poem insists we choose only one of the variants; but the presence of the variants insists on the impossibility of doing so" (*Choosing*, 42). In other words, only one of the available pieces can be made to work at a time, but the variants offer many substitute parts that could "work" in the poetic machinery in order to generate different effects. Cameron's own account of this aporia alludes to the force exerted by these substitutions: "the variants exert pressure against each other in a *particular* poem and at particular places *within* that poem" (42). According to Cameron, this produces the specific nature of Dickinsonian unreadability. To examine the "apparatus" that produces such interpretive "darkness" does not dissolve the aporia, but it does place us, as we shall see, in a better position to confront the workings and the effects of Dickinson's machines, including that most distinctive graphic element or "part" of her poetic machinery—the dash.

When did the dashes start? Stonum traces the advent of "Dickinson's most idiosyncratic mark, the intralinear dash," to the revision of an 1853 poem that she inscribed into a fascicle of 1858: "We get for the first time in Dickinson's poetry a possibility of hesitation and uncertainty about how some words are linked" (*Dickinson Sublime*, 26). This is the "inauguration" of what Stonum calls "a minimal double writing" (26), a poetic operation that generates thousands of examples. Thus, for whatever reason, by whatever motivation or intention, it is here that we first encounter the invention of an idiom, the event of a poetics that would produce almost 1,800 "units." We can call this the "event" that establishes the distinctive "machinery" of Dickinson's poetics.

The "event-machine" is, therefore, operative at the advent of Dickinson's career; and the event-machine is, I believe, *at issue* in many of the poems that comprise that career. As I see it, the following are the most pressing questions posed by the notion of the event-machine for Dickinson's poetics: what is the relationship between the powerful inaugurating event that opens the poems and the machinery that constitutes the poems' textual and contextual systems? Is the machinery of the poems the apparatus for the production of poetic *events*; or does the poetic machinery constitute a response to the inaugural event, the happening of language? The poems themselves will answer the question of the relationship between event and machine in any number of ways. In some cases the opening line arrives with such force that the subsequent lines are best understood as a sustained effort to explain it: the inaugurating event sets in motion the poem's own interpretive machinery. In other cases the poem's machinations appear to be aversions from the force of the opening line, a movement away from the power of an eruptive inauguration. And in many instances this pattern is complicated further, as in those poems in which an assertive or even imperative declaration is followed by a structure of comparison or a system of elaboration—explanatory machinations—that may in turn be subjected to intricate breakdowns of logic and syntax or further decontextualization. In *Lyric Time* Cameron describes these complicated examples as "that group of Dickinson poems in that a story is begun only to be violently broken into and disrupted" (24). The bold advent of a narrative is suddenly broken off, rather like the "broken mathematics" that cannot both *count* sequentially and *account for* the event of its instantiation. Put another way, the machinery of numerical sequencing cannot account for the singular nature of the transition from zero to one, the *event* from nothing to something, even if this something leads to nought. "The Zeros taught Us - Phosphorus," we recall, and "We learned to like the Fire."

Zeros in Dickinson do not always make it to one. The poetics of aporia is not only a recurring event in Dickinson's poems: I would argue that it is *constitutive* of her poetics. Moreover, the nature of the aesthetic in Dickinson—its representations, its occurrences—is beset by aporetic conditions. There are poems that open with an impasse, poems that are inaugurated by a blockage, such as "I saw no Way - the Heavens were stitched -" (633), a poem that confronts us with what Dickinson calls a "bright impossibility." Another name for this "bright impossibility" is the aporia or *impassibility*, what Celan in "Anabasis" called the "impassable true." It is the presence of a constitutive aporia that justifies the naming of "Emily Dickinson" as an "event-machine." And it is for this reason, one inherent in the production as well as the reception of the poems, that Derrida's term "event-machine" aptly characterizes Dickinson's *oeuvre* and opens the topic of aesthetics that will lead us to a Dickinsonian aestheticism. Derrida's formulation of this figure arises from his analysis of the conceptual antinomy between the event and the machine. Event and machine are terms, says Derrida, that "appear to us to be antinomic. Antinomic because what happens ought to keep, so we think, some nonprogrammable and therefore incalculable singularity (*Without Alibi*, 72)." This antinomic thinking is nowhere more evident than in the notion of the aesthetic that is a principal legacy of the Romantic tradition: we expect the creative act to be "nonprogrammable" and therefore "singular," to emanate from the organic realm of human representation and to be divorced from everything mechanical, repetitive. And there are few poets in this tradition who seem more singular, more "nonprogrammable," more distinctive from beginning to end, more of an *event* than Emily Dickinson.

The "natural" aversion to the machine and to the "programmable" is certainly one reason that the critical interest in structuralism, at least in the Anglo-American context, proved to be so short-lived. Structuralism was perceived as "reducing" the creative, the human, the *singular* act to an effect of systems of repetition and variation: the complex mystery of aesthetic experience demystified and diminished to a mere byproduct of a linguistic program. And if the machine appeared as a threat to our investment in the aesthetic, it also appeared as a threat to our most cherished notions of history.[19] As Derrida crystallizes the historicist objection, "an event worthy of the name ought not, so we think, to give in or be reduced to repetition" (*Without Alibi*, 72). By definition, something that is singular enough to have attained the status of an event "ought not, so we think," be susceptible to repetition. Derrida extends this antinomic relationship between the machine and the event to a particular form of aesthetic judgment: "There is no thinking of the event, it seems, without some sensitivity, without an *aesthetic* affect and some presumption of living organicity" (72). With a gesture that recalls, if not repeats, "Structure, Sign, and Play"—an essay written more than thirty years earlier—Derrida puts into play a figure that invokes the "monstrous":

> If one day, with one and the same concept, these two incompatible concepts, the event and the machine, were thought together, you can bet that not only . . . will one have produced a new logic, an unheard-of conceptual form. In truth, against a background and at the horizon of our present possibilities, this new figure would resemble a monster. (*Without Alibi*, 73)[20]

This "new figure," forged from two incompatible concepts, the event-machine, "would resemble," says Derrida, invoking the language of semblance and, by extension, aesthetics, "a monster." I can think of no better way to characterize the appearance or at least the early *reception* of Emily Dickinson than as such a "monstrosity." Even to reviewers who are clearly moved and impressed by her "absolute originality," the poetry, to quote from Col. Higginson's 1890 preface to the *Poems by Emily Dickinson*, "will seem to the reader like poetry torn up by the roots."[21] Higginson's famous comparison with Blake strikes a chord with another early reviewer, Caroline Kirkland: Higginson "likens [Dickinson's] peculiar, untainted originality to the genius of William Blake," writes Kirkland. "There is much similarity in spirit. Both were abortive geniuses; both were, in a certain way, monsters in the poetic world" (*EDR*, 119). Thus does Dickinson, even to an admirer, "resemble a monster." While Richard Henry Stoddard was noting in 1892 that "Dickinsonese" had passed from a literary "fad" to "a mild epidemic," the poetry is repeatedly characterized by readers sympathetic and otherwise as "anarchic" and "grotesque," "mad" and "monstrous": "without rhyme and without reason," declares Stoddard (*EDR*, 287, 424).

It can always be a satisfying exercise to isolate the blindness of ignorant contemporaries, especially when we have investments, critical or otherwise, in once-misunderstood or ill-treated writers. But in this instance it is more illuminating to see how many of Dickinson's early reviewers, hostile as well as sympathetic, are groping about for a language to reckon with her poems and latch upon figures that seem uncanny in their ability to identify the singular event of this poetry. "Literary crimes," declares one reviewer, stricken "almost with aphasia" (*EDR*, 471, 181). Maurice Thompson does not intend to pay the poetry a compliment when he writes that *Poems of Emily Dickinson* appears "like a crude translation of freshly discovered Greek lyrical fragments" (*EDR*, 98); but his comment captures both the sense of the Dickinson event and an awareness of the lexical, syntactic, and rhetorical defamiliarization that readers encountered with the first volume of her poems. Thompson's dismissive judgment is confirmed, but revalorized by one of the poet's most ardent early supporters, Louise Chandler Moulton, who found "something in Emily Dickinson" that "made her a law unto herself" (*EDR*, 243). In this way the publication of *Poems of Emily Dickinson* fulfills Derrida's conditions of eventhood: "an event does not come about unless its irruption interrupts the course of the possible and, as the impossible itself, surprises any foreseeability" (*Without Alibi*, 73).

There are monsters, of course, and then there are monsters: the only way I know of to measure the genuine significance for Dickinson of what Derrida calls this "new figure" of the "event-machine" is not the thick catalog of contemporary responses, but the workings of her poems, many of which certainly "surprise any foreseeabilty." What Derrida calls the "antinomic relationship between the event and the machine" is at work in what Dickinson calls "bright impossibility," and sometimes to such a degree that it is no longer an antinomy, but an aporia that is riven into the heart or "crease" of the poem. Nowhere is this condition more immediately announced than in "I saw no Way - the Heavens were stitched -" (633), which *opens* with an aporia:

> I saw no Way - The Heavens were stitched -
> I felt the Columns close -
> The Earth reversed her Hemispheres -
> I touched the Universe -
>
> And back it slid - and I alone -
> A speck opon a Ball -
> Went out opon Circumference -
> Beyond the Dip of Bell -

The poem begins with the speaker's account of a dramatic and even final impasse, an account that announces the impossibility of seeing, of finding one's "way," and the experience of the closure of the heavens, "stitched" shut and unavailable. The initial foreclosure of heavenly guidance is not overturned in this poem, but—through the removal of any theological reference—transferred into the condition of subjectivity as such. In Cameron's reading, "the dead-end of the poem's beginning . . . closes the speaker off from heaven and then dramatically turns the world inside out (*Lyric Time*, 9). The speaker's initial blockage is compounded by the claustrophobic feeling expressed in the second line—"I felt the columns close"—until the earth itself "reversed her hemispheres" and the speaker "touche[s]" not "the heavens," but "the universe" (ll.2−4).

The harrowing, if sublime condition that confronts the speaker in the opening lines is compounded in the second and final stanza of the poem. The "reversal" of earth's hemispheres experienced in the first stanza is compounded by the backward slide of the universe; and the result of this double reversal is sheer and absolute solitude: "And back it slid - and I alone -/A speck opon a Ball -" (ll.5−6). With heaven stitched and the universe withdrawn, the speaker is profoundly reduced—merely "a speck opon a Ball"—but nonetheless ventures "out opon Circumference—/Beyond the Dip of Bell" (ll.7−8). We would not be wrong to read this as an allegory of Dickinson's poetics, particularly given the idiomatic association of "circumference" and poetry in many of her poems and letters. Cameron regards this aporetic beginning, which "turns the world inside out," as a poetic experience in which "language is giddy with the speaker's disorientation" (*Lyric Time*, 9). It is entirely understandable that Cameron would confuse a reader's affective response with the performance of the lines themselves; but far from being "giddy," the language of these lines strikes me as chilling in its austerity and its solitary, untethering movement. However abstract the points of reference in the first stanza may be—heavens, columns, earth, hemisphere, universe—in the second stanza reference is all but eliminated. We are confronted with a "sliding" withdrawal onto a "circumference" that is the *circumference of nothing*. This is a rarified poetry of sheerest negation, absolute "zeroing" out. If we recognize in this poem the aesthetics of the sublime—an absolute blockage that in the infinite ungrounding of the subject gives way to the touch of the universe—it is important to understand how in Dickinson the sublime is generated by an *opening* that is simultaneously a blockage.

To cite the poem as a previously unnoticed instance of what Stonum has identified as "the Dickinsonian sublime" is not only to add another example to Stonum's argument, but to situate the poem and its particularities within the conventions of aesthetics. It is, in other words, to reckon this singular poetic event in terms of an existing structure, the "machinery" of aesthetic judgment. At the same time, the power of Dickinson's poems, and especially the inseparability of that poetic force from their status as event or occurrence, prompts us to consider aesthetics not as the framework or machinery of judgments and interpretations, but as the singular, unrepeatable event that imposes itself upon us. Agamben tells us that the historical arrival of philosophical aesthetics replaces without fundamentally displacing the *structure* of theological explanations of the linguistic event.[22] For Agamben biography and psychology come to vie with aesthetics in the efforts, traditionally accorded to theology, to understand and explain the event.

Theology, biography, psychology, aesthetics: each of these domains occupies a prominent place in the history of Dickinson criticism, the efforts to secure, situate, understand, and explain the thousands of accumulated poetic events that bear her handwriting. This is an old-fashioned and perhaps foundational interpretive dilemma: does the appearance of an event prompt the attempts to contextualize it; or is it the case that an event cannot occur outside of a context by which it can be recognized and understood as such? To my mind no one has identified the nature and difficulty of this interpretive impasse more succinctly than de Man in his account of the entanglements between poetics and hermeneutics:

> Hermeneutics is, by definition, a process directed toward the determination of meaning; it postulates a transcendental function of understanding, no matter how complex, deferred, or tenuous it might be. . . . Poetics, on the other hand, . . . pertains to the formal analysis of linguistic entities as such, independently of signification. . . . The two procedures have very little in common. . . . [But] hermeneutics and poetics, different and distinct as they are, have a way of becoming entangled, as indeed they have since Aristotle and before. One can look upon the history of literary theory as the continued attempt to disentangle this knot and to record the reasons for failing to do so. (*Resistance*, 55–56)

The Dickinsonian version of this "knotted" relationship between poetics and hermeneutics has been played out in almost every available interpretive model. Generations of critics have mined versions of biographical, psychological, cultural, social, theological, and feminist hermeneutics to establish "the determination of meaning" from a poetics that—consistently composed of shifters and abstractions, deletions and unintelligibilities—often seems forged on the basis of meaning's refusal. Stonum gives this dilemma its most elegant formulation: Dickinson's poems "regularly challenge us to imagine backgrounds they conspicuously fail to specify."[23]

One of the more intriguing efforts to reconcile poetics and hermeneutics in Dickinson is Dorothy Huff Oberhaus's *Emily Dickinson's Fascicles: Meaning and Method*.[24] Oberhaus's own hermeneutic is theological; and the primary focus of her analysis is the last fascicle, the "fortieth and final booklet Dickinson assembled" (3).[25] According to Oberhaus, the "dense" and "elliptical" poems of the fortieth fascicle are only superficially "unrelated." In Oberhaus's hermeneutic, the interpretive "key to discovering" the "deep structural and thematic unity" of the poems is biblical scripture as it is mediated by the Anglophone tradition of Christian meditational poetry.[26] By virtue of this theological and even typological hermeneutic, Oberhaus concludes that the fortieth fascicle—and indeed Dickinson's entire *oeuvre*—constitutes "a spiritual and poetic *pilgrimage*" (3). This fascinating and ultimately untenable *coup de texte* is achieved by rendering the particularities of Dickinson's lyrics into a narrative and, more specifically, "a simple conversion narrative" (19). In her interpretation of Dickinson, Oberhaus claims to reveal the genuine meaning behind complex rhetorical processes and to redeem the difficulties of the poet's elliptical form. One result of such an analysis is to eliminate from the eruptive beginnings of these poems all but one event: the speaker's—and, presumably, the poet's—conversion. What Oberhaus encounters in reading Dickinson are not, as I have been arguing, the complex machinations of almost two thousand poetic events, many of which wrestle with the nature and consequences of the aesthetic, but rather one massive devotional poem.[27] Thus is Dickinson's literary production transformed from a mass of dense, acute, and elliptical lyrics into the great New England epic poem of Christian conversion.

As the title *Choosing Not Choosing* implies, Sharon Cameron's groundbreaking study of Dickinson's fascicles is much less inclined to resolve the interpretive challenges posed by the booklets the poet assembled. If Oberhaus finds the fascicles—and F-40 in particular—to provide the redeeming interpretive key to the entire *oeuvre*, Cameron interprets "the fascicle context" not in order "to arrive at a more stable interpretive situation" (*Choosing*, 32). For Cameron the fascicles *do* generate relations among the poems, but without theological certainty, typological revelation, or conversion narrative. To reckon with Dickinson's fascicles is, according to Cameron, "to arrive at a different interpretive situation than that in which the poem is read elliptically as a decontextualized utterance. It is to be confronted by a different interpretive situation just to the extent that there are relations among poems that we cannot disregard and, as much to the point, that we do not precisely know how to comprehend" (*Choosing*, 32).

These are only two examples—less and more successful—of the many efforts to reckon not so much with the obscurity of meaning in Dickinson's poetry as with the effects of what I am calling the "zeroing" of her poetics. This zeroing arrives with the force of an event and challenges any hermeneutic effort to put the pieces of this poetic machinery together (internally or externally through the relations of poems) and make it "work" interpretively. While I am not interested in demonstrating how the topic of aesthetics might make the pieces of Dickinson's poetry cohere into a meaningful whole, I am keenly interested in the ways in which her poetics of the zero both engages and disturbs her own "system of aesthetics."

"A System of Aesthetics"

The appearance of aesthetics in Dickinson as theme or performance does not resolve the knotted entanglements between event and machine or between poetics and hermeneutics. Nor does the machinery of the fascicles stabilize or isolate a Dickinsonian aesthetic. In my own reading of the poetry, I can find no *aesthetic* correlate to Oberhaus's F-40, not even the fifth fascicle, which features such relevant poems as "Artists Wrestled Here" (111), "A something in a summer's Day" (104), and "For each extatic instant" (109). In Dickinson aesthetics resides at the very heart of the interpretive dilemma I have recounted; indeed, *aesthetics is the very knot that entangles poetics and hermeneutics.* And as such, aesthetics cannot function as a *context*; but it can serve as the point or occurrence of the antinomy between poetics and hermeneutics or as the fulcrum at the aporia between the event and the machine. In Dickinson, as in Shelley or Keats, when aesthetics is regarded as the meaningful effect—or affect—elicited by the poetic structure, it appears to be an aspect of hermeneutics. On the other hand, the aesthetic can certainly be understood as the figurative "deflection" from the literal; and such an understanding would assign the aesthetic to the domain of poetics. Or, as in certain versions of aestheticism, the aesthetic is nothing more or less than a spell—what Keats calls "sable charm and dumb enchantment"—that voids meaning through the mesmerizing effect of certain poetic techniques. And it is certainly the case that for Dickinson, as for Shelley or for Keats, the experience of the aesthetic is a "spell" that appears without notice; and to "spell" that "state" would "demean" it. This is the argument expressed in "To tell the Beauty would decrease" (1689), where the "decrease" of "telling" beauty is likened to the "stating"—and thus the "demeaning"—of the "spell" or "rapture" of aesthetic experience:

> To tell the Beauty would decrease
> To state the spell demean
> There is a syllableless Sea
> Of which it is the sign
> My will endeavors for it's word
> And fails, but entertains
> A Rapture as of Legacies -
> Of introspective mines -

Telling and stating decrease and demean the auratic immediacy of the aesthetic spell. But if beauty is the "sign" of "a syllableless Sea"—a vast, inarticulate muteness we are likely to associate with the sublime—then the poem is not simply dismissing signification and embracing a spellbound aesthetic rapture. Indeed, the speaker seeks "Beauty's" "word"; and it is only through the "will's" failed "endeavor" to find that word that the "will" "entertains a Rapture," mining the depths of introspection.

The indefinable and troubling "exstasy" and "transport" produced by an aesthetic experience is the topic of "Flowers - Well - if anybody" (95). The poem is something like a sonnet, at least as close to a sonnet as Dickinson ever gets: a fourteen-line poem with a highly irregular, but intricate rhyme scheme. Here it is not the first line that marks the event, but the first *word*: "Flowers" *as* event. But it is the second word that, though grammatically a filler, carries a tonal swagger and establishes the speaker's authority to move from the sheer transporting existence of flowers to "a system of aesthetics."

> Flowers - Well - if anybody
> Can the exstasy define -
> Half a transport - half a trouble -
> With which flowers humble men:
> Anybody find the fountain
> From which floods so contra flow -
> I will give him all the Daisies
> Which opon the hillside blow.
>   (ll. 1–8)

"Flowers" are the source or "fountain" of aesthetic rapture, an "extasy" composed half of "transport," half of "trouble." The second half of the octave proposes an exchange: if anybody can define the humbling "extasy" of flowers, if anybody can discover the source from which flows the counter-floods, if anybody can identify the cause or the effects of this aesthetic experience, then, promises the speaker, "I will give him all the Daisies / Which upon the hillside blow." In other words, you give me the name and I give you the daisies. The sestet opens with another declaration of excess, but now an excess of pathos:

> Too much pathos in their faces
> For a simple breast like mine -
> Butterflies from St Domingo
> Cruising round the purple line -
> Have a system of aesthetics -
> Far superior to mine.
>   (ll. 9–14)

The trouble and transport produced by "Flowers" prompts us to assign a face to a flower. What we are tempted to call Dickinson's flower power also results in the confusion of aesthetic response, blurring ecstasy and pathos. If the poem is an extended declaration of the aesthetic power of "Flowers," it is simultaneously a repeated admission of the failure of her own "system of aesthetics" to reckon adequately with the assertion of that power. Three times the poem registers this failure to define the ecstasy of flowers, to determine the source of "contra floods," to match the "system of aesthetics" exhibited by the "Butterflies from St Domingo" and their presumably unmediated relationship to the source of these aesthetic effects.

Sometimes in Dickinson the "system of aesthetics" itself—often in the form of a reference to beauty—provides the poem's inaugurating event. In one of Dickinson's most famous poems, "I died for Beauty" (448), beauty is posited as the sacrificial condition for the linguistic experience of death. Beauty becomes the rationale for the most fundamental existential aporia or impasse, the impossible passage *through* death, one that Dickinson addresses in a number of important poems. The allusion to the conclusion of "Ode on A Grecian Urn" makes "I died for Beauty" appear to be the most conventionally romantic version of a Dickinsonian aestheticism; but in fact the topic of aesthetics and the speaker's aestheticist gesture serves primarily as the occasion for the poem's reflection on the shuttling between poetry and death. A more sustained engagement with the source and effects of the aesthetic is "Beauty - be not caused - It is -" (654), a poem that makes beauty into the inaugurating word of a line that functions as one of those strange Dickinsonian adages. Here the declaration of a causeless beauty initiates the poetic reflection on the transience and arbitrariness of this aesthetic force. And yet the poem is less a genuine reflection on the nature of beauty than a sort of parable:

> Beauty - be not caused - It Is -
> Chase it, and it ceases -
> Chase it not, and it abides -
>
> Overtake the Creases
>
> In the Meadow - when the Wind
> Runs his fingers thro' it -
> Deity will see to it
> That You never do it -

The opening line announces the occurrence of beauty as an unprovoked event, the happening secured by the copula; and it is an occurrence that is both singular and subject to disappearance. The poem's stanzaic division makes it appear to posit a conventional comparison between beauty and the wind. "Deity" presides as the ultimate arbiter, the force that prevents any human overweaning "overtaking."[28]

The "being" or "spelling" of beauty in Dickinson often takes the form of a "veiling," which is precisely how Benjamin would describe the auratic nature of beauty. For Benjamin, "'the beautiful is neither the veil nor the veiled object but rather the object in its veil'—this is the quintessence of the ancient aesthetic. Through its veil, which is nothing other than the aura, the beautiful appears [*scheint*]."[29] How better to understand the series of "somethings" that serves as beginning and topic of Dickinson's "A something in a summer's Day" (104) than the auratic appearance of the aesthetic? There is a "something" in a "summer's Day," in a "summer's noon" (l.4), and "within a summer's night" (l.7) that, respectively, "solemnizes" (l.3), "Transcend[s] extasy" (l.6), and is "transporting bright" (l.8). This "something" is indeed nothing other than the aura, the veil through which "the beautiful appears." It is no accident that the figure and the occurrence of veiling are revealed after the third and final "transporting" "something":

> And still within a summer's night
> A something so transporting bright
> I clap my hands to see -
>
> Then vail my too inspecting face
> Lest such a subtle - shimmering grace
> Flutter too far for me -
>
> (ll.7–12)

One might conclude that the referent of this last "something" "within a summer's night" is readily inferred, that this "still," "bright" "something" is nothing other than the moon. But the poem insists triply on a *something* that is "so transporting bright" that the speaker's "too inspecting face" must be "vail[ed]": it is only through "vailing" that the effects of excess scrutiny can be avoided and the object remain the something that maintains "a subtle - shimmering grace." To turn once again to Benjamin, this "subtle - shimmering grace" is thus an effect neither of "the veil nor the veiled object but rather the object in its veil."

Dickinson's exploration of the aesthetic effects of veiling is revisited in "A Charm invests a face" (430), a poem that takes the operation and effects of veiling as its conceit: "A Charm invests a face / Imperfectly beheld - / The Lady dare not lift her Vail - / For fear it be dispelled -" (ll.1–4). The poem belongs to that class of Dickinson poems in which an adage—"A Charm invests a face / Imperfectly beheld"—and the expectations attached to it are subjected to an inversion. With the second stanza, the poem shifts its gears and moves from a face being seen, "a face / Imperfectly beheld," to the act of a veiled seeing: it is "the Lady" herself who "peers beyond her mesh - / And wishes - and denies -/Lest Interview - annul a want/That Image - satisfies" (ll.5–8). The "charm" that "the Lady" "fear[s]" "dispelled" is not—or at least not solely—that of her own face presented to the world, but those at which she "peers beyond her mesh." Thus does the poem reveal the structure, even the machinery—the "vail," the "mesh"—of an aestheticized seeing, one that generates desire, a "wishing" and a "wanting." This is an aestheticized seeing that produces an "Image" that would be "annul[ed]" by "Interview," by close critical scrutiny.

Ford examines a version of this structure of perception in a series of poems that invoke or describe "films," as in "The thought beneath so slight a film -" (203). For Ford, "the film is clearly not a barrier that impoverishes or renders the speaker inarticulate. On the contrary, it appears to make thought more distinct" (*Gender and Excess*, 54). Or, in the terms we are exploring, the film *aestheticizes* thought. But the auratic experience, the aesthetic "something," is not limited to the visual dimension of the "vail" or the "film." To return to "A something in a summer's Day," for instance, a subsequent "something," the "something in a summer's noon," involves more than one sense: it is the cumulative effect of a range of sensory engagements. This "something" is the measuring of "A depth," the visual distinction of "an Azure," the olfactory experience of "a perfume" (l.5), all of which taken together in something approaching synaesthesia are "Transcending exstasy" (l.6). The effects of these "somethings" are precisely those conjured in the prose fragment with which we began: they are the "somethings" that "overtake the mind."

If aesthetic "somethings" prompt and dominate the poem's first three stanzas, the subsequent stanzas address the natural and rhetorical machinery that promises the repetition or, better yet, the continued production of this auratic experience: "the purple brook" (l.14), the "amber Flag" of the "East" (l.16), the sun's "Caravan of Red" (l.18). But what is perhaps most striking about these lines is the repeated appearance of the word "still" that occurs four times in the space of four short lines. After Keats—and certainly after Spitzer and Krieger on Keats—our ears are tuned to the play of and pun on "still": "the fusion in it of the opposed meanings," as Krieger puts it, "never and always, as applied to motion."[30] In "A something in a summer's Day," the compression of "stills" makes the word function both as an adjective ("And still within a summer's night/A something so transporting bright" [ll.8–9]) and three times in consecutive lines as an adverb ("Still chafes," "Still rears," "Guides still" [ll.15,16,17]). If the modifying function of "still" is more stable in this poem than in "Thou still, unravish'd bride of quietness," the cumulative effect of such repeated "stilling"—as well as the resonance of the reversal in "Guides still"—produces the experience of what Krieger calls "'still' moving as a forever-now movement, always in process, unending" (91). And it is a future repetition that is anticipated in the poem's conclusion: "So looking on - the night - the morn/Conclude the wonder gay - /And I meet, coming thro' the dews/Another summer's Day!" (ll.19–22). As it comes full circle, the poem leaves us poised, "still" awaiting "Another summer's day" and the advent of yet another "something."

"A something in a summer's Day" demonstrates that the nature of the aesthetic as an event and the machinery of its recurrence are more important to our understanding of Dickinson's poetics than her conventional iconography of aesthetic experience. For if "A something in a summer's Day" explores aesthetic experience in familiar terms (ecstasy, transport, transcendence), elsewhere Dickinson pursues different registers of aesthetic sensation. "Delight - becomes pictorial -" (539), for instance, demonstrates that in Dickinson's aestheticizing, even pain can be regarded as the heightening of delight rather than its negation:

Delight - becomes pictorial -
When viewed through Pain -
More fair - because impossible
That any gain -

(ll.1–4)

"Pain" is the veil that places "delight" at a distance, an ungainable remove, and renders it "more fair" in the process. The poem's second stanza functions as an implied analogy to those initial accounts of aesthetic veiling. If "Delight - becomes pictorial -/When viewed through Pain" just as "The Mountain - at given distance -/In Amber - lies -" (ll.5–6), then amber is to the mountain as pain is to delight: both pain and amber "aestheticize" a perception. But the relationship of the stanzas is troubled by the way that the mountain "lies." This is a mode of punning on resting/deception that we have seen Shelley exploit in "On the Medusa"; and the basic grammatical elements of the stanza—"The Mountain . . . lies"—cannot but call to mind the relentless epistemological disturbances of "Mont Blanc." In Dickinson's poem the mountain seems to lie or rest preserved "In Amber" "at a given distance," but this preservative effect is nothing less than a lie; and when "Approached - the Amber flits - a little -" (l.6). The flitting of amber, rather like the aesthetic experience of the blur in the visual field, reveals the structure of an optical illusion, itself a perceptual "lie" or deceit. If this pun is valid and if the poem is indeed an extended analogy, the effects of such a lie extend back to the opening stanza and reveal that, as with any form of veiling, pictoriality itself is necessarily a lie. Such a reading is confirmed by the sudden shift in tone and theme: the poem seems initially to be about the experience of pain—a common enough topic in Dickinson, to be sure—but it quickly abandons the pathos of painful affect altogether as it enters the register of perceptual aesthetics.

These poems demonstrate that Dickinson's poetic engagements with the aesthetic often involve a sustained reflection on the act of looking, viewing, beholding: the structures of seeing that catch or even constitute an aesthetic "something." But Dickinson's commitment to an aesthetic *vision* is complicated by her fascination with blindness. This attention to the negation rather than the mere veiling of sight is apparent in "I saw no way - The heavens were stitched" (633), where the opening impasse is rendered as an inability to see. It is also apparent in "Like eyes that looked on wastes" (693), where the elaborate dependent clause that opens the poem not only sets the terms of the comparison, but does so in the form of blank sublimity, rather than sensuous apprehension:

> Like Eyes that looked on Wastes -
> Incredulous of Ought
> But Blank - and steady Wilderness -
> Diversified by Night -
>
> Just Infinites of Nought -
> As far as it could see -
> So looked the face I looked opon -
> So looked itself - on Me -
>
> (ll. 1–8)[31]

"Infinites of Nought": seeing has become a form of blindness, a mirroring blankness that generates multiple lookings, but nothing *seen*. We might call it "what the zeros saw." Dickinson's fascination with blindness is perhaps most acutely apparent in another poem about blindness and insight, "Before I got my eye put out -" (336). Here, the powerful opening line refers to the antecedent event of a blinding:

> Before I got my eye put out -
> I liked as well to see

As other creatures, that have eyes -
And know no other way -

                    (ll.1–4)

In the time before the event, the condition of sight is the given, normative condition of life: available to "other creatures," there is nothing auratic in what is recalled as the default mode of perception. "But were it told to me, Today"—in the time after the event—"That I might have the Sky/For mine, I tell you that my Heart/Would split, for size of me -" (ll.5–8). The event of blindness renders the prospect of a restored sight as an unbearable joy, an excess that has nothing to do with *knowing* the world and everything to do with *having* it. After blindness, sight is imagined as a form of incorporation— "As much of noon, as I could take -/Between my finite eyes" (ll.12–13) - that bestows possession of and title to the world—"The Meadows - mine -/The Mountains - mine -/All Forests - Stintless stars -" (ll.9–11).

Though the speaker ultimately imagines that the mere "news" of such a liberated seeing—"to look" "when I liked"—would be enough to "strike" her "dead" (ll.16, 17), she momentarily conjures a deeply aestheticized vision, "The Motions of Dipping Birds -/The Morning's Amber Road" (ll.14–15). Clinging instead to caution and safety, the speaker turns away from the entitlements offered by this vision of an aestheticizing sight:

So safer Guess -
With just my soul upon the Window pane -
Where other Creatures put their eyes -
Incautious - of the Sun -

                    (ll.18–21)

To look with "just the soul" is to turn away from all sensory apprehension; and thus the poem would seem to constitute an aversion to the aesthetic and the heart-splitting dangers of too much looking. But if the speaker seems cautious enough of the dangers of staring into the sun to avert her eyes from sensory excess, the poem itself plays on the antecedent event and, in the interval of the conditional tense, produces a glimpse of aestheticism. In other words, the poem is itself a kind of veiling: the potential pain of blindness may render the "pictorial" vision and its "shimmering grace" unavailable to the speaker, but it is made available in the poem. By way of its shutter-effect—what would be and what is not—the poem generates its own "something," its own veiling, its own "system of aesthetics."

"Bright Impossibility"

Many important Dickinson poems address aesthetic experience as something more definitive than "something." While these poems do not constitute a comprehensive or even consistent Dickinsonian understanding of the aesthetic, they do announce the topic of the aesthetic in the form of a definition, often in the pseudo-definitional mode of the adage or the aphorism that is a feature of many of the impersonal opening lines. I want to conclude this chapter by considering four poems in which the issues that concern us here converge: the status of opening lines as events, the workings of poetic machinery, and the effects of aesthetic experience. In these poems the radicalization or "zeroing" that is a principal procedure of Dickinson's poetics gives rise to events that are fully aestheticized, events that demand the speaker and the poem—and perhaps even Dickinson's poetics—to confront the dilemma of aestheticism.

This is the case in "This was a Poet" (446), a poem that seems to provide the definition of a poet, since the seventeen lines that follow the opening declaration offer the discernments and delineations that satisfy the conditions of a genuine definition. But if the poem supplies a definition of the poet, it must technically be classified as "obsolete," since the definition as well as the poet no longer appears to obtain. "This *was* a Poet" can certainly be interpreted as an elegy: this dead person whose poems I am now reading qualifies as a poet because the poems achieve the status of poetry by producing a "distillation" (yet another name for the radicalization or "zeroing" I am describing). If indeed an elegy, "This was a Poet" would be a rare, if not singular example of the genre, an elegy entirely shorn of pathos and delivered by way of a trail of pronouns and pointers to the mechanisms of poetry. The deictic dimension of the opening line, an emphatic "This," points to the relationship of *this* to poetry as such, to reckon with the connection between linguistic indication and the nature of poetry. And thus does "this" lead to "that": the opening line poeticizes the sheer linguistic act of pointing and directs us to the impersonal pronoun that follows in the next line and begins the machinery of explanation:

It is That
Distills amazing sense
From Ordinary Meanings -
And Attar so immense

From the familiar species
That perished by the Door -
We wonder it was not Ourselves
Arrested it - before -

(ll.2–9)

If the poem is routinely invoked as a straightforward account of Dickinson's poetics, the crucial temporal and rhetorical disjunction between the poem's opening declaration and its subsequent elaboration is often neglected. The grammatical tension between the first and second lines is heightened by the sense of temporal dislocation: instead of the expected "this was," we read "that was," which is followed by the present tense "it is." However conventional may be the notion of "distillation" that Dickinson proposes, the way in which the poem figures its origins and its effects is not. In the terms of my argument, poetry is figured here as an impersonal machine, an "it," by which "Attar immense" and "amazing sense" are so "distilled" from "Ordinary Meanings" and "the familiar species" that we "wonder" whether "it was not Ourselves" who "Arrested it," whether it was not the readers who might be responsible for the effects that have befallen us. In other words, genuine poesis produces a metalepsis, an aesthetic distillation powerful enough to result in the reader's confusion of cause and effect.

The poem's final two stanzas appear to return us to the human agency involved in the process: "Of Pictures, the Discloser -/The Poet - it is He -/ Entitles Us - by Contrast -/To ceaseless Poverty -" (ll.10–13). I understand the dash at the end of the poem's opening line to serve as an implied colon; and if we believe the dash at the end of the ninth line performs a similar function, we can interpret the third stanza as moving from the particular poet "that was" to the species of poet. And here the consequences of such aesthetic "disclosure" are rather less conventional: the poet "Entitles Us" to nothing good, nothing but "ceaseless Poverty"; and he achieves this by means of "Contrast"—figures, distinctions, differences—that belong to the rhetorical materials of poetry.

As it is with "Pictures," so it is with "Portion": "Of Portion - [he is] so unconscious - [that]/The Robbing - could not harm -/Himself - [since] to Him - a Fortune - [is]/Exterior - to Time" (ll.14–17). If my gloss of these lines is plausible and the final stanzas of the poem do take us back to "a Poet," the compounded inversions of the third person pronouns do not humanize the process, but, quite to the contrary, deliver us into the syntactical and grammatical machinery of the pronoun and in the process remove poetic "Fortune" from the register of human temporality, something "Exterior - to Time." My effort to understand the poem—the choices I have made here to stabilize its syntactic play and eliminate some of its grammatical incompleteness— illustrates the very process I am describing: the poem offers the poetic pieces of a machinery that is itself "arrested," "Exterior - to Time," mere parts of an apparatus that requires supplementation in order to be rendered into a meaningful narrative. I have, in other words, proposed a plausible, but scarcely definitive interpretive arrangement of the pieces of this poem to demonstrate how "arrested" it is and to suggest that however we may look to the poem to supply a definition of Dickinson's poetics, what we are in fact left with are the *workings* of poetry.

The aesthetic deixis of "This was a Poet" is present in an earlier and ostensibly less complex poem, "Artists wrestled here!" (111). If this brief exclamatory poem is much less often discussed than "This was a Poet" or "I died for Beauty," "Artists wrestled here!" immediately confronts the reader with the entanglements of aesthetics, the event, and context that we have been wrestling with—*here*:

> Artists wrestled here!
> Lo, a tint Cashmere!
> Lo, a Rose!
> Student of the Year!
> For the Easel here
> Say Repose!

We are justified in reading the first line as the exclamatory indication of an aesthetic event, the witnessing of a work of art, the only evidence of which is available to the speaker. And in the absence of an immediate referent— neither the poem nor the fascicle suggests *where* the "here" is—we are given only two features of the work of art in question, features that are announced as discoveries: "Lo, a tint cashmere! / Lo, a rose!" (ll.2–3). The poem is ekphrastic; but unlike the examples of the genre we explored in Keats and Shelley, the nature of the visual object is withheld: Dickinson offers no Renaissance painting or Elgin Marble, only the emphatic *assertion* that the speaker is in the presence of a work of art. The five line-ending exclamations give the poem its sense of elevation and, coupled with the deictic repetition of *here*, its sense of immediacy.

This immediacy is itself elevated by the verb "wrestled," as if the speaker were visiting a scene of physical strife. The agonistic dimension of the poem is confirmed by the fact that the speaker reports the outcome of a plural struggle: "*Artists* wrestled here," as if what "Reposes" on the "Easel" were the result of an aesthetic contest. But the poem moves from the plural to the singular, from "Artists" to "Student of the Year," and from wrestling to "Repose," from activity to its cessation. As urgent as it is deictic, the poem is in essence a highly agitated act of literary pointing; and it also implies in the course of its six brief lines the narrative trajectory from artistic struggle and strife to the stillness of the finished object, "Reposed" on "the Easel here." But the word *repose* has a meaning other than rest and stillness, a meaning derived from the domain of painting and available to Dickinson: in reference to a painting, *repose* means the "harmonious arrangement of figures or colours, having a restful effect upon the eye" (*OED*). Thus would the poem not only be ekphrastic—a literary representation of a visual work of art—it would also constitute an aesthetic judgment of that visual representation: the result of the artistic struggle is an easel, right here, that says, "Repose!"

In fact, the poem's ekphrastic dimension is not diminished, but deepened if we regard its deixis as self-referential, as an account of its own "wrestling." For as Krieger argues, "the ekphrastic dimension of literature reveals itself wherever the poem takes on the 'still' elements of plastic form which we normally attribute to the spatial arts. In so doing, the poem proclaims as its own poetic its formal necessity, thus making more than just loosely metaphorical the use of spatial language to describe—and thus to arrest—its movements" (*Play and Place*, 90). Dickinson's poem "takes on the 'still' elements of plastic form" by borrowing its principal terms from the realm of painting and by making use of the apparatus of visual art to "proclaim as its own poetic its formal necessity," its coming into existence *here* on the fascicle page. "Artists wrestled here!" can be understood as an ekphrastic poem about its own capacity—and the capacity of this "Student of the year"—to bring something into existence from nothing: "Lo, a tint Cashmere! / Lo, a Rose!" (ll. 2–3). Thus does the poem become the record of its own event as art, its own "wrestling" into being and toward the declaration of "repose."

Or maybe it's just a poem about a sunset. Maybe "Artists wrestled here!" is a poetic description of a dramatic sunset, one sufficiently beautiful and distinctive that it should win a prize. Perhaps this is a poem about a sunset so compelling, so auratic that it no longer seems a thing of nature, but appears to be a work of art in which the colors in the evening sky look as if they were produced by artists: sheer, abstract swaths of color reposing on an easel. If this *was* a poem that "pointed" at a singular sunset, most likely sometime in the summer of 1859, it has *become* a poem that turns its pointing at itself, a poem that erases every empirical marker or natural referent until it becomes nothing more than a radically aestheticized poetic event. From the perspective of Dickinson's own poetics of "zeroing," it doesn't matter if there was once such a sunset: the radicalization of the poem uses its deixis to eliminate any empirical reference and point the poem to its absolute aestheticization.

If "This was a Poet" and "Artists wrestled here!" are two poems about aesthetic experience that epitomize what Hollander has called the "opacity" of prepositions in Dickinson's poetry, they also demonstrate the *capacity* of her prepositions.[32] If modern linguistics has classified pronouns as "indicators of the utterance" (Benveniste)—a classification they share with other features of discourse such as "here" and "this"—Dickinson's poetry consistently exploits and explores this deictic dimension of discourse, perhaps more than any other poet in nineteenth-century Anglo-American poetry. And Dickinson's exploitation and exploration of deixis consistently deliver the poems back to the *occurrence* of discourse, to the *event of language*. This is how Agamben describes the work of these "indicators of the utterance": "Pronouns and the other indicators of the utterance, before they designate real objects, indicate precisely *that language takes place*. In this way, still prior to the world of meanings, they permit the reference to the very *event of language*, the only context in which something can only be signified."[33] "This was a Poet," "Artists wrestled here!": these poems not only demonstrate, but enact this temporal dimension of language, and they do so in the context of aesthetic experience. The poems thus demonstrate the relationship between deixis—the linguistic event-machine—and aesthetic judgment, the pointings or indications that are necessarily elicited in the here and now. These are signs that the aesthetic has imposed itself, demanded attention, elicited a pointing that "artists [have] wrestled here!"

I want to conclude this discussion of Dickinson's radical poetics of aestheticization by considering two poems in which the very project of her poetics— the representation of her calling or vocation as poet—confronts in its own workings the aestheticism it produces. The form and force of Dickinson's aestheticism is present in "I would not paint - a picture -" (348), another of her poems that opens with the ironic force of a conditional negation and then, in a Keatsian vein, posits immersive images of aesthetic experience:

I would not paint - a picture -
I'd rather be the One
It's bright impossibility
To dwell - delicious - on -
And wonder how the fingers feel
Whose rare - celestial - stir -
Evokes so sweet a torment -
Such sumptuous - Despair -
                    (ll. 1–8)

The speaker's opening disregard for the act of painting makes way for the desire to exceed the mere representation of the aesthetic in order to reside there, to "breathe its pure serene," as Keats would describe it. The analogies to Keats do not end here, for the lines are marked by the oxymoronic figures of a heightened aesthetic experience—sumptuous despair, sweet torment—that we have long associated with the Romantic poet for whom Dickinson expressed admiration. We can understand the opening stanza as choosing the act of beholding over the act of painting: thus, "I'd rather be the One" *who* "dwell[s] - delicious[ly] - on / And wonder[s]" at the "bright impossibility" of the painting. But the poem is not ekphrastic, at least not in the conventional or restricted sense (there are no details of or even references to a picture that any real or imagined artist has painted); and thus "a picture" functions *in the poem* as a "bright impossibility." There is no picture to behold or to name or to describe, and as a result the poem becomes an allegory of aesthetics. Most acutely, the poem "dwells" in the "wonders" of this "bright impossibility,"another name for the oscillation between artistic production and aesthetic reception. For if the stanza begins by choosing looking over painting, that apparently clean opposition gets muddied by the course of an aesthetic experience—the "dwell[ing] - delicious - on"—that leaves the looker wondering "how fingers feel," presumably those very fingers that "Evoke" the feelings of "sweet" "torment" and "sumptuous - Despair."

If the knotted relationship between making and beholding is "bright impossibility," it is not *impassability*: the poem proceeds to record two further versions of this aesthetic wonder, moving in succeeding stanzas from painting to music to poetry. In the second stanza, the speaker disdains "talk[ing]" *like* "cornets," choosing to be the recipient and not the producer of music:

I would not talk, like Cornets -
I'd rather be the One

Raised softly to the Ceilings -
And out, and easy on -
Through Villages of Ether -
Myself endued Balloon
By but a lip of Metal -
The pier to my Pontoon -

(ll.9–16)

But if this stanza begins by reaffirming the first stanza's opposition between producer and recipient, it arrives somewhere else. If the speaker would "rather be the One" who *listens* to the music, the lines quickly identify the speaker-listener with the music itself, collapsing the act of listening with the music: "I'd rather be the One / Raised softly to the Ceilings - / And out, and easy on - / Through Villages of Ether"—*precisely like the music itself*. As Cameron puts it, the speaker is "a listener who is moved, as if she *were* the music, to a place where the music is" (*Choosing*, 167). That "place," of course, is the non-place of aesthetic experience, the peculiar *event* that makes one feel as if one were "the One" who could pass through "Villages of Ether." The poem's contraction results in the self-reflective figure of "Myself endued Balloon," a figure in which the speaker imagines herself assuming the qualities of that ethereal object. The compounding of figures extends further, since we can take "endued" to mean "to be clothed with": in conveying the nature of *being* music, the figure "endued" is simultaneously a figure for the aestheticized experience of music.

If it is fitting for the poem to come full circle and turn in the third and final stanza to the figure of poetry, the gesture is troubling and even self-canceling, for it disclaims the vocation exemplified by its own lines. Here the speaker chooses the listener's "Ear" over the poet's hand:

Nor would I be a Poet -
It's finer - Own the Ear -
Enamored - impotent - content -
The License to revere,
A privilege so awful

(ll.17–21)

If it is "finer" to "Own the Ear" than to "be a Poet," that possessed ear would be "Enamored - impotent - content -" and thus the image of a *dispossession*. Such powerless, enraptured contentment would itself be an "awful" "privilege," the "License" of an auratic reverence. In this stanza, the suppositional is made declarative: It *is* "finer" to hear poetry; and the "privilege" conveyed through this declaration is gained by plumbing the depths of aesthetic experience. And then the poem's final supposition, one that seems as close to "negative capability" as one can imagine: "What would the Dower be, / Had I the Art to stun myself / With Bolts - of Melody!" (ll.22–24). The final lines suppose the endowments and the risks of an aestheticism that is experienced as if it were self-created, as if the distinction between producer and recipient were collapsed in this stunning instant. More precisely, the lines present the endowments of such an aestheticism as the self-stunning risk of "Bolts - of Melody!"

In Cameron's stunning interpretation of the poem, "the claimed incapacity reveals capacity. . . . The suppositional is shown to be actual. 'Had I the Art' becomes *having* the art. And this explains the relations within the series 'Enamored - impotent - content.' For the passive or 'impotent' infatuation turns into 'content,' as it turns into power" (*Choosing*, 167–68). I call her interpretation stunning because, as with everything Cameron writes about Dickinson, it demonstrates this critic's power as a reader, in this rare case her power to have the poem say what it hasn't: "Had I the Art" does not, as I read it, become "*having*" it, and impotence is not turned into power. In my view the poem supposes the radical contentment of *being done to* without ever "actually" reclaiming that power or capacity. This is the radical condition reached by the poem, a condition from which Cameron turns away.[34] The poem's final stanza demonstrates that the "zeroing" power of Dickinson's aestheticism proposes a crisis for her own project of poetics that remains or insists in these last lines. In the final stanza the speaker tells the reader (which the poet may have supposed would only ever be herself) *in poetry* that she would *not* "be a Poet" *because* the disempowerment of the aesthetic experience is "finer," indeed a "privilege so awful." And it is consistent with the logic of the first two stanzas to read the final three lines as offering something other than the *being* of a poet: the lines suppose some strange self-stunning "Art" made "With Bolts - of Melody!"

My final example is another allegory of this process, a single poem that features Dickinson's version of radical aestheticism and presents its consequences for our understanding of her poetic vocation. It is one of her most magnificent verses, "To pile like Thunder to it's close" (1353). I believe we need an understanding of the event-machine—of the nonhuman production of a poetic event—in order to confront the radical aestheticism of "To pile like Thunder to it's close." The poem offers, among other things, a rare ex-

ample of an infinitive verb initiating a powerful opening line; and it goes on
to make that bold infinitive into the very definition of poetry:

> To pile like Thunder to it's close
> Then crumble grand away
> While everything created hid
> This - would be Poetry -
>
> $$(\text{ll. }1-4)$$

A sudden and unpredictable "piling" of might that comes to "it's close" only to
"crumble grand away," leaving nothing but the remnants of its collapse: "This -
would be Poetry -." In any event, *this* would certainly be Dickinson's poetry.
Ford notes how the lines present us with the characteristic Dickinsonian "poetic structure identified by Porter: emphatic assertion followed by formal disintegration" (*Gender and Excess*, 41) or what I have been calling the event and
its aftermath. Here the first line—"To pile like Thunder to it's close"—*is* the
very event it figures. Moreover, the enfolded form and the strained logic of
this figure—the complicated double comparison—make it into a catachresis,
as if to demonstrate how poetry itself is constituted by an originary torquing
or perverting of tropes, the broken engines of poetic production.

Ford is as painstaking a reader of Dickinson as one can hope to find; and
she insists that we regard the crucial differences between this poem and the
structure Porter identified and that I have adapted. "Terms like 'crumble' and
'disintegration,'" writes Ford,

> can distract us from the potency of this metaphor. For while poetry is compared
> to thunder, whose might is transitory, thunder, in turn, is compared to stone: it
> first resounds like stones being violently heaped together (as in the spewings of
> volcanoes . . .), and then it recedes, not weakly but grandly, like centuries-long
> crumbling away of the mountains. (*Gender and Excess*, 41)

Lest we be "distracted" by the ostensible poetics of disintegration, Ford alerts
us to the contrary adverbial work of "grand" to describe the crumbling effect:
the aftermath of this event is not a weak dissipation, but something powerful,
mighty. And Ford is right to note that if poetry is likened to the transient force
of thunder, the power of the opening line derives not merely from that sudden shock, but from *thunder's* comparison to "stones being violently heaped
together." On the face of it, nothing could seem less *aestheticized*, indeed less
artful than stones "violently heaped together." A *heap* can always seem something insufficiently aestheticized, as in the early review of Géricault's *Raft*

of the Medusa that I referred to in the introduction: "a heap of corpses from which one turns away." But in "To pile like Thunder," poetry is precisely the event of this violent and random heaping of force; and it is also something from which, as the poem's final line suggests, one must turn away. In the face of this experience of poetry—this violent heap, this piling of might— "everything created hid." Far from belonging to the world of creation, in other words, poetry takes place in the very evacuation of the creative and the created. "*This,*" indicates the poem, "would be Poetry."

"Or Love," as one of Dickinson's grandest line and stanza breaks tells us, since "the two coeval come -" (l.5). Poetry and love are of contemporaneous origin; and neither is created: they "come."

> We both and neither prove -
> Experience either and consume -
> For none see God and live -
> (ll.6–8)

What does the poem say about our relationship to the "coming," to the events, of poetry and love? "We" are not the source or medium for poetry or for love; and indeed "we" are only admitted into this poem after the event and implications of both. The two are so bound up, so indistinguishable, that we "prove" or demonstrate or make good "both and neither." And in thus aligning amorous with aesthetic "experience," the poem designates an activity that has no ethical or social or political dimension: it is simultaneously supersaturated and void. This is the excess that yields nothing, for "Experience either and consume -": we are likely to read the negation of transitivity in the second verb as implying the participle ("experience either and" *be consumed*). But the terrible power of the line (which is immediately theologized) resides in its sense of the absolute: "consume" as the negative horizon of intransitivity. This would be an experience of a pure and intransitive consuming that is also a *consumption*: and it consumes no one thing but must take *everything*, "For none see God and live -" (l.8). From this "experience," one must turn away to live.

"This - *would* be Poetry -" but it *isn't*, at least not in this poem. The reading of "To pile like Thunder" that I have outlined ignores the conditional; and the conditional changes everything. In spite of the way in which the poem presents a forceful reiteration of Dickinson's poetic machinery, in spite of a powerful opening line that announces itself with the audacity of an event, and in spite of the way in which the "experience" described here is recognizable as Dickinson's aesthetics, "This" is not "Poetry." Not *yet*, perhaps, or not *now*, but certainly not *here*. There are so many ways we might try to fulfill the terms of the conditional: "This - would be Poetry -" *if* there were a poetics to accommodate it? *if* there were a "system of aesthetics" capacious enough to recognize such complete consumption? *if* we were able to "see God and live -"? As in "I would not paint - a picture -," we are presented with another "bright impossibility," an aestheticism so complete, so undoing that it can only be *supposed by*, but not *realized in*, poetry. These are poems in which Dickinson's poetic machinery produces an event that the poetics cannot realize or "prove," an event that points to zero, to those "Infinites of Nought." And thus by this Dickinsonian "Circumference" (the poetry of the zero), we find ourselves back to "The Zeros taught Us - Phosphorus -" where we recall another "bright impossibility": we recall that "Eclipses - Suns - imply -." How better to understand the poetic crisis—the "grand crumbling away"—posed for Dickinson's representation of this vocation than the "bright impossibility" of radical aestheticism? This is the teaching of the zeros.

Dickinson, "Like Eyes that looked on Wastes" (detail)

Different cloud floating over [Sun]

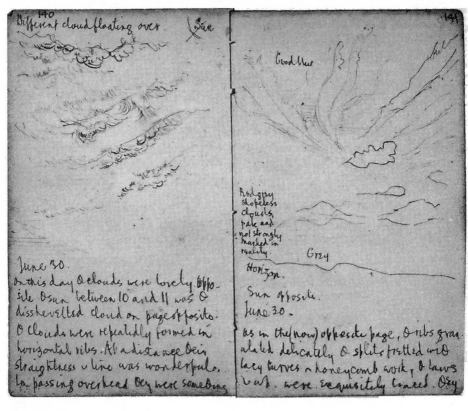

Good blue

Red grey
shapeless
clouds,
pale and
not strongly
marked in
reality.

Grey

Horizon.

June 30.
On this day O clouds were lovely. Opposite O sun between 10 and 11 was O
disshevelled cloud on page opposite.
O clouds were repeatedly formed in
horizontal ribs. At a distance Oein
straightness v line was wonderful.
In passing overhead Oey were sometime

Sun opposite.
June 30.
As in the (now) opposite page, O ribs gran-
ulated delicately O splits fretted wiO
lacy curves n honeycomb work, O laws
v wh. were exquisitely traced. Oey

Journal pages, June 30

FOUR

Hopkins's Sighs

"Let Him Oh! With His Air of Angels Then Lift Me, Lay Me!"

What are the poetics of a *sigh*? It is my premise that to read Hopkins is to confront that question. Interjections, exclamations, apostrophes—all just so many cries and sighs—punctuate Hopkins's poems early and late. Rarely do these sighs affect the *meaning* of the poems as such; and yet the experience of Hopkins's poetry is inconceivable without them. In the line from "Henry Purcell" quoted above—"Let him oh! with his air of angels then lift me, lay me!" (l.9)—the ejaculatory "oh!" that occurs in the midst of the imperative seems simply to mark the stress of a breath, the sudden excited aspiration prompted by the inspiration of Purcell's music.[1] In a letter to Bridges, Hopkins would describe this Purcellian inspiration as the "soul . . . which breathes or stirs so unmistakably in his works" (*L* I, 177). If the interjection of the "oh!" does not alter the meaning or address of the line, its appearance just prior to "his air of angels" links it not only by proximity, but by sound to the essence of Purcell's music. From "oh" to "air" to "angels," the sigh connects this poem about the power of music directly to the originary resources of sound in the productions of breath.

But the line and the sonnet in which the sigh appears address not only the music of Purcell, but the very nature and activity of the aesthetic. Thus, to declare "Let him oh! with his air of angels then lift me, lay me!" is to announce a desire to *submit* to the force of Purcell's music: to be "lifted and laid" is to give oneself over to the "air of angels." And precisely in the form of its passivity, the line is an aesthetic imperative, an announcement that the speaker will submit to the sensory apprehension of sound. Such a declaration of submission to the aesthetic runs counter to the project or vocation of Hopkins's poetry, which, as he puts it, is "charged" with the desire to find or "meet" the absolute, to make visible in language that which has been obscured, most specifically the "grandeur of God." This project is initiated in 1875 with *The Wreck of the Deutschland*, a poem that follows a seven-year renunciation of verse. The story of Hopkins's decision in 1868 to take religious orders and burn his verses is well known: to Bridges he writes, "I saw they wd. Interfere with my state and vocation" (*L* I, 24). In his journal, what Hopkins calls the "slaughter of the innocents" is followed three days later with this declaration: "resolved to be a religious." When poetry is reintroduced into that religious resolve, the aesthetic experiences it recounts are intended to serve this revelation of the divine. "Henry Purcell," for example, authorizes submission to the aesthetic in the sestet only after the octave has, as Hopkins writes to Bridges, declared its "hope [that] Purcell is not damned for being a Protestant" (*L* I, 177). In other words, ecstatic submission to the aesthetic is granted when its theological justification is also secured.[2] This means in the case of "Henry Purcell" that the composer's music must be the medium for God's message, Purcell's "airs" the "air of angels."

Because of that theological necessity, the aesthetic always bears for Hopkins a burden and a risk, the nature of which is expressed throughout his letters and journals. When, for instance, in a letter to Baillie, Hopkins recalls his youthful ambitions to be a painter, he writes "that the higher and more attractive parts of the art put a strain upon the passions" that he believes "it unsafe to encounter" (*L* I, 63). Hopkins's phrasing of his aesthetic anxiety is worth noting, for it is the "higher and more attractive" aspects of painting that possess a force that exerts its "strain *upon* the passions." Though he does not elaborate on this danger, one could speculate that Hopkins regards the sensuousness of painting as producing a strain from which, for the sake of "moderation," he must turn away. But as any reader of Hopkins knows, his turn away from painting prompts a turn to poetry that in no way avoided this "strain upon the passions": indeed, Hopkins's poetry is itself a demonstration that such stress and strain is inherent to the aesthetic as such.

A measure of this stress and strain is apparent in an important earlier letter to Baillie, the letter in which Hopkins spells out his distinctions between the "Parnassian" and genuine "inspiration" in poetry. "I am coming to think much of taste myself," writes Hopkins, "good taste and moderation, I who have sinned against them so much" (*L* I, 28). Of course, it is the very "sin" of poetic excess that seems almost indistinguishable from poetic inspiration, or what Hopkins describes as "poetry proper" (*L* I, 23).[3] By "inspiration" he means "a mood of great, abnormal in fact, mental acuteness, either energetic or receptive, according as the thoughts which arise in it seem generated by a stress and action of the brain, or to strike into it unasked" (*L* I, 23). While this formulation of a heightened poetic state is conventional enough, it is the emphasis on "stress and action," which either arises in the brain or "strikes into it unasked," that situates it within Hopkins's distinctive idiolect. Inspiration is thus an action of "stress" produced in and through a "great, abnormal" "acuteness" that separates "poetry proper" from the "Parnassian" idiom, the poetic language that "genius speaks as fitted to its exaltation . . . but does not sing" (*L* I, 24). It is this "fit," or what we have come to call adequation, that makes the "Parnassian tongue" a kind of poetic signature: "In a poet's particular kind of Parnassian lies most of his style, of his manner, of his mannerism if you like" (*L* I, 24). The moment of genuine inspiration—such as the "I say more" that opens the sestet of "As kingfishers catch fire"—is thus marked by the "surprise" that exceeds poetic identity. Genuine inspiration gives rise to a non-fit between the said and the saying that is no longer attributable to a personal "style" and that is "stressed" into song.

In the case of Hopkins, of course, poetic inspiration cannot be separated from divine inspiration.[4] Thus the "stressing" and torquing of language into genuine poetic song, what Hopkins calls a "creative violence," is an instance of what J. Hillis Miller has aptly described as "being twisted or wrung," "the violence of what God does to man through grace."[5] To Hopkins the words that are left on a page in a poem that has come through the wringer of inspiration are sufficiently "wrung or twisted" to make their stress *felt* as well as heard. And in this sense poetry is exemplary of what Hopkins calls the "work of corresponding with grace" in which the only human act necessary is the "saying Yes, the 'doing-agree'" (*S* 156). Such a "correspondence" requires the merest sign of assent, nothing more than a sigh: "this least sigh of desire, this one aspiration . . . is in answer to an inspiration of God's spirit" (*S* 155). It is what in *The Wreck of the Deutschland* Hopkins calls God's "arch and original breath" (l.194), the breath of the *arche*. Hopkins's poems are always "wrung" between inspiration and aspiration; and the poems are often so "wrung" that it becomes difficult to discern whether they are an act of human intention or an occurrence in language, something on the order of an event. The strange diastolic oscillation between poetic inspiration and aspiration in Hopkins is the place where his poems explore and exploit the relationship between poetic act and event; and it is also the site of the most acute tensions between theology and aesthetics. As I see it, the poetic "wringing" between inspiration and aspiration in Hopkins results at certain critical moments in the emission of a sigh and in the "ringing" of a radical aestheticism.

A radical aestheticism is the last thing that Hopkins intends to achieve through his poetry. For if Hopkins's speculations on aesthetics and poetics are as singular and adventurous as anything produced in the century, everything in those speculations—and everything in the *conception* of his poems—labors to resist the temptations of a heathen aestheticism, whether radically or conventionally conceived. It certainly resists the "aestheticism" that Hopkins would have associated with his Oxford years and with the figure of Pater in particular.[6] Nevertheless, I believe that at certain moments of certain poems—in nothing more or less than the space and time of a sigh—Hopkins arrives at a radical aestheticism.

As with the examples of Shelley, Keats, and Dickinson, a radical aestheticism requires, in the first instance, a poetic reflection on art; and the reflections we find in Hopkins's poems on the relationship between art's sensuous aspects and its theological justifications are exemplary. As we have seen in these earlier examples, a poem can be ascribed to an *aestheticism* in the widest sense when the course of that reflection (which necessarily entails a self-reflection) severs the relationship between art and truth by subsuming the latter into the former. For Hopkins, any form of aestheticism would create a crisis for the orthodox relationship between aesthetics and theology in which art is understood to be the sensory manifestation of God's grace; but, as we shall see, the theological ramifications of these differing versions of aestheticism are themselves quite distinctive. Though Hopkins would never *profess* an aestheticism of any sort, I am convinced that we encounter in his poetry moments or instances of this most radical of aestheticisms. I describe them as *moments* or *instances* because they are indeed that, passing moments or fleeting instances that, in Hopkins's own idiom, appear and must be "caught," and in

the catching create the conditions of a crisis, not only for theological ortho-
doxies, but for the versions of aestheticism—such as Pater's—that are predicated on the mission of "art for art's *sake*." In other words, these poems constitute something on the order of a radical aestheticism when they are taken
through what Hopkins would call a "Heraclitean fire" to its root elements
and reveal a self-origination that is simultaneously a self-nullification. Radical
aestheticism in Hopkins is the experience of a poetics, already radicalized,
that exerts such a pressure on his theological aesthetics that we encounter
something that risks, in Hopkins's words, a "flame out" to the everything and
the nothing of a breath.[7]

In order to arrive at something as unlikely as a radical aestheticism in a
poet such as Hopkins, one might expect an examination of all the "scarred
flesh" ("St. Alphonsus Rodriguez") on display in Hopkins. And in our current, more colloquial sense of the term, a *radical* aesthetic might be found in
the "dismembering" force of Hopkins's poetry, in the "fastenings" of flesh
and the "breaking" of bones that litter the poetry's somatic landscape with
scenes of corporeal violence. Indeed, Hopkins's poems constitute a catalog
of the body *in extremis*. But as racked and riven and wrung as the body is in
Hopkins, it is not the site of his poetry's radical aestheticism. The body in
Hopkins remains the site of a poetically tense and erotically charged, but
ultimately negotiable relationship between theology and aesthetics. Rather, it
is in that form most ephemerally, but constitutively related to the body—the
breath, the aspiration, the sigh—that we encounter aestheticism's radical in
the poetry of Hopkins.

Hopkins's Breathturns

In Hopkins the poetic extension of a fundamentally divine inspiration means
that the agency and the work of poetry originate outside human activity, as
something that is not so much done *by* as done *to* the poet: Hopkins's poems
happen because he has been *done unto*. My emphasis on the "being-done-to"
of Hopkins—what we could call his poetics of submission—contravenes the
recent critical emphasis on the performative dimension of the poems. It is
certainly the case that a careful reader of Hopkins will come away from his
work with a highly developed understanding of the many rhetorical, thematic,
rhythmic, and formal things that poetry can do. Indeed, an attentive reader
of Hopkins is likely to believe that she has explored the extents to which lan-

guage can be said to be a genuine act. Speaking, spelling, saying, singing, "selving": these are but some of the many well-chronicled poetic activities that occur in Hopkins, activities that the poems both discuss and perform. And without presuming to add anything new to the long and rich critical discussion of "sprung rhythm," one could safely say that it represents one of the great efforts *to do something with* the inherited tradition of English poetics.

By any measure, then, it is certainly the case that few poets in the English tradition are as explicitly performative in their theory and practice as Hopkins. The letter to Bridges on the topic of "Spelt from Sybil's Leaves" demonstrates Hopkins's emphasis on its performativity: "Of this long sonnet above all remember what applies to all my verse, that it is, as living art should be, made for performance and that its performance is not reading with the eye but loud, leisurely, poetical (not rhetorical) recitation. . . . This sonnet shd. be almost sung" (qtd. in Sprinker, *Imaginary Relations*, 64–65).[8] At such moments one can certainly understand why Hopkins's poetry, so thoroughly populated by instances of and references to speech acts, suits the recent critical explorations of performativity.[9]

But the qualities of performativity in Hopkins's poetry do not consolidate or extend our conceptions of the power and purchase of speech act theory so much as they compromise or unsettle it. Miller has explained how performativity in Hopkins is linked to the poetry's theological commitments: "like the words of the priest in the communion, poetry must not describe things as they are but make something happen."[10] In a subsequent essay on Hopkins called "Naming, Doing, Placing," Miller explicitly addresses the performative dimension of the poetry, its capacity to "make something happen" (*Topographies*, 152). Miller argues that any critical consideration of performatives in Hopkins must address the fact that many of the instances that initially resemble speech acts do not in fact meet Austin's conditions of a "happy performative," and not merely because Austin excludes as "true performatives" those utterances contained in a poem (*Topographies*, 153). Where one often thinks one should find a speech act—in the many instances of the first-person present indicative—one finds that act compromised by a constative. "Whatever there may be of the speech event or speech act in Hopkins's poems," writes Miller, "more particularly speech acts truly performative, will be intertwined with a strong constative component" (*Topographies*, 161).[11]

Miller locates the genuinely performative dimension of Hopkins's poetry in the evocatives and interjections, the "'O's,' 'Oh's,' and 'Ah's'" that interrupt the declarations and that "punctuate" the poems (*Topographies*, 162). The evocative in Hopkins is never a mere poetic adornment; and the interjection is not the linguistic effect of spiritual exuberance. Rather, these exclamations implicate every aspect of Hopkins's poetic project; and, as we shall see, they are in a crucial sense the *reason* for the poetry. Yeats, in the introduction to his edition of the *Oxford Book of Modern Verse*, directs his acute but condescending remarks on Hopkins to the shuttling of air and sound, breath and word that is bound up with the poetry's meaning: Hopkins's "meaning is like some faint sound that strains the ear, comes out of words, passes to and fro between them, goes back into words. . . . [T]he stoppage and sudden onrush of syllables were to him a necessary expression of his slight constant excitement."[12] Other than the disapproval registered in Yeats's modifiers ("faint" and "slight"), his characterization of the relationship between meaning and sound in Hopkins demonstrates how closely he had read and *heard* Hopkins. Paul Fussell finds the "justification" for the experiments with sprung rhythm in the aesthetic and affective dimensions of Hopkins's breathwork: "tears and O's and Ah's and ecstatic wonder are Hopkins's staples, and it is in the service of these effects that sprung rhythm justifies itself."[13] I would extend the implications of Fussell's assessment: Hopkins's entire poetic project exists "in the service of these effects." This means that when we look into Hopkins's poetic catalogue of the sigh we find precisely the inverse of what Miller proposes: the moment that a Hopkins poem "sighs" is not the moment it "does things with words," but the moment it marks its *being done to*.[14]

What, then, is the relationship between a *sigh*—the suspension or interruption of language's grammar and syntax—and a *speech act*? Aspiration and inspiration originally meant the same thing: *the action of blowing on or into*. Inspiration has come to mean "the act of breathing in or inhaling" and figuratively as a divine influence, what the *OED* calls "a special immediate action or influence of the Spirit of God upon the human mind or soul." Aspiration came to mean the opposite: in the physical sense, the "action of breathing out or exhaling," and in the figurative sense a fundamentally *human* "desire or longing." If inspiration and aspiration can be construed both as physical acts and as spiritual events, how do we construe the agency or performative status of a sigh? The meaning of "sigh" is a braid woven from the physical and spiritual dimensions of *spirare*: a sigh can be an "involuntary expression of fatigue or grief" (*Webster's*) *and* an act of lamentation or yearning. In the *OED*, a sigh is "a sudden, and *more or less* audible respiration, indicating *or* expressing dejection, weariness, longing, pain, or relief" (emphasis added). And up through Hopkins's day, "sigh" could be more than the linguistic representation of these physical and spiritual conditions of breathing and longing: the word itself was understood in the reflexive sense "to bring a certain state or condition," as when a lover in longing presses his head to a window and "sighs the glass dim." A sigh in a Hopkins poem can mean any of those things: it is the sign of breath that also indicates or expresses affect. And while his sighs can indeed be registered as "involuntary expressions," they can also be apprehended as a poetic act that courts theatricality, the heavy breath that draws attention to itself and is not only meaningful, but that "means too much."

I know of no better way to describe how Hopkins mobilizes the intricate resources of the sigh into a poetic theory and practice than what Paul Celan called the "breathturn" (*Atemwende*). Celan's curious compound word *Atemwende*, which is the title of a 1967 volume of his poems, first appears in the extraordinary *Meridian* address of 1960, where it is proposed tentatively, provisionally as the essence of poetry: "Poetry is perhaps this: an *Atemwende*, a turning of our breath. Who knows, perhaps poetry goes its way—the way of art—for the sake of just such a turn?"[15] Perhaps the very *Atemwende* he discerned in Hopkins prompted Celan to compose poems in his own edition of Hopkins's work. Perhaps Hopkins's own "breathturns" constituted for Celan the very vocation of poetry: "the radical putting-into-question of art" ["radikale In-Frage-Stellung der Kunst"] (Celan, *Collected Prose*, 47). Hopkins represents, in other words, a turning in and of and toward the breath, not only for its animation, but for its blankness. And I believe that Hopkins's "breathturns" deliver us to the "bucklings" of aesthetics and theology in the poetic dilations of inspiration and aspiration.

Much is at stake, then, in the poetics of the breathturn, particularly insofar as Hopkins's understands the "self" to be something of a "breath-effect." Borrowing from musicology, Hopkins will write in his sermons of the "unspeakable stress of pitch" that constitutes an individual's "selving, this self-being of my own" (*S* 123). But if Hopkins conceives of *being* as inseparable from aesthetics, the latter is also inseparable from his theology. "God's Grandeur" presents Hopkins's Scotist aesthetics in as straightforward a fashion as one will find in the poet's work. There is nothing either *radical* or *aestheticist* about the poesis described and enacted in "God's Grandeur": indeed, the poem is a celebration of poetry's capacity to reproduce the fundamentally animating power of God. "The world is charged with the grandeur of God," writes Hopkins, and this "charge," this worldly animation, is what the poem seeks to recover or rekindle: "It will flame out, like shining from shook foil." If we do not now behold or "catch" this good flame, it is because for Hopkins's the world "is seared with trade: bleared, smeared with toil." But "for all this," as Hopkins writes in the sestet, God's animating capacity is never exhausted, because "the Holy Ghost over the bent/World broods with warm breast and ah! bright wings" (ll.13–14): "nature is never spent/There lives the dearest freshness deep down things" (ll.9–10).

"God's Grandeur" spells out a relationship between theology and aesthetics that can be discerned throughout Hopkins's poetry: the aesthetic domain is understood to be the sensory manifestation of God's grandeur made available to our senses, because, as von Balthasar puts it, Christ is "God's greatest work of art."[16] As Hopkins writes in one of his sermons, "all things therefore are charged with love, are charged with God and if we know how to touch them give off sparks and take fire, yield drops and flow, ring and tell of him" (*S* 195). Language itself "gives off sparks and takes fire"; it "rings and tells of him," because, as Garrett Stewart says apropos "God's Grandeur," "origin of the world, God is also the authoring cause of its divergent tongues and terms, the poet-priest his mystic etymologist."[17] Hopkins's "poet-priest" is also God's celebrant, as in "Pied Beauty," where the poet declares that "Glory be to God for dappled things," because "he fathers-forth whose beauty is past change: Praise him." (l.1, 10). Here the possibility of worldly, sensuous beauty is predicated upon the animating presence of a God whose own beauty is not subject to mutability, but is "past change," and for which the act of praise is the only response.[18] "Beauty's address is rhetorical without restraint," as the theologian David Bentley Hart describes it in an account of God's grandeur that could constitute a gloss of Hopkins's "God's Grandeur" or "Pied Beauty": "negating nothing, simply unfolding ever more variously and intricately throughout the entirety of creation's display, resisting all reduction. God's glory and creation's goodness are proclaimed with equal truthfulness in each moment, each interval within being, in an endless sequence of *excessive* statements of that glory and goodness" (*Beauty of the Infinite*, 21).

But in the case of Hopkins it is just such poetic *excess* that makes the theological animation of the aesthetic the source of risk, one that does not always result in the relative stability of "God's Grandeur" or "Pied Beauty." In "As kingfishers catch fire," for example, the sonnet must both "catch" the occurrence of that theological animation *and* be that very event. In this poem the process of selving—the "deal[ing] out that being indoors each one dwells," the "Crying *What I do is me: for that I came*"—recorded in the octave is supplemented by the bold first-person indicative "saying" that opens the sestet: "I say more," it says, than the selving that is recorded in the opening lines. In other words, the selving "caught" in the octave generates an excess above and beyond the identity of doing and being that it "speaks and spells," an excess that spells—and *spills*—into the sestet. Like the excess that separates the true poetic genius from the Parnassian, the octave generates a remainder that says more than "I," though it calls upon the "I" to say it. And the more it says is this: "Christ plays in ten thousand places, / Lovely in limbs, and lovely in eyes not his / To the Father through the features of men's faces" (ll.12–14). By catching the kingfisher's catching fire, the poem has caught the Scotist notion of *haeccity* or "thisness." For Duns Scotus, the "individuating entity," the *thisness* of a being is its "ultimate reality" (*ultima realitas*).[19] And thus when Giorgio Agamben, for instance, discusses the *principium individuationis* in Scotus, he could very well be offering commentary on this same process in Hopkins's poem: "Duns Scotus conceived individuation as an addition to nature or common form . . . —an addition not of another form or essence or property, but of an *ultima realitas*, of an 'utmostness' of the form itself . . . : there is no difference between common nature and *haeccity*."[20] The sestet of "As kingfishers catch fire" thus becomes the "taking place" of this "utmostness;" and the aesthetic for Hopkins would be the catching of this *haeccity* always latent in the world, the *haeccity* that is always available to "catch fire." The aesthetic, in other words, is the marking, the signature of God's giving of beauty "throughout the entirety of nature's display."[21]

Though this articulation may seem unlikely at first glance, Benjamin's conception of the auratic dimension of art "catches" Hopkins's Scotist aesthetic and his poetics of "instress." Benjamin conceives of art's "aura" as its capacity to produce a kind of reverential contemplation that tends toward entrancement. When, for instance, Hopkins writes in his journal that "contemplation in its absoluteness is impossible unless in a trance" (*J* 124), he is describing the aesthetic disposition that Benjamin would call "auratic." Though the notion of the aura plays its most decisive role in Benjamin's "The Work of Art in the Age of Its Technological Reproducibility," perhaps the most succinct definition of the "aura" is to be found in his "Little History of Photography": "a strange weave of space and time: the unique appearance or semblance of distance, no matter how close the object may be."[22] Through this "strange weave of space and time," the auratic image generates the effect of a "*unique appearance or semblance*," much like the "utmostness" we find in Hopkins's understanding of Duns Scotus. Benjamin understands the auratic experience as a quasi-religious illumination, a blurring synaesthesia in which perception is transformed into *breath*, seeing into *breathing*: "While at rest on a summer's noon, to trace a range of mountains on the horizon, or a branch that throws its shadow on the observer, until the moment or the hour become part of their appearance—that is what it means to breathe the aura of those mountains, that branch" (518–19). What occurs in the "breathing" of the aura, what "takes place" in the inspirations and aspirations of the aesthetic experience, is thus the sense of the subsumption of time by space: in the phenomenology of the auratic experience, time itself becomes "part of" the image's "appearance" and temporality collapses into a sheer presence.[23] Benjamin's conception of the aesthetic "aura" helps explain the tendency of Hopkins's poems to transform the experience of singularity and the marking of time's contingencies into the signs of "God's better beauty, grace" that is "past change."

The late sonnet "To what serves mortal beauty?" explicitly undertakes the task of justifying mortal beauty and subordinating it to "God's better beauty, grace." "How meet beauty?" the poem asks, "Merely meet it; own / Home at heart, heaven's sweet gift; / then leave, let that alone" (ll.12–13). Though beauty is "heaven's sweet gift," it is not a gift to be indulged. The encounter with beauty should be temporary: it should be "met" then "left, let" alone, lest it consume. "Meet" beauty when it comes or falls or "flashes off frame and face" (l.11) the poem tells us, but dwell not in beauty for its own sake. In "The Leaden Echo and the Golden Echo," beauty is to be encountered and returned, a gift to be given to its giver: "Give beauty back, beauty, beauty, beauty, back to God, beauty's self and beauty's giver" (l.19).

This Hopkinsian "golden echo"—the entrancing repetition of "beauty, beauty, beauty" that suspends with a kind of stutter the force of the imperative—is precisely what Benjamin describes as the "aura" of aesthetic experience. David Ferris stresses that for Benjamin the aura "is not at all an attribute of the work of art; rather it is a way of experiencing a work of art; the aura exists as perception, not as art."[24] But the example of Hopkins's poetry complicates this observation, for his poems often address—and even seem to issue from—auratic experience. To elaborate on the role of perception in auratic experience, Ferris quotes an important passage from Benjamin's essay "On Some Motifs in Baudelaire": "To perceive the aura of an appearance means to invest it with the ability to return our look."[25] Benjamin's own footnote to this statement is even more to the point of my argument: "this endowment [the aura of an appearance] is a wellspring of poetry" (354). I believe that we could certainly describe it as a "wellspring" of Hopkins's poetry: when beauty appears to us in one of his poems, we perceive the "aura" or *charis* of "God's better beauty, grace."[26] Thus the experience of the aura in Hopkins's poetry occurs through the convergence or, better yet, the *compounding* of the aesthetic and theological, a compounding that is lexically confirmed and perhaps even constituted by the compounding of nouns, adjectives, and adverbs that pervades the poems. Either way, theology and aesthetics in Hopkins are woven at the level of poiesis, a weave that not only demonstrates the degree to which the aesthetic retains a theological investment, but the degree to which Hopkins's poetry and poetics are unthinkable without it.

I am also convinced that no one can read Hopkins closely without developing a strong sense of the fragility of the relationship between aesthetics and theology and the stress and strain required to maintain its "harmony." For as the term "harmony" suggests, the relationship between theology and aesthetics is an unstable one, subject to the play of stress and pitch; and in Hopkins the harmony of aesthetics and theology is an achievement and not a given. If the aesthetic as Hopkins conceives it is made possible by God's "fathering-forth" as it is exemplified in the Incarnation, if aesthetics is the worldly and sensuous effect of "God's grandeur," then it is also the case that Hopkins's rendering of this Scotist doctrine is saturated by aesthetic metaphors. The debate over Christ's beauty is the site at which the compounding of aesthetics and theology reaches its "utmostness" and courts a genuine theological danger. Hopkins can on the one hand write eloquently, even sensually and with open desire of the physical beauty of Christ, as in the 1879 Bedford Leigh sermon on "Christ our hero":

> There met in Jesus Christ all things that can make men lovely and lovable. In his body he was most beautiful. . . . [H]is body was framed directly from heaven by the power of the Holy Ghost. . . . I leave it to you, brethren, then to picture him, in whom the fullness of the godhead dwelt bodily, in his bearing how majestic, how strong and yet how lovely and lissome in his limbs. . . . [F]or myself I make no secret that I look forward with eager desire to seeing the matchless beauty of Christ's body in the heavenly light. (*S* 35–36)[27]

On the other hand, Hopkins will also stress the "danger" of physical beauty in his letters as well as his poems. The opening line of "To what serves mortal beauty?" begins by adding to the "mortal beauty" of the title the crucial adjective—"To what serves mortal beauty—/dangerous."

The critical tradition has certainly never overlooked this "dangerous" relationship between theology and aesthetics in Hopkins. But with the exception of some notable examples, Hopkins scholarship has characterized this relationship along predictable lines: either Hopkins's Scotist theology is invoked to explain his poetic theory and practice, or the tension between the spiritual vocation of the priest and the aesthetic project of the poet is emphasized, sometimes to the point of irreconcilability. In more biographical forms, the same relationship is represented in terms of the stress of the sensual beauty and spiritual yearnings, or as a predominantly psychological strain. Even Michael Sprinker's illuminating ideological and rhetorical analysis of the intertwining of aesthetics and theology in Hopkins ultimately preserves a familiar picture of the split between the calling of a priest and the project of a poet, one that dates at least as far back as I. A. Richards's interpretations of "As kingfishers catch fire" that first appeared in *Dial*. According to Sprinker, the disarticulation of the poetic "spelling" in a poem such as "As kingfishers catch fire" is produced necessarily at the expense of its putative aesthetic harmony and Scotist theology: "The poem is not aesthetic," Sprinker concludes, "and cannot, therefore, be like Christ" (*Imaginary Relations*, 71). I, too, am interested in the "buckling" of Hopkins's theological aesthetics (or aesthetic theology). I, too, am interested in those poetic events we encounter in Hopkins that cannot adequately be explained by references to Scotist concepts of the incarnation or individuation. But one important implication of Sprinker's argument is that counterpoint is invariably dissonant and, by extension, that Hopkins's poetry results in the transgressive disruption of his theological orthodoxy. I believe that we do more justice to Hopkins's poetics when we resist the temptation to regard Hopkins's poetry as transgressive—a temptation invited by the poet himself—and examine instead the ways in which that poetry is *regressive*. I mean this not in a political or theological sense, but in the sense suggested by Garrett Stewart's practice of "phonemic reading": according to Stewart, Hopkins is always "dragging . . . meaning back toward its source in a dispersion of phonetic material awaiting articulation. . . . The pulse of language is thus heard beneath utterance, heard bringing itself to utterance" (*Reading Voices*, 25). It is thus precisely this "regressive" quality in Hopkins's sighs, his "dragging meaning back toward its source" that opens his work to what I am describing as a radical aestheticism.

When we pursue the "regressive" poetics of Hopkins's "breathturns" to their source, we see that theology and aesthetics cannot be split into discontinuous domains, nor do they cohere in a single unity; on the contrary, aesthetics and theology produce at certain crucial moments a compound that results in aesthetic radicalization. In other words, Hopkins's radical aestheticism does not occur at the expense of his theological project or through some clandestine or unacknowledged rupture between the aesthetics and the theol-

ogy, but by their highly volatile *compounding*. If at some special moments the
poetry reveals Hopkins to be a radical aesthete, it is not in spite of his religious devotion, but precisely because of it. We encounter his radical aestheticism in those places where, as Hopkins writes in "Spelt from Sybil's Leaves,"
"selfwrung, selfstrung, sheathe- and shelterless, thoughts against thoughts in
groans grind," and in this shelterless grinding, generate something else than
the "dearest freshness deep down things." The occurrences of a radical aestheticism are most discernible or "audible" in the auratic sighs and sounds
that Miller has catalogued. The aspirations that respond to the divine and poetic inspiration that evokes them are the sites where the doing of inspiration
and aspiration converge: these are the sites where the strain of the event and
the stress of the act, where aesthetic experience and theological commitment,
collide, and, in the singular achievement of Hopkins's poetry, result in "a fire
that breaks."

"The Fire of Stress"

The "fire that breaks" is the effect of the "fire of stress," the poetic stress
of a theological "fire" of the sort that Hopkins confronts in *The Wreck of
the Deutschland*, the poem in which theological "calling" and aesthetic manifestations first converge. In the first stanza of *The Wreck*, God performs all
the acts: it is his "mastering" that results in the gift of "breath and bread."
The only "doing" in these lines that one might attribute to the human is an
undoing: "Thou hast bound bones and veins in me, fastened me flesh,/And
after it almost unmade, what with dread,/Thy doing" (ll.5–7). But in spite
of the efforts of this "unmaking," God's "touch" is renewed: "Over again I
feel thy finger and find thee" (l.8), a "finding" that is given like grace, "felt"
from the touch of God. The poem's recording of human actions begins with
the famous "yea saying" of the second stanza: "I did say yes/O at lightning
and lashed rod;/Thou heardst me truer than tongue confess/Thy terror, O
Christ, O God"; (ll.9–12). This affirmation and exclamation, compounded
and enjambed—"yes/O"—confirms at the edge of signification a breath prior
to speech, "truer than tongue." The "yes" the poet reports is an aspiration to
God's inspiration. It is here, in the pulsations of this stanza, that we encounter
the "fire of stress": "And the midriff astrain with leaning of, laced with fire of
stress" (l.16). Nothing in Hopkins seems more apt in describing his poetry
thematically, formally, or rhetorically than this line, for his best poems are

indeed "astrain with leaning of, laced with fire of stress." But to whatever degree it can be said that Hopkins's poetry exhibits this "fire of stress," the lines declare that this is something *that happens* to the poet-speaker and to the poem.

If we are looking in *The Wreck* for something like the first act of the speaker, one that could be characterized rigorously as performative, we must wait until the fifth stanza, where the poem commences the discourse between stress and instress. "I kiss my hand," says the speaker, an act that comes both as a greeting and as an aesthetic judgment: "I kiss my hand / To the stars, lovely-asunder / Starlight . . ." (ll.33–35). But if this is a speech act, one that occurs in the first-person present indicative, it is also not only an acknowledgment of the "lovely-asunder / Starlight" or "the dappled-with-damson west" (l.37), but a stressing of God's mystery. In other words, the stanza spells out a kind of poetic hailing, an aesthetic appreciation that comes as a response to that divine mystery, like the "meeting" of beauty described in "To what serves mortal beauty?" The feeling of God's instress must thus be stressed or "spelt" as it is in these lines. And in the stanza that follows, we learn that this stress "springs" not from God's "bliss" (ll.42, 41), but from the "dense and driven Passion" (l.53) that allows us to understand the event of the wreck.

What is this event? And what is the relationship between the story of the wreck and the first part of the poem? "The poetic text" in Hopkins, says Gerald Bruns, "is not a document but an occasion" (*Inventions*, 138). So where in *The Wreck* is the "occasion" and where is the "occasion" *of* the document? If "Part the first" precedes the story of the wreck as what Benjamin might have called a poetico-theological prelude to the narrative, "Part the first" is nonetheless chronologically afterward and *inspired* by the event. Inspiration certainly seems the best way to describe this relationship, for it confirms the two-part structure that we have noted in Hopkins's theological poetics: in this poem, the inspiration of the wreck can be said to produce the aspiration of the poetic response. But this interpretive structure resolves the question prematurely and reasserts a model of causality that Hopkins's poetics teases out to the point of "wrecking." *Where*, in other words, is the poem's "event"? Is it the wreck itself, the crying of the tall nun, the account of Hopkins's conversion, the poem, or all of these together? Hopkins scholarship has often turned to the Scotist doctrine of the incarnation in order to explain the poem's representation of the event, an interpretation invited by the phrase "before-time-taken" that Hopkins uses to describe the sacrifice of Christ in stanza 21 (l.174).[28]

Instead of turning to Scotist doctrine as the explanatory key to the poem, I want to pose the question in a different manner and consider how the poetic event in Hopkins is the site of the convergence of aesthetics and theology. This allows us to reckon the stakes attendant to this often violent convergence, a "wreck" of its own that always risks what Agamben calls "the originary event of its own word as nothing." Hopkins's sighs point to just such an event: the emergence of the word or the mark, the spacing of the breath, the force of the ejaculation caught between its status as poetic-linguistic phenomenon and as aspiration and response. Each and every "ah" or "oh" in Hopkins is caught in and registers this predicament, such as the "ah" that announces the turn to the present in the eighteenth stanza of "The Wreck":

> Ah, touched in your bower of bone
> Are you! turned for an exquisite smart,
> Have you! make words break from me here all alone,
> Do you!—mother of being in me, heart.
>
> (ll.137–40)

The "ah" that inaugurates this stanza possesses the force of an event, marking the turn from the story to the reckoning in the form of apostrophic interruptions, apostrophes that are accusations of and to the heart that has both been done to ("touched" and "turned") and that does ("make words break from me"). Moreover, the sigh announces it as a violent event that happens both spatially and temporally in the here and now of composition: "words break . . . here."

The "breaking" continues; and it reaches a crisis of sorts in stanza 28, where it results not in an ejaculation, but in a desperate stutter, an acute if temporary breakdown of syntax:

> But how shall I . . . make me room there:
> Reach me a . . . Fancy, come faster—
> Strike you the sight of it? look at it loom there
> Thing that she . . . There then!
>
> (ll. 217–20)

This poetic aphasia, a kind of signifying *in extremis* that echoes the nun's own physical "extremity," is "cured" (l.222) by the very next words of the poem: "the Master, / *Ipse*, the only one, Christ, King, Head" (ll.220–21). We might call this the "naming cure," but however theologically sound it may be, the string of names uttered or invoked to rescue the poem from this grammatical "wreckage" generates its own rhetorical malady, since the accumulation of disparate, if conventional metaphors for the "son of God" implies that the naming might never stop. Thus, if *The Wreck* "makes room" for openings such as this, the force of their rupture and their resolution—whether as ellipsis or ejaculation or rhetorical excess—produces a "strain" upon the poetry that, to return to Hopkins's sense of painting, "makes it unsafe to encounter." The danger is renewed with every act of reading, as Hopkins describes of his own rereading of that other poetic "shipwreck," *The Loss of the Eurydice*: "I read some lines, reading, as one commonly reads whether prose or verse, with the eyes, so to say, only, it struck me aghast with a kind of raw nakedness and unmitigated violence I was unprepared for" (*L* I, 124). In order for the poet to read his own poem without turning away, in order to make it "all right," he must "*take breath* and read it with the ears" [emphasis added] (*L* I, 124).

Hopkins encounters this "unmitigated violence" repeatedly; and, according to Isobel Armstrong, his poetry "cannot bear the 'stress' of this effort."[29] Armstrong's fine analysis of Hopkins as "agnostic reactionary" focuses on the syntactic stress and strain of the poems, in particular the burden placed on his syntax by his practice of doubling metaphors. The result, claims Armstrong, is a poetry that is "always threatening" the breakdown of the copula. Armstrong's attention to the burdens the poems place upon the copula poses an important question for my consideration of the event in Hopkins: can there *be* an event if the copula has broken down, if the grammatical system of signification cannot tell it? A grammatical collapse of this magnitude would have profound theological implications, because in Hopkins's theology, Christ *is* the copula. Even if the poetry enacts nothing more than a breakdown in the *human* system of meaning, one that does not threaten the divine discourse that precedes and transcends it, how can that divine discourse be imparted through a copula that has "buckled"? How can we be sure of its meaning? Or is the very breakdown of the copula itself an event, in fact the event *of* the poetry? If the bifurcation between aesthetics and theology in *The Wreck* is most apparent in the poem's two parts, it is also at work in the very structure of the poem's stanzas. The poem pulls inspiration apart from aspiration, theology from aesthetics; and this wrenching results in the collapse of the copula we encounter in stanza 28. In the context of my argument, this poetic event is not the sigh that marks the compounding of aesthetics and theology, but the ellipsis that marks their fissure, a fissuring manifested by the forms of violence at work throughout the poem.

Critics of Hopkins have rightly stressed the revolutionary quality of *Wreck of the Deutschland*, by any measure one of the most formally, metrically, and thematically adventurous literary works of the century. Almost everything that Hopkins addressed in his subsequent poems can indeed be found in one form or another in *The Wreck*. Hopkins never again embarked on a poem as ambitious in scope or practice as *The Wreck*; and many critics relate the disappointment of its refusal to Hopkins's turning away from the extravagant poetic practice it opened, as if in the wake of the poem's failure to find a readership Hopkins's poetry faced its own "shipwreck." Sprinker argues that the scale of the risk ventured with *The Wreck* and the nature of its failure was of such magnitude that Hopkins would never again return to the sublime mode in his later poetry, prompting the poet to turn instead to the safer terrain of the sonnet form. If this conventional picture is in its own way true enough—Hopkins would never again undertake the scope of a poem such as we find in *The Wreck*—I believe that we can understand the poetic crisis of *The Wreck* and its place in the trajectory of Hopkins's career in a different light. If we assess the nature of Hopkins's poetic adventurousness as I propose it—by considering the instances and outcomes of the compounding between the aesthetic and the theological—then *The Wreck* no longer appears as the great road not taken.

I have noted that Celan was so taken by Hopkins's poetry that he would on occasion compose his own poems in his edition of Hopkins.[30] If *The Wreck of the Deutschland* shows Hopkins's aesthetic and theology "sprung" into form and reaching for the sigh opened between inspiration and aspiration, it is in the "terrible sonnets" at the end of his career that we find the closest anticipation of Celan's own project. I believe the anguished poems of the Dublin years to be among his most powerful; and if, as Hopkins said of "No worst, there is none," they were "written in blood" "against his will," we might expect to find in them an aestheticism that has reached radicality. They are, to be sure, poetic sighs, aspirations of sheer grief and lamentation. If these sonnets are what Hopkins describes in "I wake and feel"—"cries like dead letters sent"—they recount not only the poet's "spiritual droughts," his "wrestling" with God in the "now done darkness," they lament God's "distance" from the poems: "And my lament/Is cries countless, cries like dead letters sent/To dearest him that lives alas! away" (ll.6–8). But while the animating charge of "God's Grandeur" is not evident in these poems "pitched past pitch of grief" ("No worst" l.1), neither is the compensation of the aesthetic. In the terms of my argument, the "terrible sonnets" are desiring poems of longing aspirations without divine inspiration, sonnets in which the "pain of fire" has reached the point of suffocation, their aspirate vowelings a grasping for breath and breath itself "our *memento mori*" ("The shepherd's brow")—a poetics of *expiration*. Here the sigh is the gasp of a missed "correspondence" with the divine, the cry of the "dead letter sent." Adorno's powerful description of Celan's poems applies to the terrible sonnets: "their truth content itself becomes negative. They imitate a language beneath the helpless language of human beings, indeed beneath all organic language: it is that of the dead speaking of stones and stars . . . his poetry is without aura."[31]

But for all their wrenching and nullifying power, these poems do not reach aestheticism's radical for the very reason that they take place *without the aura*. If the *aura* has been extinguished from these sonnets, it means that the "utmostness" that defines aesthetic animation for Hopkins has vanished alongside it. In "Carrion Comfort," for instance, the poem concludes with a "cheer," but the lines recall the speaker's inability to know who is being cheered:

> Cheer whom though? The hero whose heaven-handling flung me, foot trod
> Me? or me that fought him? O which one? is it each one? That night, that year
> Of now done darkness I wretch lay wrestling with (my God!) my God.
>
> (ll.12–14)

The questions that mark a separation, a gulf between the speaker and his "hero," remain unanswered, deepening the fissure that they describe between inspiration and aspiration and between the theological and the aesthetic. If "Carrion Comfort" and the other "terrible sonnets" demonstrate many of the same formal features of Hopkins's earlier poems—the same wild buckling of figure, the same wide opening of the mouth in vowelings that say "O"—here the apostrophizing of God brings no fire. If these sonnets are events, they are events as black holes from which no light can escape, sonnets of that "now done darkness" for which the only comfort is not that of the resurrection, but a "carrion comfort." Thus, as radical and severe as the poems are, their radicality and severity are not "aestheticist" in the sense we have been exploring, for if God has become distant in these poems, withdrawn from the poet's hailing, the poems mark that withdrawal with the expiration of the aesthetic.

For Hopkins's deepest encounter with poetry's radical aestheticism, one might be tempted to look to one of the late poems in which inspiration has returned, such as "That Nature is a Heraclitean Fire and of the Comfort of the Resurrection." That we might find a radical aestheticism in a poem devoted at least in part to nature should not be surprising: as in "God's Grandeur" or

"Pied Beauty," the thematics of nature is most often the occasion for Hopkins to engage aesthetic experience. But as the title indicates, the poem in question engages nature not as it is charged with "God's grandeur," but as a "Heraclitean fire," and thus the version of aesthetics at work there is both Paterian and pagan. Prompted by the movement of clouds, "chevy[ing] on an air—/Built thoroughfare" and "glitter[ing] in marches," the delight of this image mutates in these remarkable lines in which linguistic change, the "flaunt[ing] forth" of its linguistic play, echoes the shifting play of the clouds and does not immediately connect with its theological origins. In a poem so riven by Hopkins's strange diacritical caesuras that it almost splits into two columns, "nature's bonfire burns on," but it is a fire that burns without illumination:

> But quench her bonniest, dearest | to her, her cleavest-selvèd spark
> Man, how fast his firedint, | his mark on mind, is gone!
> Both are in an ùnfathomable, all is in an enormous dark
> Drowned.
>
> (ll.10–13)

The spiraling into darkness and drowning escalates as "vastness blurs and time | beats level" (l.15). Suddenly the movement stops and the monotonous "level beat" of time ceases. "Enough!" the poem says, putting an end to this blur and beat by announcing "the Resurrection," the event that would dismiss "grief's gasping" with the inspiration and illumination of eternal life: "Across my foundering deck shine/A beacon, an eternal beam" (ll.18–19). By catching sight of this eternal illumination, the speaker catches his breath and avoids shipwreck. By catching sight of this perpetual illumination, the poem tells us that beyond "world's wildfire" that "leave[s] but ash," the speaker is "in a flash" cast by the beam and beacon of the Resurrection, "all at once what Christ is." The closing lines would thus seem to describe the process of reaching the radical, where the transformation from "Jack, joke, poor potsherd,/Patch" mutates not randomly, as it would in a Heraclitean fire, but according to the restoration of time in the Resurrection, as "matchwood" in the fire that makes this "Jack, joke, poor potsherd" into the "immortal diamond" that Christ always already "is."[32]

Despite the poem's exploration of this Heraclitean fire, it does not produce the compounding of theology and aesthetics that would engender a radical aestheticism. Instead, it poses the prospect of a Heraclitean aesthetic and pursues its implications through a spiraling into the kind of darkness that haunts the terrible sonnets. Should nature be a Heraclitean fire, language would indeed be anarchic and senseless, signifying mutation without end, a sheer abyss, "an enormous dark drowned." But then the speaker says "enough" to these speculations and turns away from their implications to declare his identity with Christ—"I am all at once what Christ is"—and to celebrate the "comfort of the resurrection." In this sense the poem interrupts what, following Stewart, I have called Hopkins's *regressions* and in the process replaces a potentially abyssal aestheticism with a theological shelter, even if that shelter harbors the fire that reduces all to "immortal diamond."

In the end it is not in the origins of Hopkins's poetry or in its latest versions that we find the sighs that signify a radical aestheticism; it is, rather, in a poem that would seem to mark the most triumphant version of his Scotist aesthetics, a poem from which very few readers of Hopkins have "turned away": "The Windhover."

"The Fire That Breaks"

"The fire of stress," the "pain of fire," "catching fire," "nature's bonfire": the list of fires in Hopkins extends throughout his poetry. Like the sighs we have been considering, the fires mean different things at different times. In almost every case I am aware of, however, fires are like sighs in that they mark a kind of event in Hopkins, a happening that the poem either records or enacts. I want to conclude this chapter of the relationships between act and event, between the inspiration of theology and the aspiration of the aesthetic in Hopkins, by turning to one of his most celebrated poems. "The Windhover," written in the wake of *The Wreck*, begins by recounting a very different kind of event, the speaker's "catching" of a bird's motion and movement. All the breathless and breathtaking "riding" and "striding" of this extraordinary sonnet's extraordinary octave—one sentence propelled over six densely packed, internally woven, and highly enjambed lines—seems to erupt from the opening utterance: "I caught." Everything that I have suggested about the wavering status between act and event, doing and being-done-to is "caught" by the poem's opening play upon the meaning of catch as "to seize" or "to be seized by":

> I caught this morning morning's minion, king-
>   dom of daylight's dauphin, dapple-dáwn-drawn Falcon, in his riding

> Of the rólling level underneath him steady air, and striding
> High there, how he rung upon the rein of a wimpling wing
> In his ecstasy! then off . . .

(ll.1–5)

All that has actually happened—the event being "caught"—happens above.
All the force and play, all the "riding" and "striding" and "ringing," all the
"ecstasy" happens away and above; and readers of Hopkins can "catch" the
allegory of sprung rhythm in the relationship between the bird's dramatic and
unpredictable movements and the "steady air" he rides. The opening line also
calls to mind the intransitive sense of "catching" that occurs in "As kingfishers
catch fire." In "The Windhover" the speaker catches the event of the bird's
movement and, as a result, his "heart in hiding" is "stirred" by the "achieve
of, the mastery of the thing" (l.8) to which he is witness, spectator, beholder.[33]
To catch the event of the "dapple-dáwn-drawn Falcon, in his riding," then,
is to *behold* the windhover as a work of art and to make "The Windhover" an
ekphrastic poem.

Like the generations of critics that have preceded me, I am taken by the
turn of the sestet and the "buckling" that occurs as an event between the
"brute beauty" of the bird "AND the fire breaks" from the poem's addressee:

> Brute beauty and valour and act, oh, air, pride, plume, here
> Buckle! AND the fire that breaks from thee then, a billion
> Times told lovelier, more dangerous, O my chevalier!

(ll.9–11)

The turn is, at first glance, a curious one, for as J. R. Watson notes, the sestet,
"instead of turning reflective, drives the excitement yet further."[34] But the
opening of the sestet is not simply a continuation of the octave, for the sestet
actually marks two turns, from past to present and from the "brute beauty"
of the bird's flight to the "fire that breaks" from Christ. But before it breaks,
it moves through the fragile and tenuously balanced stasis of the ninth line,
stringing a series of nouns interrupted by the interjection "oh" before the last
word of the line, which seems itself a "break" in time and place: "Brute beauty
and valour and act, oh, air, pride, plume, here / Buckle!" (ll.9–10). And as with
every formal and thematic aspect of this extraordinary sonnet, the line seems
to manufacture an almost rhizomatic permutation of divergent readings: the
nouns can be read as a continuous string merely punctuated by the ejaculation; *or* the "oh" can be understood to be the fulcrum *or* the hole that balances

or separates beauty, valour, and act from air, pride, and plume, a balance that is then broken *or* connected by the reference to the line: "here, / Buckle!"

This is one of the most widely and variously discussed line breaks in Hopkins: an almost painful postponement of the verb and its dramatic arrival, which corresponds with the break. And in light of the poem's and poet's reflections on the nature of linguistic and spiritual performance, it is worth noting the way in which the verb "buckle" mimics the effect of the line itself, as if the poem is here doing what it is saying. What Agamben has said of enjambment in general seems particularly relevant to these crucial lines in Hopkins: "in the very moment that verse affirms its own identity by breaking a syntactic link, it is irresistibly drawn into bending over into the next line to lay hold of what it has thrown out of itself."[35] In the breaking of the syntactic link in lines nine and ten in "The Windhover," the poem attempts to "lay hold of what it has thrown out of itself"—the "fire that breaks"—and in that instant offers a discourse on the poetic enjambment it performs.[36]

In the poem's "laying hold of what it has thrown out of itself," we encounter a simultaneous breaking and linking that marks the poem's buckling of the past with the present and the aesthetic with the theological. Simultaneously an articulation and a disarticulation, a catch and a collapse, this buckling is at once a model of deconstructive undecidability and, as in William Empson's definitive reading of the poem, an exemplification of the "seventh type" of ambiguity—which may indeed be but another way of saying the same thing. According to Empson, this constitutive ambiguity, its highest form, "occurs when the two meanings of the word, the two values of the ambiguity, are the two opposite meanings defined by the context, so that the total effect is to show a fundamental division in the writer's mind."[37] In Empson's account of "The Windhover," everything hinges on the "buckle" that, as he puts it, "admits of two tenses and two meanings" and produces "two things thought of as incompatible, but desired intensely by different systems of judgments" that are "forced into open conflict before the reader" (225, 226). This is marked by the emphatic and the fully capitalized conjunction "AND" that announces the "fire that breaks." It is as if the poem requires such a capitalized conjunction to make the articulation, to secure the connection, to overcome the force of the disjunction present in that other sense of "buckle." As if to demonstrate the weight of this moment, this connection that generates such dangerous beauty, the capitalized "AND" becomes a typographical indication that invests the paratactic connection with hypotactic force. As Empson puts it, "this enormous conjunction, standing as it were for the point of friction between the two worlds conceived together, affects one rather like shouting in an actor" (226). Another name for "how this affects one," "like shouting in an actor," is *theatricality*; and the "two worlds" typically brought to "the point of friction" in that dramatic context are those of art and reality, which in Hopkins translates to those of aesthetics and theology.

The "fire that breaks from thee then" is the fire that by the poem's logic "breaks" or erupts from the "buckle." Moreover, by the force of temporality and even causality indicated in the "then," the fire asks to be read as an effect and not a cause of the poem. This reading is confirmed by the following line, which celebrates the beauty of Christ: "a billion, / Times told lovelier, more dangerous, O my chevalier!" (ll. 10–11). Both the fire that breaks and the immense loveliness of Christ are sprung, we might say, from that "buckle," that point of articulation and disarticulation. Hopkins may well be referring to the "telling" of Christ's story in the Gospels, but the force of the lines, of the "fire that breaks" and the "then" that establishes the temporality of the eruption relate this in the poem to the moment of "buckling." But if "buckle" has rightly been the word that attracts most critical attention, the self-referential gesture of the lines—"here / Buckle!"—refers us back to that other "buckle," the ejaculatory sigh, the "oh" of the ninth line. In fact the explicit "buckling" can be read simply as the articulation of the aspiration, the sigh, the "oh" born of "air," that *then* like "the fire that breaks" "here / Buckles!" The poetic event, in other words, is nothing more or less than the "oh" that the subsequent lines try to render into something meaningful.

"No wónder of it," begins the closing reflective tercet, commenting on the lines that have provoked the very wonder they express. But to diminish our sense of wonder at the breaking of the fire, Hopkins employs two images of the appearance of beauty that are themselves quite divergent:

> No wónder of it: shéer plód makes plóugh down síllion
>   Shine, and blue-bleak embers, ah my dear,
>   Fall, gáll themsélves, and gásh góld-vermíllíon.
>
>   (ll. 12–14)

The first of these, the tilling of the soil that "makes plough down sillion / Shine," is the result of a human activity, "culture," in one of its oldest definitions. Agamben reminds us that the English word "verse" is derived from the Latin word *versura*, the "word that indicates the place (and the moment) where the plough turned round at the end of the furrow" (*Idea*, 40), the "síllion" left "shining" in its wake. The second image is the effect of a burning that requires no human intervention: it simply happens, and our only role is to "catch" its occurrence, a catching that prompts the ejaculation of the apostrophe to the beloved Christ: "ah my dear." Here again we encounter a kind of buckling: these disparate animations, colorings of the world, are linked by their compounding in the figure of Christ addressed by, but not *yet present* in the poem.

Critics who stress the poem's subversive "underthought" overlook the ways in which the "catching" of theology and aesthetics is not only indispensable to its structure and effects, but is achieved only through its *auratic* qualities. At the same time, critics who emphasize the happy reconciliation enacted in the poem surely miss not only the poem's violence, its explosive breaking and buckling, but the breathless effects of its Petrarchan addresses: "ah my dear," "O my chevalier." Of course, all readers know full well that the poem is addressed to Christ. But the status of the poem's dedication—or is it a subtitle?—acquires a curious resonance in the wake of the poem's sighs. On the one hand, the proper love object is secured only with the supplementary address of the subtitle. And yet the poem's auratic and erotic force make it felt as a love letter, a "cry," not unlike that which in "I wake to feel the fell of dark, not day" is addressed to "dearest him that lives alas! away." If in Hopkins's "terrible sonnet" the cry is uttered as a "lament," a "dead letter sent," in "The Windhover" the "cry" is formed as an auratic aspiration that might find the inspiration it names, and in naming conjures.

If the convergence between theology and aesthetics is everywhere evident in Hopkins, it achieves a special "compounding" in "The Windhover." Here that compounding generates "the fire of stress" that produces the event of a radical aestheticism, one in which the nothing of the breath or the sigh conjures through the beauty of its auratic love a "Christ our Lord." In other words, Christ is the consequence of this radical aestheticism; and this is a consequence that no theological aesthetics can accommodate. Christ's occurrence in "The Windhover" is "wrung" from the singular compounding of an aesthetics and a theology that would claim him for its source, but who is in fact the poem's effect. As it is caught by this Hopkins poem, the sigh produces a poetic "ringing and "telling"—a "billion/Times told lovelier and more dangerous"—giving off sparks that take fire "AND" "tell of him" it would call to being.

Rossetti, *Giotto Painting Dante* (Harvard Art Museums / Fogg Museum, Bequest of Grenville L. Winthrop, 1943.488; Imaging Department © President and Fellows of Harvard College)

FIVE

Superficiality: What Is Loving and What Is Dead
in Dante Gabriel Rossetti

To Art: I loved thee ere I loved a woman, Love.

— DANTE GABRIEL ROSSETTI

On the Surface . . .

. . . no artist appears more appropriate than Dante Gabriel Rossetti for inclusion in a study of the aestheticism that emerges in the wake of Romanticism. "Five English Poets," the late sonnet-sequence Rossetti composed on the topic of Romantic poetry, is arguably the most engaged Victorian *reading* we have of Romantic poetics and is one index of Rossetti's acute sense, even late in life, of his participation in what Wilde called "our Romantic movement." Indeed, one consequence of Rossetti's various reflections on and reprises of Romanticism is to restore the aestheticism that was always at work in those "Five English Poets." Art-Lover, Art-Catholic: on the surface, no Victorian writer appears more suited than Rossetti to an examination of the aestheticism of which he was accused and that he courted.

And yet none of the writers I am considering seems a less likely candidate than Dante Gabriel Rossetti for an exploration of the *radicality* of aestheticism. Rossetti's aestheticism seems too obvious, too *apparent* to be regarded as radical in any genuine sense. From the beginning with Rossetti there has been the perception of slightness, in the poetry, the pictures, and the subsequent criticism of both. Each of the authors I have addressed to this point has elicited a distinguished record of criticism. The same cannot be said for Rossetti: with some notable exceptions, the history of Rossetti criticism possesses none of the power or distinction of the critical heritages of Shelley or Keats, Dickinson, or Hopkins.[1] This is not to say that there have not been insightful contributions to Rossetti criticism from distinguished scholars; but there is something about the work of this poet-painter from which our major critics have turned away, something in Rossetti that fails to elicit the kind of book or article in literary studies that everyone in the field is expected to read, something that prevents scholars from engaging Rossetti's poetics in the way that Wasserman reads Shelley or that Cameron reads Dickinson. Whether it is the dense and often forbidding sonnets, many of which exhibit a musicality almost bereft of meaning, the depthless surfaces of the paintings, the rhetorical acrobatics of the poems, or the apparently superficial images and merely decorative details of poems as well as paintings, Rossetti's work provokes either cultish connoisseurship or critical aversion. It is not merely that Rossetti's contribution appears too slight to warrant sustained critical attention: there is something about Rossetti and his poems and pictures that strike readers and viewers as superficial. It is my belief that such a judgment of Rossetti is not so much wrong as its fundamental "rightness" has been fundamentally misevaluated. My argument here is that the genuine significance of Rossetti—and the special form of his acute engagement with a radical aestheticism—is best grasped not in spite of, but by virtue of his *superficiality*.

I invoke "superficiality" both as a description and as a judgment, the latter of which is more ethical than aesthetic in nature, and one that is routinely invoked not only in the case of Rossetti's painting and poetry, but as a response to any form of aestheticism. If, for example, we follow Hegel and understand the aesthetic as "the sensory manifestation of the Idea," this understanding implies the perpetual risk not only that "sensory manifestation" might obscure or even negate the "Idea," but that mere sensory manifestation might itself come to be regarded *as* the Idea. By definition the superficial is simply that which pertains to the surface or that which takes place on the surface. As such superficiality refers to an inherent quality of the medium of painting and is particularly pertinent for the pictures of this poet-painter for whom the name "Pre-Raphaelite" referred to the immediacy of the surface in the old Italian artists he most admired. This "superficiality" is visible in the image reproduced above: *Giotto Painting Dante's Portrait* (c.1859), a *faux* fresco (actually watercolor, gouache, and graphite composition on cream woven paper) that attempts to conjure the Giotto effect. This Pre-Raphaelite picture depicts on its surface two of the "pre-Raphaelite" figures whose aesthetic its painter seeks not only to represent, but to "re-activate."

But for many viewers and readers of Rossetti another and now more prominent meaning of superficiality applies to this picture and to the entirety of his painting and poetry–namely, an exclusive concern with what is on the surface. Superficiality is "therefore apparent or obvious," as the *OED* defines it, "lacking depth or thoroughness; not deep, profound." In fact the "shallowness" of the superficial can imply duplicity, that which has "only the outward appearance of being what is denoted; only apparent or on the surface, not real or genuine." At this point, where the superficial implies ontological inauthenticity, we pass from technical description to ethical judgment. It is the sort of judgment often leveled against Rossetti by his detractors, a judgment that his most avid supporters always feel the need to address. David Riede, for instance, stresses "Rossetti's obsession with surfaces," but only to insist that "his illumination of the surface and his disregard for physical depth do not indicate that he is, in the pejorative sense, superficial" (161–62). And if there is no more "superficial" "obsession with surfaces" than that of the narcissist, reflecting upon his reflection in the mirror, how else are we expected to interpret the frequency with which mirrors and their images appear in Rossetti's poems, much less the overt acts of narcissism represented in poems and paintings?

Only by looking into—or, more precisely, looking *at*—Rossetti's "obsession with surfaces" can we understand what is loving and what is dead in his poetry. This means that the relationship between death and love in Rossetti is not only a constitutive one, but a relationship always present on the surface in everything Rossetti writes or paints. For Rossetti any conception of aestheticism, radical or otherwise, must be gleaned from the surfaces and semblances of the dead and loving that populate his poetry and paintings. Indeed, the question of superficiality is, at least for Rossetti, inextricable from the status of his aestheticism. If, as Jerome Buckley puts it, "the charge of aestheticism has been repeated often enough to condition the poet-painter's whole reputation," Rossetti also remained "as suspicious as Ruskin of a declared aestheticism" and even "feared the autonomy of art."[2]

There can be no doubt that as an escape from temporality and a reminder of death, art for Rossetti is not only the most powerful way to represent love, art is the closest thing to love itself. At the same time, Ovid's dictum—*Arte regendus Amor,* which prescribes art's sovereignty over love— certainly seems applicable to Rossetti, particularly in light of his own fragmentary "versicle" to art that serves as this chapter's epigraph. To say "to Art" that "I loved thee ere I loved a woman" not only addresses art as the first love, but implies that aesthetic love is the precondition of "fleshly love." In this private message Rossetti declares his fidelity to art in light of his dalliances with women, reassuring his "Love" of her privileged place in his heart. But the fragment can also be read otherwise: "To Art" can be understood as the destination of this message—its "superscription"—and Rossetti can be interpreted as declaring the primacy of Love (in the allegorical sense) over any worldly, empirical love. Understood in this light, the fragment is not a love letter to Art, but a note about Rossetti's understanding of Love that is *sent* to Art.

The entanglements of Art and Love are not only prominent features of Rossetti's poems and pictures, they define his project as a poet-painter. And yet this project must reckon with figures of death: of all the "kindred Powers" "marked" and allegorized in the permutations of Rossetti's poems, Death is that which, as in "Bridal Birth," "light[s] the halo" of "Love," giving it its special aura, paradoxically *animating* it.[3] If the subtitle of my chapter is rendered in the form of a question—just what *is* loving and what *is* dead in the poetry of Dante Gabriel Rossetti?—the answer produced by so many of the poems and the paintings is "everything." In his most famous "double-work," "The Blessed Damozel" is portrayed as both dead and loving. The very nature of her love, as the speaker "sees" it, is predicated on her death, the "gold bar" that separates her from the realm of the living and frames her as the object of love.

In the sonnets that compose the sequence of *The House of Life*—the project to which Rossetti devoted so much of his literary energies—each poem seems to offer another variation on the baroque intricacies of the allegory of Love and Death. In an early note that he drafted "To the Reader of The House of Life," Rossetti implores his readers not to read the poems autobiographically: "these poems are in no sense 'occasional,'" he writes. "The 'life' <recorded> involved is neither *my* life nor *your* life, but life <representative> purely and simply as tripled with Love and Death." The highly compressed and intricately wrought sonnets of this sequence certainly demonstrate that when "life <representative>" is "tripled with Love and Death," such multiplications are far from pure or simple. The first installment of this calculation appears in the much quoted introductory sonnet, where the opening lines declare the form itself, appearing as it does in Italian love poetry before the time of Raphael and canonized by Dante's own sonnet sequence, to be inextricable from death: *"A Sonnet is a moment's monument, — / Memorial from the Soul's eternity / To one dead deathless hour"* (ll.1–3). Both "monument" and "memorial" to the "moment," the sonnet is a time-fetish sent like a love-letter from "the Soul's eternity" to mark the hole of death.[4]

Or, as the sestet defines it, "A Sonnet is a coin," a two-sided surface: "its face reveals / The soul, — its converse, to what Power 'tis due" (ll.9–10). Perhaps no figure is more insistent in Rossetti's poetry and painting than the face that reveals. To identify this visage as the surface of the sonnet is to assert that the soul is apparent in the face and that there is nothing *beneath* the soul of the sonnet. Life, Love, and Death — each of them "kindred Powers" — are to be found, individually or in some combination, inscribed or even "super-scribed" on the flip-side of the sonnet-coin. There are many variations on this game of heads and tails, none more haunting perhaps than the closing couplet of "Death-in-Love," where we "behold" the image, delivered by a "veiled woman," of the identification of love and death: "'Behold, there is no breath: / I and this Love are one, and I am Death'" (ll.13–14).

Rossetti's project is there for everyone to behold: the project is Love, the poetic cultivation of an amatory aesthetic experience that, mirroring the figures and faces in the poems and pictures, might catch the reader or viewer in an erotic spell, a kind of stilled rapture that is closest to an allegorical Death. Unlike the poetic projects of Shelley, Keats, Hopkins, and Dickinson, there is no inherent disjunction between Rossetti's painterly project and his poetic undertakings. In fact, unlike politics, ethics, theology, or poetics — the rubrics that have oriented my readings in each of the previous chapters — love and aesthetics enjoy a relationship of such mutual reciprocity that they can appear indistinguishable without the intervention of a critical discourse. It is not only the case that Rossetti's aesthetic project appears on the surfaces of his poems and paintings; that project *is* its appearance on the *surfaces* of his poems and paintings. The question posed by Rossetti's project for everyone who beholds it can be characterized in this way: can Love — or at least the poetics of Love that is measured by a breathless, rapturous aesthetic experience — be the home of a critique? In other words, *can Love "house" a critical function?* Or is the aesthetics of Love by definition a spell, perhaps *the* defining and originary spell of auratic mystification, which can only be dispelled by revealing a deeper structure or mechanism of desire, one that can be identified and denounced or even mobilized into a form of critique?

"One Face Looks Out"

Feminist critics as well as professional biographers have long understood something like Love to be Rossetti's mission; and they have demonstrated that the dead and loving are entwined not only in the poetry and painting, but in the *life* of Dante Gabriel Rossetti, as well. To offer one prominent example, Elisabeth Bronfen identifies Rossetti's lived relationship with Elizabeth Siddal as a paradigmatic instance of what Bronfen calls the "knotting" of "death, femininity, and the aesthetic."[5] For Bronfen, "The Blessed Damozel" is an acute example of "the dead beloved as muse," an aesthetic model that she places alongside cognate examples in Poe and Nerval:

> Dante Gabriel Rossetti's poem "The Blessed Damozel" (1873), composed ten
> years after the death of Elisabeth Siddall, stages the poet's dialogue with a dead
> beloved, who like his own wife is ten years dead. He reanimates his lost beloved
> so as to fashion an image of himself after death, for the speech she delivers in his
> vision anticipates his entrance into heaven and describes how she will initiate him
> into celestial mysteries. Though inspired by the dead beloved, his invocation in
> fact endows her with speech, and the object of her discourse is a representation of
> his resurrection after death and a legitimation of his earthly love by virtue of its
> perfect celestial repetition. (367–68)

Bronfen's gloss of the poem is sufficiently incisive in its analysis of the structure of desire that animates the poem that we can forgive, if not overlook, her mistake: first published in *The Germ* in 1850, "The Blessed Damozel" was composed in 1847–48, at least a year or so before Rossetti had even laid eyes on Elisabeth Siddall. But this fact ironically confirms and even radicalizes Bronfen's assertion that "in the absence of the beloved, the poet can best picture her, namely as his creation, with a reference not so much to any historical reality as to his poetic gift" (368). Thus the beloved is by definition absent and never a "historical reality": already dead, "Elizabeth Siddall" simply serves to occupy the position of absent beloved that this poetic structure has prescribed for her. In this regard, we should take Jonathan Freedman's argument quite literally: "the Pre-Raphaelite woman," says Freedman, "*comes to being* under the sign of mortality; particularly in the death-obsessed work of Rossetti, she is envisioned as both the vehicle through which death is confronted and the means by which it may (or may not) be transcended" (*Professions*, 210, emphasis added).

Of course, this is a story that, if not as old as the hills, is at least as old as Petrarch. It is a story whose uncanny retellings continue to circulate throughout the critical discourse of cultural representations. "For an astonishingly long time in the contentious modern history of literary criticism," remarks Lisa Freinkel, "we've been telling ourselves essentially the same story about psychoanalysis, gender, religion, and Renaissance lyric poetry" ("Shakespearean Fetish," 109). It is the story of the silencing of Diana, and it sets the stage of a poetical theatre in which legions of mute Lauras and Lizzies are paraded before us for our fetishistic enjoyment. In Freinkel's account, the most established version of this story in contemporary Renaissance criticism is the work of Nancy Vickers, whose critique of Petrarchan poetics is, in turn, deeply indebted to Laura Mulvey's influential account of the gaze in classic narrative cinema. And, as if to fulfill the terms if the chiasmus, Mulvey's version of psychoanalysis is, in its turn, as indebted to the Petrarchan legacy as it is to Freud and Lacan. For my part I am not as interested in challenging the validity of such an interpretation of Rossetti as I am in "revaluing" its assumptions about love, desire, and aesthetics. Above all, I am interested in how someone christened Gabriel Dante Rossetti came to devote his poetry and painting to the love-and-death story of looking at surfaces and in the process gave himself a new life and a new name.

McGann characterizes Rossetti's translation of *Early Italian Poets* as "an act of extreme linguistic devotion, as resolute as a cultic or ritual performance" (*DGR and the Game*, 59). Thus does Rossetti repeat by way of translation the "acts" of "extreme linguistic devotion" already on display in the *Vita Nuova*. It is in his role as translator that Rossetti—uninterested in poetry, indolent in painting—can be said to embark on the project that fully engages his literary and artistic impulses, what Jan Marsh calls "a poetic apprenticeship through translation."[6] "It is true," writes Rossetti in the introduction to his translation, "that the *Vita Nuova* is a book which only youth could have produced, and which must chiefly remain sacred to the young; to each of whom the figure of Beatrice, less lifelike than lovelike, will seem the friend to his own heart" (77). "Less lifelike than lovelike": the terms of the comparison suggest an amatory aesthetic of semblance that insists itself throughout Rossetti's work. And yet Rossetti's own account of his relationship with the "figure of Beatrice" suggests that the semblances generated by this "lovelikeness," if not "superficial," are nonetheless immature, "something which must remain sacred chiefly to the young." Despite Rossetti's "devotion" to the Dante translations, despite his belief that "a translation . . . remains perhaps the most direct form of commentary" (61), it is also an act of love that reveals—in part by virtue of its object, a work produced by young man—its youthful lack of depth.[7] "The task of the translator," writes Rossetti, "is one of some self-denial" (62): to translate is thus to attempt to give oneself to the other, to dedicate oneself to another language in the hopes of producing a genuine semblance of the original. The effort is bound to fail, of course; and the translation is destined by its very nature to be secondary, a *mere* semblance.

Pater regarded the relationship between the two Dantes as much more than nominal or nationalist, more than mere emulation or derivation. According to Pater, for Rossetti as for Dante, "life is a crisis at every moment." Rossetti's poetics does indeed belong to what Agamben calls the "legacy that the love lyric of the Duecento has imparted to European culture," in particular the "nexus of eros and poetic language, the *entrebescamen* of desire, phantasm, and poetry in the *topos outopos* of the poem."[8] Rossetti does not simply belong to this Duecento legacy of the love lyric; he participates as poet and painter in its recovery and translation. Rossetti's translation of this "nexus of eros and poetic language" brings love and death together, insisting on the dimension of mourning inscribed in desire. It is present from the earliest period of Rossetti's poetry—"The Blessed Damozel"—and, as we shall see, it is woven rhetorically and formally throughout the sonnets of *The House of Life*. Agamben's account of the "displacement from desire to mourning" in Romance poetry announces a displacement of its own, from a thematic concern of the poems to an understanding of poetry itself as the "site" of this shift from "Eros" to "Thanatos":

> [The] essential textual tension of Romance poetry will be the displacement from desire to mourning: Eros will yield to Thanatos its impossible love object so as to recover it, through a subtle and funereal strategy, as lost object, and the poem will become the site of an absence yet nonetheless draws from this absence its specific authority. (*Stanzas*, 129)

Agamben is telling the history of the lyric, one that he calls a "poetic process whose emblematic temporal extremes are Petrarch and Mallarmé." Rossetti not only participates in the last days of this "poetic process," his poetry and paintings revisit and unearth the Petrarchan elements of its origins, that other "temporal extreme," thematizing, formalizing, *repeating* the structures by which "Eros yields to Thanatos." This yielding of Eros to Thanatos, as well as the "funereal strategies" by which Eros is projected as "lost object" in poems that mark its absence, characterizes the trajectory of *The House of Life* as a sequence of sonnets.[9]

In Bronfen's account of the relationship between the masculine artist and his feminine model-muse, "Eros yields to Thanatos" when the "virility and immortality" of Rossetti's status as artist are predicated upon the obsessive representations of Siddall as the "beautiful figure of *melancholia*, of feminine beauty signed by death, in the liminality between life and death" (*Her Dead Body*, 174, 170). In other words, what is virile, living, immortal in Rossetti's painting and poetry is precisely the "deanimating" depiction of the iconic woman as dead or dying. What makes this structure even more disturbing is its apparent capacity to exceed the boundaries of artistic representation, constituting the nature of Rossetti's love for Siddal and even prefiguring her death. As Barbara Gates puts it, Elizabeth Siddall seems "to have decided to live—and die—a fiction."[10] And in case we have missed the point, Griselda Pollock spells out precisely why this aesthetic structure is to be deplored: Elizabeth Siddall becomes "a cipher for masculine creativity inspired by and fulfilled in love for a beautiful feminine face."[11] For Bronfen the relationship between Rossetti and Siddall is paradigmatic enough of the structure of "death, femininity, and the aesthetic" to become one of her "case studies." These are Bronfen's conclusions regarding this strange painter-poet and his model-muse:

> The cultural conventions and representations of their times seem to have entered literally into the lives of Siddall and Rossetti as they repeatedly enacted a deanimation of the feminine body as engendering an animation of the artist, a production of images and poems, resurrecting the deanimated body as source and theme of these representations. (*Her Dead Body*, 177)

Bronfen's account so neatly summarizes an influential strain of psychoanalytically informed feminist analysis of the gendered nature of the image that it could serve as its own "case study." For my own interests, I want to highlight two features of Bronfen's argument: first, that the structure she discerns is repeated consistently enough to eliminate the need for close analysis of any single painting, because, we must assume, what the paintings "mean" is entirely visible on the surface.[12] Second, Bronfen's conclusions assume a porous relationship between art and life: there is an assumed, if unexplored mechanism by which artistic representations "seem to have entered literally into the lives of Siddall and Rossetti" (*Her Dead Body*, 177).[13]

None of this would have been news to those who were closest to Rossetti: in fact, Bronfen's analysis is fully anticipated in the accounts of his siblings and colleagues. Rossetti's friends knew of his obsession with Siddal or "Gug-gums," one of her many nicknames; and they knew he drew and painted her picture over and over again. "He showed me a drawer full of 'Guggums,'" recounts Ford Maddox Brown, "God knows how many. It is a monomania with him. Many of them are matchless in beauty however and one day will be worth large sums."[14] Nothing captures the nature of Rossetti's "monomania" better than his sister's sonnet "In the Artist's Studio," a sonnet that explicitly addresses the structure of desire and the mirror-effects of the paintings. "We found her hidden just behind those screens, / That mirror gave back all her loveliness," she writes, "One face looks out from all his canvases, one selfsame figure" (ll.3–4, 1–2). The sonnet anticipates with such compressed acuity the analyses and judgments that have been produced in the wake of psychoanaly-sis and feminism to make those latter-day commentaries appear as superflu-ous iterations.

If Christina Rossetti's sonnet is routinely invoked as an illuminating and critical reading of her brother's painting, there is an overlooked aspect of Christina's analysis that I would like to consider: by positioning the speaker of the sonnet in the first-person plural, *we* participate in the "discovery" of the love-object: "we found her hidden." Thus the poem anticipates the ap-parent necessity of repeating this analysis, just as it anticipates the appar-ent superfluity of attending closely to any individual painting, since "every canvas means / The same meaning, neither more nor less" (ll.7–8). What the paintings repeat in "every canvas" is the "vampyric" relationship that crystal-lizes the structure of idealization and deanimation described by Bronfen: "He feeds upon her face by day and night, / And she with true kind eyes looks back on him / . . . . Not as she is, but as she fills his dreams" (ll.9–10, 14).

Christina Rossetti is not unearthing something that her brother's own po-ems perform unaware. "The Portrait," for instance, is explicit in its recount-ing of an act of artistic enshrinement that has accomplished ("Lo! It is done" [l.9]) what Bronfen calls the "animation of the artist" by way of the "deanima-tion of the feminine body." The sonnet's octave is a prayer the artist addresses to "Love" as he undertakes the picture of his beloved: "O Love! let this my lady's picture grow / Under my hand to praise her name" (ll.2–3). In the space between the octave and the sestet, the sonnet becomes ekphrastic and points at a portrait that not only makes "her face" "her shrine," but that grants the artist the supreme "gift" of "love," exclusive access to his beloved: "Her face is made her shrine. Let all men note / That in all years (O Love, thy gift is this!) / They that would look on her must come to me" (ll.12–14). The sonnet demonstrates that Rossetti is fully aware of what his paintings do: it is there on the surface, just as "her face" is there on the surface for all "that would look on her." If we have learned from feminism and from psychoanalysis to understand how the thing called Desire underwrites Rossetti's poetics and opens its critique, the lesson is learned only by overlooking the gift Rossetti calls Love.

"A Blunder of Taste"; or, What Would Clement Greenberg Say?

Critical condemnation of Rossetti is not, of course, limited to ethical judgments of his gendering of love and death in the poetry and paintings. Though the histories of the critical responses to Keats and Shelley or to Hopkins and Dickinson have exhibited everything from outraged attack to outright neglect, Rossetti continues to be afflicted with the kind of critical ambivalence that relegates his work to a persistent nether-canonical status. If for Bronfen the poetry of Rossetti is symptomatic of a particular artistic pathology, for Clement Greenberg the paintings of Rossetti and the Pre-Raphaelites are guilty of "a blunder of taste," especially when the "timidity" of their undertaking is compared to the powerful epochal achievement of their French contemporary, Manet:

> By being juxtaposed more abruptly, without gradual transitions and blurrings, the different shading tones of greys or browns come through more purely—which means more flatly. For the sake of luminousness Manet was willing to accept this flatness. . . . The Pre-Raphaelites, too, had wanted to do brighter pictures, but were unwilling to accept flatness, and so they imposed detailed shading on their heightened color, imitating the Quattrocento Italians. But whereas the latter could get away with it because in their time and place they could get away with anything that served to increase the sculptural realism of their art, the Pre-Raphaelites could not. Their timidity in the face of the tradition of sculptural illusion led them into what proved to be a blunder of taste more than anything else. (A decade separated the beginnings of Pre-Raphaelitism [1848] from Manet's own beginnings, but the difference between them in artistic culture seems more like an aeon.)[15]

On the face of it, nothing appears flatter than the early paintings of the Pre-Raphaelite Brotherhood: they are characterized by the substitution of sculptured drawing with light tentative lines, the abandonment of illusionistic depth for a series of shallow plains in which bright, ornate, "secondary" details assert themselves and dissolve the distinction between foreground and background. These are features that Robert Buchanan describes simply as "a great indifference to perspective" (26). The Pre-Raphaelite paintings from 1848 to 1850—in particular, Rossetti's *The Girlhood of Mary Virgin* and *Ecce Ancilla Domini!*, Millais's *Isabella* and *Christ in the House of His Parents*, and, to a lesser degree, Hunt's *Rienzi*—are bright, awkward, and unstable compositions that seem perpetually on the verge of spilling onto the viewer. In this regard the comparisons between the early paintings of the PRB and the project of the French avant-garde appear justified. Indeed, Elizabeth Prettejohn argues that "the Pre-Raphaelites were no less radical than the French painters in their opposition to the dominant modes of painting in their own art world" (*Art of Pre-Raphaelites*, 38). But Greenberg's judgment has prevailed: far from being "radical," the Pre-Raphaelite challenge to "the tradition of sculptural illusion" is characterized by a "timidity" that led them into a regressive "blunder of taste" in their "imitation" of the Quattrocento Italians. For Greenberg the formal solution to this historical impasse—luminousness gained by way of flatness—could be achieved only by an artist with Manet's audacious, *critical* force, one whose "paintings became the first Modernist ones by virtue of the frankness with which they declared the surfaces on which they were painted" (*Collected*, 86). From the perspective of this narrative of European painting, the Pre-Raphaelites, though Manet's contemporaries, are quite the opposite of an avant-garde: flat enough only to be superficial, and thus "aeons" in arrears in terms of "artistic culture."[16]

For Michael Fried, Manet marks the same historical "breakthrough" assigned to the painter in Greenberg's narrative; but Fried reckons the nature of the painter's achievement in terms of his ongoing—and now canonical—analysis of the relationship between absorption and theatricality in the Western tradition of visual representation. Unlike Greenberg, Fried makes no mention of Pre-Raphaelite painting, even as a point of comparison or departure; but his principal points of reference, absorption and theatricality, illuminate important aspects of Rossetti's pictures. Though all paintings would seem, by definition, to be made in order to be shown and seen, Fried argues that French painters, from the time of Chardin and Greuze onward, began to make their paintings refuse this fundamentally *theatrical* condition of beholding by composing scenes and models of *absorption*. According to Fried, this anti-theatrical impulse, one in which the beholder is ignored, negated, or even merged into the painting itself, achieves its artistic zenith in the breathtaking canvases Courbet painted after 1848. But soon thereafter—"by 1860"—the "means and conventions by which French painting for more than a century had sought to establish the ontological illusion . . . that the beholder did not exist had nearly come to the end of their efficacy"; and we are thus confronted with the most radical "response to this crisis"—namely, Manet's "modernism."[17]

Though Fried insists that it is not the "aim" of his readings of French eighteenth- and nineteenth-century painting (his initial point of reference) "to make value judgments that turn on the issue of theatricality," he acknowledges that his critical project "does provide food for thought" about such evaluations given that "painters of the stature of David, Géricault, Millet, and Courbet all sought to defeat the theatrical in their art" (*Courbet's Realism*, 51). And, as Robert Pippen has argued, Fried implies that to defeat the theatrical is to defeat the "inauthentic."[18] In other words, theatricality in painting implies an *ethical failing*, an inauthenticity of being often referred to as superficiality. When Rossetti's pictures are compared to those of his brilliant French contemporaries who, like Courbet, were developing unprecedented methods and devising extraordinary strategies to resist theatricality, they certainly appear theatrical, inauthentic. Rossetti's painterly provocations appear as superficial also-rans when placed alongside those of Manet, who, says Fried, was "systematically avoid[ing] or subvert[ing] absorptive or potentially absorptive motifs" (*Manet's Modernism*, 405) in order to confront the beholder with "certain truths about the painting-beholder relationship it was no longer feasible to deny" and thus, "with extreme provocation," manufacturing a "revolution" in painting (*Courbet's Realism*, 200–1). Manet's "revolution," the nature of his "extreme provocation," is no longer merely formal: Manet demands that his canvasses be regarded, *beheld* as *critique*. When Rossetti's pictures are considered in that context—the context of painting *as critique*—they appear in the most pejorative sense to be *theatrical, inauthentic, superficial*.

Robert Buchanan launched his notorious critical assault on Rossetti's poetry with this same "theatrical analogy." We tend to regard "The Fleshly School of Poetry" as an attack on Rossetti's representation of sensuality in general and in particular on the "shameless" depiction of "amorous sensations" in "Nuptial Sleep."[19] But, according to Buchanan, the principal crime of "Nuptial Sleep" is not Rossetti's depiction of sensuality (Swinburne is much more extreme in this regard), but that Rossetti "parades his private sensations before a coarse public, and is gratified by their applause" (28). Buchanan's fundamental accusation is that Rossetti is guilty of what is known in theater as "gagging"—guilty, in other words, of the most superficial and inauthentic form of theatricality (27, 24). Rossetti's sins are not confined to a single poem: "the fleshly feeling is everywhere." Buchanan discerns the same sense of "fleshly" superficiality in the poems that he sees in Rossetti's paintings: "There is the same thinness and transparence of design, . . . the same sense of weary, wasting, yet exquisite sensuality; nothing virile, nothing tender, nothing completely sane; a superfluity of extreme sensibility, of delight in beautiful forms, hues, and tints." (26) Almost by necessity does such "superfluity of extreme sensibility" make Rossetti's poems appear not only "deficient in sincerity," but guilty of an "excess of affectation" that is "not natural" (31). More subdued and restrained versions of these charges recur throughout the history of Rossetti criticism; and Harold Wetherby's judgment regarding the poetry's superficiality crystallizes this strain of the tradition: Rossetti's "surfaces are overwrought, not because they are, comparatively speaking, exceedingly ornate but because there is often no solid fabric beneath them."[20]

And, as I see it, Wetherby was right. Rossetti did not, of course, believe that this was what he was doing. Not only does he chafe at the charge of "gross sensuality," Rossetti was particularly angered by Buchanan's assertion that the members of the "fleshly school" "wish to create form for its own sake" ("Fleshly School," 37). But if, as Bowra claims, for Rossetti the flesh "somehow was the visible image of the soul," his attention to the visibility of the surface can always appear to neglect what rests beneath.[21] Even as sympathetic a reader of Rossetti as Baum acknowledges that the poet "often disguised his meaning under a cloud of gorgeous phrasing" (*House of Life*, 3). This leads any reader to ask whether Rossetti's poetry is nothing more than "a cloud of gorgeous phrasing" and whether that "cloud of gorgeous phrasing" *is* its "meaning." McGann's early influential essay on "Rossetti's Significant Details" makes the case for the poet's refusal of symbols and, in the example of "My Sister's Sleep," the "religious 'meaning'" it seems to invoke: "Rossetti's art here is highly self-conscious: he wants us to seek and fail to find the religious 'meaning' in his stanza, and failing to find it, to recognize the purely sensational value of the lines."[22] According to McGann, Rossetti "forces the reader to attend to the surface, insists that the greatest significance lies there, unburied" ("Rossetti's Details," 54); but it is precisely this insistent attention to the formal fact of the picture-surface that leaves Rossetti open to the charge of superficiality.

Rossetti and Manet: the comparison remains instructive, particularly given Rossetti's complicated, but ultimately defensive rejection of his French contemporary, whom his friend Fantin-Latour identified as the principal figure among the new painters in Paris.[23] The Pre-Raphaelites in general and Rossetti in particular thus seem guilty of doing both too much and too little, being simultaneously excessive and yet always falling short of a genuine critique (Bronfen) or formal achievement (Greenberg). Manet accomplishes both, exposing and undoing the gendered nature of the gaze in the Western tradition while—and *by*—achieving the decisive formal and critical breakthrough. From this historical perspective, one in which aesthetic solutions can be understood to constitute ethical representations, the Pre-Raphaelites in general and Rossetti in particular appear doubly dubious. But one of the most fascinating aspects of the judgments of Bronfen and Greenberg, feminist and formalist, is how closely they echo the judgments and observations of many of Rossetti's contemporaries, including those who were closest to him. Intimations of Greenberg's modernist evaluations of Rossetti *vis-à-vis* Manet are certainly anticipated by the often harsh assessment by Fantin-Latour and, as Marsh has suggested, seem to be implied in the envious irritation Rossetti expressed about his highly championed French counterpart.

We know that Rossetti saw *Olympia* and that Manet's masterpiece suggested some of the compositional ideas Rossetti would take up in *The Beloved* (*The Bride*) (1865–66), perhaps Rossetti's most Manetian painting. Indeed, Marsh calls the controversial placement of the black boy in the left lower foreground of the *The Beloved* "a straight steal from *Olympia*"; but this pilfered image only alerts the viewer to other aspects of Manet's looming presence in this ambitious painting. If the depiction of the beloved herself bears Rossetti's painterly signature, Manet's presence is registered in the frankly reciprocal gazes of the female attendants who frame the central figure. Though the centrality of the beloved is only solidified by this framing strategy, the compression of the composition and the lushness of the drapery produce a crowded, even cluttered surface that suggests less a wedding procession than a kind of strange, single, composite entity. And, above all, the viewer is presented with eyes, a flowering of eyes. Thus does Manet's influence serve to make the differences between *The Beloved* and *Olympia* feel even more pronounced. *The Beloved* is a strange and even haunting picture; but it possesses none of the audacious critical power of Manet's canvas. Here and throughout the principal works of this mature stage of his career, Rossetti's attention to the surface does not participate in the stringent critique that characterizes Manet's important paintings in this period. The comparison between *Olympia* and *The Beloved* is exemplary; for the accumulation of eleven eyes in Rossetti's painting cannot approximate the unnerving power of that one look from Olympia.[24]

It is precisely the powerful dimension of critique discernible in *Olympia* that allows the painting to be regarded not only as an extraordinary aesthetic achievement and a formal breakthrough of historic proportions (Greenberg, Fried), but also as an ethical and even *political* intervention (Clark, Berger, Nochlin) in the culture of painterly representations. If Manet's modernism is indeed what Fried calls "the face of painting in the 1860s," it is a face that consistently and "with extreme provocation" and "shocking confrontation" addresses the themes and structures of desire, not only in *Olympia*, of course, but manifestly in *Le Déjeuner sur l'herbe* (*Manet's Modernism*, 153). If the topic of the gendered structure of the gaze has become a commonplace of certain models of feminist criticism, Fried's inquiries into Manet's figures of the gaze, his "direct but uncommunicative confrontation of the beholder," is especially relevant: if these faces—or the one face of Victorine Meurent—"*gaze back* at the viewer," it is with an "emptiness and abstractness" that "may be the purest emblem in Manet's art of a face or an eye that, for all its liveness of address, lacks the merest hint of psychology, of subjective depth" (*Manet's Modernism*, 323). The flat, discomforting frankness with which Manet's Meurent returns the viewers' gaze is registered—then and now—as the kind of undoing achieved by the most rigorous critical analysis of desire.

None of this can be said about Rossetti, and not merely because he is technically inferior as a painter. Rather, in *The Beloved* and in so many of the pictures in the 1850s and 1860s, Rossetti is not painting *desire*, but *love*; and this is what love looks like. But to assert this only seems to confirm Rossetti's superficiality. From the perspective of the critical tradition aligned with Manet—one that continues to the present in the forms of our *critical* theories of art and culture—"desire" is always something that runs deeper than love: desire is the fundamental structure for which "love" is always only the ideology, the veil, the aura. Therefore, the best way to understand the project of Rossetti's paintings—and, as I will argue, his poems—is not to approach that project as a form of *critique*—i.e., the laying bare of the constitutive elements of desire in the beholding of the painted (female) figure—but in an altogether different, *uncritical* mode as the thoroughly auratic semblance of love. Unlike Manet or, in a different sense, Courbet, whose anti-theatrical strategies of painterly absorption demonstrate what Fried calls "their predilection for subjects involving two or more personages engaged in something like significant human action" (*Courbet's Realism*, 223), Rossetti's pictures tend not only to avoid but to eliminate "significant human action," at least in its most social forms. If it is difficult to miss in Manet the elements of painterly critique and thus an *ethics*, it is as difficult to find either in Rossetti.[25] Looking for love, Rossetti's pictures ask the viewer to surrender to the image: they solicit a relationship that is not ethical, but erotic.[26]

"Love Is Addressed to the Semblance"; or, What Would Jacques Lacan Say?

Slavoj Žižek also believes Chrisina Rossetti when she writes that for her brother "every canvas means/The same meaning." In *The Metasteses of Enjoyment*, Žižek prefaces a discussion of filmmaker "David Lynch as Pre-Raphaelite" with Christina's diagnosis of her brother's art. In Žižek's pop-Lacanian idiom, "the Lady,"—"deprived of every real substance"—"functions as a mirror on which the subject projects his narcissistic ideal."[27] Žižek's account of Pre-Raphaelite painting, one that is derived from his brief treatment of two pictures by Hunt rather than Rossetti, echoes much of the most pejorative responses to the Brotherhood's painting from the time of their earliest exhibitions and reviews:

> The first thing about their paintings that strikes the viewer is their flatness. This feature necessarily appears to us, accustomed as we are to modern perspective-realism, as a sign of clumsiness: Pre-Raphaelite paintings somehow lack the "depth" that pertains to space organized along perspective lines which meet at a distant point—it is as if the very "reality" these paintings depict is not a "true" reality but, rather, a reality structured as in bas-relief. (Another aspect of this same feature is the "dollish," mechanically composed artificial quality that clings to the depicted individuals: they somehow lack the abyssal depth of personality that we usually associate with the notion of "subject.") (114)

Žižek's account of Pre-Raphaelite painting is worth noting not for the originality of his observations, but for the critical functions he assigns them. The naive artificiality of Rossetti's depictions, the doll-like qualities of the figures, the depthlessness of human subject and painted canvas, are precisely the qualities that, according to Žižek, give the paintings their unnerving power and—this is Žižek's real interest—help us comprehend the aesthetic experience of Lynch's cinema, *Blue Velvet* in particular. For Žižek the critical value of any work of art—its genuinely meaningful achievement—resides in its capacity to "open up a hole in reality" and deliver us to "the void of the Thing." The way to get there—to the "void of the Thing"—is not, according to Žižek, through the redemptive power of works of art. In the case at hand, Žižek is not interested in rehabilitating the Pre-Raphaelites or revising the views of generations of art critics and historians who regard the pictures as flat, depth-less, clumsy, and artificial: these are precisely the qualities that, from Žižek's point of view, enable the paintings to dissolve the "reality" of the symbolic. For Žižek "every canvas" *does* indeed "mean the same meaning," and this is what gives the paintings their special power. In other words, the symptom of narcissistic desire in Rossetti's paintings was not something hidden beneath the surface that feminist critics have now made visible: it was there all along for everyone to see on the very surface of these pictures; and far from reveal-ing a masculinist pathology of desire to be deplored, it touches at the truth of desire.

Žižek's account of the Pre-Raphaelites, like his entire critical project, is in-formed by and dedicated to Lacanian psychoanalysis. Perhaps no topic in La-can is more important to Žižek's thought than the analysis of courtly love; and this is especially apparent in Žižek's invocation and deployment of Rossetti and Pre-Raphaelite painting in his discussion of "Courtly Love, or, Woman as Thing." Lacan's account of courtly love does not "explain" Rossetti's poetics; rather, French psychoanalysis and British Pre-Raphaelite poetry and painting come from the same place. In the 1972–73 seminars devoted to "the limits of love and knowledge," Lacan offers this "definition" of "courtly love": it is "for man—in relation to whom the Lady is entirely, and in the most servile sense of the word, a subject—the only way to elegantly pull off the absence of the sexual relationship."[28] While courtly love may materialize in highly spe-cialized poetic conventions and originate under particular historical condi-tions, Lacan argues that the "techniques of courtly love" address an inherent truth of desire—namely, its "fundamentally narcissistic" character.[29] Thus the "idealizing exaltation" we associate with the poetry of courtly love—and with its reiteration in the paintings and poems of Rossetti—is caught up in a mirror-play from which there seems no historical extrication:

> And the element of idealizing exaltation that is expressly sought out in the
> ideology of courtly love . . . is fundamentally narcissistic in character. . . . The
> mirror may on occasion imply the mechanism of narcissism. . . . But it also fulfills
> another role, a role as limit. It is that which cannot be crossed. And the only orga-
> nization in which it participates is that of the inaccessibility of the object. (*Ethics of
> Psychoanalysis*, 151)

There are many reasons one might subscribe to or reject the Lacanian analysis of desire; and that debate, once central to literary and cinema studies, has found its second coming of sorts in the work of Žižek. But my own interest here is more modest and local: Lacan's project appears to help us think about the relationship between amatory and aesthetic experience in Rossetti's poetry. Lacan's characterization of courtly love—the fundamental narcissism of its "idealizing exaltations," the double role of the mirror as self-reflection and limit—seems to illuminate the "idealizing" examples of Rossetti's poetics of "lovesight," his own most Dantean inheritance. "When do I see thee most, beloved one?" asks the speaker of "Lovesight," "When in the light the spirits of mine eyes / Before thy face, their altar, solemnize / The worship of that Love through thee made known? (ll. 1–4). Posed as a question, the lines crystallize in this chiasmic mirror the poetic tradition Lacan is engaging. This tradition is even more conventionally evident in "The Lamp's Shrine," a sonnet Baum describes as a "very favorable example of Rossetti's Early Italian or Dantesque manner" (*House of Life*, 114). When, for instance, Lacan says of the troubadours that "all the poets seem to be addressing the same person" (*Ethics of Psychoanalysis*, 149), we can discern the quality of interchangeability among Rossetti's models, as well as the fact that "the same person" is often addressed and depicted by all the painters associated with the Brotherhood. And what Lacan says of Dante regarding the deanimation of the feminine object can be—and has been—said of his inheritor: "In this poetic field the feminine object is emptied of all real substance. That is what made it easy subsequently for a metaphysical poet such as Dante, for example, to choose a person whom we definitely know existed . . . and make her the equivalent of philosophy or indeed, the end, of the science of the sacred" (*Ethics of Psychoanalysis*, 149). It is only by emptying the feminine object of real substance—any human or subjective "depth"—that one can attend to a relationship that is by its nature superficial.

There are certainly examples enough of "Rossetti's Early Italian or Dantesque manner" throughout the poet's career to regard it as the Victorian reiteration of the structure that Agamben and Lacan identify in Dante and the troubadours. And there is something uncanny—if historically traceable—in the way the psychoanalytic *and* feminist accounts seem equally capable of explaining the structure of desire in Rossetti, even when they do not address his poems or his pictures. But the very adequacy of this explanatory model, its very "fit," suggests that something is awry. In other words, Rossetti seems not to challenge our interpretive efforts, but to conform to them all—*but all too readily*. Rossetti's poetry seems to yield to the feminist critique of its "idealizing deanimation"; but this critique is defused by the fact that no critique was necessary, because the object of that critique was already there on the surface. If Rossetti's paintings can be regarded as "a blunder of taste" for their display of formal as well as thematic *shallowness* that never achieve the force of a critical *flatness*, it is a shallowness that the pictures seem not only to display, but to flaunt "theatrically." If Rossetti's poetry reveals features that are deeply indebted to his namesake, displaying a structure of courtly love interrogated by Lacan's analytic techniques, it is the Lacanian techniques that are superfluous and unnecessary, given the transparence of this structure in Rossetti's work.

We are so accustomed to the challenges posed by textual interpretation—and perhaps to the theological impulse behind hermeneutical exegesis that still informs it—that we tend to be suspicious of such easy fits. This makes it oddly difficult to see why these critical models feel less and less adequate the more we read Rossetti's sonnets or look at his pictures, because the source of this inadequacy is not something deeper, something unearthed, a hidden kernel of meaning or smoldering critical impulse that awaits to be reignited. The source of the *critical* incompatibility is the aestheticization that "draws" or "traces" or "marks" a pattern (of courtly love, of idealization, of superficiality) into its surfaces. It is the "flashing jewel" that "deigns to shine" in Rossetti's most "Dantesque" of sonnets, such as "The Lamp's Shrine," the "flashing jewel" that comes at "Love's shrine."[30]

When Lacan circles back to the topic of love in his 1972–73 seminar "On Feminine Sexuality, the Limits of Love and Knowledge," he joins love to another cognate of the aesthetic, *semblance*: "Love . . . is addressed to the semblance," the relational structure that precedes and accommodates being (*On Feminine Sexuality*, 92, 95). Rossetti's poetics of love in the pictures and the poems is just such an "address to the semblance." For Schiller, of course, the aesthetic is famously the realm—both *Reich* and *Staat*—of semblance [*Schein*]; and semblance is "the very essence" of the "fine arts."[31] In order to preserve the values of this properly aesthetic semblance, Schiller must distinguish it from "logical semblance": "It goes without saying," says Schiller, "that the only kind of semblance I am here concerned with is aesthetic semblance (which we distinguish from actuality and truth [*Wirklichkeit und Warheit*]) and not logical semblance (which we confuse with these): semblance, therefore, which we love just because it is semblance, and not because we take it to be something better. Only the first is play, whereas the latter is mere deception"

(*Aesthetic Education*, no. 26). In the British Romantic tradition semblance does not possess the unquestioned value Schiller assigns to *Schein*, whether because it never seems "to go without saying" that aesthetic semblance can be so easily distinguished from logical semblance or because the "essence" of the "fine arts" is never identified as "semblance."[32]

When "semblance" does figure in Romantic and post-Romantic discourse, it tends to imply a *superficial* property or aspect, as when Wordsworth, negotiating the extraordinarily complex play of light and dark in the "Intimations" ode, addresses "exterior semblance": "Thou, whose exterior semblance doth belie/Thy soul's immensity;/Thou best philosopher, who yet dost keep/Thy heritage, thou eye among the blind" (ll.109–12). Semblance often implies an "appearance or outward seeming of something that is not actually there," a "seeming" that conceals the true substance. But in a more neutral register, semblance can also designate "the form, likeness or image of a person or thing" considered in relation to another that is similar, as in "resemblance." As such, semblance implies "the fact or quality of being like something." As a "likeness" it implies a fundamentally aesthetic quality, one in which the tropological nature of similitude converges with the visual act of presenting to view. Thus the meaning of semblance oscillates between something purely relational—between surface and depth, between seeming and substance—and an apparent quality of its own.

The variability of range in the definitions of semblance offers an index to the critical ambivalence toward Rossetti's painting and poetry. It is apparent, for instance, in the ways in which critics have viewed the painter-poet's obsession with the "form, likeness, and image" of his serial Beatrices, as well as the "resemblances" among the various models. And it is apparent in the charge, leveled time and again, of superficiality, a charge based on the judgment that the paintings and poems exclusively address the semblances, playing at and on the surfaces and thus neglecting the "soul's immensity" and those "thoughts which lie too deep for tears." But semblance not only offers us a way to understand the various views of Rossetti, it also affords us the best way to see how Rossetti himself *sees*, how he sees love, of course, but also how he views the fundamentally erotic nature of vision. "Lovesight," for instance, concludes with the speaker reflecting on the prospect of losing the *image* of love's eyes: "O love, my love! if I no more should see/Thyself, nor on the earth the shadow of thee,/Nor image of thine eyes in any spring, . . ." (ll.9–11). In "The Portrait," the speaker addresses Love as "the Lord of all compassionate control" and beseeches him to "let this my lady's picture glow/Under my hand to praise her name" (ll. 1–3). Should this auratic wish be granted, the semblance will do more than represent his lady's likeness: it will "show / Even of her inner self the perfect whole" (ll. 3–4). In "Hand and Soul," the artist Chiaro's soul appears before him as a semblance, an outward appearance: thus is the soul not hidden in the depths, but made manifest as an image or, to use Rossetti's emblematic pun, *drawn*. Throughout *The House of Life*, "souls" are semblances, images surfacing in poem after poem as offerings to the "Breath" of Love. Its epitome perhaps is the concluding lines of "Youth's Antiphony," a sonnet whose octave is comprised entirely of the clichéd dialogue of young lovers caught in their most absorptive superficiality, "while Love breathed in sighs and silences / Through two blent souls one rapturous undersong" (ll. 13–14).

If, as Lacan puts it, "love is addressed to the semblance," we see in Rossetti the mirror-image: the semblance is addressed to Love. It is the aesthetic experience of Love and not the analysis of desire that is Rossetti's poetic (and painterly) project. This is not say that Rossetti's project cannot be subjected to Bronfen's demystification or that Žižek is misguided to seek a fundamentally critical dimension to Rossetti's paintings. But both of these accounts, mirror images of each other, are made possible by the intervention of a critical discourse of desire, one that it is unearthed *beneath* the poetic and painted surfaces or "semblances" of love. But Lacan shows us that Love and Desire — like phenotext and genotext or like ideology and its critique — derive from the same origin. And if that critical discourse of desire, articulated in opposing images by Bronfen and Žižek, is already present in the sonnet by Christina Rossetti, Dante Rossetti also "already" understands the superficiality of his Love language and images. The discourses of Love and Desire might well be inseparably braided, but Dante Rossetti's superficial project is dedicated to drawing out the deathlike states of aestheticized Love in poems and pictures: the promises of love are those made directly on the glass.

The Promises of Glass

Rossetti knew that any claim he might stake as a major poet would inevitably rest on the judgments of *The House of Life*; and this awareness may account for his particularly defensive response to Buchanan's review of the volume and for the extent of his revisions of the sonnets that comprise it.[33] If the sonnets of *The House of Life* are not characterized by thematic or expressive "depth," they are without question characterized by overwrought density, surreal personification, and extreme rhetorical compression. These sonnets are highly allegorical "chambers" from which narrative "sequentiality" is invoked and just as often expelled. For Pater the originality of the sonnets derives from their "conveyance of a poetic sense which recognized no conventional standard of what poetry was called upon to be" (*Appreciations*, 206). Identifying Rossetti as a formal innovator in the Romantic tradition, Pater anticipated the charge that Rossetti's innovations may constitute little more than "mere tricks of manner": "At a time when poetic originality in England might seem to have had its utmost play, here was certainly one new poet more, with a structure and music of verse, a vocabulary, an accent, unmistakably novel, yet felt to be no mere tricks of manner" (206). "Utmost play" is an especially pertinent term to describe this poetic originality when we consider Rossetti's efforts in the poems to figure love itself as "utmostness." Indeed, much of what contributes to Rossetti's "poetic originality," what makes him seem "one new poet more," is his rejection of rhetorical moderation, his refusal of comparisons that might subdue the heightened tone of the poems, and his rejection of the worldliness that might ground the represented extremities of love and death. "When," as in the sestet of "The Love-Letter," "through eyes raised an instant, her soul sought/My soul," the result is a union that not only creates the experience of "utmostness," but does so as the aestheticization of love:

> Fain had I watched her when, at some fond thought,
>   Her bosom to the writing closelier press'd,
>   And her breast's secrets peered into her breast;
> When, through eyes raised an instant, her soul sought
> My soul, and from the sudden confluence caught
>   The words that made her love the loveliest.
>
> (ll.9–16)

To "catch" the words that make "love the loveliest": this is the nature of Rossetti's commitment in *The House of Life* to the essence of Love *as* its idealization. Given this "confluence" of love and aesthetics in a poetry devoted to catching "the words" that make love the "loveliest," what would its *radicalization* look like? Is it something that would lend these poems a "sudden" and unexpected critical force, a dispelling of that frozen, tremulous state? Would a radical aestheticism in Rossetti be that which pierced the surfaces or the semblances and undid the promises of glass?

"The Lovers' Walk" offers one version of Rossetti's poetic formulation of these questions. The lush summer scene developed in the octave—"An osierodoured stream that draws the skies/Deep to its heart" (ll.4–5)—features the lovers, "two souls," "mirrored eyes in eyes" (ll.6, 7). In the sestet, however, the path of this relationship takes an extravagant turn:

> Even such their path, whose bodies lean unto
>   Each other's visible sweetness amourously,—
>   Whose passionate hearts lean by Love's high decree
> Together on his heart for ever true,
> As the cloud-foaming firmamental blue
>   Rests on the blue line of a foamless sea.
>
>   (ll.9–14)

The "infinite truth" of "Love's high decree" is, in other words, a stunning visual trick, the sublime optical illusion of the "firmamental blue" appearing to "rest" on "the blue line of a foamless sea." Moreover, the revelation of such an illusory condition in this exquisite if impossible analogy does nothing to diminish "Love's high decree," which is never anything more or less than "mirrored eyes in eyes." Isobel Armstrong beautifully describes the cumulative emotional effects of this poetic extremity, the paradoxical compound of sublime intensity and absolute absence in *The House of Life*:

> The sonnets are the great conjurers of emptiness in this period. A contentless world, of cold, waste, shadow, and annihilation belongs to them. But it is a world where the pressure of physical form *has* been or might be. Meaning hovers beyond or beneath the material form, or the physical hovers beyond or beneath the state of loss, always incommensurate, always unrealised. (*Victorian Poetry*, 453)

"A contentless world": there is no better way to describe the poetic landscape one enters when reading these extraordinary sonnets. The effect of sonnet after sonnet is to hollow out extreme spaces in which the adamantine figures of love can be spun untethered to the worldly demands of meaning.

But if we entertain Fried's notions of painterly absorption and theatricality in the context of a poet-painter whose ekphrastic impulses always invite it, Rossetti's figures of love's "utmostness" and, for that matter, his disposition for rhetorical spectacle can only be regarded as *theatrical* gestures, excessive declarations of love in its most extravagant personification. At the same time, however, even a poem such as "Mid-Rapture," denounced (or celebrated) for its theatrical displays of eroticism—its patent exhibitionism—is constructed from the most *absorptive* of figures. The poem's final line—"O lovely and beloved, O my love"—may necessarily ring theatrical as a mode of amatory address; but the variations of love are taken to the point of *polyptoton*, one that is, moreover, an apostrophic reiteration of the poem's opening address. In other words, if the line cannot help but sound entirely theatrical, its theatricality is the result of compressed and absorptive repetitions; and thus the line—as with so many of the lines of these sonnets—is a theatre that cannot escape the figurative enclosures of love.

The rhetorical bravura of "Mid-Rapture"—similes mutating into chiasms, apostrophes composed of *polyptotons*—is on display throughout the sonnets. The peculiar nature of this rhetorical compound would prompt Pater to believe that Rossetti's work constituted "a really new kind of poetic utterance, with effects that have nothing else like them" (*Appreciations*, 210). For Pater, as for many of his contemporaries, the most distinctive figure in this strange rhetorical brew was Rossetti's use of personification and what Pater would call the "forced and almost grotesque materializing of abstraction" (210). Browning denounced Rossetti's personification of love in the name of worldly love: "Then how I hate 'Love' as a lubberly, naked young man putting his arms there & his wings there, about a pair of lovers—a fellow they would kick away in the reality." Even a reader as sympathetic and sensitive as Pater described Rossetti's excessive use of personification as a kind of poetic "*mania*": "The insanity which follows a vivid poetic anthropomorphism like that of Rossetti may be noted here and there in his work" (*Appreciations*, 209). The personification of love in "Heart's Haven," for instance, is familiar and comfortable enough to provide "haven": "And Love, our light at night and shade at noon, / Lulls us to rest with songs, and turns away / All shafts of shelterless tumultuous day" (ll.9–11). But in such a "vivid anthropomorphism" as that of "The Stream's Secret," the elaborate personifications of "Love" are sensuous and seductive enough to make the reader forget that there was ever an "I and she" in the first place:

> Say, hath not Love leaned low
> This hour beside thy far well-head,
> And there through jealous hollowed fingers said,
> The thing that most I long to know,—
> Murmuring with curls all dabbled in thy flow
> And washed lips rosy red?
>
> (ll.6–12)

It may be the case that Rossetti's readings and translations of his namesake's poems, particularly of *La Vita Nuova*, are the source of his own reliance on personification, the "well-head" of his own poetics. "Another of his conformities to Dante," writes Pater, who believes "the really imaginative vividness . . . of [Rossetti's] personifications" achieves a rhetorical force that exceeds the poet's control and acquires its own compulsive agency: "his hold upon them, or rather their hold upon him, with the force of a Frankenstein, when once they have taken life from him" (208). Thus does the personification of love not only become a life and death matter in the poetry of Dante Gabriel Rossetti, but a potentially monstrous one, at least the monstrosity of a rhetorical force that exceeds the "hold" of human agency.

For Jonathan Freedman Rossetti's personifications issue from a Romantic problematic and constitute an "explicit turn to the allegorical," one that confirms de Man's deconstructive reading of the Romantic relationship between symbol and allegory. Freedman quotes these famous sentences from de Man's "Rhetoric and Temporality" that spell out the symbol's "undoing" by allegory:

> [W]hereas the symbol postulates the possibility of an identity or identification, allegory designates primarily a distance in relation to its own origin, and, renouncing the nostalgia and the desire to coincide, it establishes its language in the void of this temporal difference. In so doing, it prevents the self from an illusory identification with the non-self, which is now fully, though painfully, recognized as a non-self. It is this painful knowledge that we perceive at the moments when early romantic literature finds its true voice. (de Man, *Blindness and Insight*, 207)

According to Freedman, Rossetti "provides the 'true voice' of Romantic practice . . . which the Romantics themselves devoted much of their own energy to denying, evading, or recasting" (*Professions*, 28–29).[34] Ironically, it is Rossetti's aestheticism that demonstrates the "good conscience"—and even the "authentic" "true voice"—of an allegorizing poetry that foregrounds its constitutive figurative dimension.[35]

Freedman's account of the deconstructive impulse inscribed in Rossetti's poems is an attractive one: the invocation of de Man enlists an unexpected critical dimension and an unlikely critical authority to these poems. Freedman's turn to de Man derives, yet again, from the urgency to locate a critical function in Rossetti's poetic aestheticization of love. But the self-conscious display of rhetoricity does not itself, at least for de Man, constitute a "deconstruction" of the order he spells out in "The Rhetoric of Temporality."[36] If it is the case that the allegorical dimensions of these poems undo our symbolic expectations (as well as the aesthetic judgments that issue from them), if the rhetoricity is not only foregrounded but made "utmost," if the "soul" itself in Rossetti is understood to be a rhetorical projection, and if these are indeed sonnets that demand to be understood as superficial, this does not yet account for what I would call their *aestheticism*. But the path of rhetoricity is the best way to get to the particular aestheticizing effects of figuration in these sonnets: it allows us to assess what Rossetti in "Love-Letter" describes as "the sudden confluence" of forces and figures that make "love the loveliest."

If the sonnets display Rossetti's propensity for elaborate figures of repetition, they do not produce a *deepened* understanding of the linguistic relationship to the experience of love; they are, rather, eruptions of the variations spun out by a single root, superficial permutations. The sonnets present us with figures of love that no longer mediate the relationship between lover and beloved, but begin to banish them, and thereby leave us with repeated and increasingly minute variations on "Love," as if to bathe in the stream of their apparently endless permutations. Baum's disapproving gloss of "The Lovers' Walk" addresses another version of this process of allegorical rarification: poetic conceits in which abstractions are made "even less concrete" as they unfold. "This sort of architectonics is not difficult to understand," says Baum, "but its appeal is to a rather limited and highly cultivated taste, for it verges on the artificial" (*House of Life*, 84). "Verging on the artificial," the prevalence in Rossetti's poetry of allegoricizing figures, such as personifications, repetitions, and chiasms, as well as the tableaux-like flatness of so many of the scenes, makes it difficult for *The House of Life* to fulfill its narrative expectations as a sonnet sequence, especially those symbolic-organic expectations of wholeness and completeness.[37] If we are asked to understand the sequence as offering a "dramatic personae of the soul" and if the two parts of the work seem organized by a progressive temporalization, the experience of reading is one of arrested development rather than organic unfolding. The trajectory of the sonnets is perpetually open to the sudden suspension and spatial dislocation of narrative movement.

If the "really imaginative vividness" of Rossetti's personification of love was the rhetorical feature Pater found most striking (and that Browning most detested), and if the loops of repetition demonstrate Rossetti's allegorizing impulse, the chiasmus is not only one of the most obvious tropes in Rossetti's poetry, but the figure that best accounts for the thematic and formal dimensions of Rossetti's project. It is, moreover, through the twists and turns of his chiasms that we can best experience the most adventurous force and effects of Rossetti's aestheticism, which is to say his superficiality. Indeed, nothing better characterizes Rossetti's sonnets than the way in which his most prominent figures avail themselves to chiasmic involutions. In "Love's Lover's," for instance, the allegorizing repetitions of love are spun into an elaborate chiasmus: "My lady only loves the heart of Love:/Therefore Love's heart, my lady, hath for thee . . ." (ll.9–10). If we understand the figure of chiasmus in its most capacious form as "a placing crosswise" that produces the spatial image of the *x*, then the insistence of this fundamentally pictorial figure offers us the best way to understand the relationships between painting and poetry in Rossetti.[38] Indeed, the relationships between poetry and painting in Rossetti's sonnets exhibit the same cross-hatched structure as the chiasmus: poetry is to painting as painting is to poetry. If we cannot necessarily look to chiasms to *explain* the criss-crossing of Rossetti's career as poet and painter, there certainly seems to be no better figure to *describe* it. Even when Rossetti declares in 1870 that he is "a poet primarily" and that it is his "poetic tendencies that chiefly give value" to his pictures, he is postulating a permeability between these two media and the importability of one principle to the other. The very best critics of Rossetti's work, from Pater to McGann and Stein, have always emphasized what Stein calls the collusions between "painting and poetic form." When Pater describes Rossetti's poetic style, he does so not only in terms of drawing, but in terms of the tracing of a surface: "The control of a style which did but obediently shift and shape itself to the mental motion, as a well-trained hand can follow on the tracing paper the outline of an original drawing below it" (*Appreciations*, 206). Pater's description not only emphasizes the crossings between painting and poetry in Rossetti's work, but restores the almost technically superficial dimension of this relationship, figures that are always on the surface and the aesthetic forms that are devoted to that superficiality.

If the representation of love in Rossetti always lends itself to personification, it is ultimately the figure of the chiasmus by which the experience of love in its various narcissistic forms is represented: this is where and how the semblance gets addressed to Love and Love to the semblance. If nothing seems more reductive than to characterize the erotic relationship as a rhetorical figure, it is this particular figure that repeatedly gives form to the irreducible superficiality of the love relationship, insofar as it insists upon the irreducibility of narcissism from the erotic relationship. Indeed, the mirrorings that appear in Rossetti's poetry and painting thematize this rhetorical condition, as in the mutual encounter of the doubles placed crosswise in *How They Saw Themselves.*

As Rossetti's poems reflect upon the kinds of aesthetic experience they long to produce, they are inevitably drawn to the chiasmus that becomes the figure of ekphrasis, the crossing from the pictorial into the literary and the inversions inherent to this crossing of media. This is what the sonnet "Transfigured Life" calls "Art's transfiguring essence" (l.12), the "transfigurations" that produce the experience of "sweet interchange" (l.4). This sonnet, the initiating poem of the second part of the sequence, traces the crossing of properties—"likenesses"—from their appearance in the child back to the features of the parents: "As growth of form or momentary glance/In a child's features will recall to mind/The father's with the mother's face combin'd,—/Sweet interchange that memories still enhance:" (ll.1–4). "And yet," as the poem develops this establishing analogy, the provenance of those origins is erased "as childhood's year and youth's advance": "The gradual mouldings leave one stamp behind,/Till in the blended likeness now we find/A separate man's or woman's countenance: . . ." (ll.5–8). The octave recounts the ways in which the cross-hatched production of the figure is erased by the "one stamp," a "blended likeness" that leaves us with one "countenance": the crossing of figures giving rise to a single face that cancels the history of its production. "Love's Testament" offers a particularly delirious example of the swirling effects of this chiasmic play, one in which the triangulated—and even quasi-trinitarian—relationship between lover, beloved, and Love is wound tighter and tighter until the speaker feels his beloved's "breath to be/The inmost incense of [Love's] sanctuary" (ll.4–5). At this point the distinctions among the three figures begin to dissolve, "blending" into a chiasmic identity: "intent/Upon his will, thy life with mine hast blent,/And murmured, 'I am thine, thou'rt one with me" (ll.7–8).[39] This is Rossetti's account of "Art's transfiguring essence," its ability to transform its double origins in the pathos of "Joy and Pain" into the surface of a song.

The nature of the chiasmic dimensions and effects of this aesthetic relationship become more acute in "The Monochord," that great and forbidding late sonnet that William Michael Rossetti called "the most obscure" "of all the sonnets in *House of Life.*" The sonnet is structured as a series of unanswered questions, prompted perhaps by the effect of the title figure. These questions point repeatedly at "it," at "this" in order to discern the nature of a force that asserts itself mortally and in the present upon the speaker:

Is it the sky's vast vault or ocean's sound
That is Life's self and draws my life from me,
And by instinct ineffable decree
Holds my breath quailing on the bitter bound?
Nay, is it Life or Death, thus thunder-crown'd,
That 'mid the tide of all emergency
Now notes my separate wave, and to what sea
Its difficult eddies labour in the ground?

Oh! what is this that knows the road I came,
The flame turned cloud, the cloud returned to flame,
The lifted shifted steeps and all the way? -
That draws round me at last this wind-warm space,
And in regenerate rapture turns my face
Upon the devious coverts of dismay?

Baum, in his notes to the sonnets, calls this "a prime example of poetry striving towards the condition of music—and almost ceasing to be intelligible" (*House of Life*, 187–88). If this is true, then the sonnet is "striving towards" its originating state, for, as Baum also notes, "the sonnet was inspired by Rossetti's listening to a certain piece of music; it is therefore the monument to a musical moment" (*House of Life*, 188). Thus does the poem itself become its own chiasmic site, the crossing point between something issued from and returning to music: music turned poetry, poetry returned to music. If the sonnet seems to be abandoning the demands of intelligibility as it crosses the horizon of musical abstraction, it is also the occasion for the convergence of these two art forms. As Stein puts it, "what is clear is the relation of the very complexity of the poetry to the pressure of a second art" forceful enough to cross into the first (*Ritual*, 201). This is a conclusion that seems inescapable, for even if we take the sonnet's opening question, and indeed each subsequent question, to be addressing not the effects of some unspecified piece of music, but the experience of hearing "the monochord," the power of this experience is such that it effaces its origin.

In the earlier version of the sonnet published in *Poems 1870*, the musical inspiration is made explicit. Not only is the title accompanied by the parenthetical subtitle, "Written during Music," but this version of the sonnet opens by asking whether it is "the moved air or the moving sound / That is Life's self." When Rossetti includes "The Monochord" in *The House of Life*, he replaces the technical questions of sound with the iconic figures of the sublime—"this sky's vast vault or ocean's sound"—and thus insists on its aesthetic dimension. This might appear to confirm Stein's interpretation of the sequence that Rossetti's late "poetry is less immersed in compelling human situations than in the first sonnets" and "as the increased use of allegory suggests, he tends to view life at a distance, as the subject of abstract speculation" (*Ritual*, 202). But this implies that allegory is by definition removed from "compelling human situations," that the aesthetic is necessarily experienced at a "distance." It is an ethical imperative that prompts this conclusion, but such an assessment fails to account for the tone and tense of "The Monochord"—urgent, immediate—or for the deeply *immersive* experience it presents for speaker and reader, both of whom are likely to feel themselves "'mid the tide of all emergency," caught *now* in its "difficult eddies" and "drawn" into "regenerate rapture" (ll.6, 7, 13).

The sonnet regards the aesthetic experience to which it alludes to be deeply "compelling," indeed, a question of "Life or Death." Whatever the insistent "it" pointed at by the poem may be, it is experienced as "Life's self," which, in an obvious painter's pun, "draws my life from me." For McGann the pun on *draw* is invoked by Rossetti "at signal moments in his writing to create an even more potent iconic urgency in his texts" (*DGR and the Game*, 80). Indeed, the appearance of *draw* in the sonnets is often and all at once, iconic, erotic, aesthetic: "thine eyes," concludes Rossetti in "Love's Testament," "Draw up my prisoned spirit to thy soul" (ll.13–14). If the pun on *draw*, like the pun on *mark* that also reappears in the sonnets, aestheticizes this experience, it also makes it an entirely urgent, if unanswered question. And if the sonnet offers no answer to this or to any of the questions that constitute it, in each case the "this" or "it" to which the speaker points is something that is prior and it is something that "knows," although the knowledge it possesses is structured as a chiasmus: "Oh! what is this that knows the road I came, / The flame turned cloud, the cloud returned to flame, / The lifted shifted steeps and all the way?" (ll.9–11). In the moment of an aesthetic experience, "knowledge" is not the possession of the subject, but quite the reverse: it is as if the "this" to which the poem refers possesses the knowledge that has been evacuated from the speaker and that makes all these questions both necessary and unanswerable. What is *this*? asks "The Monochord," "That draws round me at last this wind-warm space, / And in regenerate rapture turns my face / Upon the devious coverts of dismay" (ll.12–14).

In this remarkable moment the speaker is not "turned" away but, in "regenerate rapture," turned "*upon*" the "devious coverts of dismay." If we are not given access to the surface forms taken by the "devious coverts," we see a speaker who is "turned upon" them. What "The Monochord" gives us is the poetic experience of aestheticism, not one referred or alluded to, but offered entirely on its surface in the presentation of its questions. The aesthetic object, which reduces the speaker at that moment to sheer deixis, to pointing at *this* or *it*, leaves him and us with the semblances of knowledge that pivot around the figure of the chiasmus. Indeed, the properties of that object vanish in the time of the question posed by this experience. In Rossetti radical aestheticism is this pervasive condition of superficializing, forcing everything to the surface, where, as in "The Monochord," it becomes susceptible to the crossings of the visible and the blending of the voices.

Thus a radical aestheticism in Rossetti is not so much an event, a singular and crisis-ridden occurrence, as it is the manifest pressure of the surface—the semblance, the glass, the sheet, the image, the mark, the face—upon everything that is painted or written. Its radicality, in other words, is the insistence of its superficiality. But if a radically superficial aestheticism is present in Rossetti as a kind of currency of forces, it remains for us to consider the effects of this radical aestheticism for the most insistent "Life or Death" topic in this poet-painter's work: the representation of love. I opened this chapter with Rossetti's fragmentary superscription "to Art"; and I want to close the chapter with "A Superscription," one of the final daunting sonnets of *The House of Life* and perhaps the best place to assess the fate of love in the face of a radical aestheticism. There is nothing slight in topic or tone about a sonnet McGann calls "one of the most astonishing poetical works in our language" (*DGR and the Game*, 137), a description that is apt for the poem's capacity to provoke wonder and amazement as well for the archaic meanings of astonish as that which stuns, paralyzes, or stupefies (*OED*). The sonnet begins with a series of ponderous compound names for what William Michael Rossetti called "the Sense of Loss." But if few of Rossetti's poems could seem less superficial than "A Superscription," it is also a poem drawn from the conceit of a surface: a "superscription" is, among other things, an inscription on or above a surface, here the "face" of a glass into which we are summoned to "look."

> Look in my face; my name is Might-have-been;
> I am also called No-more, Too-late, Farewell;
> Unto thine ear I hold the dead-sea shell
> Cast up thy Life's foam-fretted feet between;
> Unto thine eyes the glass where that is seen
> Which had Life's form and Love's, but by my spell

Is now a shaken shadow intolerable,
Of ultimate things unuttered the frail screen.

Mark me, how still I am! But should there dart
  One moment through my soul the soft surprise
  Of that winged Peace which lulls the breath of sighs,—
Then shalt thou see me smile, and turn apart
Thy visage to mine ambush at thy heart
  Sleepless with cold commemorative eyes.

William Michael Rossetti's summary attempts to look past the surface and recover the sonnet's deeper subject, "chiefly, the sense of loss in the death of one supremely beloved." He then broadens the poem's ostensible topic to include "the sense of loss in any lost opportunity, any duty irrecoverably neglected, and the like," which "reassert[s] itself with direful force at moments when the soul feels beguiled into happiness or contentment" and which provokes "the ache of unforgiving memory" (*House of Life*, 216). In his own commentary, Baum notes the oblique gravity of "any duty irrecoverably neglected," one of "the many pregnant phrases scattered long the whole course of William Michael Rossetti's fraternal biographical notes and commentaries" (*House of Life*, 216). Baum is referring to Dante Rossetti's unrelenting self-reproach and sense of culpability in the death of Elizabeth Siddal; and one implication is that her death and the corpse it left behind are the "subject" that rests unquietly beneath the surface of this poem, another of Bronfen's case studies of poetry "superscribed" "over her dead body."

In this context it may well seem not only superficial, but unethical to insist on what the poem actually says, to keep looking at poetic surfaces that are, as William Michael Rossetti suggests, "worded with great condensation." If for many readers the sonnet cannot help but conjure the biographical depths of painful regret as well as the ethical dilemma that haunts Rossetti's aesthetics, the poem makes explicit demands that the reader "look" and "mark" its mirrored surface, delivering us back to the exquisite narcissism that is constitutive of Rossetti's aesthetics of love and death. The poem's sense of depth, in other words, its *gravitas* as well as its pathos, is the projected effect of its superficiality, much like the sublime illusion generated by the convergence of sea and sky in "The Lovers' Walk." Here, however, it is the proper name of non-convergence—as well as its aliases—that prompts us to supply the narrative: "Might-have-been" *aka* "No-more," "Too-late," "Farewell."

But to whom exactly is this particular superscription addressed? And precisely who or what is speaking? Are we to assume the speaker addresses himself? If the questions are as pressing and urgent for this poem as for any in the tradition we are considering, there is nothing inside the poem or out that answers them, particularly given the fact that Rossetti also understood a superscription to be the address of a letter or even its signature. Moreover, the tone of the poem's second-person address—imperative, exclamatory, accusatory—elicits the reader's guilty complicity much as Keats's "This Living Hand." The performative dimensions of both poems are constituted by disruptive gestures: Here it is, I hold it toward you, says this sonnet, "the glass where that is seen / Which had Life's form and Love's, but by my spell / Is now a shaken shadow intolerable." Perhaps what is *meant* by this is less important than what is *done* here, the confrontation with the reader of his or her own disfigurement brought on by the "spell" of the glass: the "reflection of the "form" of Life and Love "now a shaken shadow intolerable." If this is no "*frail spell*," it is a "frail screen" that does not utter the "ultimate things." Or, perhaps this is how we are seduced into paraphrase by the last line of the octave: "Of ultimate things unuttered the frail screen." The poem demands that we look at the unresolved relationship that marks all of Rossetti's work, the relationship between the depth of "ultimate things"—the "enthronement" or "enshrinement" of the "kindred Powers" of Love and Death—and the aesthetic experience of the "frail screen." If we are drawn by the line into restoring what we assume to be the elided preposition—to say "Of ultimate things unuttered *by* the frail screen"—the *by* remains the very thing "unuttered," and the lines themselves refuse the grammatical connection, leaving those "ultimate things" suspended at yet another surface, the literal superficiality of the "frail screen."

The sestet of "Superscription," which Baum calls "remarkably dramatic and powerful," opens by making another demand delivered with such forceful immediacy that it makes it difficult to remain superficial: "Mark me." Behold, you who "look in my face," "how still I am!" Readers of Lacan will find it difficult to resist the temptation to read the "superscription" of the title as the *anamorphosis* that he identifies as the very truth of distortion in Hans Holbein's *The Ambassadors*. Once we have entered into the critical relationships between vision and desire, once we have learned—as have Mulvey, Vickers, and Bronfen before us—the Lacanian lesson that *The Ambassadors* is "simply what any picture is, a trap for the gaze," it is difficult not to apply that lesson of the entrapping gaze to a sonnet that not only demands the gaze of the reader, but that refuses to tell the reader what it is he or she sees.[40] As Lacan writes of the strange smear or blur suspended in the foreground of Holbein's painting, "what is this object?":

> You cannot know—for you turn away, thus escaping the fascination of the picture.
>
> Begin by walking out of the room in which no doubt it has long held your attention. It is then, that turning round as you leave—as the author of the *Anamorphoses* describes it—you apprehend in this form . . . . What? A skull.
> (*Four Concepts*, 88)

To readers schooled in Lacanian psychoanalysis, the critical lesson we discern in Rossetti's sonnet on the looks of Love is that we must *not turn away* from the "glass where that is seen / Which had Life's form and Love's," but rather to "*look awry*." This is, of course, how Žižek describes Lacanian beholding, the perspective necessary to "mark" the open secret of death's inscription. And like Holbein's "magical floating object," the superscription is a *memento mori*: "It reflects our own nothingness," says Lacan, "in the figure of the death's head" (*Four Concepts*, 92). *That* is what we would see smiling at us precisely at the moment that our soul experiences "the soft surprise / Of that winged Peace which lulls the breath of sighs." *That* is the "ambush" of the "heart," one that makes us to "turn apart" our "visage," "sleepless with cold commemorative eyes."

The Lacanian route to Rossetti is the route to desire and its critique. But from the perspective of love, that route is a trap: it is close enough to what Rossetti offers us that we find ourselves drawn into the critical discourse of desire when the poems insist on the auratic aesthetics of love. Lacan himself always insisted that though the "structure of the gaze" "captures the subject" in "an obvious relation to desire," that "obvious relation" "*remains enigmatic*" (*Four Concepts*, 92, emphasis added). But it is precisely this insistence on the "*enigmatic*" aspect of an "obvious relation" that disappears from the established versions of cultural *critique* that have issued from Lacanian psychoanalysis. In this regard the work of critics such as Bronfen is both symptomatic and emblematic of an ethically motivated (and professionally institutionalized) critical impulse to "demystify" the "frail screen" of auratic love and to reveal and explain the deep structure of desire at work beneath it.

How difficult it is, then, as much in our context as in Rossetti's, to stay superficial, to maintain an "obsession with surfaces," to resist the critical discourses of desire, and to remain a Rossettian reader of love. But even a sonnet

as darkly haunting as "A Superscription" resists the temptations of depths—
"ultimate things"—that it invites. The same lines that hail the reader with a
deathly summons also place him or her in a funhouse of first- and second-
person pronouns: "Mark *me*, how still *I* am! But should there dart / One moment through *thy* soul the soft surprise / Of that winged Peace which lulls the
breath of sighs,— / Then shalt *thou* see *me* smile, and turn apart / *Thy* visage to
mine ambush at *thy* heart" (ll.9–13, emphases added). The "mirrored eyes in
eyes" of "The Lovers' Walk" have become the mirrored *thou*'s and *thy*'s of "A
Superscription." In this spinning mirror of subjective pronouns and parts—
"visage," "eyes," and "heart"—there is literally no place to "turn apart" *from*,
only *to*. This is perhaps the poem's most terrifying aspect: the final "ambush"
is not the utterance of "ultimate things," but an endless looking "sleepless
with cold commemorative eyes."

The critical discourse of desire and the auratic experience of love: "ultimate
things" and the "frail screen." If we are once again drawn near to another
chiasmic formulation, perhaps it is because love and desire are as inseparable
from the sonnet, perhaps, as love and death, or the two sides of a coin, one
that "reveals / The soul,—its converse, to what Power 'tis due." One of the
most difficult things about reckoning with the radicality of Rossetti's aestheticism is the irreducibly superficial aspect of this relation: "A sonnet," says the
sonnet to the sonneteer in the introduction to *The House of Life*, "is a coin:
its face reveals." Mark its aspect, draw its visage, trace its figures, "look in my
face," for what it reveals is in its surface. As the last sonnets of this remarkable
sequence demonstrate, those directives remain as much as a challenge to the
reader as to the sonneteer. They are the superficial demands Rossetti's radical
aestheticism places upon its writer and its readers: whether they worship Love
or Death, the sonnets are not critical, but "reverent" of their own "ardent fulness": "Look that it be, / Whether for lustral rite or dire portent, / Of its own
arduous fulness reverent" (ll.3–5). When Rossetti's sonnets accomplish this
with "words" that "make love the loveliest," our gift, as the introductory sonnet describes it, is "a flowering crest impearled and orient"; and our challenge
is its flipside, the "frail screen" upon which we gaze, sleepless, in "regenerate
rapture," with "eyes mirrored in eyes."

Rossetti, *The Beloved* (Tate, London / Art Resource, NY)

Moreau, *Salomé dansant* (*Salomé Dancing Before Herod*) (© RMN–Grand Palais / Art
Resource, NY)

SIX

"Rings, Pearls, and All": Wilde's Extravagance

> As for extravagance . . . the virtues of prudence and thrift were not in my own nature or in my own race.
>
> — DE PROFUNDIS

The Soul of Man Under Aestheticism

Oscar Wilde poses a new and singular challenge to my argument. In each of the previous chapters, the author's implicit or explicit project is something other than aesthetics as such. In the case of Keats, for instance, it is the poetry of a "humanized" ethical regard; for Dickinson the project is the event of poetry itself, figured as originary *poesis*. In each chapter I explored the ways in which writers in this strain of Romanticism produced a poetry of and about aesthetic experience as an integral part of the projects they undertake, a poetry that on occasion results in an aestheticism. And in each chapter I have attempted to demonstrate how the poetic solicitation of aesthetic experience and aestheticism results under the right conditions in a radicalization that not only undoes the poet's ethical or theological or political project, but poses a more fundamental problem for our understanding of the relationship between aesthetics and politics or ethics or theology. Moreover, to the extent that each of these projects was conceived either implicitly or explicitly in ethical or political or theological terms, the threat posed by an aestheticism, however radical, can be conceived as something *external, heteronomous.*

My final chapter proceeds from a different perspective, one that can be characterized most simply by the following question: can a radical aestheticism befall a project that already identifies itself as aestheticist in theory and undertakes that aestheticism in practice? In other words, can "art's undoing" extend to a project dedicated to art itself? My answer, perhaps predictably enough by this point, is "yes." Less predictable, I believe, are the forms and consequences of such a radicalization. To take up this question and its implications, I want first to revisit the structure as well as the content of Wilde's aestheticism.[1] More specifically, I want to examine Wilde's aestheticism from the point of view of *its point of view.* I begin by returning to "The English Renaissance of Art," the inaugural lecture of Oscar Wilde's 1882 North American tour. Wilde's account of this "vital" but subordinate and even subversive "romantic movement" establishes the historical contours of my book, one that locates the origins of radical aestheticism in the poetry of Shelley and Keats and reaches its culmination here, with what I call Wilde's extravagance. "Our romantic movement," Wilde tells his audience, is characterized by "the desire for a more gracious and comely way of life, its passion for beauty, new forms of art, new intellectual and imaginative enjoyments."[2] Of course, the aim of "The English Renaissance of Art" is not solely that of historical appreciation. What Wilde calls "*our* romantic movement" is not something of the past to be evaluated and appreciated, but, to those co-conspirators hailed by its objectives, an *imperative*: "Love art," he promises, "and all the things will be given to you" (268). That is the promise for the soul of man under aestheticism.

It has been a premise of this book that the aestheticism of "our romantic movement" appears in the form of espousals, exhortations, celebrations. And if it is a movement, "Hymn to Intellectual Beauty" and *Endymion* become, however retrospectively, its conversion story and its poetic manifesto. By the time we reach Oscar Wilde, aestheticism itself has become "a vital tendency," something that exists to be *professed*, to be taught, learned, cultivated, and—crucially—*lived.* This is both a rhetorical position and a pedagogical mission, and it is as inherent and indispensable to the practice of Wilde's aestheticism as its content. Aestheticism's "point of view," the vantage point of its "espousal," activates its tenets and beliefs; and it is the perspective of espousal that accounts for the effective flourishing of Wilde's aestheticism when it is presented on the theatrical stage or in the lecture hall. For the better part of a year Wilde traveled across North America promoting and defining aestheticism: "I have defined it about two hundred times," he said to an interviewer on only the second day of his tour, "but I am here to diffuse beauty."[3] Indeed, Wilde's aestheticism *is* this point of view, the vantage point from which he may "diffuse beauty"; and it is never difficult to identify that position in his poems, his criticism, his dialogues, his interviews, and even—with one decisive exception—his plays. Wilde often indicates explicitly this "point of view," as in these coupled maxims from the Preface to *The Picture of Dorian Gray*: "From the point of view of form, the type of the arts is the art of the musician. From the point of view of feeling, the actor's craft is the type" (3). Even as Wilde makes a sophisticated and compelling case for "the truth of masks" in the dialogue by that name, it is rarely difficult there or elsewhere in his work to determine *which* mask is true. Wilde's comedies may be virtuoso performances of the performativity of identity; and yet even in the most subtle and daring of the comedies, *The Importance of Being Earnest*, the authoritative vantage point is always discernible.

The perspective or vantage point not only *activates* Wilde's aestheticism, but makes it *critical*: the aestheticist maxim is deployed or the art-loving epigraph delivered from the point of view of the cultural critic, and not merely that of the specialized connoisseur. The aestheticist perspective accounts for the tone and tenor of the "dialogues" on art and culture; and it is this "point of view" that allows Wilde's presentation of "The Soul of Man Under Socialism" to avoid the spurious identification with the downtrodden, to resist the sentimentalism of Victorian charity, and even to reject "ethical sympathies" as "an unpardonable mannerism of style." I invoke Wilde's most explicitly political essay in order to stress the decisive role of the preposition *under*: "the soul of man" should be placed "under" the purview of aestheticism (which is not at odds with Wilde's version of socialism). In this game of over and under, aestheticism always assumes the superior or "elect" position: in *De Profundis*, Wilde describes Pater's *Studies in the History of the Renaissance*, the first full flowering of British aestheticism, as "that book which has had such a strange influence over my life" (1022). This is the nature of Wilde's project I hope to explore in this chapter: I want to examine Wilde's aestheticism from the point of view of the "strange" and extravagant influence of art—and aestheticism— *over* life, over everything.

From the vantage point of the lectern at Chickering Hall, Wilde made his aestheticist promise to the multitude gathered to hear him speak: "Love art and all the things will be given to you." This extravagant promise is itself the promise of extravagance, one that is not merely an allusion to, but uncanny invocation of Luke 12:31: "seek ye the Kingdom of God; and all these things shall be added to you." The verses identify "these things" as those that sustain the body: food, drink, and shelter. But Christ's imperative to the multitude gathered to hear him derives from the parable that warns against covetousness, the parable prompted by a question from the assembled crowd about the division of property. Christ responds by refusing to adjudicate and by rejecting the economic calculation entirely: "Man, who made me a judge or a divider over you? . . . Man's life consisteth not in the abundance of things which he possesseth" (12:14–15). Reject this worldly, restricted economy *and then* you will get it all. But what does this mean for Wilde? What is this "all," this "everything" promised for *this* world and not the one hereafter? The best account of it I know appears as a representation of its impossibility, a Paterian vision that Dorian Gray helps his narrator realize: it is the "wild longing" that can be touched only in "the unreal shadows of the night," one that departs from the "same wearisome round of stereotyped habits" and posits the utopian vision of a "world that had been refashioned" for "our pleasure."[4] For more than a century Wilde's readers have sought to give this phenomenon a name. I call it extravagance.

By celebrating and luxuriating in art as it invokes scripture—scripture as such and these verses in particular—Wilde's aestheticism announces itself as both the vehicle and the gift, an extravagance that promises more extravagance. It is this double sense of the term, both means and end, that is crucial to understanding what is at stake in Wilde's aestheticism. Rejecting ethical imperatives and appropriating religious proscriptions, Wilde posits art and beauty as the good and the sacred. And thus Wilde's aestheticism is by definition extravagant: "excess prodigality of wastefulness in expenditure," as well as that "quality of exceeding just or prescribed limits of decorum" (*OED*). There is an older meaning of extravagance, obsolete in general use, but operative, if latent, for Wilde: before it meant "profligacy in expenditure," extravagance was a wandering from the prescribed path and the "*position* or fact of *erring*" or deviation (*OED*). Strictly speaking, *extra-vagari* is this vagrancy, this deviation from the way. In its obsolete noun form an "extravagant" was the one who wandered, the vagrant, the foreigner, the one who failed or refused to keep within "ordinary or reasonable limits." It should take little persuasion to regard Wilde as an extravagant; and in this sense the extravagance of Wilde's aestheticism is as much constituted by his perspective—*extra-vagari*—as it is by its content. "The only thing that can console one for being poor is extravagance," he declares in "A Few Maxims for the Instruction of the Overeducated," a "consolation" predicated upon the vantage point of poverty.

The best way I know to understand an artistic extravagance that wanders from any "ordinary or reasonable limits," that "exceeds the bounds of moderation in expenditure," is Georges Bataille's notion of *dépense*, a "nonproductive expenditure" that has "no end beyond itself."[5] Wilde's aestheticism is indeed a form of "nonproductive expenditure," one that refuses the "principles of classical utility" (*Visions*, 118, 116) and from the perspective of bourgeois economics or "philistine" "meanness" appears as sheer profligacy, sumptuous decadent excess. Like Wilde's aestheticism, Bataille's expenditure needs its espouser. And in the end—the far end—Bataille's expenditure is as "redeemable" as Wilde's aestheticism. Give yourself, says Bataille, to a "poetic expenditure" that "ceases to be symbolic in its consequences" and you will gain genuine uselessness, "the insubordinate function of free expenditure" (*Visions*,120, 129). We might call it "the soul of man in excess," a world in which the principle of expenditure and the force of the sacred create a social structure no longer founded on capitalist production and bourgeois accumulation, but on the luxurious extravagance of art and play and excess.[6] Bataille illuminates the extravagance of Wilde's aestheticism; moreover, I would argue that the notion of expenditure—at least as it is developed in Bataille's critical writings in the late 1920s and 1930s—*is* an aestheticism of the same order of extravagance. This makes the relationship between Bataille and Wilde unique among the pairings I have explored in this book. If, for instance, Walter Benjamin's notion of the "aura" gives us a flexible critical term by which we might better understand the forms of aesthetic "spelling"—"frail" and otherwise—in Shelley's poetry, the "constellations" of his historical thinking not only establish a critical idiom for Shelley's poetics of historical "kindling," they suggest the "unacknowledged" affinities that connect the German critic and British poet. Roland Barthes's late criticism reveals his own aestheticist disposition; but it also illuminates the critical dimension of Keats's indolence and the ethics of his weakness. By contrast, the relationship between Wilde and Bataille is more continuous historically and conceptually. Bataille's idiom, his tone, and the objects of his study are certainly not to be found in Wilde's poems, plays, stories, or criticism; but Wilde's model of "the critic as artist" applies to Bataille and in the same manner that Wilde conceives it. The relationship between Bataille and Wilde, in other words, cannot be called *criti-*

cal. This derives not merely from the considerable overlap between Wilde's aestheticism and Bataille's "expenditure," but from their shared positional extravagance as "espousers" rather than critics.

In that New York lecture Wilde identifies "the poetry of Shelley and Keats" as "the most complete and perfect utterance" of the "two most vital tendencies of the nineteenth century," which, "to the blind eyes of their own time, seemed to be as wanderers in the wilderness, preachers of vague or unreal things" (*WCW* XIV, 259). "The blind eyes of their own time": their own Romantic *moment* lacked the "untimely" perspective necessary to recognize "the vital tendency" of Shelley and Keats. They are, in effect, *extravagants*, poets who made the place of poetic excess, "errancy" of thought, troubadorian vagrancy, and even exile the vantage point of their "utterance."[7] And though neither poet is known to have eaten locusts or wild honey, Wilde's account conjures Mark's description of John the Baptist, though in this nineteenth-century version, Wilde hears "the voices of *two* crying in the wilderness." Of course, John the Baptist probably never believed he was a "preacher of vague or unreal things"; that was simply what his preaching looked like from the perspective of the Roman or the Philistine. One wonders just how many times during that American tour Wilde might have been described, as he was in the *Chicago Inter-Ocean*, as "the John the Baptist of the religion of art" (*Oscar Wilde in America*, 57). Even in 1882, of course, this is a *marginal* position; and, risking anachronism, I contend that it constitutes the position of an aesthetic vanguard or *avant-garde*, a notion that is of course predicated both politically and artistically on its own anachronicity. From Wilde's historical vantage point, Shelley and Keats achieve their vitality as a result of the extravagance of a "preaching" that, though unacknowledged in their own moment, kindled a cultural movement comparable to the Renaissance that is realized as aestheticism. John the Baptist, Shelley the Democrat, Keats the Aesthete: these icons of extravagant wandering, "preachers of vague or unreal things," all converge historically or, as Benjamin would have it, are "reconstellated" in Wilde himself: he is the final *extravagant* in this subversive tradition.[8] Oscar Wilde, peddler of aestheticist extravagance, embarking this night on his own westward "wandering" in the wilderness of the northern Americas, "preaching the doctrine" of the "sacrament" of art (*WCW* XIV, 268), lecturing on the "vague and unreal" things of beauty, and equipped with nothing but an aesthetic point of view.[9]

Christ the Romantic, Christ the Dandy

When at Chickering Hall Wilde professes the poetry of Shelley and Keats to represent the "most vital tendencies of the nineteenth century," he identifies not only the Keatsian "tendency to value life for the sake of art," but also the "democratic and pantheistic tendency" that finds its "most complete and perfect utterance in the poetry of Shelley" (*WCW*, XIV, 265). While it is the former "tendency" we identify with Wilde's aestheticism, the Shelleyan strain is also discernible throughout Wilde's poetry and criticism. Moreover, the Shelley Wilde invokes in his poems is not the delicate Shelley of the late love lyrics to Jane Williams; it is, rather, the Shelley for whom poetry and politics are thoroughly interwoven, the Shelley, for instance, of "To Wordsworth," in which the elder poet's apostasy reveals the political stakes of poetry's commitment to and betrayal of democratic principles. It is by way of Shelley's example that Wilde lays claim to Milton's legacy. In "Quantum Mutata," Wilde declares that Milton's poetic "estate" would still be paying its cultural-political dividends were it not for the economic profligacy—a "luxury" of "barren merchandise"—that blocked its entrance: "How comes it then that from such high estate/We have thus fallen, save that Luxury/With barren merchandise piles the gate/Where noble thoughts and deeds should enter by:/Else might we still be Milton's inheritors."

On the face of it, nothing could seem further removed from the "high estate" of Milton the Puritan than the figure of Wilde's dandy, the aesthete whose own "luxury" is an art devoid of morality and for whom the preface to *The Picture of Dorian Gray* serves as an apostle's creed. What Wilde's Milton shares with Wilde's dandy—and indeed with Christ—is a vantage point, one that is critical and rhetorical *before* it is moral or ethical. Here and elsewhere in Wilde, the *function* of the "point of view" precedes its content. As a critical *position*, one that activates an aestheticism, it is a perspective that can be occupied by any number of figures: Henry Wotton, Algernon Moncrief, Vivian, Shelley, Christ. It is the position of the "elect" to whom, in yet another of those epigrams from the Preface to *Dorian*, "beautiful things mean only beauty." When it is the dandy who occupies this position, it is never one of moral or ethical superiority: "Dandyism," asserts Wilde in "A Few Maxims," "is the assertion of the absolute modernity of Beauty." The dandy is not what Paul Bowles might call "the complete outsider," but an extravagant, an errant excess that comes from within. The practice of the dandy is, of course, predicated on the careful manipulation and not complete disregard of the operative social codes. Wilde's dandy is always fully aware of the extent of his complicity and the nature of his contingency.

If the dandy is not the outsider, he might be the one who points us the way out. This is Michel Foucault's argument in "What is Enlightenment?," an essay that belongs to the "Bataille-mode" of Foucault's thought, its explorations of transgressions and limit-cases.[10] The essay takes its title and its point of departure from the answer to that question Kant published in 1784 in the periodical *Berlinische Monatschraft*. "A minor text," Foucault acknowledges. But "without giving it an exaggerated place in Kant's work," he nonetheless stresses "the connection that exists between this brief article and the three *Critiques*" (*Foucault Ethics*, 308). In this "minor text," Kant goes on to "describe Enlightenment as the moment when humanity is going to put its own reason to use, without subjecting itself to any authority," the moment when humanity begins to "be released from the status of immaturity" (*Foucault Ethics*, 308, 305). "Kant says that this Enlightenment has a *Wahlspruch*," says Foucault, "a heraldic device, that is, a distinctive feature by which one can be recognized, and . . . also a motto, an instruction that one gives oneself and proposes to others" (*Foucault Ethics*, 306). Kant's "heraldic device" may not be the little green flower worn in the button-hole of the lapel; but its identifying function is the same: it is a sign, a badge, and a promise.[11]

When, in the second half of his essay, Foucault turns from Kant to Baudelaire, he does so not to pose a challenge to Kant's *Aufklärung*, but to fulfill it, or, more precisely, to find and describe the theater of its realization. The Baudelaire that Foucault invokes is the Baudelaire of *The Painter of Modern Life*, the Baudelaire who "defines modernity as 'the ephemeral, the fleeting, the contingent,'" the Baudelaire who proposes and professes "a deliberate attitude" toward this modern condition: "*dandysme*" (*Foucault Ethics*, 310, 311). It is an "attitude" that requires a "discipline more despotic than the most terrible religions": this is the asceticism of aestheticism, realized at this historical moment in "the asceticism of the dandy who makes of his body, his behavior, his feelings and passions, his very existence, a work of art" (*Foucault Ethics*, 312). To this characterization of the Enlightenment Foucault adds— emphatically—"one final word": "this ironic heroization of the present, this transfiguring play of freedom with reality, this ascetic elaboration of the self—Baudelaire does not imagine that these have any place in society itself or in the body politic. They can only be produced in another, a different place, which Baudelaire calls art" (*Foucault Ethics*, 312). For Foucault, then, the only viable *Ausgang* that *Aufklärung* both produces and points out is that of aestheticism; and the Enlightenment is the "different place," the disposition, and even the *ethos* through which the subject learns "the transfiguring play of freedom with reality" and "dares to know" how to become an (art) object. Wilde's version is much more succinct: "one should either be a work of art, or wear a work of art," he declares in "Phrases and Philosophies for the Use of the Young."

We do not need to know how highly Wilde valued Baudelaire's poetry to recognize the relevance of Foucault's argument for Wilde's own version of *dandysme*. "I treated art as the supreme reality," Wilde writes in *De Profundis*, "and life as a mere mode of fiction" (1017). This is Wilde's summation of his own version of the "transfiguring play of freedom with reality," that daring practice of theatrical performativity that offers as its own "way out" the subject's "very existence" as "a work of art." This reaches its apotheosis in *The Picture of Dorian Gray*, not merely because the novel depicts this vision of the subject's "transfiguration" into "a work of art." The novel's representation of the transfer of physical and affective features from Dorian the man to Dorian the picture is a narrative "literalization" of the more subtle transfiguration in Dorian, which takes place early in the novel once he is exposed not only to his portrait, but to the extravagance of Lord Henry Wotton's perspective.[12] As agents or apostles of "transfiguration," Wilde's dandies do not get us "out" any more than Baudelaire's do. But if they point us toward the *Ausgang*, it is by way of an aestheticism *as* vantage point. And the epigram, as it is deployed in Wilde's critical dialogues, lectures, prefaces, and plays, is his aestheticism's most effective tool.

For Foucault, Kant's "Enlightenment" is predicated on the "audacity to know"—Wilde calls it "intellectual daring" (1017)—a critical "attitude" that one adopts and practices (*Foucault Ethics*, 309).[13] Foucault is keen to distinguish this Kantian account of *Aufklärung* from humanism and to undermine our received ideas of the Enlightenment as "general truths" that achieve universal assent. Wilde's adoption of the epigram involves the same rhetorical maneuver and produces the same effect. Wilde remains true to convention in his crafting of epigrams as propositions that, in aphoristic form, express "general truths." The didactic function of "Phrases and Philosophies for the Use of the Young," for instance, is explicit. And yet the truths that Wilde deploys are characteristically reversals of those received truths, and even of the prescriptive mode itself. In this sense, the epigram as Wilde composes and delivers it is constituted on an antithetical gesture. For an epigram or a maxim to "work"—for such a speech act to be received as such—assent or acceptance of its authority is required. Wilde's epigrams uniformly dismiss such general acceptance even as they appropriate the epigram's "positional" and rhetorical authority, as in "A Few Maxims for the Instruction of the Over-Educated." In the preface to *The Picture of Dorian Gray*, for instance, Wilde pronounces "an ethical sympathy"—that which can be understood as the foundation of a Victorian universalist aesthetics and that might be expected to elicit assent—to be nothing more than "an unpardonable mannerism of style" "in an artist."

Given the significance of the "vantage point" for Wilde's aestheticism—an aestheticism that functions by the authority of its declarations and the force of its espousals—one might predict that the collapse of this vantage point would result in the demise of Wilde's aestheticism. How can an aestheticism survive when the perspective on which it is predicated no longer exists? Can there be an aestheticism *behind bars*, subjected to "hard labor"? The extraordinary document we know as *De Profundis* (but that Wilde titled "In Carcere et Vinculis") demonstrates that the profound crisis of Wilde's life does not signal the end of his aestheticism. *De Profundis* demonstrates that, while the immediate worldly effectivity of his aestheticism may have been temporarily curtailed, Wilde reclaims the vantage point "underneath," the singular perspective of the depths. This reclamation of the vantage point is, therefore, constituted on a strict reversal of positions that leaves its authority, its perspective intact.

But while *De Profundis* is a document of heights and depths, it does not announce its reversal of positions and their relative values up front. Instead, Wilde begins his epistle by claiming the high ground of the victim. In the tone of Wilde's address to Bosie, in his posture and his position, Wilde never relinquishes his superiority, one that is ethical and intellectual as well as aesthetic.[14] Indeed, throughout much of the letter, Wilde locates the source of all extravagance and excess in "the froth and frivolity" of Bosie's proclivities. "I was often bored to death by it," he recounts, "and accepted it as I accepted your passion for going to music-halls, or your mania for absurd extravagances in eating and drinking" (987). This was but one manifestation of the generalized profligacy and excess that he identifies with Bosie, who, unlike Wilde, could never have appreciated "the ideal" of "*plain living and high thinking*": Bosie's "insistence on a life of reckless profusion" is the source of Wilde's own "entire ethical degradation," an "extravagance" that "was a disgrace" to them both (983, 984). Wilde acknowledges that he allowed himself "to be lured into long spells of senseless and sensual ease," but these were the results of a susceptibility to Bosie's seductions that brought him low: "tired of being on the heights I deliberately went to the depths in the search for new sensations" (1018). The language is not merely that of a moral and ethical fall, but one born of the profound loss of the singular and authoritative vantage point of "a man who stood in symbolic relations to the art and culture" of his age: "few men," he declares, "hold such a position in their own lifetime and have it so acknowledged" (1017). Having "lain in prison for nearly two years" and "passed through every possible mood of suffering," Wilde finds himself dispossessed of it all, reduced to a man "down in to the dust" (1017, 1018).[15]

From the prison point of view, it is not merely the case that Bosie's own excesses laid waste to Wilde's life and brought him down. Bosie's lack of ethical principles or moral scruples played on Wilde's own "weakness" for excess and displayed an "inexhaustible greed" that sought to consume Wilde's "entire existence" (985). The ultimate effect is not merely the shame of public humiliation and the degradation of imprisonment and poverty, but the sense having been consumed by extravagances, not only Bosie's unrestrained excesses of behavior, but the extravagance of Wilde's surrender to those same behaviors. This compounding of excess and degradation sounds like one of Bataille's many examples of the experience of "nonproductive expenditure," the dimension of human activity that cannot be accommodated to the bourgeois principles of classical utility. From the perspective of the restricted rational economy, the circulatory loop of "production" and "consumption," nonproductive expenditure appears as exorbitant and "pathological" (*Visions*, 116–17). Indeed, within the terms of a dominant bourgeois economy, "pleasure, whether art, permissible debauchery, or play, is definitively reduced . . . to a concession, . . . to a divergence whose role is subsidiary" (117).

Bataille's project in "The Notion of Expenditure" is not only to theorize and describe, but to promote and espouse this "useless" excess he calls nonproductive expenditure. Bataille "reserves the use of the word *expenditure* for the designation of . . . unproductive forms, . . . activities which, at least in primitive circumstances have no end beyond themselves" (118); and one legitimate way to approach the range of Bataille's creative as well as critical undertakings—the theories, the "anthropologies," the histories, the pornography—is to understand them all as exemplifications or enumerations of expenditure. In the 1933 essay Bataille "illustrates" the principle of "unconditional expenditure" through "a small number of examples taken from common experience:" "beautiful and dazzling" jewels that, though functionally useless, are like "cursed matter that flows from a wound," the "bloody wasting of men and animals in *sacrifice*," extravagant wagers, and "artistic productions" (119). Bataille initially distinguishes music, dance, and "architectural construction," which he calls "*real* expenditures," from that of "*symbolic* expenditure"—namely, literature and theater. But while poetry may belong to this "secondary" symbolic category, Bataille asserts "that the term poetry . . . can be considered synonymous with expenditure; it in fact signifies, in the most precise way, creation by means of loss. Its meaning is therefore close to that of *sacrifice*" (120). In other words, while poetry may appear merely to *represent* expenditure in, for example, the amatory discourse engendered by the tradition of the sonnet, Bataille claims the *term* poetry (and *not* the vast majority of its examples) as another name for expenditure, the creation of extravagant things by means of loss. Moreover, in rare and special cases, poetry is such a losing game that it passes into the category of "real expenditure"; and at that moment, it is the poet who loses himself in the act: for the "rare human beings who have this element at their disposal, poetic expenditure ceases to be symbolic in its consequences," and at this moment "the function of representation engages the very life of one who assumes it" (120). Nothing "positive" is achieved in this "engagement": when poetry "ceases to be symbolic," when poetic expenditure touches life, it reaches back to the *poet*, and its effects are wholly consuming and altogether undoing. Genuine poetic expenditure "condemns" the poet "to the most disappointing forms of activity, to misery, to despair, to the pursuit of inconsistent shadows that provide nothing but vertigo or rage" (120). I can think of no better way to understand the sacrificial logic and affective register at work in *De Profundis*, this autobiographical account of a poet, "a man who stood in symbolic relations to the art and culture" of his age and is reduced to using "words only for his own loss," "profoundly separated from society as dejecta are from apparent life" (120).

If the Wilde of *De Profundis* can declare that "neither Religion, Morality, nor Reason can help" him at all, the love with which he reads the life of Christ should demonstrate that, while the discourse of the aesthetic arises alongside the historical process of secularization, aestheticism is not (yet) secular. Or, more precisely, it is secular in one of the oldest definitions of the term: the member of the religious order who is marked as departing for the world or, in other words, on his "way out." When Wilde declares "Religion does not help," he also paints an image of

> an order for those who cannot believe: the Confraternity of the Fatherless one
> might call it, where on an altar, on which no taper burned, a priest, in which heart
> peace had no dwelling, might celebrate with unblessed bread and a chalice empty

of wine. . . . Agnosticism should have its ritual no less than faith. It has sown its martyrs, it should reap its saints, and praise God daily for having hidden Himself from man. (1019–20)

If this is not a religious order, it is indeed a sacred one. In every manifestation of his aestheticism, Wilde regards the sacred as the poetic production of beautiful things. By the time of *De Profundis* this sacred poetic act comes to be understood as only Bataille can explain it, as fully *sacrificial*. However much it is Wilde's project throughout his career to *consecrate* art, in *De Profundis* consecration becomes that which—as Bataille puts it in his essay on "The Sacred"—"*consumes* and *destroys* the one it *consecrates*" (*Visions*, 245). Suffering is the affective dimension of this logic; and suffering is both the vantage point of *De Profundis* and what links the privileged position of Wilde's dandy to his notion of Christ. When Wilde revisits his own earlier work, rereading passages from *The Soul of Man* or "The Critic as Artist," he comes to recognize explicitly that suffering—"the Sorrow that abideth for Ever"—is "the ultimate realization of the artistic life" (1027). It is there that Wilde comes to see the "intimate and immediate connection between the life of Christ and the true life of the artist" (1028). Certainly one point at which Bataille's work crosses with Wilde's is the point at which Christ's passion and its celebration constitute a sacred aestheticism, a "privileged instant" prior to Christ's ascension to heaven and the restoration of the social order (*Visions*, 241). It is a site of art's fragile, fugitive appearance.

In one of the most compelling sections of *De Profundis*, Wilde declares that "Christ's place indeed is with the poets"; and anyone familiar with "our romantic movement" is likely to be reminded of Keats's own prediction: "I think I shall be among the English poets after my death." It is not merely the pathos of sacrifice that produces this resonance. If "Shelley and Sophocles" are of Christ's "company," the Keatsian oxymoron is the Romantic trope by which Wilde reads "the whole life of Christ," one in which "Sorrow and Beauty [are] made one in their meaning and manifestation" (1029). Wilde remarks that, should he ever write again after his release from prison, one of only two subjects he wants to write about is "Christ, as the precursor of the Romantic movement in life." The remarkable pages in *De Profundis* devoted to Christ—as a discourse on art and not faith—constitute a draft of this project. Wilde is explicit about the distinction between Christ as artist and Christianity as moral imperative, recalling a conversation with Gide "in some Paris café" in which he claimed that, though "Metaphysics had but little interest for me, and Morality absolutely none," "there was nothing that either Plato or Christ had said that could not be transferred immediately into the sphere of Art, and there find its complete fulfillment" (1027).[16] To revisit, for instance, Wilde's scriptural allusion to Luke 12:31, when Christ says "seek ye the Kingdom of God; and all these things shall be added to you," Wilde understands this directive not as a moral order, but an *ethos*, one that finds its "complete fulfillment" in his aestheticist creed: "Love art and all the things will be given to you."

Christ is, according to Wilde, "the true precursor of the romantic movement in life" because the "very basis of his nature was the same as that of the nature of the artist, an intense and flamelike imagination" (1027). Throughout this section of *De Profundis*, the "meaning and manifestation" of Christ is as indelibly a feature of romantic aesthetics as Shelley's notion of poetry in the *Defence*: "Christ's own renaissance" "produced the Cathedral of Chartres, the Arthurian cycle of legends, the life of St. Francis of Assisi, the art of Giotto, and Dante's *Divine Comedy*," but was "interrupted and spoiled by the dreary classical Renaissance" epitomized by Petrarch, Raphael, Pope (1032). "But," says Wilde in his most Shelleyan voice, "wherever there is a romantic movement in Art, there somehow, and under some form, is Christ, or the soul of Christ" (1032). At the same time, Wilde understands Christ's "poetical" teaching as an aestheticism of its own, indeed, the very origins of the aesthetic movement. As Wilde reads it, those whom Christ "saved from their sins are saved simply for beautiful moments in their lives" and "all that Christ says to us by way of a little warning is that *every* moment should be beautiful" (1036). Indeed, in Wilde's scriptural exegesis, beauty extends to sin itself, though in a "manner not yet understood." This is, Wilde says, not only Christ's "creed," but one of his most "dangerous ideas": "he regarded sin and suffering as being in themselves beautiful, holy things, and modes of perfection" (1037). The beauty of sin cannot be understood in the moral order and must call upon art to find its realization, its "mode of perfection." This, then, is *Christ's* extravagance, himself a wandering "extravagant" whose teachings, always exceeding the prescribed limits of decorum, are "fulfilled" by the extravagance of aestheticism. "Indeed," says Wilde, "when all is said," "the charm about Christ" is that "he is just like a work of art himself. He does not really teach anything, but by being brought into his presence one becomes something" (1037).

Whether we regard Wilde's account of "Christ the Romantic" as an accommodation extorted under duress, both physical and psychological, or as an understanding reached through the crucible of sorrow and suffering, what

Wilde gives us is an extravagant reading, one that remains both "dangerous" and "beautiful"—which is to say "aestheticist." One might have anticipated that for the aesthete who predicated his critical and artistic career on the maxim that life is in the service of art, a radical crisis would come in the form of the maxim's violent reversal, life's ugly and brutal intrusion. But if *De Profundis* chronicles in painful detail the profound crisis life posed for Wilde, it did not produce a crisis for his aestheticism. Indeed, one can read *De Profundis* as aestheticism's final flowering, its "fulfillment." The extravagance of Wilde's letter is still the extravagance of the vantage point, the singular point of view that, whether from above or below, authorizes and enables the perspective of the work of art. It is not the crisis of life addressed in and by this letter that radicalizes Wilde's aestheticism. The crisis of aesthetic radicalization in Wilde had already taken place, not with the violence of an ugly worldly intrusion, but by the simultaneously immersive and dispersive power of his most extravagantly aestheticized work, that "beautiful coloured, musical thing" called *Salomé* (1042).

The Cost of a Kiss

When at Chickering Hall in January 1882 in New York Wilde looks back on "The English Renaissance of Art," he makes the (perhaps extravagant) claim that "our romantic movement"—the trajectory that runs from Shelley and Keats to Wilde—matches that earlier English Renaissance in every genre but one: tragedy. It would take Wilde almost another decade to turn his own attention to the tragedy of Salomé; and to the end it remained the completed work that mattered most to him. It was here that Wilde claimed to take "the drama, the most objective form known to art, and [make] it as personal a mode of expression as the lyric or the sonnet" (1017).[17] This is indeed a "daring" achievement, a "lyricization" of the tragic mode of drama that derives from the lyric's origins in a personal perspective, a distinctive and subjective vantage point.[18] Here as elsewhere I take lyricization to be yet another name for aestheticizing, one linked to the personal perspective that is the animating position of Wilde's aestheticism.[19] But inherent in this lyrical and personal vantage point—in fact its mechanism—is the infinite transferability and thus the impersonality of the personal pronoun. That antinomy, which finds its most precise twentieth-century formulation in Benveniste, always hovers about Wilde's texts—in the form of the animating nominalism, for instance, of *The Importance of Being Earnest*—and manifests itself most extravagantly in the sacred performance of Salomé's kiss. It is a kiss that activates the full range of meanings of this capacious word "extravagance" and radicalizes its effects and implications for Wilde's aestheticism.

The route to the extravagance of that kiss passes through a luxurious language, through each of the senses and perhaps first and foremost through what Jokanaan calls "the lust of the eyes." The lustful eyes in question belong to the princess Salomé, but the lustful eyes of the desiring gaze are to be found everywhere in this play. And certainly, if we are seeking the play's vantage point or perspective, it will be established by way of the look or the gaze. Indeed, represented or reported acts of gazing are so prevalent in the play— and the gaze so thoroughly thematized and theatricalized—that *Salomé* can be read as a play devoted to the production and nature of the gaze as well as its effects and consequences. The primary dramatic action of this one-act tragedy revolves around Herod's obsessive gaze at his stepdaughter Salomé: Herod's wayward obsession leads him to promise Salomé anything "up to half of his kingdom." The play lurches from death to dance to death, its actions interpolated by long discourses on the powers and dangers of the gaze. Every event in the play—whether it is the suicide of the young Syrian captain or the dance of the seven veils or merely an offhand comment about the moon— seems to be elicited as the effect of looking and gazing. In *Salomé*, looking is doing; and looking acquires the full status of dramatic action.

The play's obsession with the gaze is announced in its opening lines. The young Syrian captain, Narraboth, gazes at the off-stage Salomé and remarks on her beauty while Herodias's Page, standing next to the captain, gazes at the moon and comments on its strange "air": "Look at the moon. How strange the moon seems! She is like a woman rising from the tomb. She is like a dead woman. One might fancy she was looking for dead things" (583). The passage presents the spectator with a form of double vision that it will continue to feature throughout: two acts of looking occurring simultaneously and that enter variously into symbolic or metaphorical or metonymic relations. Here the Page's remarks prompt Narraboth to face and comment on the moon, as well, and to confirm and extend the Page's description: "She has a strange look. She is like a little princess who wears a yellow veil, and whose feet are of silver. She is like a princess who has little white doves for feet. You would fancy she was dancing" (583). But it is not entirely clear from the text who the "she" is: without a stage direction, we cannot know that the young Syrian has turned his attention away from Salomé and toward the moon, since what he says might be applied to Salomé, as well. But however the director points his actor—toward the moon or the princess—the effect is a form of stereo-optics or "wall-eyed" looking that may or may not refocus on the same object. The similes that register and describe this looking are themselves instances of multiple likenesses that contribute to the layered diffusion.

I argued in the preceding chapter that Dante Rossetti's project was, against appearances and received critical opinion, a discourse of love and not desire. *Salomé*, on the other hand, is saturated with a desiring that from the start is severed from love: "the lust of the eyes" rather than "lovesight." And on the face of it, *Salomé* is a play for which the strain of feminist critical discourse we have come to associate with Laura Mulvey's project would have genuine analytical and explanatory value. The opening scenes introduce a visual dynamic that reaches its culmination in Salomé's "Dance of the Seven Veils": an inherently voyeuristic relationship in which the woman is positioned as the passive object of the male subject's active and objectifying gaze. Without rehearsing in detail the psychoanalytic principles and feminist tenets that inform this interpretation, it is important to note how the structure of the gaze is understood by the proponents of feminist film theory to define and delimit the domain of visual culture as such: the double role of woman as "lack" and as the threat of castration is constitutive of the visual field. According to this critical paradigm, patriarchal structures respond to this inherent threat to the stability and consistency of the visual field by assigning a subjectivity to femininity that is "inevitably bound up with the structure of the look and the localization of the eye as authority."[20] As a result, woman's "self-image" is always a "function of her being for another," a consequence of her position as object to the male gaze. As Joan Copjec argues in her account of this scopic relationship, the very structure of the gaze "guarantees that even [woman's] innermost desire will always be not a transgression but rather an implantation of the law."[21]

Salomé invites such an interpretation; and it is tempting to read the play and the biblical passage on which it is based as an allegory of the foundational story of the male gaze. The princess is explicitly positioned as the object of Herod's voyeuristic desires, and his wish to have her dance for him—as well as her decision to perform the dance—confirm her status as nothing other than an object to be looked at. It is, therefore, no coincidence that when Rosalind Krauss describes the masquerade of femininity in the photographs of Cindy Sherman, she does so in terms that not only invoke a pivotal aspect of Lacanian psychoanalysis, but that could equally serve as program notes for a production of *Salomé*: "The dance of her 'to-be-looked-at-ness' is a veil covering this nothing, which Lacan . . . designates as 'not-all' [pas-tout]."[22] Krauss's remarks not only describe the situation of Salomé within the play's visual field in general, but the nature of the "dance of the seven veils" in particular. The subsequent course of the play could confirm this reading, for when the Princess makes the effort to move from the object of voyeuristic gazes to an active desiring subject fully in possession of her own "lustful" looking upon the prophet Jokanaan, the effort is regarded as an intolerable transgression. In the course of her move from the passive object of desire to the acquisition of a desiring agency, Salomé extracts from Herod the most conventional displace-ment for castration—namely, the decapitation of Jokanaan. The psychoana-lytic allegory would seem to be confirmed by the fact that, once decapitated, the head remains the fetishized object of Salomé's lavish desire. Once the na-ture of this desire is revealed—the "device bared"—the play fulfills the para-digm of male castration anxiety present in the scopophilic gaze by abruptly silencing—killing—the castrating female and thus implanting the law in the wake and at the site of her transgression.

I spell out the armature of this allegory of the gaze not to discredit it, but to stress one of its obvious features—namely, that it relies upon the *singular* perspective of the male gaze. This does not mean that the validity of feminist film theory's adaptation of the Lacanian model rests upon the presence of a single gazer: the structure of the gaze precedes and positions the spectator as well as his object and can thus accommodate multiple viewers who occupy this position. But the allegory of the gaze does not accommodate *Salomé*'s dis-persive visual network, its various and crossed spectatorship; and, as we shall see, it does not account for the way in which its sensual excess of sound and vision cannot be accommodated by the theatrical "rectangle." *Salomé*'s visual economy is better understood as massed and discordant *adventures* of the gaze. The play presents its viewers with a wandering field of crossed and crossing looks, splittings and accumulations of the gaze that both short-circuit and exceed the model presented and analyzed by film theory. I stress this in part because a primary concern of film theory has been the *meaning* of the gaze for the gendering of subjectivity and the patriarchal systems in which subjectiv-ity is inscribed. But neither the princess nor the play called Salomé lingers much on the meaning of the gaze. When, in an apparently incidental early passage, Salomé asks what Herod's gaze means, it is a question she answers in her next line: "It is strange that the husband of my mother looks at me like that. I know not what it means. In truth, yes, I know it" (586). "In truth, yes," Salomé and *Salomé* know perfectly well what the gaze means and know it from the beginning. By announcing up front the meaning of the gaze, the play abandons knowledge as its goal and thus effectively dismisses the hermeneutical or allegorical domains of meaning in the process of orienting itself and its audience toward its more pressing concerns with the performance and effects of the gaze.

Even the most cursory attention to *Salomé* reveals that the performances of the gaze in the play are not restricted to men looking at women. Men look at women with desire, but at other men, as well; and Salomé looks at Jokanaan with all the active desire of Herod's gaze. And then there is that orbiting extravagant called the moon that everyone looks at and that, however conventionally feminized, acquires an oscillating status of mirror and screen in the course of the play. It is this bit of stagework that reminds us that *Salomé* is not merely a thematics, but a theatrics of the gaze. This dimension of the play, another obvious if often overlooked feature, must be acknowledged both for the play's inclusion of the audience in the dynamics of looking and for the uncertainty regarding how all this looking is staged from one production to another, a feature made more uncertain given the paucity of Wilde's stage directions for *Salomé*. Directors have always had the textual opportunities and the theatrical resources either to restrict or accentuate an audience's discomforting implication in the play's economy of looking and desiring; but it is impossible to disguise entirely the fact that we watch characters who gaze and, more importantly, that we watch characters who watch the gazing. The result is not the triangulated relationship of the gaze, but an overloaded circuitry of looking: watching *Salomé*, we see, for instance, Herod gazing at Salomé, and we watch Herodias watching her husband's gaze upon her daughter. We see the young Syrian captain gazing at Salomé and we see Herodias's Page watching that gaze, while the Page himself looks longingly at the young captain. We see the princess Salomé gazing at Jokanaan; and we see both Herod and the young captain watching in vexation at her obsessive longings to look upon the "holyman." And we see just about everyone in the play look at the moon. As a result *Salomé* participates in the wild economy of the looking it produces and presents, a proliferation of gazing, watching, beholding that continues not only in spite of, but because of the many injunctions and warnings it issues about the dire consequences of gazing, watching, beholding.

There is, of course, an exception to this elaborate exchange of the gaze, an element that occupies the place of refusal within this disjointed economy. If Salomé sees Herod's gaze and "knows what it means," if she is aware that the gaze of the young captain is a desiring one, she is also aware that Jokanaan *refuses* his "to-be-looked-at-ness": "Who is this woman looking at me?" asks Jokanaan; "I will not have her look at me . . . with her golden eyes under her gilded eyelids" (589). Salomé sees that she is not looked at by the prophet; and it is his refusal to reciprocate her gaze, his refusal to occupy the place of the *desiring subject* that makes his (non-gazing) eyes appear "terrible" to her: "It is his eyes above all that are terrible." And she goes on to liken them to "black lakes," "black caverns," "black holes," because in refusing to look, the eyes give no light: like "black holes," the eyes of Jokanaan absorb all the light of seeing, sucking it into caverns of their orbs. If *Salomé* is the theatrical equivalent of a glittering planetarium, Jokanaan, ironically enough, is its candidate for dark matter, a refractory force, a black hole that warps the visual field, super-saturated with looking.

Thus it is not the simple accumulation of gazes and gazers that overloads and destabilizes the optical structure and visual field of the play. Nor is it simply the fact that the prophet refuses to look and resists being looked at. The destabilization of the visual field in *Salomé* results from the play's dramatic presentation and thematic representation of a feature of the gaze that, far from being a unilinear activity issued from a single perspective, is on this "mirrored stage" always subject to splitting and *multiplication* and dispersal, what Jeff Nunokawa describes as "this infinite universe of visual splendor."[23] It is not an accident that the play opens with an example of this fissure in the structure and perspective of the gaze. When the Page likens the moon to "a woman rising from the tombs," this line is juxtaposed with the young Syrian captain's observations that "she is like a little princess who wears a yellow veil, and whose feet are of silver," a juxtaposition that seems to imply an identification between the moon and Salomé. But, as we have seen, the ambiguity of the pronoun "she" persists and demands that the director intervene and decide whether to block the scene in such a way that the relationship between the moon and the princess is made either into a metaphor or a metonymy. What the scene announces is not only the thematic and dramatic significance of the moon, but the way in which the allegorical force of the identifications (moon = princess / dancing = death) comes about through a splitting of the gaze as it is staged before us. Indeed, Lacan's enigmatic remark that "the point of the gaze always participates in the ambiguity of the jewel" is confirmed and complicated in the play by the jeweled oscillation of the moon's status as mirror or screen or perhaps even point of view.[24]

Whether the "point of the gaze" in *Salomé* is its "participation" in the "ambiguity of the jewel" or in its many-jeweled *ambiguities*, the effect is not only to complicate our notion of the power of looking by the accumulation of "looks" (though the play does indeed do that), or to disclose a splitting of the gaze that occurs in the process of identification (though the play does this, as well). But this excess of looking and this division in the look are themselves features of a more general extravagance of the gaze in *Salomé*: they are features of an optical economy that gives too much and receives in turn only the spectacle of loss. It is an economy for which the male gaze of feminist psychoanalytic film theory is less pertinent—and less "rich"—than Bataille's account of the deconstituting "anguish" of the desiring gaze. If in both critical accounts it is through the medium of the gaze that the subject desires "to take hold of the object in order to possess it," for Bataille this act of appropriation is always a losing game in which the subject and not the object "loses itself," an experience that goes by the name of "rapture." "As long as *ipse* perseveres in its will to be *ipse*," writes Bataille in *Inner Experience*, "anguish lasts, but if *ipse* abandons itself and knowledge with it, if it gives itself up to non-knowledge in this abandon, then rapture begins."[25] The gaze in *Salomé* insists from beginning to end on its failure to know and to master the object; and it results in the subject's surrender of itself. It is for this reason that it is neither the object nor the subject of the gaze, but the gaze itself that, in both phenomenological and epistemological senses of that term, *appears* to possess power: this is what accounts for the power of "being looked at" in *Salomé*.

Salomé capitalizes on this power when she dances the "dance of the seven veils" for Herod and, it should be stressed, for all who sit and watch. We are likely to be seduced by the history of eroticized orientalism and by the history of the play's production to believe the dance to be an elaborate striptease; but it is important to stress that Wilde left no directions for its performance other than the enigmatic allusion to the "seven veils." After Salomé concludes her dance, and once Herod's "rapture" ends and his sense are restored, he reflects first on the troubling effects of Salomé's beauty and then on the dispossession generated by the "anguished" gaze: "Thy beauty has troubled me. Thy beauty has grievously troubled me, and I have looked at thee too much. Nay, but I will look at thee no more. One should not look at anything. Neither at things, nor at people should one look. Only in mirrors should one look, for mirrors do but show us masks" (601). If this epigrammatic conclusion is a familiar Wildean *topos*, it is also a sign of the theatrical excess of looking that only the narcissistic gaze—the mirrored point of view—can be regarded as healthy, the only gaze that preserves itself from the anguish of loss. Salomé herself is fully aware of this. Her decision to dance for the king is not prompted out of a latent exhibitionist impulse; it is, rather, a calculated decision: the princess knows that to dance for the king will result in his dispossession, the rapturous loss of his own subjectivity, and that he will give her the thing the wants. She sees in advance that Herod will lose himself in his looking and that this loss will yield an extraordinary extravagance.

In this theater of the gaze, how are we to regard the way in which Wilde produces the images we look at with his Herod and his entourage? These are both theatrical images to be seen and dramatic images about seeing and its consequences. When Barthes writes his "confession" about "Leaving the Movie Theater," he proposes two modes of the spectator's response. Although Barthes is quite specific that this is a response to the particular "lure" of the *cinematic* experience—the specific *dispositif* of the reception of the movie-image—he turns nonetheless to Brecht's epic theatre for his shorthand account of an art that might produce the "spectator's critical vision" (*RL*, 348). "It is still possible to conceive of an art," he writes in the closing paragraph of the essay, "which will break the dual circle, the fascination of film, and loosen the glue, the hypnosis of the lifelike (of the analogical), by some recourse to the spectator's critical vision (or listening); is this not what the Brechtian alienation-effect involves?" (*RL*, 348). When at the end of "Visual Pleasure and Narrative Film" Mulvey calls for the production of a cinema that would break the hold of the gaze by "destroying" the "pleasure" of film, she is not only, as Barthes would say, "armed by the discourse of counter-ideology," she is invoking yet another version of the "Brechtian alienation-effect."[26]

Does the gaze in *Salomé* belong to or anticipate the Brechtian mode? Or does it not only *present* rapt, auratic fascination to its audience, but *elicit* and even *demand* it from them? It is certainly possible to imagine a "successful" production of the play that draws generously from the repertoire of epic the-atre—stylized staging, textual intrusions, segmented tableaux, quotable ges-tures, and "poor" acting—that heighten further and then *comment* on the acts of looking in the play and in the process break the "auratic" and "fascinated" hold of the spectator's gaze. But as ethically satisfying as this might well be as political theatre, the Brechtian mode issues from the vantage point of a triumphant critical superiority that Wilde's play of multiplying gazes sim-ply overwhelms. More relevant to this particular piece of theatre is Barthes's other—and preferred—"way of going to the movies": not the critical position of the ironic production or the skeptical spectator, but a *doubled* fascination of "the image and its surroundings" (*RL*, 349). Barthes's description of this effect is particular to the movie theater; but the doubling effect itself seems entirely applicable to the sensual saturation of the "*Salomé* theatre": it is "as if I had two bodies at the same time," says Barthes, "a narcissistic body which gazes, lost, into the engulfing mirror, and a perverse body, ready to fetishize not the image but precisely what exceeds it: the texture of sound, the hall, the darkness, the obscure mass of the other bodies, the rays of light, entering the theater, leaving the hall," in short a thorough aestheticization not only of the "relation" between the spectator and the image, but of the "situation" of the spectator (*RL*, 349). Far from any "counter-ideological" "ungluing," it is a doubled fascination that is at work in *Salomé*'s theatre of the gaze, something closer to Bataille's "story of the eye." Bataille's eye is not the instrument of a panoptical vantage point, but the embodied eye that both looks and then, as Foucault describes it, "rolls back in ecstasy" as it gazes upon "the mute and exorbitated horror of sacrifice" (*AME*, 83). This is precisely how a director might motivate the actress playing the part of the Princess as she gazes upon the dismembered object of her desire *or* how one might imagine an audience beholding the spectacle of this sacred theater.[27]

Anyone familiar with Wilde's work might well expect the sharp wit of Wilde's language to "unglue" us from this spellbound fixation of the gaze. And it is true that almost every referenced act of looking or reference to looking in *Salomé* comes with an injunction or a warning or an omen; and much of the play's talking—its dialogue and its voluminous monologues—*addresses* the excesses of the looking, the imperative to turn away from the object of the gaze. To return to the Lacanian register, we might be tempted to say that the play's language, specifically the many warnings about and prohibitions against looking, imposes the law of the Symbolic order against the insurrectional force of the Imaginary: language charged with the task of "overseeing" the visual field. But the words as written and spoken in *Salomé* do not correspond to this formula: if they invoke what Steven Shaviro calls "the harsh imperatives of the Symbolic order," they do so only in order to mock and exceed it.[28] If the play is a running litany of warnings about the dangers of the gaze, this is also its longest running gag, since no one ever heeds any interdiction against looking. *Salomé* cannot, in other words, be understood as a cautionary tale about the dangers of the gaze or a witty "counter-ideological" struggle to dismantle its apparatus. Rather, in a logic once again closer to Bataille than to Brecht, the warnings exist *precisely* to be ignored, prohibitions asserted only to be transgressed.[29]

Far from operating as the discursive limit to the adventures of the gaze, spoken language in *Salomé reflects* the looking. And this specular relationship is not merely that of linguistic "reflections" or meditations upon staged acts of looking: the play's mirroring of seeing and saying is not the comfortable dramatic convention of a parallel between the performative dimension of the gaze and the constative dimension of language. Language and looking mirror each other in *Salomé* with an intimacy that places both within the same register, a shared zone of seductions and temptations that makes them both equally sensuous and affective. This intimacy finds its fulfillment in the synaesthesia of Salomé's last monologue. Addressing the decapitated head of Jokanaan, Salomé says, "When I looked at thee I heard a strange music"; and there is nothing in the play itself that would have us doubt that looking has this musical effect. Indeed, Wilde in *De Profundis* likens *Salomé* to "a piece of music" whose "refrains" and recurring *motifs* "bind it together as a ballad" (1026). Jokanaan, whose voice possesses its own musicality, not only demands that he not be looked at by Salomé, but that she not speak to him, because he equates the sound of her feminine voice with that of woman's introduction of evil into the world: "By woman came evil into the world. Speak not to me. I will not listen to thee. I listen but to the voice of the Lord God" (590). In the play's reflective intimacy, the forms and effects of excess—the "too much" of desire and fear—extend to the speaking as much as the looking. In *Salomé* the rhythmic incantations of the voice make it as much an auratic medium of obsession as the gaze, and this serves to *compound* its effects. If it "works" in production, the compounding of the play's sensuous experience would produce a fusion of what Northrop Frye calls *melos* (the physical rhythms of musicality) and *opsis* (the representation of the visual) that would result in a "magical imprisonment" (*Anatomy of Criticism*, 280).

What makes the voice an object of desire in the play is a hypotactic lyricism that repeatedly suspends rather than sustains its narrative trajectory. Wilde has fashioned for his principal characters a jeweled speech that may enchant or enthrall, but that is often indifferent to dramatic action as it is conventionally understood.[30] *Salomé* is punctuated by lavish monologues, linguistic spectacles that feel as if they have more to do with their own performative exuberance than with plot or allegorical significance. One measure of the play's rhetorical extravagance is its concentrated investment in figurative modes that not only attract attention to themselves, but appear as rhetorical emblems of each character. Salomé's speech, for instance, is marked by synchronic figures, principally metaphor and simile, *lyric* figures that—as we have learned from Jakobson if we failed to learn it from the poets—are not figures of narrative action.[31] So prominent are these figures in her addresses and descriptions that they seem to reflect on the metaphoric capacity of language, not to *present* likenesses or even to *produce* them, but to fail its basic function of resemblance.[32] "How wasted he is!" says Salomé when she first sees the "prophet": "He is like a thin ivory statue. He is like an image of silver. I am sure he is as chaste as the moon is. He is like a moonbeam, like a shaft of silver. His flesh must be cool like ivory. I would look closer at him" (589).[33] None of the similes is necessary to the dramatic action or even to Salomé's description; but they mark the princess as a maker of similes. That she shares this metaphoric mode with the young Syrian captain demonstrates that this figural disposition is not an *expression* of character, but the rhetorical projection of the "character-effects" we call "Salomé" and "Narraboth."

Herod is another story. No mere likenesses for Herod: his dominant rhetorical mode is metonymic; and his occasional metaphor or simile is encased in a kind of metonymic envelope that conveys the provenance, magnitude, and preciousness of his possessions. But Herod's metonymies do not correspond to the Jakobsonian scheme: they neither participate in the *play's* narrative unfolding, nor do they contribute to its "reality effect." And if these metonymies by definition take a narrative form, they do so as lyric entries in the dramatic *catalogue* of Herod's great Palace collections. Consider, for instance, the third of Herod's three lavish offerings to Salomé after she has danced the dance of the seven veils:

> Listen. I have jewels hidden in the palace—jewels that your mother even has never seen; jewels that are marvellous. I have a collar of pearls, set in four rows. They are like unto moons chained with rays of silver. They are like fifty moons caught in a golden net. On the ivory of her breast a queen has worn it. . . . I have opals that burn always with an ice-like flame, opals that make sad men's minds, and are fearful of the shadows. I have onyxes like the eyeballs of a dead woman. I have moonstones that change when the moon changes, and are wan when they see the sun. I have sapphires big like eggs, and as blue as blue flowers. The sea wanders within them and the moon comes never to trouble the blue of their waves. . . . I have a crystal, into which it is not lawful for a woman to look, nor may young men behold it until they have been beaten with rods. In a coffer of nacre I have three wondrous turquoises. He who wears them on his forehead can imagine things which are not, and he who carries them in his hand can make women sterile. These are great treasures above all price. They are treasures without price. . . . What desirest thou more than this, Salomé? (602–3)

"Treasures without price" or, in other words, extravagance. But what constitutes it as such? Those last "three wondrous turquoises" with magical powers?

The entirety and secrecy and impossibility of the collection? Herod's rhetorical capacity to produce such figures of excess? The irony—and the challenge for any director of the play or actor of Herod—is the leveling, horizontal effect of the accumulation of jewels and figures that makes what Rossetti might have called "utmostness" into a sheer profusion and accumulation of items that, in spite of the escalating and even violent claims for their singularity, become substitutable.[34] And, of course, from Herod Antipas to Robert Plant, Western cultural history is populated by desiring men who promise the objects of their desire "all" they've "got to give: rings, pearls, and all."

When Herod shifts to the metaphoric register, he strains to the breaking point the notion of metaphor as a substitution predicated on resemblance and reveals his personal and political power to be implicated in the fragile venture of that figure. In the performative universe of Wilde's play, Herod's power derives from his rhetorical capacity as a maker of figures. And yet the metaphors he makes often subvert the ordered hierarchy that metaphor depends on, the hierarchy that enables the proper distinction between a figure and its true intent, the reliability of a substitution. For Herod—and, I believe, for Wilde—tropes of resemblance do not refer to an existing relationship, but create that relationship and, moreover, *transfigure* and *transvalue* the very relationship they have ushered into existence. Shortly before Salomé agrees to dance for Herod, the Tetrarch reflects on his fevered emotional state and upon the metaphorical capacity of language and its worldly consequences: "Ah! I can breathe now. How red those petals are! They are like stains of blood on the cloth. That does not matter. You must not find symbols in everything you see. It makes life impossible" (599). If it is unwise to "find symbols in everything," if to do so creates a symbolic universe so laden with meanings and omens that it "makes life impossible," it also appears within the very same passage that it is "impossible" for Herod—and for Wilde—to avoid. Herod's next lines demonstrate that he has not escaped this hyper-symbolic condition: "It were better to say that stains of blood are as lovely as rose petals. It were better to say that. . . . But we will not speak of this" (599). Herod understands that similes are as dangerous as they are inevitable, not because of their content, but because of the potential reversibility of the tenor and vehicle. As Herod gives voice to this realization, he refuses to consider it further: "But we will not speak of this," for to "speak of this" is to embark yet again on the instability of this figure, which makes it seem "impossible" for life.

Herodias shares neither her husband's exuberant investments in rhetorical pyrotechnics nor his anxiety regarding the risks of figurative of language for life. Committed to language's literal dimension, Herodias is the play's great demystifier, the deflator of rhetorical excess. If we were to give the play over to the epic theatre, Herodias would be its "Mother Courage" and hers would be its critical vantage point. Shortly after Herod's initial entrance, he gazes at the moon and begins spinning the kind of metaphoric identifications that almost every character in the play seems obsessively to undertake. After eroticizing the moon by noting her "nakedness," Herod likens the moon he sees "reeling" "through the clouds" above him to a "drunken woman": "I am sure she is looking for lovers. Does she not reel like a drunken woman? She is like a mad woman, is she not?" (592). Herodias's response is as piercing as it is terse: "No, the moon is like the moon, that is all" (592). But Herodias is a positional, rather than definitive demystifier; and if the clear-eyed force of her deflations serves a critical—and comic—function, they never solidify into the play's authoritative perspective. Herodias's literality comes after the figure's deployment: in both senses of the word, Herodias is positioned *behind* the figurative excess of Herod and the play's other characters, including her daughter: the literal both follows or comes after and is "clouded" or "veiled" by figurations that precede it. The literal in *Salomé* is always too little and too late, always trying through the character of Herodias to catch up and respond to the effects of its rhetorical extravagance. Although Herodias says "no" often enough to the linguistic and theatrical excesses she hears or beholds, her utterances never function in the play as an *effective* negation: indeed, *Salomé* is until the end a theatre without negation, a theatre that perpetually reignites the linguistic capacity for extravagance that, however much it may point to an emptiness of reference, generates effects and produces affects.[35] The seductions of language in this play do not merely entice us with the epistemological whirligig of the figurative and the literal; rather, *Salomé* presents us with a world in which the effective (and indeed critical) difference collapses between the literal and the figurative, between language and looking.[36]

Salomé is a play based on a sacred text and saturated with references to sacred content that nonetheless makes its readers and spectators *feel* what happens when the performance of language spins off to the far horizons of meaning, remote from any sacred *terra firma*. We may recognize the utterances of the prophet Jokanaan, and we may know how to interpret his allegorical language as prophecy. But *Salomé* does not authorize that allegorical perspective, and Jokanaan's utterances certainly sound sacred, but are not, in the context of the play, necessarily true or divine. Instead, they are regarded *in* the play as the mad ravings of a holyman, indecipherable incantations; and I would argue that they are understood *by* the play as the fissuring of the sacred from the truth. If in Matthew the teaching of the Baptist derives its power from its prefiguration of Christ's mission, the power of Jokanaan's speech in the play is derived not from the truth of its content, but from its power or force as a spell.[37] Officially, *Salomé* was banned by the English censors on the grounds that it depicted biblical personages on the stage; and Wilde's representation of the language and comportment of Jokanaan justifies their concern, since the play suspends his subsequent Christian identification as John the Baptist and presents his utterances not as transparent or even allegorical vehicles of God's truth, but as a wild and severe discourse.[38] "Rejoice thou not, land of Palestine," declares Jokanaan, "because the rod of him who smote thee is broken. For from the seed of the serpent shall come forth a basilisk, and that which is born of it shall devour the birds" (587). The princess becomes obsessed with the prophet not because she believes in anything he says, but solely because his "voice is as music to her ears." It is the seduction of his "strange voice," the power of his saying that entices her to listen to and to eroticize him without knowing what he says. The play recaptures in Jokanaan what the Christian vantage point can no longer recognize in the canonized figure of Saint John the Baptist: an itinerant *extravagant* whose excess is but another name for a linguistic extravagance.

Jokanaan's apocalyptic utterances and Salomé's seductive speeches are drawn closely enough to Revelation and the Song of Songs to create the aura of scriptural citation; but while Wilde's "citation-effect" often conveys the *effect* of something sacred, it never makes these moments feel like confirmations of biblical authority. Indeed, *we* know that the story of Salomé derives from the Christian gospels; but the play does not acknowledge that vantage point. Instead, *Salomé* simply ignores any "vertical" authority and indulges instead in a "horizontal" and discursive collision between Roman, Judaic, and other Semitic cultures.[39] There is nothing in *Salomé* that cannot ultimately be accommodated by the Christian narrative; but in the ancient world staged by the play, that Christian vantage point is only one element of a diverse and volatile theological and political milieu. Rather than appearing as the *necessary* overcoming or "sublation" of the pre-Christian theologies, the Christianity that is yet to come simply adds to the proliferation of contending sacred discourses. In fact, after the play's opening exchange between the young Syrian captain and Herodias's page over the beauty of Salomé and the strange aspect of the moon, the dialogue turns to an expansive and humorous theological exchange between a Nubian ("The gods of my country are very fond of blood"), a Cappadocian ("In my country there are no gods left. The Romans have driven them out"), and Roman soldiers ("The Jews worship a God you cannot see"), an exchange that serves both as dramatic exposition (it tells us about Herod, Herodias, and Jokanaan) and as an introduction in tone and tenor to the play's depiction of political and religious "disputes."

Exchanges such as this contribute to the de-theologizing and even de-sacralizing force of a play that never confirms the truth of a transcendent or even mystical experience. Miracles are a given, but represented in the form of carnival tricks performed by itinerant hucksters. The play devotes long stretches of its monologues and dialogues to fleshly desire and material excess. And yet despite its lavish attentions to the profane and despite its critical demystifying, the play still *feels* sacred. This "feeling" derives not from its scriptural origins, but from its aesthetic qualities: Wilde reestablishes the relationship between the sacred and the aura *from the perspective of the auratic experience itself* and not from the authority of sacred texts. Benjamin understands the aura to be the effect of a sacred authority, its epiphenomenon or aesthetic manifestation, which was severed by the Kantian critical discourses on aesthetics that marked its effective secularization. More recently the forces of production—technological developments and the artistic practices they usher into existence—are understood to be responsible for the "waning" or the "withering" of the aura. In the context of Benjamin's narrative of "the work of art in the age of its technological reproducibility," *Salomé* not only saturates the stage with auratic experience, it also reestablishes the relationship with the sacred, but entirely from the perspective of dramatic effects and thus after the fact, and divorced from the sacred authority of scriptural references.

Salomé's reconstitution of the sacred is produced by and through its immersion in extravagance and possesses no *effective* theological content. For Wilde as for Bataille, the experience of the sacred does not, as Rebecca Comay puts it, "presuppose an originary plenitude, the serene presence of truth."[40] For Wilde as for Bataille, "sacrifice is nothing other than the production of sacred things." When in exchange for Salomé's dance Herod offers her "the largest emerald in the world," when he offers her scores of "jewels that are marvellous to look at," even when he offers her "half of his kingdom," he—and we—may regard these offerings as an inventory of extravagance, for in this royal display of excess Herod has indeed, as we say, offered to "sacrifice a fortune." But for Salomé none of this is enough: unlike the true object of her desire, Herod's spectacular catalogue of possessions remains *measurable*, profligacy in a *restricted* economy. "I will give thee the mantle of the high priest," he declares at last, "I will give the veil of the sanctuary" (603). The shocked exclamations of the Jewish attendants mark this moment as the shift to a sacred discourse; yet, again, for Salomé it is not enough. Her refusal of Herod's offer of these items—regardless of their sacred origins and their sig-nification as royal wealth and might—renders them profane and reassigns the objects to the world of substitution and exchange.[41] Only the sacrifice of this "holyman," only "the head of Jokanaan," is sufficient for Salomé; and it is only the head of this holyman for which there is no equivalent. But however much Herod is frightened by the prospect of Jokanaan's beheading, it is not the head as such that is extravagant. For her part, Herodias regards the demand as a perfectly reasonable exchange for her daughter's dance; and there is nothing about the beheading itself—fully authorized by the perspective of biblical scripture—that creates a crisis for the play or Herod's or Wilde's aestheti-cism. Herod attempts to dissuade Salomé from her demand by telling her that "the head of a man cut from his body is ill to look upon. . . . It is not meet that the eyes of a virgin should look upon such a thing. What pleasure," he asks rhetorically, "could you have in it? None, No, no, it is not what you desire" (600). But Herod's disbelieving remarks only demonstrate that in spite of his material excess, he belongs to a conventional economy of aesthetic pleasure and decorum, a *restricted aestheticism*.

For Wilde the *killing* of Jokanaan, however spectacular, does not rise to the level of the sacred. It is Salomé's *kiss*—this act of desire in Wilde's theatre of the sacred—that prompts what Bataille calls a "sacred horror," the "richest and most agonizing experience, which does not limit itself to dismemberment but which, on the contrary, opens itself, like a theatre curtain, onto a realm beyond the world, where the rising light of day transfigures all things and destroys their limited meanings."[42] *Salomé* presents its audience with just such a "theatre curtain," one that "transfigures all things" as it "opens itself" onto "a realm beyond the world" in which the "rich and agonizing experience" of Jokanaan's beheading gives the princess an object that she makes sacred for all who witness her kiss, a kiss that destroys "limited meaning," including that of the Christianity that would redeem or sanctify it.[43] "What is sacred," says Bataille in *The Theory of Religion*, "attracts and possesses an incomparable value, but at the same time it appears vertiginously dangerous for that clear and profane world where mankind situates its privileged domain."[44] The act of sacrifice—that act which produces sacred things—"draws the victim out of the world of utility and restores it to that unintelligible caprice" (*Theory of Religion*, 43). "Vertiginous danger," "unintelligible caprice": these are other names for the act of love that Salomé displays. It is solely this act of love that places the play's sense of scale into crisis, an act of love that takes all who behold it—theatergoer or tetrarch—beyond the world of meaning and utility and exchange, beyond the immense and profuse, but still measurable economy of Herod's possessions. It is, in other words, the meaningless extravagance of sacred love committed by one extravagant upon another. "The mystery of love is greater than the mystery of death," says Salomé as she prepares for that one act. "Love alone should one consider" (604).[45]

When Salomé addresses the decapitated head of Jokanaan carried on a charger—addresses it, caresses it, *kisses* it—when she asks whether there was the "taste of love" on her lips and decides that it was indeed the "the taste of love," she has *tasted* the sacred.

> Ah! I have kissed thy mouth, Jokanaan. I have kissed thy mouth. There was a bitter taste on thy lips. Was it the taste of blood . . . ? But perchance it was the taste of love. . . . They say that love hath a bitter taste. . . . But what of that? What of that? I have kissed thy mouth, Jokanaan. (605)

When, as the stage directions specify, "a moonbeam falls on Salomé," it does not so much illuminate her as *"cover* her with light." This is the moment of serious moonlight, the moment Wilde's play and his aestheticism achieve extravagance; and it is no coincidence that this sacred and unredeemable moment occurs where the play departs from any scriptural fidelity. In an 1893 review of the play, the reviewer for *The Times* called *Salomé* "an arrangement in blood and ferocity, morbid, bizarre, repulsive, and very offensive in its adaptation of scriptural phraseology to situations reverse of sacred."[46] None of what the reviewer says is wrong, of course, but as we often say, it depends on one's perspective; and from the play's point of view, this excess is not the "reverse of sacred," but its very definition, what Bataille would call its "sacramental element."[47] But Herod, that (non-radical) aesthete, "turns away" from the sacred act as the moonbeam covers Salomé with its light and gives his final order—"kill that woman!"—which his soldiers carry out as the curtain falls. With her "monstrous" act in which everything is lost, extravagance is gained, its impossible perspective singled out by a moonbeam and covered with light.

It is a love carried out in the vertiginous language of an aestheticism that has exceeded the claims of beauty and pleasure with which it is most identified and *tasted* its radical.

To point to this one moment in this one play and call it radical aestheticism poses yet another version of the problem of the "vantage point." *Salomé* is, of course, a theatrical text, or at least the published script of a drama that has been variously produced on the stage for more than a hundred years. In every version of a radical aestheticism that I have proposed to this point, it is something we read or, more precisely, something that happens to us when we are reading. In the case of *Salomé* we might well encounter this radicalized aestheticism when we read the text, but it also might be something that we actually see on the stage before us; and in any case it is certainly something we read as if it were *something to be seen*. If I claim to have "seen" this radical aestheticism, it is only in my own mind's sensorium or "spectatorium," in a performance that was barred from the stage by an actress no one now living has ever seen. I "see" it as Arthur Symons *would* have described the way Sarah Bernhardt *would* have played the role of the princess: with "a kind of absolute peril" in a performance that "was like a passionate declaration offered to someone unknown . . . as if the whole nervous force of the audience were sucked out of it and flung back, intensified, upon itself" (quoted in Powell, *Wilde and the Theatre of the 1890's*, 43). This is how one "performs" a radical aestheticism; and this is how one would experience that performance.

The irony that *Salomé* presents for my broader argument is that the play does not *turn away* from this radical aestheticism, but distills it from the spectacular extravagance of its multiple vantage points into this one final, sacred moonlit image for all to see. This was not the case for Hopkins, say, or for Dickinson, in which the text could never avow the "event" of the radical aestheticism; and this was not the case for Shelley or for Keats, in which a radical aestheticism appears in failed texts and at the point of their failure— in fragments, remains, burn-outs. Radical aestheticism here is the play's denouement, in the open, illuminated and named. And yet the turning away starts immediately, with Herod, of course, whose response to this image he beholds is an emblem of the turn. The British censors, of course, turned away long before this final image, the scene of an aestheticism that has radicalized itself and given rise to the crisis, for the project the play was supposed to exemplify is there for everyone to see, and yet they do not. Not even Wilde himself, at least not in such terms, since he always held out hope for something more.

Covered with Jewels

When asked in 1882 where the aestheticism he called his "Romantic move-ment" would end, Wilde responded that "there is no end to it; it will go on forever; just as it had no beginning. I have used the word *renaissance* to show that it is no new thing with me. It has always existed."[48] And yet for Wilde's radical aestheticism the end of *Salomé* is the end of the line. With Wilde as with Shelley, Keats, Dickinson, Hopkins, and Rossetti, radical aestheticism does not have the last word in a writer's career: it arrives without warning, a dead-end or blank spot, after which there may be more poems or plays, but no "advances," nothing that *progresses* from this moment, this blank pseudo-event of a radical aestheticism. Wilde did not turn away from *Salomé*. If after *Salomé* he went on to write the plays and stories and novel and essays that we have come to regard as his most important contributions to each genre, *Salomé* remained his most precious creation. "You set me to wrestle with Cali-ban," Wilde tells Bosie, and the ugliness of those trials and tribulations pre-vented him from devoting himself to "making beautiful coloured, musical things such as *Salomé*, and the *Florentine Tragedy*, and *La Sainte Courtisane*" (1042). The last on the list is the play Wilde was working on in 1895 when the troubles began. The play exists only as a fragment because, as the story goes, in Paris two years later Wilde left the almost completed manuscript in a cab. Still, it is instructive to consider what Wilde did write when he returned to the dramatic mode that resulted in the radicalization of his aestheticism.

La Sainte Courtisane revisits not only the "beautiful coloured, musical" di-mension of *Salomé*, but also its crossings of the sacred and profane. The stage of *La Sainte Courtisane*, however, is a far cry indeed from Herod's palace and, as if purified of the excess of that earlier glittering theatre, is as stark as any-thing from Beckett: "*a corner of a valley in the Thebaid. On the right hand of the stage is a cavern. In front of the cavern stands a great crucifix. On the left, sand dunes*" (734). But the austerity of the scene only heightens the play's resem-blances to *Salomé*, as if Wilde had bound its distilled structural elements and linguistic properties like the "recurrent motifs" that for Wilde made *Salomé* "so like a piece of music" (1026). Honorius is the "beautiful young hermit" who "will not look upon the face of a woman" (734) and who dwells in the cavern of this desert world populated by Christian hermits or *extravagants*.

La Sainte Courtisane opens with two men, one who appears to belong to one of the secret religions that flourished in the region, engaging in a descriptive "dialogue" about Myrrhina, the "courtesan saint" and "daughter of the Emperor." As much Herod as Salomé, Myrrhina is both object of desire and rich and powerful beyond measure: indeed, she is rich and powerful beyond measure *because* she is *the* object of desire. "I took the minion of Caesar from Caesar and made him my play-fellow," she says to Honorius in a "monologue" that is both a catalog of her conquests and an act of seduction. "He came to me at night in a litter. He was pale as a narcissus, and his body was like honey" (737). And yet as she addresses Honorius with these tales of her conquests and her power, it is only at its end of her address that we can be certain that she is not confessing, but seducing: "The dust of the desert lies on your hair and your feet are scratched with thorns and your body is scorched by the sun. Come with me, Honorius, and I will clothe you in a tunic of silk. I will clothe you in hyacinth and put honey in your mouth. Love—" (737). Honorius interrupts her profane extravagance with a sacred declaration: "There is no love but the love of God" (737). From there Honorius undertakes his own account of a Christian love that issues from "the Son of God" who was "born of a virgin" and that disdains the body as "vile." When Myrrinha reasserts "beauty," Honorius cuts her off by declaring that "the beauty of the soul increases till it can see God. Therefore, Myrrhina, repent of thy sins" (738). And, without pause, she does. It is at that very same and unmarked moment that Honorius undergoes his own profane "conversion" experience and declares to his "courtesan saint" "covered with jewels": "Myrrhina, the scales have fallen from my eyes and I see now clearly what I did not see before. Take me to Alexandria and let me taste of the seven sins" (738).

In what remains of the brief manuscript, there is no event, no "taste of love," no instance or occurrence of a radical aestheticism that marks art's undoing, only an unexplained and perhaps inexplicable double conversion. From a rhetorical perspective we are made witness to a theatrical chiasmus, the fluid crossings of the sacred with the profane. If we were to give this play its own musical score, it is not Strauss that is conjured by this dramatic fragment, but Debussy: if not the delicate serenity of "Claire de Lune," the more mediated and plaintive, if static tension of "La Terrasse des Audiences du Clair de Lune," a piece that alludes in its title to the terraces of "moonlit audiences" that are features of both *Salomé* and *Le Sainte Courtisane*. As with Debussy's prelude, the eventless double conversion of the latter play gives it the feeling of an aftermath. Without the event that makes *Salomé* a unique experience, *La Sainte Courtisane* restores in effect the chiasmic crossing of Christianity and aestheticism that Wilde spells out in *De Profundis*. There is nothing here that broaches a *radical* aestheticism, certainly nothing from which one turns away; and yet neither is there any of the giddy enthusiasm or Olympian wit that exemplifies the "affirmative" aestheticism of Wilde's Vivian or Henry. In *Le Sainte Courtisane* the espousals, seductions, and conversions loop without authority or conviction. I think of the play as that which radical aestheticism bestows "our Romantic movement": a partial world jeweled, but unredeemed, a fragmented no-man's zone of the chiasmic crossings of the sacred and the profane.

This is the aftermath world of the courtesan saint, now converted *and* covered with jewels. This has also been Wilde's afterlife, at least one of them, the form of martyred sainthood that he treasured in Saint Sebastian, one whose public sufferings give us the example of a passion that, as Richard A. Kaye argues, establishes Wilde's "posthumous sainthood," his "role as the leader of a certain kind of community or fellowship—namely, sexual dissidents."[49] But if Saint Oscar long ago became an aestheticist cliché, there is an extravagant and unclaimed remainder of his project that solicits a kind of impossible, but passionate identification. When in *De Profundis* Wilde envisioned his "Confraternity of the Fatherless," he invoked an "agnosticism" that "should have its ritual no less than faith. It has sown its martyrs, it should reap its saints." And in Wilde's play we come to see how "our romantic movement" carries within it a radical aestheticism that "has sown its martyrs" and "should reap its saints." In the moment that Salomé performs her miracle—the single sacrament of her sacred community—Saint Salomé of the Severed Head joins an elect group of radical aestheticism's impossible martyrs and unredeemable extravagants: Keats's burnt-out Hyperion and living hand, Shelley's disfigured "what-was-once" Rousseau, Hopkins's gloriously buckling bird, the "bright impossibilities" of Dickinson's haloed zeros, Rossetti's Saint "Might-have-been." It's the shrine of art's undoing, the kind of shrine one might visit with the trepidation of the young Keats, poised before an aesthetic experience that lays waste, that consumes and gives nothing back. It's the kind of unredeemable literary confraternity from which one might well turn away.

INTRODUCTION: "FROM WHICH ONE TURNS AWAY"

1. Marc Redfield, *The Politics of Aesthetics: Nationalism, Gender, Romanticism* (Stanford: Stanford University Press, 2003), 11. Redfield's book established a critical touchstone for the constellation of issues that are the concern of this book. I will have occasion to return to Redfield's reading of Shelley in Chapter 1; but the argument Redfield develops throughout the book—especially in its careful teasing out of the conceptual relationships between Romanticism, aesthetics, and ideology—informs much of what I undertake in this project. With the exception of Shelley, I turn to different authors, and throughout my book I arrive at conclusions with which Redfield would most likely disagree. But my thinking about the conceptual framework of this project is deeply indebted to and engaged with Redfield's work.

2. Immanuel Kant, *Critique of Judgment*, trans. J. H. Bernard (London: Collier Macmillan, 1951), 44.

3. Oscar Wilde, "The English Renaissance of Art," in *The Collected Works of Oscar Wilde*, ed. Robert Ross (Boston: John W. Luce, 1908), 14:268.

4. The invocation of the *radical* informs such divergent projects as Ernesto Laclau and Chantal Mouffe's conception of "*radical and plural democracy*" and Northrop Frye's *Anatomy of Criticism*. For Laclau and Mouffe, "pluralism is *radical* only to the extent that each term of this plurality of identities finds within itself the principle of its own validity, without this having to be sought in a transcendent or underlying positive ground for the hierarchy of meaning of them all and the source and guarantee of their legitimacy"; Laclau and Mouffe, *Hegemony and Socialist Strategy: Towards A Radical Democracy* (London: Verso, 1985), 167. For his part, Frye makes use of the notion of the radical to argue for the rhetorical basis for genre: "The basis of generic distinctions in literature appears to be the radical of presentation. . . . The basis of generic criticism in any case is rhetorical"; Frye, *Anatomy of Criticism: Four Essays* (Princeton: Princeton University Press, 1970), 246, 247. My point is not to suggest hidden affinities between a landmark work of radical political theory and one of the great achievements of Anglo-American literary studies. Nor do I wish to be understood as attempt-

ing to enlist either Laclau and Mouffe or Frye—radical democracy or liberal humanism—in the project of a radical aestheticism. My invocation of both is related here to their uses of the "radical"; and, as I will spell out below, Frye's account of the lyric's mode of radicality is particularly crucial to my thinking about a radical aestheticism.

5. Though this is an argument I made in 2002, Arkady Plotnisky's version of this metaphor is more informed; see Plotnisky, "Beyond the Inconsumable: The Catastrophic Sublime and the Destruction of Literature in Keats's *The Fall of Hyperion and Shelley's The Triumph of Life*," in *Cultures of Taste/Theories of Appetite: Eating Romanticism* (New York: Palgrave, 2004), 168–69.

6. Paul de Man, "Kant and Schiller," in *Aesthetic Ideology* (Minneapolis: University of Minnesota Press, 1996), 147. On the question of de Man and the aesthetic, see in particular Andrzej Warminski's introduction to *Aesthetic Ideology*, 1–33; Cynthia Chase, "Trappings of an Education," in *Responses: On Paul de Man's Wartime Journalism*, ed. Werner Hamacher, Neil Hertz, and Thomas Keenan (Lincoln: University of Nebraska Press, 1989), 44–79; Michael Sprinker, *Imaginary Relations: Aesthetics and Ideology in the Theory of Historical Materialism* (London: Verso, 1987), 237–66; and Rodolphe Gasché, *The Wild Card of Reading* (Cambridge, Mass.: Harvard University Press, 1998).

7. As Rei Terada puts it, "de Man both points out how Schiller edits Kant's troubled *Third Critique* into a system that raises fewer questions, and admires Kant for his relative inability to paper over its problems"; Terada, "Seeing Is Reading," in *Legacies of Paul de Man*, ed. Marc Redfield (New York: Fordham University Press, 2007), 169. Terada's work cuts through the conceptual and figurative antinomy of the relationship between seeing and reading that shadows my own project. Of the many indispensable accounts of the legacy of Paul de Man, I know of none which more lucidly addresses the role of "phenomenal cognition" in the aestheticization of Kant's own legacy and what this might mean for the tricky relationship between figures of seeing and figures of reading. "For de Man," writes Terada, "the foundering of Kant's transcendental system in material vision is a failure of redemption, the nontragic failure of materiality to be transformed" (164). I also find Terada's conclusion—that "the word 'seeing' in all its ambiguity" and "understood as internally and enigmatically divided, can be a rather honest figure, one that does not necessarily resemble aesthetic ideology's appropriation of it" (163,164)—to be richly suggestive and even critically promising, though I am also convinced that a reading of what I am calling the radical aestheticism of these poets will *not* make good on that promise.

8. Friedrich Schiller, *On the Aesthetic Education of Man in a Series of Letters*, trans. Reginald Snell (New York: Frederick Ungar, 1954), 27.

9. Emil Brunner, *The Divine Imperative: A Study of Christian Ethics*, trans. Olyve Wyon (London: Butterworth Press, 1937).

10. *The Rules of Art: Genesis and Structure of the Literary Field*, trans. Susan Emanuel (Stanford: Stanford University Press, 1996) and *The Field of Cultural Production*, ed. Randal Johnson (New York: Columbia University Press, 1993)

are Pierre Bourdieu's most influential books. In the context of North American literary and cultural studies, John Guillory's *Cultural Capital: The Problem of Literary Canon Formation* (Chicago: University of Chicago Press, 1993) remains the most important sustained critical engagement with the principles and practices of Bourdieu's sociology; see especially 325–40, where Guillory offers a provocative supplement to Bourdieu's analysis of the aesthetic disposition. Guillory rightly notes that "what is genuinely problematic in Bourdieu's theory" is "the adequacy of a socio-logic to express the illogic of social existence." But in a move that is ultimately reassuring to idealist conceptions of aesthetic value, Guillory proceeds to identify the "the remainder" of this inadequacy as "nothing other than aesthetic experience" (327); see also Peter Bürger's "The Problem of Aesthetic Value," trans. Shaun Whiteside, in *Literary Theory Today*, ed. Peter Collier and Helga Geyer-Ryan (Ithaca: Cornell University Press, 1990), 23–34), an astute assessment of the challenge and limitations of Bourdieu's sociology. Burger is especially helpful in demonstrating Bourdieu's blindness to the historical and institutional effects of artistic *material*. The most comprehensive rejoinder to and illuminating reading of Guillory's book is Redfield's "Professing Literature: John Guillory's Misreading of Paul de Man," in *Legacies of Paul de Man*, 93–126, which is much less "pugnacious" than the title suggests.

   11. The most explicit formulation of Levinas's iconoclasm is his 1948 essay; see Emmanuel Levinas, "Reality and Its Shadow," reprinted in *The Levinas Reader*, ed. Sean Hand (London: Blackwell, 1989), 131, in which aestheticism is defined as that which "situates art *above* reality and recognizes no master for it, and it is immoral inasmuch as it liberates the artist from his duties as a man and assures him of a pretentious nobility." But, of course, that is not Levinas's last word on the matter; and this very fact makes his understanding of the relationship between ethics and aesthetics interesting and complicated. If, as Blanchot declared, "Levinas mistrusts poems and poetic activity," it is also the case, as Gerald Bruns has demonstrated, that "Levinas could not get such things out of his mind, for he frequently found in poetry and art conceptual resources for his thinking, which perhaps helps to explain why the ethical in his work is never far removed from the aesthetic"; Bruns, *On the Anarchy of Poetry and Philosophy: A Guide for the Unruly Perspectives in Continental Philosophy* (New York: Fordham University Press, 2006), 176. Much of Derrida's late work is deeply beholden to Levinas, and this exchange may come to be regarded as one of the most significant philosophical engagements of the twentieth century. See especially Derrida's moving "good-bye" to Levinas, which ushers in another installment in Derrida's meditation on Levinasian themes: Jacques Derrida, *Adieu: To Emmanuel Levinas*, trans. Pascale-Anne Brault and Michael Naas (Stanford: Stanford University Press, 1999); see also Judith Butler's title essay to her volume *Precarious Life: The Powers of Mourning and Violence* (London: Verso, 2004), 128–52. Jill Robbins's *Altered Reading: Levinas and Literature* (Chicago: University of Chicago Press, 1999) remains to my knowledge the most careful and sustained study on Levinas and the problem of the literary. I suspect I will be distinctly in the

minority when I express my disappointment over this "ethical turn" in Derrida's work, prompted at least in part by his responses to Levinas, or when I regard it to be a derailment from the critical-linguistic analysis that characterized Derridean deconstruction from the 1960s to the early 1980s.

12. "The rapture of this [Christian] kind of experience in faith is quite different from what is called estheticism." Though von Balthasar definitively draws the line that separates the immersive experience of aestheticism from the raptures of Christian faith, his "theological aesthetics" is a magisterial examination of the crucial role of aesthetics in Christian theology. For von Balthasar, a "theological aesthetics" is "a theology which does not primarily work with the extra-theological categories of a worldly philosophical aesthetics (above all poetry), but which develops its theory of beauty from the data of revelation itself with genuinely theological methods"; Hans Urs von Balthasar, *The Glory of the Lord: A Theological Aesthetics*, vol. 1, *Seeing the Form*, trans. Erasmo Leiva-Merikakis (San Francisco: Ignatius Press, 1982), 117. Von Balthasar regards the aversion to aesthetics—in the work of Rudolf Bultmann, for instance—to be a theological "dead-end." For Bultmann "the idea of the beautiful is of no significance in forming the life of Christian faith, which sees in the beautiful the temptation of a false transfiguration of the world which distracts the gaze from 'beyond'"; cited in von Balthasar, *The Glory of the Lord*, vol. 4, *The Realm of Metaphysics in Antiquity*, trans. Brian McNeil, et al (San Francisco: Ignatius Press, 1989), 27n11. Von Balthasar's account of Bultmann's argument is quite pertinent to any discussion of aestheticism: "in all that Bultmann writes there is a deep seriousness which comes from having been seized . . . by Christ. But this is a gravity which, alas, is full of anguish because of its total lack of imagery and form: a real dead-end for Protestantism"; von Balthasar, *Theological Aesthetics*, 52. Von Balthasar stresses that this aversion to aesthetics is not exclusively the result of a Protestant iconoclasm: "the word 'aesthetic' automatically flows from the pens of both Protestant and Catholic writers when they want to describe an attitude which, in the last analysis, they find to be frivolous, merely curious and self-indulgent" (51). The dangers of aestheticism—what von Balthasar calls the "stupor" or what Keats would call the "dumb enchantment" of a benumbed aesthetic contemplation—is avoided, according to von Balthasar, if one "keeps ones eyes set" on the "form" of Christ: "If one really has within one's vision this living and divine form [of Christ] which sovereignly stamps its shape on the world then there is no danger that one will stultify in an 'aesthetic' contemplation of dead images and have to be awakened from this stupor by an ethical actualism that destroys all images" (550).

13. "What is ultimately at stake," declares Badiou for philosophy's "return to itself," "can be formulated in terms of the question which weighs upon us and threatens to exhaust us: can we be delivered, *finally* delivered, from our subjection to Romanticism?"; Alain Badiou, *Theoretical Writings*, trans. Ray Brassier and Alberto Toscano (London: Continuum, 2004), 22. For Badiou, Romanticism is another name for "the aura of the poem," that seductive aesthetic light

of the poetic object that "seemingly since Nietzsche, but actually since Hegel" "grows ever brighter" (25). It reaches its culmination in Heidegger. According to Badiou, the "essence of the process of Heideggerian thought"—its constitutive gesture—is Romantic: it involves a "subtraction" of the poem "from philosophical *knowledge*, to render it *truth*"; Badiou, *Infinite Thought*, trans. Oliver Feltham and Justin Clements (London: Continuum, 2003), 72, 73. The trajectory of Heidegger's thought leads him to "restore, under various and subtle philosophical names, the sacral authority of the poetic utterance, and the idea that the authentic lies in the flesh of language" (*Infinite Thought*, 73–74). There are, says Badiou, "three possible regimes of the bond between the poem and philosophy," "regimes" that are distinguished by varying philosophical dispositions of philosophy and the poem. The first of these, which Badiou calls the "Parmenidian," "organizes a *fusion* between the subjective authority of the poem and the validity of statements held as philosophical. Even when 'mathematical' interruptions figure under this fusion, they are definitely subordinated to the *sacred* aura of utterance, to its 'profound' value, to its enunciative legitimacy. The image, language's equivocations, and metaphor escort and authorize the saying of the True. Authenticity resides in the flesh of language" (*Infinite Thought*, 72). In Badiou's schema the Platonic and the Aristotelian "regimes" break with this Parmenidian "fusion": Plato "distances" the "undermining fascination" of the poem from philosophy simply by banishing the poets; while for Aristotle, "the poem is no longer thought in terms of the drama of its distance or its intimate proximity, it is grasped *within the category of the object*" and becomes "a regional discipline within philosophy," that which will come to be called "Aesthetics" (*Infinite Thought*, 72). As Badiou sees it, Heidegger misses the opportunity "of inventing a fourth relation" between poem and philosophy; instead, he removes the poem from the domain of knowledge and restores, via Heraclitus, its Parmenidian essence, its sacred aura—which is, of course, another way of calling it an *aestheticism*.

14. I will quote the eloquent closing sentences of Guillory's book to give a sense of the difference between his argument and my own: "If there is no way out of the game of culture, then, even when cultural capital is the only kind of capital, there may be another kind of game, with less dire consequences for the losers, an *aesthetic* game. Socializing the means of production and consumption would be the conditions of an aestheticism unbound, not its overcoming. But of course, this is only a thought experiment"; Guillory, *Cultural Capital*, 340. To this I would respond that in spite of the apparent materialism of the phrase "socializing the means of production and consumption," the final formulations of Guillory's provocative "thought experiment" are distinctly more Schillerian than Marxist.

15. In the present "precarious position of art," "each of the two alternatives negates itself with the other. Committed art, necessarily detached as art from reality, cancels the distance between the two. 'Art for art's sake' denies by its absolute claims that ineradicable connection with reality which is the polemi-

cal *a priori* of the attempt to make art autonomous from the real. Between these two poles the tension in which art has lived in every age until now is dissolved"; Theodor Adorno, "Commitment," in *Aesthetics and Politics*, ed. NLR (London: New Left Books, 1977), 178. On the question of Adorno and the aesthetic, see in particular Fredric Jameson, *Late Marxism: Adorno, or, The Persistence of the Dialectic* (London: Verso, 1990); J. M. Bernstein, *The Fate of Art: Aesthetic Alienation from Kant to Derrida and Adorno* (University Park, Penn.: Penn State University Press, 1992), 188–274; and Terry Eagleton, *The Ideology of the Aesthetic* (Oxford: Blackwell Press, 1990), 341–65.

16. Karl Marx's "Marginal Glosses" on Arnold Ruge, quoted in S. S. Prawer, *Karl Marx and World Literature* (Oxford: Clarendon Press, 1976), 69. One fascinating and pertinent aspect of Marx's response is not merely his attack on "purely formal activity," but his obvious distaste for the inherent theatricality of aestheticism, "stylistic exercises in public."

17. Walter Benjamin, "The Work of Art in the Age of Its Technological Reproducibilty," in *Selected Writings*, vol. IV (1938–1940, ed. Howard Eiland and Marcus Bullock (Cambridge, Mass.: Harvard University Press, 2003), 254, 256.

18. "A concatenation of the aesthetic with the meaning-producing powers of language is a strong temptation to the mind but, precisely for that reason, it also opens up a Pandora's box. The aesthetic is, by definition, a seductive notion that appeals to the pleasure principle, a eudaemonic judgment that can displace and conceal values of truth and falsehood likely to be more resilient to desire than values of pleasure and pain"; de Man, *The Resistance to Theory* (Minneapolis: University of Minnesota Press, 1986), 64. As Andrzej Warminski argues in his introduction to *The Aesthetic Ideology*, the aesthetic according to de Man is that which invites its own "turning away" from the constitutive materials of the literary text: "whether by 'evasion' or 'omission,' the recourse to the stability of the aesthetic ends up turning away from that which de Man calls the 'materiality' of the text" (Schiller, *Aesthetic Ideology*, 3).

19. If many readers of de Man and Adorno have noted their affinities, to my knowledge no one has done more than Fredric Jameson to place these two great inheritors of the Kantian legacy into genuine engagement. While his book on *A Singular Modernity* begins by describing the recent "resuscitation of aesthetics" as another of the "intellectual regressions" of the "current age," Jameson goes on to develop a fascinating account of de Man's project in light of Adorno's, one that orbits around the problem of aesthetic autonomy; see Jameson, *A Singular Modernity: Essay on the Ontology of the Present* (London: Verso, 2002), 3. Jameson's "Deconstruction as Nominalism" remains to my mind the single most illuminating account of de Man's project from a Marxist perspective; see Jameson, *Postmodernism; Or, The Cultural Logic of Late Capitalism* (Durham: Duke University Press, 1991), 217–59.

20. Terry Eagleton, *Ideology of the Aesthetic*, 9. If I find Eagleton's model of aesthetic autonomy to lack nuance, I would also like to stress that some of our best readers of Romanticism and the problem of aesthetics have presented the

logic of spatialization in more complicated and productive forms than "idealized refuges" by demonstrating how the aesthetic does not simply retreat from its historical moment but incorporates it, takes it into itself. Thomas Pfau, for example, has described this as "the capacity of the aesthetic to encrypt its own contingent historical situation"; Pfau, *Wordsworth's Profession* (Stanford: Stanford University Press, 1994), 3. Redfield offers an acute analysis of the aesthetic as the secret space of historicist criticism, its unacknowledged crypt. Even when historicist critics seek to disavow or disallow the aesthetic in the name of politics, Redfield asserts, they do so only by *encrypting* the aesthetic itself: in their efforts to abolish it, the aesthetic "becomes the *impensé*, the encrypted and cherished secret, of historicist-political criticism" (*Politics of Aesthetics*, 178).

21. Hegel, *Aesthetics: Lectures on Fine Arts*, vol. 1, trans. T. M. Knox (Oxford: Clarendon Press, 9). This argument, which is legible in much of the Frankfurt School, is concisely summarized by Eagleton, *Ideology of the Aesthetic*, 65; and it is presented as the "project" of J. M Bernstein's *The Fate of Art*. The permutations of the notion of aesthetic autonomy and their ethico-political valences are enough to "tease us out as doth infinity." I continue to believe that Louis Althusser's discussions of art and aesthetics are the richest of the tradition; see in particular, "A Letter on Art in Reply to Andre Dapre" and "Cremonini, Painter of the Abstract," in *Lenin and Philosophy and Other Essays*, trans. Ben Brewster (London: NLB, 1971), 221–28; 229–42. Michael Sprinker's account of this dimension of Althusser's thinking is precisely to the point: "Scandalously—but with complete consistency—Althusser insists that the ideological (and therefore the political) effectiveness of artworks derives from their aesthetic power, namely, from their production of an 'internal distance' in relation to the ideology that they present . . . . Art's aesthetic power is the source of its pedagogical, scientific function"; Sprinker, "Art and Ideology: Althusser and de Man," in *Material Events: Paul de Man and the Afterlife of Theory*, ed. Tom Cohen, et al (Minneapolis: University of Minnesota Press, 2001), 43–44. In the years since his untimely death, Sprinker's contributions to our understanding of the relationship between aesthetics and ideology and between de Man and Althusser appear stronger and more compelling than ever; see especially Sprinker, *Imaginary Relations*.

22. Historicist criticism over the past twenty-five years has worked to extricate criticism from the seductions of the aesthetic experiences generated by Romantic poetry by turning to Romanticism's constitutive historical and social contexts. This particular historicist project (which includes the many cogent critiques of its assumptions, protocols, and results) may have run its course. But what was conspicuously absent from such contextualizing was even an acknowledgment that the discourse of aesthetics itself constituted a meaningful and primary context, the one with which I am most interested in here. William Keach's account of the role of "arbitrary power" in the literature and politics of the period offers a compelling account of the centrality of the aesthetic: "The aesthetic, even when placed most conspicuously at the service of transcendent

'spirit' or 'idea' was above all invented to provide new philosophical grounds for valuing the sensuous, and therefore raised new questions about the materiality of form in artistic representation"; Keach, *Arbitrary Power: Romanticism, Language, Politics* (Princeton: Princeton University Press, 2004), 23.

23. Peter de Bolla, *Art Matters* (Chicago: University of Chicago Press, 2001), 12.

24. De Man, "Intentional Structure of the Romantic Image," *The Rhetoric of Romanticism* (New York: Columbia University Press, 1984), 7.

25. David Bentley Hart's engrossing "defense of the suasive loveliness of Christian rhetoric" opens with what amounts to a gloss—entirely unacknowledged—to the most famous aestheticist formulation of British romanticism. "Christian rhetoric," asserts Hart, "must inevitably make an appeal to beauty. Beauty, that is, rather than simply 'truth'; or, rather beauty as inseparable from truth, as a measure of what theology may call true"; Hart, *The Beauty of the Infinite: The Aesthetics of Christian Truth* (Grand Rapids, Mich.: Eerdmans, 2003), 5, 3. I will have the opportunity to revisit Hart's project—by turns pugnacious and thrilling, fascinating if not convincing—in my discussion of Hopkins in Chapter 4. Here it will suffice to note that however much Hart might dismiss the "postmodern" impulse in contemporary European philosophy (much of the book is devoted to critical broadsides leveled against Derrida, Deleuze, Lyotard, Levinas, and Heidegger), and however much I find myself in disagreement with Hart's characterizations and assessments of these philosophers, his uncompromising orthodoxy recovers in unexpected forms the necessity of the aesthetic, one that verges on the brink of aestheticism: "In the moment of the beautiful, one need attend only to the glory that it openly proclaims, and resist the temptation to seek out some gnosis secretly imparted" (25). Hart's theology "begins only in *philokalia*, the 'love of beauty'"; and it is a theology that "should always remain at the surface (aesthetic, rhetorical, metaphoric), where all things, finally, come to pass" (28).

26. Jacques Rancière understands these two "vital tendencies" to be inseparable. The recent phase of Rancière's work restores the connections between aesthetics and politics precisely by locating a fundamentally and ineradicably democratizing impulse in the "absolute singularity of art," an impulse that announces the emergence of "the aesthetic regime of art." Having broken from the Platonic or "ethical regime of images" and the Aristotelian or "representative regime of art," the "aesthetic regime of art" "strictly identifies art in the singular and frees it from any specific rule, from any hierarchy of the arts, subject matter, and genres. . . . In the aesthetic regime, artistic phenomena are identified by their adherence to a specific regime of the sensible, which is extricated from its ordinary connections and is inhabited by a heterogeneous power, the power of a form of thought that has become foreign to itself: a product identical with something not produced, knowledge transformed into non-knowledge, *logos* identical with pathos, the intention of the unintentional, etc."; Rancière, *The Politics of Aesthetics*, trans. Gabriel Rockhill (London: Continuum, 2004),

23, 22–23. In other words, the aesthetic regime is distinguished by the way in which "non-identity" is registered to the senses in the form of a "defamiliarization": "The idea of a regime of the sensible that has become foreign to itself, is the invariable core in the identifications of art that have configured the aesthetic mode of thought from the outset" (23). Rancière collapses the local generational or socio-historical periodizations of Western art: from Vico through Kant and Schiller and Schelling to Proust and Mallarme and Bresson and Godard, art is characterized by iterations of this "invariable core" of the "aesthetic regime." Rancière's understanding of the aesthetic regime of art is made all the more relevant when we recognize that its historical emergence corresponds to that which we commonly call Romanticism. According to Rancière, the emergence of the aesthetic regime abolishes the Aristotelian or representative regime of art "without *ending* it." Indeed, both the representative regime of art and the older Platonic ethical regime of images continue to be operative long after their "abolition" by the aesthetic regime. In his afterward to *The Politics of Aesthetics*, Slavoj Žižek describes Rancière's project as the "*aestheticization of politics*": "the assertion of the aesthetic dimension as *inherent* in any radical emancipatory politics" (76). Thus has this protégé of Althusser become Schillerian through and through.

In a different critical idiom, Bruns makes much the same point about the relationship between poetry and aesthetics at this pivotal moment in Western art: the Romantics "pressed the question of what sort of thing poetry might be if it is not (as both ancient and Medieval traditions of poetics had taught) a form of mediation in the service of other fields of discourse—namely, the versifying of meanings derived from various contexts of learning, or the rehearsal of traditional themes of religious and erotic experience"; *On the Anarchy*, 177.

27. Jerrold Hogle, "Shelley's Texts and the Premises of Criticism," *Keats-Shelley Journal* 42 (1993): 72. Hogle goes on to argue that Shelley conceives of this historical spirit in terms of a "dynamic so disruptive of conventional thinking and writing that it undercuts the stated positions of some its poets with 'words which express what they understand not.'"

28. For Badiou, "'Romanticism' is an aesthetic religion," one that we "must be done with" by "deconsecrating the work" and "divesting the artist"; Badiou, *The Century*, trans. Albert Toscano (London: Polity, 2007), 154. And in a different medium John Berger's judgment of Delacroix's *Massacre at Chios* demonstrates that aestheticism is often regarded as an inherent tendency of Romanticism in the broadest sense of that term, such that, when Romanticism "degenerates," it "degenerates into effete aestheticism." What is perhaps most interesting about Berger's judgment is that this degeneration is, as he says, "confirmed" not by Romanticism's failed or minor works, but "most strikingly by the work that represents Romanticism at its height; Berger, "Delacroix's *Massacre at Chios*," *Selected Essays* (New York: Pantheon, 2002), 60.

29. Gary Lee Stonum, *The Dickinson Sublime* (Madison: University of Wisconsin Press, 1990), 33.

30. See *Emily Dickinson's Reception in the 1890s*, ed. Willis J. Buckingham (Pittsburgh: University of Pittsburgh Press, 1989). Higginson first makes the comparison to Blake in "An Open Portfolio," published in the *Christian Union* in 1890. There he notes that "the conception" of "I died for Beauty" is "weird enough for William Blake" (6). In his preface to *Poems by Emily Dickinson* published later that year he makes the oft-quoted comparison to Blake: "It is believed that the thoughtful reader will find in these pages a quality more suggestive of the poetry of William Blake than of anything to be elsewhere found" (14).

31. I suspect that this claim is much less controversial among Romanticists than it may be among specialists in nineteenth-century American literature. When, for instance, Anne-Lise Francois places Dickinson alongside Words-worth and Hardy in the central chapter in her field-changing book, *Open Secrets: The Literature of Uncounted Experience* (Stanford: Stanford University Press, 2008), this constellation is proposed without any special pleading.

32. "Wordsworth: The Poetry of Enshrinement," in *The Ideology of Imagination: Subject and Society in the Discourse of Romanticism*, by Forest Pyle (Stanford: Stanford University Press, 1995), 59–93.

33. Wilde, *De Profundis: Complete Works of Oscar Wilde*, 5th rev. ed. (London: Harper Collins, 2003), 1017.

34. De Man, *Blindness and Insight* (Minneapolis: University of Minnesota Press, 1983), 8. Of course, de Man also goes on to say that "the rhetoric of crisis states its truth in the mode of error. It is itself radically blind to the light it emits" (16). While I hope to demonstrate that the "light emitted" by certain moments in certain texts is best understood as a radical aestheticism, I recognize that for de Man, one cannot know one's own crisis. The famous essay in which de Man makes these claims, an essay called "Criticism and Crisis," begins and ends with a discussion of a lecture Mallarmé delivered in London in 1894, a lecture that with supreme irony, declares a "*crise de vers*." For de Man, the "crisis" Mallarmé alludes to is a "screen" or "pretext" for the poet to examine how, in Mallarmé's words, "the act of writing scrutinized itself to the point of reflecting on its own origin": thus, Mallarmé's lecture is "a text that pretends to designate a crisis when it is, in fact, itself the crisis to which it refers" (7).

35. Timothy Bahti, *Ends of the Lyric: Direction and Consequence in Western Poetry* (Baltimore: Johns Hopkins University Press, 1996), 11.

36. Roland Barthes, "On Leaving the Movie Theatre," trans. Richard Howard, in *The Rustle of Language* (New York: Hill and Wang, 1986), 347.

37. Perhaps a classic example of wanting to have one's cake and eat it, too; though I prefer to understand it as an oscillation between what Hillis Miller calls the optic and semiotic. In "'As the Poets Do It': On the Material Sublime" (*Material Events*, 10), Andrzej Warminski offers a concise and precise account of de Man's practice of reading—what he calls a "reading-motion"—that is particularly relevant to the issues I am posing here: "a reading-motion like

de Man's . . . goes *from* the all-too-poetic lyric . . . that declares, performs (in its synaesthesia), and values sheer aesthetic ideology *to* an infratext underneath that threatens to disarticulate the poem's transcendentalizing tropes and end up in 'the stutter, the *pietinement* of aimless enumeration.'" To invoke another loaded spatial metaphor also employed by de Man, one moves from aesthetic effects as a "superstructure" (and almost by definition delusive "false consciousness") to the text's material base, its textual mode of production. The question asked in various ways by each of these chapters is something like this: what happens when what, following Warminski, we might call the lyricizing synaesthesia of aestheticism performs that disarticulation, leaving us without access to any material "infratext underneath"? Though this question seems to appear in almost every essay de Man wrote, I will limit myself to referring the reader to the most immediately pertinent: "Anthropomorphism and Trope in the Lyric," in *The Rhetoric of Romanticism*, 229–62; "The Resistance to Theory"; and "Reading and History," in *The Resistance to Theory*, 3–20, 54–72. The question is one of scale as well as proximity, for, as in the case of so many Dickinson poems, even the most compressed lyric can make it seem as if there is nothing beyond it or beneath it. I am interested in the effects and affects of that phenomenon, yet another of those instances where the intricacies between phenomenality and materiality, painting and literature, seeing and reading assert themselves as they do in theme and figure throughout the texts of this tradition.

38. In a similar and entirely relevant context, Norman Bryson describes the composition of Caravaggio's early, disorienting *Basket of Fruit* in terms of a "principle of heaping" that "obscures the particularity of individual form and mass"; Bryson, *Looking at the Overlooked: Four Essays on Still Life Painting* (Cambridge, Mass.: Harvard University Press, 1990), 78.

39. Michael Fried, *Absorption and Theatricality: Painting and Beholder in the Age of Diderot* (Chicago: University of Chicago Press, 1980), 154, 153.

40. Murray Krieger's 1965 essay, "The Ekphrastic Principle and the Still Movement of Poetry; or, *Laokoon* Revisited," in *The Play and the Place of Criticism* (Baltimore: Johns Hopkins University Press, 1967), 105–28), remains unsurpassed in its precision and insight into the aesthetic and epistemological issues posed by *ekphrasis*. His essay famously hinges on the aporetic experience of a "still movement" in poetry that informs my thinking not only about Keats, but Shelley, Dickinson, and Rossetti, as well. I take what Krieger calls his "final claim" as my point of departure: "I would like finally to claim that the ekphrastic dimension of literature reveals itself wherever the poem takes on the 'still' elements of plastic form that we normally attribute to the spatial arts. In so doing, the poem proclaims as its own poetic its formal necessity, thus making more than just loosely metaphorical the use of spatial language to describe—and thus to arrest—its movements" (108). Frye's account of the musical and pictorial impulses in the lyric demonstrates how this visuality constitutes its "formal necessity": not only are there "thousands of lyrics so intently focused on visual

imagery that they are, as we may say, set to pictures," but the very "typographical appearance of a lyric on a printed page" shows us that the lyric is "so to speak, overseen as well as overheard" (*Anatomy*, 274).

41. Julian Barnes, *A History of the World in 10½ Chapters* (New York: Vintage, 1990), 125, 127.

42. Denis Hollier, "The Dualist Materialism of Georges Bataille," *Yale French Studies: On Bataille*, ed. Allan Stoekl, no. 78 (1990): 138–39.

43. But it is important to stress something here that we will explore in the chapters on Keats and, especially, Wilde: Bataille's theory of "expenditure" is not a *solution* but a *problem*. Indeed, the efforts by Bataille and some of his followers to make "expenditure" into the basis of a program or project bears uncanny resemblance to those who espouse aestheticism. Allan Stoekl, one of Bataille's most insightful Anglophone interpreters, offers an excellent characterization of the problems attendant to what I am calling an espousal of expenditure: "the problems in Bataille's approach," argues Stoekl in his editor's preface to an important collection of essays on Bataille, "arise exactly to the extent that his work repeats—or mimics, parodies—the orientations of an optimistic Hegelian model of historical development. . . . Throughout the three volumes of *The Accursed Share*, we never really get a convincing portrayal of the virtually utopian future that awaits us, when 'expenditure' will be taken into account in governmental planning, and the great nation States will be devoted to the same aims as those held for millennia by 'primitive chiefs, lovers, and mystics'"; *On Bataille*, 3. Referring to some of the responses to Derrida's influential early work on Bataille, Stoekl notes that many of "Derrida's critics (including Foucault) maintain" that "Bataille's positions, such as they are, gain coherence only by losing any contact with, and effect in, the world" (3). What Stoekl goes on to say about Bataille's novels, *Blue of Noon* and *L'Abbe C.*, also has particular resonance for my thesis about these authors' projects: "it may be that as soon as one recommences a project, no matter how rigorously devoted it is to a 'sheer expenditure,' it will always lead back to a social and even moral environment or context because writing as coherent project (even if its theme is the challenge to all coherency) is itself betrayal" (5).

1. "A LIGHT MORE DREAD THAN OBSCURITY":
SPELLING AND KINDLING IN PERCY BYSSHE SHELLEY

1. Unless otherwise indicated, quotations of Shelley's poetry and prose are from *Shelley's Poetry and Prose*, ed. Donald H. Reiman and Neil Fraistat (New York: Norton, 2002); hereafter *SPP*.

2. This is the function of the aesthetic in such a late and exquisite poem as *The Witch of Atlas*: there the "sweet visions" of beauty are bestowed as an extraordinary gift, entirely unearned, which the beneficiary experiences "*as if* some control / Mightier than life, were in them" (ll.597–98). Even the Witch's participation in "the peopled haunts of humankind" (l.524) is itself the result

of an aesthetic judgment: "To those she saw most beautiful, she gave / Strange panacea in a chrystal bowl" (ll.593–94).

3. Carol Jacobs, *Uncontainable Romanticism* (Baltimore: Johns Hopkins University Press, 1989), 203n15.

4. Compare in this context what one of our own most rigorous contemporary theologians of the beautiful, David Bentley Hart, has to say on the visitation of beauty: "Whatever 'beauty' means is grasped only by analogy, by constant exposure to countless instances of its advent, and through constant and continuous revision (this because, in theological terms, God is the 'primary analogate' to whom beauty is ascribed); and in the more radically ontological sense, that beauty is not some property discretely inherent in particular objects, but indwells the analogical relationship of all things"; *The Beauty of the Infinite*, 18. Hart says that this is what "'beauty' *means*," and yet I think it is more to the point of his own argument to say that this is what and how beauty *teaches*: by the making of analogies, "by constant exposure to countless *instances* of its advent," beauty instructs us about the "primary analogate," what Hopkins would call "God's better beauty, grace." If for the Shelley of the "Hymn," "beauty" is also "grasped only by analogy," by "countless instances of its advent," the *radicality* of Shelley's conception of beauty is that the countless instances of its advent occur in likeness without "primary analogate," which would be but another of Shelley's "frail spells." The teaching of beauty in the "Hymn" is the teaching of an aestheticism.

5. Alain Badiou would no doubt say that this narrative of beauty's descent is formally and thematically nothing more than the "frail" but persistent "spell" of romanticism itself. It is, after all, this very romanticism from which Badiou seeks at last to deliver *us* in order for philosophy to bestow its gift of truth: "What is romanticism? . . . Art is the descent of the infinity of the Ideal into the finitude of the work. The artist, elevated by genius, is the sacrificial medium of this descent. This is a transposition of the Christian schema of the incarnation: the genius lends Spirit the forms it has mastered so that the people may recognize its own spiritual infinitude in the finitude of the work. Since in the end it's the work that bears witness to the incarnation of the infinite, romanticism cannot avoid making the work sacred. . . . What we are calling 'romanticism' is an aesthetic religion"; Badiou, *The Century*, 154. Given the poem's overt deployment of what Badiou calls the "Christian schema," I doubt that Shelley's painstaking discrimination between the nature and the effects of "the phantoms of a thousand hours" and the "poisonous names with which our youth is fed" would satisfy the French philosopher that the performance of this hymn to "O awful LOVELINESS" constitutes anything more than the positing of an "aesthetic religion."

6. To evaluate the nature of this idealist, but genuinely political critique of the actuality of the nation-state, one needs only to situate it alongside Samuel Taylor Coleridge, *On the Constitution of Church and State*, ed. John Colmer (1829; Princeton: Princeton University Press, 1976). For Coleridge, of course, there

is an idea of the nation; and what he calls the "ever-originating idea" of nation is understood to precede and inform the "Idea of a Constitution" (12) and the institutions of the nation-state. The origins of this "ever-originating idea" are not, moreover, empirical in nature: Coleridge regards the origin of the nation as a "pure fiction" (14), but one that is the very condition of its effectivity. For the idea of the nation to secure the state and overcome the class divisions that threaten to undo the sense of a national community, the national fiction must be entrusted to what he calls a "permanent class of order," a "national clerisy." It is thus this national clerisy—a secular poetic intelligentsia—that would effect and administer what Coleridge would openly acknowledge as the "spell" of that "ideal object" called the nation.

7. Badiou would no doubt classify himself as one of Plato's *legitimate* heirs; but the question he poses for the relationship between philosophy and politics is a reiteration of Shelley: for Shelley as for Badiou, it is not enough to ask "Can there be a just politics?" One must also ask whether there can be "a politics which *does justice* to thought?"; Badiou, *Infinite Thought*, 52.

8. Earl Wasserman, *The Subtler Language: Critical Readings of Neoclassic and Romantic Poems* (Baltimore: The Johns Hopkins University Press, 1959), 228. If Wasserman's Shelley remains "unsurpassed," Jerrold E. Hogle has certainly "matched" his precursor: Hogle, *Shelley's Process: Radical Transference and the Development of His Major Works* (New York: Oxford University Press, 1988) is without question the most important sustained interpretation of the poet's career since Wasserman. Hogle's thesis—that Shelley's poetic and discursive thought is activated by (and reveals) a radical and mobile process of transference—is as supple a way of grasping the course of the poet's career as it is illuminating of individual works. Hogle's account of the process of displacements and transferences in "Mont Blanc" casts its shadow over everything I want to say about the poem (73–86). And see "God, Ghosts, and Shelley's 'Atheos,'" *Literature and Theology* 24 (2010): 4–18, for Geoffrey Hartman's recent powerful reading of the poem that I believe complements both Wasserman and Hogle by developing the historical theater of the poem's political and theological implications. Demonstrating how Shelley's poem refutes the mountain's theological iconicity, Hartman's reading stresses the "affirmative" force of "the 'atheos' writ large by [the] poem": "In the face of the power associated with the mountain, Shelley reclaims the matching human power of independent thought" (18).

9. Hogle, "Shelley's Texts and the Premises of Criticism," 68.

10. Michael Davidson, "Refiguring Shelley," *Keats-Shelley Journal* 42 (1993): 49.

11. Compare, for instance, Wilde's characterization of Shelley alongside the latter's account of Milton's relationship to his own historical moment: "Milton stood alone illuminating an age unworthy of him" (*SPP*, 520). In "The Soul of Man Under Socialism," Wilde argues that the fact of Shelley's self-imposed exile from England helped him escape the fate of Byron, whose "personality was terribly wasted in its battle with the stupidity, and hypocrisy, and Philistinism of

the English. Such battles do not always intensify strength: they often exaggerate weakness. Byron was never able to give us what he might have. Shelley escaped better. Like Byron, he got out of England as soon as possible. But he was not so well known. If the English had had any idea of what a great poet he really was, they would have fallen on him with tooth and nail, and made his life as unbearable to him as they possibly could. . . . Still, even in Shelley the note of rebellion is sometimes too strong. The note of the perfect personality is not rebellion, but peace" (*Collected Works of Wilde*, 262–63).

12. The work of Michael Scrivener has long illuminated the extent and power of Shelley's influence and has demonstrated that this influence is not limited to the Chartists, but reaches back to the development of a radical artisan poetry in the 1810s and 1820s; see, in particular, Scrivener, *Radical Shelley: The Philosophical Anarchism and Utopian Thought of P. B. Shelley* (Princeton: Princeton University Press, 1982).

13. Edward Aveling and Eleanor Marx Aveling, *Shelley's Socialism* (London: Journeyman Press, 1975).

14. Quoted in Henry S. Salt, *The Company I Have Kept* (London: George Allen and Unwin, 1930), 51.

15. In the end this might well be more an index of Edward Aveling and Eleanor Marx Aveling's political distinctions between the poets than those of the elder Marx. I have never been able to locate this sentence in Marx's published writings, his notebooks, or his correspondence; and others have questioned the legitimacy of this attribution. In any event, what is most worthy of note in this passage is the alignment of an aesthetic and a political avant-garde in a form that Jacques Rancière finds "in accordance with Schiller's model": namely, "the aesthetic anticipation of the future. If the concept of the avant-garde has any meaning in the aesthetic regime of the arts, it is . . . on the side of the invention of sensible forms and material structures for a life to come"; Rancière, *The Politics of Aesthetics*, trans. Gabriel Rockhill (London: Continuum, 2004), 29. See also Badiou's account of the links "forged" "between artistic avant-gardes and politics," in Badiou, *Century*, 133. Badiou is interested in the forms through which political and artistic avant-gardes—especially communists and painters— developed a defining model of twentieth-century self-understanding. Though this is conventionally understood to be a modernist project, Badiou stresses the romanticism imprinted in the very notion of the avant-garde. Moreover, Badiou's description of the twentieth-century avant-garde's commitment to a *collective* and *historical* project helps us understand a strain of thought that runs throughout Shelley's political poetics and offers a new way to read the manifesto we call *A Defence of Poetry*. "For the avant-gardes," writes Badiou, "art is much more than the solitary production of works of genius. Collective existence and life itself are at stake. Art can no longer be conceived without an element of violent aesthetic militancy" (*Century*, 134).

16. See, for instance, the 1816 sonnet "Feelings of a Republican on the Fall of Bonaparte" and the final poem published during Shelley's life, "Written on

Hearing the News of the Death of Napoleon," perhaps the bleakest of any poem Shelley would write. It should be acknowledged that the putatively "Marxist" differentiation between Shelley and Byron fails to appreciate the simultaneously penetrating and narcissistic power of the latter's analysis of Napoleonic desire in the third canto of *Childe Harold's Pilgrimmage*.

17. Michael Palmer, "Some Notes on Shelley, Poetics, and the Present," in *Active Boundaries: Selected Essays and Talks* (New York: New Directions, 2008), 199. It is worth noting that no such "rediscovery" is necessary for the German poetic tradition, where Shelley was never a poet "under erasures." If Brecht is "our father" of German Modernist poetry, he claims Shelley as *"mein Brüder."*

18. Walter Benjamin, "On the Concept of History," in *Selected Writings*, vol. IV (1938–1940), ed. Howard Eiland and Marcus Bullock (Cambridge, Mass.: Harvard University Press, 2003), 396. In his most immediate circle, one thinks of such "irreconcilables" as Scholem, Adorno, Brecht, Lacis. Later in the century Benjamin becomes the nexus for another such "constellation saturated with tensions": Marxism (Jameson, Eagleton, Berger), deconstruction (de Man, Derrida, Jacobs, Balfour), theological poetics (Agamben), "anthropological poetics" (Taussig). I would like to acknowledge my good fortune over the past twenty years to have enjoyed extended conversations about Benjamin with some of the most knowledgeable scholars of his work: Ian Balfour, John McCole, Mick Taussig, and Irving Wohlfarth.

19. As with so many of Benjamin's contributions to our critical vocabulary, the notion of the "constellation" is as formidably difficult as it is richly provocative: in fact, the principal passages in which it is defined are often among those that demand the most exposition. I will, nevertheless, cite two passages that are indispensable to my own understanding of the term. The first is taken from the "N" convolute of the *Arcades Project*: "It's not that what is past casts its light on what is present, or what is present its light on the past; rather, image is that wherein what has been comes together in a flash with the now to form a constellation. In other words, image is dialectics at a standstill. For while the relation of the present to the past is a purely temporal, continuous one, the relation of what-has-been to the now is dialectical: is not progression but image, suddenly emergent"; Benjamin, *The Arcades Project*, trans. Howard Eiland and Kevin McLaughlin (Cambridge, Mass.: Harvard University Press, 1999), 462; N 2a, 3. The second passage appears under the heading "A" in an early draft of the theses "On the Concept of History": "Historicism contents itself with establishing a causal nexus among various moments in history. But no state of affairs having causal significance is for that very reason historical. It became historical posthumously, as it were, through events that may be separated from it by thousands of years. The historian who proceeds from this consideration ceases to tell the sequence of events like the beads of a rosary. He grasps the constellation into which his own era has entered, along with a very specific earlier one. Thus, he establishes a conception of the present as now-time shot through with splinters of messianic time" (*SW*, IV, 397). Further evidence of this "secret agreement":

in 1922 Benjamin conceived of a journal to be named *Angleus Novus* inspired by the Klee painting he owned at the time. In his unpublished "announcement" of the journal, Benjamin writes that "the vocation of a journal is to proclaim the spirit of the age"; *Selected Writings*, vol. 1 (1913–1926), ed. Marcus Bullock and Michael W. Jennings (Cambridge, Mass.: Harvard University Press, 1996), 292.

Giorgio Agamben is certainly among Benjamin's most illuminating interpreters; and Benjamin's conceptions of time and history are often the topic if not the occasion of his many essays and books. My understanding of Benjamin's conceptions of history is especially indebted to Agamben, *Infancy and History: Essays on the Destruction of Experience*, trans. Liz Heron (London: Verso, 1993), and *The Signature of All Things: On Method*, trans. Luca D'Isanto, with Kevin Attell (New York: Zone Books, 2009); see also Max Pensky, "Method and Time: Benjamin's Dialectical Images," in *The Cambridge Companion to Walter Benjamin*, ed. David S. Ferris (Cambridge: Cambridge University Press, 2004), 177–98.

20. As it turns out, the "agreement" between Shelley and Benjamin is not such a "secret," and is more congested than a "one-way street": Shelley, an object of intense identification for Brecht, is also taken up by Benjamin during the course of their extraordinary discussions and correspondences. While Benjamin is working on Baudelaire and Paris, he reads Brecht's translation of *Peter Bell the Third* and transcribes nine stanzas from Part III ("Hell is a city much like London—") that are included as an entry in the "M" convolute in *The Arcades Project* (*Arcades*, 449; M18). Shelley's poem and, most likely, Benjamin's conversations with Brecht about politics, the lyric, and the city prompt Benjamin's most sustained reflections on the British Romantic poet, reflections that take the form of comparisons between Shelley and Baudelaire over their allegorical impulses. Benjamin concludes that "the incisive effect" of *Peter Bell the Third* "depends, for the most part, on the fact that Shelley's *grasp* of allegory makes itself felt. It is this grasp that is missing in Baudelaire. This grasp, which makes palpable the distance of the modern poet from allegory, is precisely what enables allegory to incorporate into itself the most immediate realities. With what directness that can happen is best shown by Shelley's poem in which bailiffs, parliamentarians, stock-jobbers, and many other types figure. The allegory, in its emphatically antique character, gives them all a sure footing" (*Arcades*, 370; J81, 6).

21. John McCole, *Walter Benjamin and the Antinomies of Tradition* (Ithaca: Cornell University Press, 1993), 3.

22. Robert Kaufman, "Aura, Still," in *Walter Benjamin and Art*, ed. Andrew Benjamin (London: Continuum, 2005), 122. I find Kaufman's essay to be a crucial point of reference and departure for my own argument. His analysis of the "matrix" of Benjamin, Adorno, Shelley, and Brecht is indispensable for anyone interested in the debates over such aesthetic notions as the aura; and it is crucial for our understanding of the Romantic origins and the recent manifestations of those debates. Ultimately, Kaufman turns from Benjamin's efforts to jettison the aura to Adorno's reappropriation of its critical dimension. In Kaufman's account,

this reclaiming of the aura "*via negativa*" is precisely what separates art and its critical autonomy from *aestheticization*.

23. And yet, as many of Benjamin's commentators have demonstrated, his formulations of the aura are not always consistent, and certainly not consistently negative. In his 1930 account of an experiment with hashish, for instance, Benjamin would take pains to distinguish the "genuine aura" from that which is "described and illustrated in vulgar works of mysticism": "the characteristic feature of genuine aura is ornament, an ornamental halo, in which the object or being is enclosed as in a case"; *Selected Writings*, vol. 2 (1927–1934) ed. Michael W. Jennings. Howard Eiland, and Gary Smith (Cambridge, Mass.: Harvard University Press, 1999), 328). An "ornamental halo," the "*genuine* aura" "wreathes" the object with what one might call the effect of divinity (328, emphasis added). And yet Benjamin preserves this "genuine aura" from the "spiritualists" and their "beloved" "magic rays": "genuine aura"—and thus, perhaps, genuine divinity—is for Benjamin an *aesthetic* effect. If there is any doubt about Benjamin's evaluation of the aura in this context, one need only to consider the example he invokes from "the age of technological reproducibility" to illustrate this effect: "Perhaps nothing gives such a clear idea of aura as Van Gogh's late paintings, in which one could say that the aura appears to have been painted together with the various objects" (328). The most nuanced and, in many ways, unsettling essay on Benjamin's aura is Samuel Weber's "Mass Mediauras; or, Art, Aura, and Media in the Work of Walter Benjamin," in *Walter Benjamin: Theoretical Questions*, ed. David S. Ferris (Stanford: Stanford University Press, 1996), 27–49; see also Agamben, "The Melancholy Angel," in *The Man Without Content*, trans. Georgia Albert (Stanford: Stanford University Press, 1999), 104–15.

24. The final chapter of Redfield's *The Politics of Aesthetics* is devoted to "Shelley's Political Poetics"; and it opens with a penetrating reading of *The Mask of Anarchy*, a reading that establishes a new benchmark for our understanding of the formal and rhetorical complexities of this "wholly political" poem in ways that are immediately applicable to the issues I raise in this chapter. In Redfield's understanding, *The Mask* demonstrates how Shelley's "critique of aesthetic ideology will always have to risk a certain 'aestheticism'" (157). "Furthermore," Redfield writes, "this aestheticization enables the satire—the identification of Murder and Castlereagh, Anarchy in King George—that made the poem unpublishable in 1819, and politically effective in the 1830s" (161).

25. See Adorno, "Extorted Reconciliation: On Georg Lukacs's *Realism in Our Time*," in *Notes to Literature*, vol. 2, trans. Shierry Weber Nicholsen (New York: Columbia University Press, 1991), 2:216–40.

26. Thus is Shelley's conception of the relationship between aesthetics and politics an "avant-garde" not in Aveling and Marx Aveling's sense of a political leadership, but as Jacques Rancière characterizes it, "rooted in the aesthetic anticipation of the future," "the invention of sensible forms and material structures for *a life to come*" (Rancière, *Politics of Aesthetics*, 29). Shelley understands, *pace Rancière*, that "political statement and literary locutions produce effects in real-

ity. They define models of speech or action, but also regimes of sensible intensity" (39).

The sonnet's implicit articulation of literary form and political history is the focus of an important reading by James Chandler, who takes the title of the sonnet for his own impressive study of "the politics of literary culture and the case of Romantic historicism." Chandler attends closely to the list of social evils that comprises the body of the sonnet and argues persuasively that "the terms of the times in Shelley's catalogue—the conditions of his tempestuous day—are not simple evils and are not simply overcome by the arrival of an enlightening '*deus ex machina.*' Rather, these conditions, these terms of social existence, are in each instance the source from which the illuminations will spring"; Chandler, *England in 1819: The Politics of Literary Culture and the Case of Romantic Historicism* (Chicago: University of Chicago Press, 1998), 30. For Chandler the ills as they are enumerated by the poem rise to the level of historical "conditions"—genuinely contradictory ones at that—that must be "*read*, like fine print, not merely seen" (31).

Chandler's argument throughout his book has the entirely salutary effect of returning our attention to the radical historicizing already at work in Shelley (or, as his other chapters demonstrate, in Scott, Byron, and Keats). Chandler achieves this, moreover, without resorting to the sort of critical contortions evident, for instance, in Marjorie Levinson's celebration of Keats's "badness": while *Keats's Life of Allegory* (Oxford: Basil Blackwell, 1988) is certainly a virtuoso performance, it also constitutes something like an end-around of the "romantic ideology." In his own assessment of the new historicism, Chandler asserts that much of the work that has been conducted under this rubric claims a "historiographical, even a political advance over any historical paradigm one uncovers in the Romantic era, but that *appearance* may itself depend on covering over . . . the complexity and density of historicist thought in Romantic writing" (*England in 1819*, 139). Chandler's understanding of the "complexity and density of historicist thought" in Shelley concentrates on the poet's notion of the "spirit of the age" that Chandler characterizes as the poet's "preoccupation with contemporaneity" (106). Chandler's Shelley is thus a poet whose work not only reflects upon his own socio-historical movement, but also "situates *itself* in that movement" (525). And yet, should Chandler's reading of Shelley's engagement with his historical "conditions" (such as those inscribed in the sonnet) have the desired (and desirable) results of prompting closer critical attention to Shelley's conceptions of history, the poetics of contemporaneity will reveal itself to be but a "case" of futurity.

27. On the disruptive and revolutionary force of the messianic, see Eric Jacobson, *Metaphysics of the Profane: The Political Theology of Walter Benjamin and Gershom Scholem* (New York: Columbia University Press, 2003): "The advent of messiah is clearly juxtaposed to the course of history shaped by the mighty and powerful. The messiah disrupts history and is determined to usher into worldly affairs a transformative age" (6).

28. "Kindling," as Deborah Elise White notes, "appears in almost every major Shelley text" as the "aesthetic transformation of a didactic encounter into an imaginative one": "kindling names an eloquence that informs and yet surpasses language"; White, *Romantic Returns: Superstition, Imagination, History* (Stanford: Stanford University Press, 2000), 133. The final two chapters of *Romantic Returns* are not only devoted to Shelley's deployments of "kindling" (133–42), "poetics of reference," and sense of history's "proof," but the finest reading of *The Revolt of Islam* I know of.

29. See Chandler's closing chapter of *England in 1819* for a compelling discussion of "history's lyre" in the *Ode to the West Wind* (525–54).

30. "On the Medusa of Leonard da Vinci in the Florentine Gallery" is not among the poems published in *Shelley's Poetry and Prose*. This text of the poem is taken from *The Posthumous Poems of Percy Bysshe Shelley*, ed. Mary W. Shelley (London: John and Henry L. Hunt, 1824), 139–40.

31. See Neil Hertz's brilliant reflection on the figurations of Medusa in *The End of the Line* (New York: Columbia University Press, 1985), 160–93; and see the critical exchange that follows Hertz's essay: a brief and straightforward historical critique by Catherine Gallagher (194–96), Joel Fineman's suggestive and more far-reaching engagement (197–205), and Hertz's reply (206–15). And see Jean-Pierre Vernant's exquisite readings of the classical accounts of the Medusa in his *Mortals and Immortals*, ed. Froma I. Zeitlin (Princeton: Princeton University Press, 1991), 111–50.

32. For descriptions of Shelley's visits to the Uffizi, see Richard Holmes, *Shelley: The Pursuit* (New York: Penguin, 1974), 565–68. In this context it is worth noting that not only is the Medusa of Shelley's poem not "of Leonardo da Vinci," but that the painting no longer even hangs in the "Florentine Gallery." Holmes has collected Shelley's much more conventional examples of ekphrastic writing from his "Notes on Sculptures in Rome and Florence," in *Shelley on Love: An Anthology* (Berkeley: University of California Press, 1980), 21–29, 233–35.

33. Theodor Adorno, "Lyric Poetry and Society," in *Notes to Literature*, trans. Shierry Weber Nicholson (New York: Columbia University Press, 1991), 1:39.

34. W. J. T. Mitchell, *Picture Theory* (Chicago: University of Chicago Press, 1994), 151–81.

35. Jacobs, "On Looking at Shelley's Medusa," in *Uncontainable Romanticism*, 5.

36. This is, of course, an invocation of Levinas, one that seems simultaneously appropriate and problematic for Shelley's Medusa: the poet's gesture, rescuing a face from violence of (dis)figuration, seems wholly appropriate until we recall that it remains *an image in a work of art*. We will return to this Levinasian challenge in the following chapter. Here I would point out among the many important responses to Levinas's work Judith Butler's *Precarious Life*, a sympathetic and pertinent account of the insistence of figuration in Levinas. There Butler demonstrates how the face for Levinas is "not exclusively a human face,"

that it can "operate as a catachresis," "as if it were a face or, rather, a face with a mouth, a throat, or indeed, just a mouth and throat from which vocalizations emerge that do not settle into words," and perhaps—as in the example of the painted image of the Medusa—are exhaled as a "thrilling vapour"; see *Precarious Life*, 128–51.

37. If the nature of Mitchell's interpretation dictates that he not confront the poem's rhetorical complications, Jacobs's genuine confrontation prompts another form of aversion at the far end of her reading, as she turns without notice from Shelley's poem to a brief closing discussion of *The Defence of Poetry*.

38. "[S]kepticism is precisely what I've been talking to you about: the difference between believing and seeing, between believing one sees [*croire voir*] and seeing between, catching a glimpse [*entrevoir*]—or not. Before doubt ever becomes a system, *skepsis* has to do with the eyes"; Jacques Derrida, *Memoirs of the Blind: The Self-Portrait and Other Ruins*, trans. Pascale-Anne Brault and Michael Naas (Chicago: University of Chicago Press, 1993), 1.

39. In her reading of these lines, Jacobs stresses that "in Shelley's text the figure for poetic inspiration . . . appears as a questionable source of poetry, a vaporous mirror that both reflects and withdraws the locus of reflection"; Jacobs, *Uncontainable Romanticism*, 13.

40. Martin Heidegger, "The Origin of the Work of Art," trans. Albert Hofstadter, in *Poetry, Language, Thought* (New York: Harper and Row, 1971), 78.

41. Paul de Man, "Shelley Disfigured," in *Rhetoric*, 97. Orrin N. C. Wang's "Disfiguring Monuments: History," in Paul de Man and Percy Bysshe Shelley, *Fantastic Modernity: Dialectical Readings in Romanticism and Theory* (Baltimore: Johns Hopkins University Press, 1996), 37–68, is to my knowledge the most illuminating and genuinely dialectical reading of the problem of history in this poem and in de Man's "disfiguring" "monumentalization" of it. And see Geoffrey Hartman's brief, but brilliant account of the poem and de Man's response to it in *Criticism in the Wilderness: The Study of Literature Today* (New Haven: Yale University Press, 1980), 106–11, 261–62.

42. For Hogle, this "shape all light" is the figure of Shelleyan "primordial transference," "transference embodied, almost more than any previous figure that Shelley has employed"; Hogle, *Shelley's Process*, 323. In an earlier attempt to come to terms with the nature and effects of this "shape all light," I called it a catachresis. I thought that I could resist the seductions of this romantic image by reading it as de Man taught us; see Pyle, *The Ideology of Imagination*, 117–20. But even if we have learned enough from his work to identify "a shape all light" as a catachresis, a worldly impossibility that issues from language's most originary power to posit, to arise from nothing, the instant we look back at the poem and *gaze* upon this "image," "all that was seemed as if it had been not" (l.385). If I permit myself here to refer to my earlier reading of *The Triumph of Life*, it is in the spirit of de Man's account of Benjamin's translator: "If the text is called '*Die Aufgabe des Übersetzers*,' we have to read this title more or less as a tautology: *Aufgabe*, task, can also mean the one who has to give up. . . . It is in that sense

also the defeat, the giving up, of the translator"; de Man, *Resistance to Theory*, 80. As I understand it, my own return to this passage in *The Triumph* marks both the revival of that task of reading and an acknowledgment that what I am doing here is the mode of "giving up," the surrender of that critical practice to the radical aestheticism I encounter in this poem.

2. "I HOLD IT TOWARDS YOU": KEATS'S WEAKNESS

1. Quotations of Keats's poems are from *The Poems of John Keats*, ed. John Stillinger (Cambridge, Mass.: Harvard University Press, 1978) and are indicated by line numbers. Quotations from Keats's letters are from *The Letters of John Keats*, ed. Hyder Edward Rollins, 2 vols. (Cambridge, Mass.: Harvard University Press, 1958), and are indicated by the abbreviation *KL*, with volume and page number.

2. *Complete Works of Oscar Wilde*, 770.

3. Gerard Manley Hopkins, *Selected Letters*, ed. Catherine Phillips (Oxford: Clarendon Press, 1990). In his strong reading of "Keats's Radicalism," *Studies in Romanticism* 25 (Summer 1986), David Bromwich also quotes this passage to emphasize how Hopkins's judgments replicate those of John Gibson Lockhart in the latter's notorious assault on the Cockney School of Poetry.

4. Andrew Motion, *Keats* (New York: Farrar, Straus and Giroux, 1997), 569.

5. Karen Swann has written "definitively on these things"—the "cloudy trophies hung" in the Keats reliquary—in a series of exquisite essays about the highly overdetermined afterlives of both Keats and Shelley, these alien and "beautiful dreamers" that "live a posthumous life, beyond life and death, but transcending neither." As early as 1820 Keats writes that he feels he is already living a "posthumous life"; and Swann demonstrates that "long before the symptoms of consumption appeared," the Keats Circle "started preparing for the fame-to-be of the dead poet," whom after the reviews of *Endymion*, they began to refer to "as poor Keats," cultivating and projecting a weakness in advance of any empirical evidence; see Swann, "The Strange Time of Reading." This essay, "*Hyperion's* Beautiful Dreamers," and "Shelley's Pod People" are installments in an ongoing project that Swann calls "The Lives of the Dead Poets." Swann's essays are to my mind the most compelling accounts of this dimension of the poet since Christopher Ricks's *Keats and Embarrassment* (Oxford: Clarendon Press, 1974), a book that only seems more right and relevant thirty years on. Famously for Ricks, Keats's great achievement is his willingness to court embarrassment, which Ricks correlates directly to the poet's capacious ethical sense: "acute to embarrassment, [Keats is] probably more widely and subtly gifted with powers of empathy than any other English poet" (24). But of course we can only be embarrassed by what we regard to be a weakness, a connection that Ricks implies when he asserts "that embarrassment is primitively connected with defencelessness" (24).

6. Paul de Man, "The Poetry of John Keats," in *Critical Writings* (Minneapolis: University of Minnesota Press, 1989), 181.

7. Timothy Bahti's indispensable account of Keats's place at the "ends of the lyric" treats this relationship without indulging the fascination of an indolent strength; see Bahti, *Ends of the Lyric*, 80. In *The Neutral*, Barthes identifies sleep as one of the states or conditions that by suspending consciousness and conflict can deliver us to the neutral. In Barthes's account, sleep even assumes an ethical dimension insofar as it produces a kind of temporary utopia; Roland Barthes, *The Neutral*, trans. Rosalind Krauss and Denis Hollier (New York: Columbia University Press, 2005), 37.

8. In the autobiography he composed in the third person, Roland Barthes acknowledged that his own "raptures over binarism" became for him a mania, "a kind of erotic object," such "a continuous astonishment" that he tacitly admits it as a form of weakness: *Roland Barthes By Roland Barthes*, trans. Richard Howard (New York: Farrar, Straus, and Giroux, 1977). While Derrida's deconstruction of the structuralist reliance on oppositions is one of the most prominent features of his early work—indeed, perhaps the *event* that constitutes a *post-structuralism*—Derrida would later maintain that he "believe[d] that [Barthes] did not believe . . . in any oppositions. He would use them only for the time of a passage. . . . [T]he concepts that seemed the most squarely opposed, or opposable, were put in play"; Derrida, "The Deaths of Roland Barthes," in *Psyche: Inventions of the Other* (Stanford: Stanford University Press, 2007), 1:267. And it is true that "raptures over binarism" constitute less a *belief* than a species of aesthetic response.

9. Barthes, "Dare to be Lazy," in *The Grain of the Voice: Interviews 1962–1980*, trans. Richard Howard (New York: Farrar, Straus, and Giroux, 1985), 339, 342.

10. Barthes's essays on Twombly are collected in *The Responsibility of Forms: Critical Essays on Music, Art, and Representation*, trans. Richard Howard (New York: Farrar, Straus, and Giroux, 1985), 158; hereafter *RF*.

11. "The key to Twombly's 'effect,'" writes Barthes, "constant in all Twombly's canvases . . . is the very general one released in all its possible dimensions by the word *Mediterranean*. The Mediterranean is an enormous complex of memories and sensations: two languages, Greek and Latin, to be found in Twombly's titles, a mythological, historical, poetic culture, a whole life of forms, colors, and light"; Barthes, *RF*, 186. So many of Keats's most compelling poems and so much of his thinking belong to this "mythological, historical, poetic culture"; and if those "two languages, Greek and Latin," are notoriously weak in this poet or if Keats's Mediterranean is seldom "serene," the poetic cessation of activity summoned by the "Ode on Indolence" is Keats's closest approximation to Twombly's luminous "Mediterranean effect."

12. Barthes, *A Lover's Discourse*, trans. Richard Howard (New York: Farrar, Straus, and Giroux, 1978), 11–12.

13. Stuart Sperry, *Keats the Poet* (Princeton: Princeton University Press, 1973), 262.

14. *The Life and Letters of Joseph Severn*, ed. William Sharp (London: Sampson, Low, Marston, 1892), 23.

15. Although Ricks does not address these sonnets in *Keats and Embarrass-ment*, he offers a more nuanced account of what he calls "the mere gape" in Keats. For Ricks this is an aspect of Keats's willingness to risk embarrassment in order to achieve his deepest "generosity." As Ricks puts it, Keats's "lines not only do not avert their eyes from the mere gape (always fascinating in its way, they do not look upon it with distaste or thwarted sympathy either; they embody a generosity that can accommodate a truthful recognition (and not be mesmer-ized)" (9).

16. This is another version of the condition that Keats recounts in "Lines on Seeing a Lock of Milton's Hair." There the speaker's ode to that "Old Scholar of the Spheres" forecloses itself: "what a mad endeavour/Worketh he,/Who, to thy sacred and ennobled hearse,/Would offer a burnt sacrifice of verse/And Melody" (ll.2, 6–10). And when the speaker sees "A Lock" of the great poet's "bright hair," "hushed" and "flushed" are paired to account for the weak mutism brought on by beholding "the simplest vassal" of Milton's great "Power": "For Many years my offerings must be hush'd./When I do speak, I'll think upon this hour,/Because I feel my forehead hot and flush'd—/Even at the simplest vassal of thy Power—" (ll.31–35). In "The Strange Time of Reading," Karen Swann's delicate and intimate reading of this poem demonstrates how the speaker's "shameful loss of composure"—his *weakness*—makes the poem acquire the force of the relic he witnesses "unaware."

17. Marjorie Levinson offers a characteristically provocative reading of "On Seeing the Elgin Marbles," in *Keats's Life of Allegory*, 248. In Levinson's account of the trajectory of Keats's "badness," the sonnet is said to convey "the weakness of the early, unself-consciously fetishistic poetry," which she contrasts to "the power of the later, determined fetishism" (247). But I don't regard that trans-formation to be the *object* of Keats's sonnet, which seems rather to explore the effects and affects of aesthetic experience and the weakness it produces.

18. Teresa Kelly's acute attention to the "tonal perplexity" of the sonnet has taught us how to understand the speaker's "unconfident, oddly provisional stance"; and it is indeed perplexing to confess to a weakness in a poetic mode that would seem to be predicated on the strength of one's descriptive pow-ers; see Kelly, "Keats and Ekphrasis," in *The Cambridge Companion to Keats*, ed. Susan Wolfson (Cambridge: Cambridge University Press, 2001), 172. Kelly demonstrates how the "ekphrastic impulse" permeates Keats's poetry, an impulse perhaps more powerfully and confidently at work in poems that are not, strictly speaking, literary representations of a visual artwork. Keats's most overtly ek-phrastic poems are often characterized not only by hesitation, uncertainty, and tentativeness, but by confessions of weakness, the crippling failure to describe.

19. I think Barthes understood his aestheticism in this way, recoiling from it at the very instant of its identification and the point of its contact. For example, he would reject the suggestion that an aestheticism—what he identifies as "a kind of higher aestheticism"—unites Twombly and Mallarmé: Twombly "has been compared to Mallarmé, but what enables the comparison, i.e., a kind of

higher aestheticism which would unite them, exists in neither"; Barthes, *RF*,
161. It is worth comparing this aversion of aestheticism to Foucault's embrace
of it in his late essays and interviews. For Foucault, an aestheticism emerges as
one of the principal results of what he calls his "genealogy of ethics." I take up
Foucault's ethics of aestheticism in Chapter 6.

20. This is how David Ferris invokes the figure of the pointed finger in his
chapter in *Silent Urns* on Keats's Hellenism and its most famous example. Ferris
reads the poem's own reading of "a Grecian Urn" and demonstrates that, far from
proposing any resolution between truth and beauty or between history and the
aesthetic, Keats's ode alludes to an aesthetic understanding that the performance
of the poem itself resists. For Ferris Keats's poem is a reminder in the midst of
our own debates that "[w]hat has still to be digested is a romanticism that no
amount of ideology finger-pointing will allow us to evade, a romanticism that
undertakes a reflection on the relation of historical knowledge and aesthetic
understanding" Ferris, *Silent Urns: Romanticism, Hellenism, Modernity* (Stanford:
Stanford University Press, 2000), 60. "Finger-pointing" is a fascinating way to
describe this contemporary aversion to the aesthetic, especially when we consider the deictic character of Keats's ekphrastic poem and of the insistence of
the aesthetic in romanticism more generally. For if Keats's poem "consistently
fails to answer its own questions about the historical status of the urn" (83), the
questions it poses—the questions it insists upon—"confound, rather than lead to,
understanding. Part of the problem that Keats *points to* in these lines is that what is
being looked at does not guide or define the poet's" questions, "questions that are
suspended because they cannot define what they ask after" (77, emphasis added).
If Keats's poem insists that "the power is there," the *there* is the urn that the poem
both indicates and addresses; and it is a persistent if recalcitrant *aesthetic* power.

21. In Austin's terms, is the poem an illocutionary or perlocutionary act?
"The perlocutionary act always includes some consequences: it is an instance of
"by saying this I was doing that"; J. L. Austin, *How to Do Things With Words*, 2nd
ed. (Cambridge, Mass.: Harvard University Press, 1975), 107. It is, in fact, these
consequences—which Austin says can be an "arbitrarily long stretch"—that
qualify the poetic utterance as a threat. But Austin also tells us that "the distinctions between illocutions and perlocutions . . . seem likeliest to give trouble"
(110), so determining whether Keats's poetic "utterance" "rises" to the level of
an illocutionary act will doubtless give us the same trouble, particularly given
the fact that we are dealing with what Austin famously terms a "parasitic" use of
language (104). The performance of an illocutionary act "takes effect" when it
"secures" what Austin calls the "*uptake*" of its audience. Does this poem—and
can any poem—constitute "an unmistakably threatening gesture" (120)? Austin's
examples are fascinating; and thus it is interesting in this context to note that
Austin distinguishes physical acts from speech acts by invoking as the "minimum
physical act, the movement of the finger."

22. Among the many reasons Barthes lists for declaring his love to Benveniste, none is more influential than Benveniste's principal role in the founding

of "a new linguistics": "the linguistics of interlocution, language, and consequently the whole world, is articulated around this form: I/you"; Barthes, *The
Rustle of Language*, trans. Richard Howard (New York: Hill and Wang, 1986),
166; hereafter *RL*. According to the principles of the "new linguistics," Keats's
subjective state—his intentions or motivations—are entirely irrelevant. The
ringing conclusion Barthes draws from "the new linguistics" possesses the power
of a slogan: "there is no 'subject' (and consequently no 'subjectivity,' there are
only locutors; moreover—and this is Benveniste's incessant reminder—there
are only *interlocutors*" (166)

23. This is de Man's definition and example in "Hypogram and Inscription":
"The trope which coins a name for a still unnamed entity, which gives face to
the faceless is, of course, catachresis. That a catachresis can be a prosopopoeia,
in the etymological sense of 'giving face,' is clear from such ordinary instances
as the *face* of a mountain or the *eye* of a hurricane"; de Man, "Hypogram and
Inscription," in *Resistance to Theory*, 44.

24. "The *author* is a modern character, no doubt produced by our society
as it emerged from the Middle Ages, inflected by English empiricism, French
rationalism, and the personal faith of the Reformation, thereby discovering the
prestige of the individual, or, as we say more nobly, of the "human person."
Hence, it is logical that in literary matters it should be positivism, crown and
conclusion of capitalist ideology, which has granted the greatest importance to
the author's person"; Barthes, *RL*, 49–50.

25. Susan Wolfson, *Formal Charge: The Shaping of Poetry in British Romanticism* (Stanford: Stanford University Press, 1997), 189.

26. It is worth noting that in his 1954 essay on "The Dead-End of Formalist
Criticism," de Man identifies the assumptions and motivations of Barthes's work
that led it to this impasse: Barthes's formalism "proceeds from a historical situation," writes de Man, and motivated by "revolutionary action" falls "all at once
into all the traps of impatient 'pastoral' thought: formalism, false historicism,
and utopianism"; de Man, "The Dead-End of Formalist Criticism," in *Blindness
and Insight*, 241. "The Death of the Author" is caught in each of these "traps."
We might be tempted to characterize the language in this essay as "militant"
were it not for Barthes's pronouncements against militant language: "I was never
a militant, and it would be impossible for me to be one because of my personal
attitude toward language: I don't like militant language" (*Grain*, 362). How do
we reconcile these positions? De Man's analysis of Barthes's position is certainly
accurate, even more than a decade before the publication of "The Death of the
Author." At the same time, however, if we can speak of a "tone" as well as a
"grain" to the voice of this critic, Barthes's "partisanship" never possesses the
tone of genuine militancy. He is more likely to conjure the plaintive indolence of
Leonard Cohen *singing* "The Partisan."

27. When de Man is assessing the strength of Riffaterre's reading practices,
for instance, he poses the most stringent tests in the language of power and
strength, the disfiguring force of language itself: "Do these readings cope with

the sheer strength of figuration, that is to say master their power to confer, to usurp, and to take away significance from grammatical universals? . . . How do they confront the trope which threatens to dismember or to disfigure the lexicality and grammaticality of the hypogram, namely prosopopoeia which, as the trope of address, is the very figure of the reader and reading?"; de Man, *Resistance to Theory*, 45.

28. But many of us do read it, over and over. "This living hand," this scrap of textual residue, has come to exert a powerful attraction for many critics, the source of a fascination that occasionally rises to the level of obsession. That this poetic fragment would be the object of such intense critical attention would have long been unthinkable. In her assessment of the crisis posed by Keats's late lyrics, Wolfson shows that, until quite recently, even the most capable readers have regarded "This living hand" and the handful of late lyrics as nothing "other than documents in agony and a sorry falling off from the Great Odes" (169). These late texts have long signaled, in other words, the descent of the poet into his final weakness. Wolfson does not tell us what changed or why; but de Man's 1966 introduction to the Signet edition of Keats's selected poems and letters might mark that event in Keats studies, the moment at which we could begin to recognize how the "violently negative form of his last poems" takes us to a place that must be confronted, "a long way [from] the early days of *Endymion*" (de Man, *Critical Writings*, 196). In what de Man calls this "new phase" of Keats's poetry, there is "a change that is so far-reaching that it requires a radical readjustment on the part of the readers" (191). De Man concludes his introduction by quoting in full "This living hand," the final installment in this "new phase." And yet he offers no reading of this poem and gives it only the most minimal of introductions: it is as if de Man were handing it to us, showing us the poem that will require our own "radical readjustments."

Certainly one such "radical readjustment" demanded by "This living hand" is not only to be addressed directly and thereby implicated by the address, but to reckon with the fact that this poetic hailing seems to crystallize not only a particular threat to the reader, but the very threat of reading as such. Perhaps "This living hand" demands something from us *now*, because it knows—and *shows*—that the threat posed by reading is the definitive form of haunting: the poem presents us with thoughts, images, feelings that never cease their visitations and that "present themselves as recurrent influences or impressions, esp. as causes of unrest" (*OED*). If "Ode on Melancholy" arrives at the figure of speech that is both a figure of strength—a "strenuous tongue"—*and* that makes "trophies" of its owners, "This living hand" presents us with a weakness powerful enough to threaten every reader. Perhaps this is why even the finest readers, such as Wolfson, Bahti, Culler, and de Man—to name only those to whom I am most indebted—invoke the poem *in closing*: in order to extend the haunting of its most lurid figures.

29. In his eloquent reading of the poem, Bahti describes this relationship as "the figure . . . of a Möbius strip" in a manner that emphasizes the implication of

the reader; *Ends of Lyric*, 91–94. Bahti's attention to the pressure that "This living hand" places upon the notion of a "handwriting" conjures the indeterminate region between printing and painting, handwriting as "hand drawing," a region Twombly explores in his own forays into Keats's Mediterranean.

30. Jonathan Culler, *The Pursuit of Signs* (London: Routledge, 1981), 153.

31. See Stephen Bann, *The True Vine: On Visual Representation and the Western Tradition* (Cambridge: Cambridge University Press, 1989), 86–87.

32. From his early work on eighteenth-century French painting through his recent work on Caravaggio, Michael Fried has made absorption and theatricality, the terms he takes from Diderot, the basis for an extraordinary career of visual analysis. The project was initiated with Fried, *Absorption and Theatricality*; and its most recent installment—one germane to this chapter—is Fried, *The Moment of Caravaggio* (Princeton: Princeton University Press, 2010). I take up Fried's critical project in Chapter 5.

33. In "Keats and Ekphrasis," Kelly demonstrates how Keats's commitment to ekphrasis exceeds the conventional boundaries of a literary representation of a pictorial representation. According to Kelly, Keats's ekphrastic impulse actually constitutes many of its seen objects as works of art to be beheld. In this way, Kelly has pointed out how to see something that she has not explicitly shown us, which is how to regard "this living hand" as art object.

34. Barthes, *Camera Lucida: Reflections on Photography* (New York: Farrar, Straus, and Giroux, 1980), 27.

35. Leo Bersani and Ulysse Dutoit, *Caravaggio's Secrets* (Cambridge, Mass.: MIT Press, 2001), 85. The resonance of the biblical allegory for my argument is made even more acute when we consider what we all recall from our youth: David slew Goliath "with a sling and a stone." Thus the sword the young shepherd grasps to cut off Goliath's head is the warrior's own weapon. On the threats and provocations that permeate Caravaggio's paintings, see Fried's *The Moment of Caravaggio*.

36. Heidegger's gloss on Mnemosyne appears in the course of his reading of Hölderlin in "What Calls for Thinking?" (351–58).

37. For a beautiful account of the discourse of the stars in *Hyperion* as it is illuminated by Deleuze's film theory, see Rei Terada, "Looking at the Stars Forever," *Studies in Romanticism* 50, no. 2 (Summer 2011): 275–310.

38. This muteness recalls the speaker's exhortation in Keats's "On Sitting Down to Read *King Lear*" to the "serene lute" to "be mute."

39. The "flush" that Apollo undergoes calls to mind one variety of Ricks's Keatsian "embarrassment" and many of the entries in Barthes's *A Lover's Discourse*. At this point in the poem, it is as if some strange illicit sexualized thing were happening between power and the aesthetic, for the *frisson* of these two spheres finally engulfs both and concludes with these "wild commotions."

40. Of the many important studies of the *Hyperion* project, Balachandra Rajan's *The Form of the Unfinished: English Poetics from Spenser to Pound* (Princeton: Princeton University Press, 1985) features a compelling exploration of "Keats's

doubly unfinished effort" that is particularly pertinent to my argument, even as it arrives at very different conclusions about this great "poem twice abandoned" (211–49).

41. This is a principal conclusion of "The Materialism of Poetic Resistance," my chapter on Keats in *The Ideology of Imagination*, 129–46. For an argument that presents a Keatsian aestheticism as a "solution" to the problems posed by his skepticism, see Ronald A. Sharp, *Keats, Scepticism, and the Religion of Beauty* (Athens, Ga.: University of Georgia Press, 1974).

42. See Marshall Brown, "Unheard Melodies: The Force of Form," in *Turning Points: Essays in the History of Cultural Expressions* (Stanford: Stanford University Press, 1997). In the course of his fine meditation on the relationships between aesthetics and form in painting and music as well as poetry, Brown offers a brief, but suggestive account of the sights and sounds of "Ode on a Grecian Urn."

3. WHAT THE ZEROS TAUGHT: EMILY DICKINSON, EVENT-MACHINE

1. Quotations of Dickinson's poems are from *The Poems of Emily Dickinson*, ed. R. W. Franklin, Variorum ed. (Cambridge, Mass.: Harvard University Press, 1998).

2. I have learned most about Dickinson's poetics of the zero from two of her most astute readers, Jorie Graham and Anne-Lise Francois. For Graham the "circumference" in Dickinson can appear as a figure for poetry and is also another name for the zero. See Thomas Gardner, "An Interview with Jorie Graham," in *Regions of Unlikeness: Explaining Contemporary Poetry* (Lincoln: University of Nebraska Press, 1999), 214–38. Anne-Lise Francois's game-changing reading of the "powers of voidance and negation" in Dickinson's poetry—its capacity for "uncounting"—convinced me that I was on the right track with my argument. I understand my own reading here as something like the "flip-side" of Francois's attention to the poetics of the zero in Dickinson. As she argues in her reading of "It sifts from Leaden Sieves," the poem, "premised on transience," "accepts the superfluity of its artistry and awakens us to negation as to an action taking place in time: more than a suspension of empirical memory, a dispensation: more than an erasure of harvests, a kind of negative harvesting or gift received when it mounts to zero"; Francois, *Open Secrets: The Literature of Uncounted Experience* (Stanford: Stanford University Press, 2008), 146.

3. While this is a topic Derrida takes up in some of the most influential essays of his early period (especially "Structure, Sign, and Play in the Human Sciences," "Signature, Event, Context," and "Limited, Inc."), my subtitle comes from a late essay by Derrida that pushes his earlier investigations of the event towards reflections on the machine; see Derrida, "Typewriter Ribbon: Limited Ink (2)," in *Without Alibi*, trans. Peggy Kamuf (Stanford: Stanford University Press, 2002), 71–160.

4. David Porter, *Dickinson: The Modern Idiom* (Cambridge, Mass.: Harvard University Press, 1981).

5. Sharon Cameron, *Lyric Time* (Baltimore: Johns Hopkins University Press, 1979), 14.

6. Charles Anderson, *Emily Dickinson's Poetry: Stairway of Surprise* (Garden City, N.Y.: Doubleday, 1966), 70.

7. Karen Jackson Ford, *Gender and the Poetics of Excess: Moments of Brocade* (Jackson, Miss.: University of Mississippi Press, 1997), 40.

8. Perhaps the most important and provocative contribution to this more complete and complex picture of Dickinson's poetic practice is Virginia Jackson's *Dickinson's Misery: A Theory of Lyric Reading* (Princeton: Princeton University Press, 2005).

9. To regard Dickinson's use of the "it" as "deliberately unspecified" makes it possible to insist on the "lyricism" of these poems. Cameron's subsequent work on Dickinson, *Choosing Not Choosing: Dickinson's Fascicles* (Chicago: University of Chicago Press, 1992), restores some of the specificities, what we might call the poetry's productive machinery, that lyricization absents. Virginia Jackson's *Dickinson's Misery* takes as its primary charge the "de-lyricization" of the poems through a "refamiliarizing" and "recontextualization." Jackson's critique is a bracing corrective to those critics, myself included, who regard Dickinson's poetics as fundamentally "lyricizing." But I think Jackson's project has only made it clearer that even when the familiarizing contexts and addresses of the poetry's occasions are restored, the poetic force of so many of the opening lines, coupled with the impersonalizing weight of "it," *produces* this decontextualization. See also Francois's response to Jackson's polemic, *Open Secrets*, 155n40.

10. Emile Benveniste, "Relationships of Person in the Verb," in *Problems in General Linguistics*, trans. Mary Elizabeth Meek (Coral Gables, Fla.: University of Miami Press, 1971), 199.

11. Agamben, *The End of the Poem*, trans. Daniel Heller-Roazen (Stanford: Stanford University Press, 1999), xii–xiii.

12. Robert Weisbuch, *Emily Dickinson's Poetry* (Chicago: University of Chicago Press, 1975).

13. Gary Lee Stonum, *The Dickinson Sublime* (Madison: University of Wisconsin Press, 1990), 22.

14. I know of no better treatment of the poet's deployment of sound and song forms than John Shoptaw's "Listening to Dickinson," *Representations* 86 (2004): 20–52.

15. Josef Raab, "The Metapoetic Element in Dickinson," in *The Emily Dickinson Handbook* (Amherst: University of Massachusetts Press, 1998), 280–81. Raab refers to the B variant of the poem for his reading, where the crucial variant for "consecrate" is "stimulate," a substitution that shifts the nature of the act from a theological to an aesthetic and physiological register. And yet the theological resonance returns in the fourth line of 1268B with the substitution of "Maker" for "Author." Ultimately Raab's characterization of the poem as demonstrating Dickinson's "fascination" "with the concept of uncontrollable language" seems an inadequate way to account for the linguistic occurrences

addressed by and reckoned with in the poem. This is especially the case in the second stanza, where it is far from certain that we are confronted with the same linguistic phenomenon—much less "concept" (can "uncontrollable language," strictly speaking, be characterized as a *concept*?)—that we have addressed in the poem's opening stanza.

16. The poem's second stanza shifts its focus from the event of the word to the grammatical and syntactical machinery of the sentence. It is an "infected" machinery, one that "breeds": "Infection in the sentence breeds/We may inhale Despair/At distances of Centuries/From the Malaria -" (ll. 5–8). The break at line five renders intransitive the more commonly transitive verb "breed": "Infection in the sentence breeds," generates, produces. The agency of this linguistic infection is even more impersonal than the opening stanza: no being, not even a "Wrinkled Author," breeds an infection that appears as if it were a virus of language itself. How different from the "consecration" or "stimulation" of an eye: the consequence of the linguistic infection invoked in the second stanza is that "we may inhale Despair," though "at distances of Centuries/From the Malaria," at the farthest remove from the source of disease, the event of its occurrence.

17. Judith Farr, *The Passion of Emily Dickinson* (Cambridge, Mass.: Harvard University Press, 1992), 246–47.

18. It is, moreover, a poetics that "absents" *eloquence*, one of the most deeply human attributes we ascribe to poetry. Alain Badiou has described Paul Celan's poetics as the "termination" of a "figure of eloquence": "If Celan's poem ["Anabasis"] is not eloquent, it is because it exposes an uncertainty concerning language itself—to the extent of presenting language only in its cut, in its section, in its perilous reparation, and practically never in the shared glory of its resource"; Badiou, *The Century*, 89. I think it would take very little tinkering for us to substitute Dickinson's name for Celan's and register the truth of this statement, though such a substitution would overthrow Badiou's larger historical claim that the poetics of the termination of eloquence is what distinguishes Celan's poems as *of the century*. And yet it is certainly this evacuation or voiding of eloquence that distinguishes Dickinson's poetic idiom from the other poets presented here, each of whom can be said to mine the "shared glory" of the resources of language.

19. This is certainly one way to characterize the debate between structuralism and historicism as it played out in a variety of disciplines and fields of study. To my mind, the most illuminating critical account of this tension remains Fredric Jameson's long "Introduction" in *The Political Unconscious: Narrative as a Socially Symbolic Act* (Ithaca: Cornell University Press, 1981), 2–91.

20. As the essay unfolds, Derrida continues to tease out the aesthetic dimensions of this relationship: "But can one resemble a monster? No, of course not, resemblance and monstrosity are mutually exclusive. We must therefore correct this formulation: the new figure of an event-machine would no longer be even a figure. It would not resemble, it would resemble nothing, not even what we call, in a still familiar way, a monster. But it would therefore be, by virtue of this

very novelty, an event, the only and the first possible event"; Derrida, *Without Alibi*, 73.

21. Thomas Wentworth Higginson's preface is included in the invaluable "documentary history," *Emily Dickinson's Reception in the 1890s*, ed. Willis J. Buckingham (Pittsburgh: University of Pittsburgh Press, 1989), 14. Subsequent references to the articles and reviews included in this volume will be indicated by the abbreviation *EDR*.

22. Agamben, "The Dictation of Poetry," in *The End of the Poem: Studies in Poetics*, trans. Daniel Heller-Roazan (Stanford: Stanford University Press, 1999), 76.

23. Stonum, "Dickinson's Literary Background," in *The Emily Dickinson Handbook*, 44.

24. Dorothy Huff Oberhaus, *Emily Dickinson's Fascicles: Meaning and Method* (University Park: Penn State University Press, 1995).

25. In her introduction of *Emily Dickinson's Fascicles*, Oberhaus presents her methods and her findings in a form that resonates with—and proposes a resolution to—the entanglements between poetics and hermeneutics described by de Man. Oberhaus's account of the importance of Dickinson's fortieth fascicle is worth quoting at length:

> Although at first this booklet appears to be simply a collection of unrelated poems in her late, dense style, in the process of grappling with these elliptical poems one discovers beneath their surface multiplicity a deep structural unity. The key to discovering this unity is in the poems' allusions to one another and to preceding fascicles, and their echoes of the Christian meditative tradition. This intertextuality forms a network of signals leading the reader to discover that the fortieth fascicle is a carefully constructed poetic sequence and the triumphant conclusion of a long single work, the account of a spiritual and poetic pilgrimage that begins with the first fascicle's first poem (3).

It is particularly interesting in the context of de Man's argument that Oberhaus claims to arrive at her theological understanding not merely through biographical information about Dickinson's beliefs, but by way of her poetics and "the process of grappling with these elliptical poems." Oberhaus does indeed attend to what de Man describes as the "interaction of poetic structures" in "the formal analysis of linguistic entitities"; de Man, *Resistance*, 56. What Oberhaus describes as her own "painstakingly careful intertextual reading" demonstrates that close and even technical attention to rhetorical figures and their constitutive role in the formation of meaning by no means delivers us to "deconstructive" conclusions.

However one regards Oberhaus's conclusions, there can be no doubt that she *initiates* the process of reading. Oberhaus consistently demonstrates an impressive command of rhetorical and formal analysis. But despite the sophistication and sheer imagination reflected in her attention to form and figure, Oberhaus's devotion to a theological hermeneutic drives her desire for an extralinguistic key of textual understanding. The method and results of Oberhaus's analysis epitomize de Man's account of the "hermeneutic enterprise": "In a hermeneutic enterprise, reading necessarily intervenes, but, like computation in an algebraic proof, it is a means toward an end, a means that should finally become transparent and superfluous; the ultimate aim of a hermeneutically successful reading is to do away with reading altogether" de Man, *Resistance*, 56. This is just what Oberhaus claims to have achieved; and nowhere is this more in evidence than in her claim that certain rhetorical figures are *inherently biblical*, as if divine scripture and not the capacities of language had produced them: "F-40's [the fortieth fascicle] tropes and rhetorical figures are those of the biblical writers: the metonym, the kenning, parallelism, the chiasm, the envelope structure"; Oberhaus, *Emily Dickinson's Fascicles*, 11.

26. Moreover, Oberhaus argues that the rhetorical figures featured prominently in the fortieth fascicle—such as metonymy, parallelism, chiasmus—"are those of the biblical writers," and this demonstrates the poet's commitment to a biblical interpretation and demonstrates that, like all great Christian allegorists, "Emily Dickinson treats the bible typologically"; *Emily Dickinson's Fascicles*, 12.

27. For Oberhaus the fortieth fascicle is the key that unlocks the entirety of the *oeuvre*: "F-40 is not only illuminated by the other thirty-nine fascicles, it also illuminates some of their most perplexing mysteries"; *Emily Dickinson's Fascicles*, 11. Oberhaus's hermeneutic and narrativizing impulse is pervasive and confident enough that she no longer even regards Dickinson as a lyric poet at all: "Understanding F-40 . . . depends upon the reader's seeing that none of its poems is fully able to stand alone as a self-sufficient, autonomous text, which may explain in part why many received little or no critical attention. So interdependent are they that the referent for one poem's pronoun is frequently found in another" (11).

28. Still, the strange detached position of the fourth line—"Overtakes the creases"—creates its own crease in the poem and complicates the argument. The detachment is syntactic as well as spatial; and it gives rise to a genuine, if not irresolvable ambiguity: while the grammatical structure of the lines prompts us to read the line as the subject of a new sentence that it initiates, one that finds its completion in the lines that follow. Understood in this way, "Overtake the Creases / In the Meadow -" is made parallel to and as equally futile as the chasing of beauty. Since we know that she wrote one copy of the poem without stanza breaks, is it simply an accident that in this draft of the poem, Dickinson makes the most interesting line in the poem a stand-alone? Is it, in other words, a line "dropped careless on a page"?

29. Walter Benjamin, "The Significance of Beautiful Semblance," in *Selected Writings*, (1935–1938), ed. Howard Eiland and Michael W. Jennings (Cambridge, Mass.: Harvard University Press, 2002), 3:137.

30. Murray Krieger, "The Ekphrastic Principle and the Still Movement of Poetry; or *Laokoon* Revisited," in *The Play and Place of Criticism* (Baltimore: Johns Hopkins University Press, 1967), 91: The poem's insistence on the word "still"

might well be enough, at least by Krieger's expansive definition, to qualify "A something in a summer's Day" as an ekphrastic poem, despite the fact that it is not about a visual work of art. This attribution is confirmed by the poem's circular structure.

31. Judith Farr situates "Like eyes that looked on Wastes" in the "Sue cycle," calling the poem the "crux of the Sue story." Farr relates the poem to the Pre-Raphaelite iconography that she believes to be deeply influential to Dickinson's aesthetic. Farr's analysis emphasizes the reciprocity of the gaze in a poem that, to my own way of seeing, seems instead to insist on a terrifying blankness; *Passion of Emily Dickinson*, 161–62.

32. John Hollander, "Of *of*: The Poetics of a Preposition," in *The Work of Poetry* (New York: Columbia University Press, 1997), 97.

33. Agamben, *Language and Death: The Place of Negativity*, trans. Karen E. Pinkus with Michael Hardt (Minneapolis: University of Minnesota Press, 1991), 25.

34. Given the principal acts represented in the poem as well as its many variants, it is not surprising that Cameron would choose "I would not paint - a picture -" as one of the principal pieces of lyric evidence for her claim in *Choosing Not Choosing* that Dickinson demands us to read the poems in terms of the fascicles. Cameron's reading of the poem appears in "The Interior Revision," the book's concluding chapter. There she moves from the problem of "not choosing" as it radiates through the fascicles (principally involving the relationships between variants and poem, between one poem and another, and among poems within a fascicle) to the way in which "the fascicles teach us the comprehensive terms by that to read Dickinson's poems taken singly" (*Choosing*, 159). In Cameron's deft hermeneutic, "Dickinson's lyrics—poems read individually . . . —illustrate the way in which not choosing governs the relation between part and whole in terms criticism has not yet, without the benefit of the fascicles, fully considered" (162). And yet, however illuminating her treatment of the contexts—or what I would call the machinery—established by the fascicles, I am not convinced by Cameron's "consideration" of individual lyrics, such as "I would not paint - a picture - ," that this hermeneutic fundamentally changes the way we read the lyrics "taken singly," beyond the observation that "choosing not choosing" becomes "a phenomenon that could be understood as a theme" (162).

4. HOPKINS'S SIGHS

1. Quotations of Hopkins's poems are from *Poetical Works of Gerard Manley Hopkins*, ed. Norman H. Mackenzie (Oxford: Clarendon Press, 1990.) Quotations of Hopkins's journal entries are from *The Journals and Papers of Gerard Manley Hopkins*, ed. Humphry House, completed Graham Storey (London: Oxford University Press, 1959) and are indicated by the abbreviation *J*. Quotations of Hopkins's correspondence are from *Selected Letters of Gerard Manley Hopkins*,

ed. Catherine Phillips (Oxford: Clarendon Press, 1990), and are indicated by the abbreviation *L* with volume number. Quotations of the sermons are from *The Sermons and Devotional Writings of Gerard Manley Hopkins*, ed. Christopher Devlin (London: Oxford University Press, 1959) and are indicated by the abbreviation *S*.

2. While I will focus on the particularities of Hopkins's negotiations between aesthetics and theology, I refer to "theology" not in terms of a particular dogmatic tradition or according to a particular ecclesiastical authority; rather, following von Balthasar, I "take this word 'theology' in its widest sense, as the understanding of the truth delivered for our belief, and this presupposes the application of reason as a striving to live by it"; von Balthasar, *Explorations in Theology: The Word Made Flesh*, trans. A. V. Littledale, with Alexander Dru (San Francisco: Ignatius Press, 1989), 120.

3. Indeed, as Michael Sprinker notes, Hopkins's reflections on the sin of Lucifer "have an intense poignancy for Hopkins, for his own aim in poetry was to achieve" what he claimed of Lucifer, "'an instressing of his own inscape.... Lucifer's song is precisely that species of unnatural music which Hopkins perpetually claimed he himself created"; Sprinker, *"A Counterpoint of Dissonance": The Aesthetics and Poetry of Gerard Manley Hopkins* (Baltimore: Johns Hopkins University Press, 1980), 88.

4. To assert in the case of Hopkins that poetic inspiration is inseparable from divine inspiration is not necessarily to assert that the former is subordinate to the latter: the inseparability between the two goes both ways and contributes to what I will call the "compounding" of theology and aesthetics in Hopkins. In this context, it is worth considering Paul Ricoeur's hermeneutics of divine revelation: not only does Ricoeur assert that in the "primordial ground of our existence" the "revelatory function is coextensive with the poetic function," but that "lyric *pathos*" itself is an indispensable component of *divine* as well as poetic inspiration; Ricoeur, *Essays on Biblical Interpretation* (Philadelphia: Fortress Press, 1980), 101–2; see also Nicholas Wolterstorff's valuable accounts of and responses to Ricoeur's biblical hermeneutics: *Divine Discourse: Philosophical Reflections on the Claim that God Speaks* (Cambridge: Cambridge University Press, 1995). And see Enda McDonagh's *The Gracing of Society* (Dublin: Gill and Macmillan, 1989) for an account of Hopkins's work as a "poetry which trembles on the edge of prayer" (126).

5. J. Hillis Miller, *Topographies* (Stanford: Stanford University Press, 1995), 160.

6. Resistance is, to be sure, a much more complicated response than mere rejection or opposition; and there can be no question that Pater's aestheticism (in both his writings and teaching) left a deep impression on Hopkins—one that, as Gardner, the editor of this following volume of Hopkins's poems, notes, is perhaps most legible in the poet's notions of *inscape*; *Gerard Manley Hopkins: Poems and Prose* (Harmondsworth: Penguin, 1953), 20–22. In 1866 Jowett arranged for Pater to be Hopkins's "coach" at Oxford, and it is evident from Hopkins's letters

and journals that Pater's influence was significant and that his aestheticism was explicit. Nevertheless, when the young coach would "talk . . . two hours against xtianity," Hopkins remained unperturbed, even in these months leading up to his conversion (*J* 138). In the summer of 1864 Hopkins had met with members of the Pre-Raphaelite Brotherhood, which Martin calls "a grand literary party," one that prompted Hopkins to imagine, as he would write to Baillie, that he might "do something in poetry and painting" (*L* III, 214). It is also clear that Hopkins preferred Christina Rossetti to her brother "for pathos and pure beauty of art" (*L* III, 213).

7.　Gerhard Nebel's *The Event of the Beautiful* poses a relevant Protestant version of this aesthetic phenomenon: "The beautiful demands of man a confrontation. . . . The aesthetic is transformed into the beautiful when the object is consumed in the flame of the event. To be beautiful is, therefore, the act in which the beautiful offers itself as a sacrifice to itself and, therefore, to Another, to a higher Being"; quoted in von Balthasar, *The Glory of the Lord*, 1:58. In this context a conventional aestheticism interrupts this process before it can offer itself in its sacrifice to "a higher Being," while a radical aestheticism reveals the "higher Being" to be its own effect.

8.　Given Hopkins's adherence to Scotist principles and his interest in renewing the Scotist-Thomist debates in which Aquinas had prevailed, it is worth noting Aquinas's strict limitations on singing in the sections of the *Summa Theologiae* devoted to religion and worship: "Jerome does not condemn singing absolutely, but he corrects those who sing theatrically, or who sing not in order to arouse devotion but to show off or to provoke pleasure"; quoted in von Balthasar, *The Glory of the Lord*, 1:123–24. Thus do the invocations of "theatricality" featured in so many denunciations of aestheticism reveal their theological sources.

9.　Though deeply if often implicitly indebted to the work of J. L. Austin, this new strain of studies in performativity has expanded the field of "performance" far beyond its relatively circumscribed place in Austin's theory. Indeed, the pioneering work of Judith Butler has inspired a notion of performativity compelling and extensive enough that one could almost be excused for forgetting that language might also possess a constative dimension, though the question of performativity—and specifically the "performance of gender"—is at the heart of Judith Butler's *Gender Trouble: Feminism and the Subversion of Identity* (New York: Routledge, 1990). Butler's subsequent work explicitly takes up Austin's theories and explores more fully the vexed linguistic and worldly relationships between speech acts and subjective identities; see, in particular, Butler, "Critically Queer," in *Bodies that Matter: On the Discursive Limits of "Sex"* (New York: Routledge, 1993), 223–42), and Butler, *Excitable Speech: A Politics of the Performative* (New York: Routledge, 1997). In the context of my argument, I find Jonathan Culler's remarks on the "appeal to the notion of performativity" to be particularly pertinent: "It is important to stress that performativity is a problem not a solution, that it draws attention to the difficulty of determining what can be said to happen, under what conditions, and to the fact that the event is not something that is simply given"; Culler, "Deconstruction and the Lyric," in *Deconstruction Is/in America: A New Sense of the Political*, ed. Anselm Haverkamp (New York: New York University Press, 1995), 43. Culler's "The Performative" is the most succinct and lucid account of "the vicissitudes of a concept that has flourished in literary and cultural theory," of its "unexpected" fortunes and unforeseeable applications; Culler, *The Literary in Theory* (Stanford: Stanford University Press, 2007), 137–65. And, finally, Culler's 1993 MLA Presidential Address, "Lace, Lance, and Pair"—specifically its engagement with the aural force and density of Hopkins's poetry and their social and affective implications—was a catalyst for my return to Hopkins; Culler's address is published in *Profession 94* (New York: MLA), 5–10.

10. Miller, *Linguistic Moment* (Baltimore: Johns Hopkins University Press, 1985), 244.

11. In his essay on "Energy and Interpretation in Hopkins," Gerald Bruns describes the way in which the poetic act for Hopkins is only one dimension of a larger linguistic event: "Such an event is an instance of speech that requires the act of writing for its preservation . . . : Hopkins is nature's amanuensis"; Bruns, *Inventions: Writing, Textuality, and Understanding on Literary History* (New Haven: Yale University Press, 1982), 130.

12. *Oxford Book of Modern Verse, 1892–1935*, ed. W. B. Yeats (Oxford: Oxford University Press, 1936), xxxix, xl.

13. Paul Fussell, *Poetic Meter and Poetic Form*, rev. ed. (New York: Random House, 1979), 61.

14. Another way to note this distinction is to compare the difference between Hopkins's poetic marking of the occurrence of an "ah" or "oh" and Shakespeare's reference to a "sigh," such as that in sonnet 30: "When to the sessions of sweet silent thought/I summon up remembrance of things past,/I sigh the lack of many a thing I sought" (ll.1–3).

15. Paul Celan, *Collected Prose*, trans. Rosmarie Waldrop (New York: The Sheep Meadow Press, 1986), 47.

16. Hans Urs von Balthasar, "Revelation and the Beautiful," in *Explorations in Theology*, 117.

17. Garrett Stewart, *Reading Voices: Literature and the Phonotext* (Berkeley: University of California Press, 1990), 177.

18. In *The Gracing of Society*, the Irish theologian Enda McDonagh turns to "Pied Beauty" to describe the shared sense of celebration at work in poetry and prayer, and offers a fine account of the power and risk of Hopkins's poetics: "Divine and human creativity in prayer and poetry share also a sense of celebration. The human and cosmic wonders, which poetry celebrates, must be recognized in their unique selfhood, 'All things counter, original, spare, strange.' Yet their 'enselving' reality and mystery cannot except at the cost of final meaninglessness, be closed off from the ultimate reality and mystery who fathers-forth whose beauty is past change: Praise him.' As Hopkins above all recognized, the

very stuff of poetry and poetic celebration must self-transcend to the ultimate, or self-destruct" (130–31).

19. John Duns Scotus, "Individuation, Universals, and Common Nature," in *Duns Scotus, Metaphysician*, ed. and trans. William B. Frank and Allan B. Wolter (West Lafayette, Ind.: Purdue University Press, 1995), 185, 187.

20. Agamben, *The Coming Community*, trans. Michael Hardt (Minneapolis: University of Minnesota Press, 1993), 17–18.

21. See Agamben's "Theory of Signatures," the pivotal chapter of his *Signature of All Things*, 33–80.

22. Benjamin, "Little History of Photography," trans. Edmund Jephcott and Kingsley Shorter, in *SW*, 2:518–19. "Beauty is the true form of distance": this is one of the principal theses of David Bentley Hart's theological aesthetics: "Beauty inhabits, belongs to, and possesses distance, but more than that, it gives distance. . . . Within the world, beauty does not merely adorn an alien space, or cross the distance as a wayfarer, but is the true form of that distance, constituting it, as the grammar of difference. This presence of distance within the beautiful, as primordially the *effect* of beauty, provides the essential logic of theological aesthetics"; Hart, *Beauty of the Infinite*, 18.

23. The absorption of temporality in the auratic experience implicates all aspects of its historicity. This is, of course, why for Benjamin the "aura" of the aesthetic experience is deeply ideological and not something to be preserved and celebrated but "destroyed." And yet, there is little doubt that Benjamin's critique of the aura is made richer and more compelling as a result of his own considerable auratic impulses.

24. David Ferris, "Introduction: Aura, Resistance, and the Event of History" in *Walter Benjamin: Theoretical Questions*, 22. Ferris goes on say that "what Benjamin defines as the aura requires, in de Man's words, a 'union of phenomenal and epistemological properties'" (22).

25. Walter Benjamin, "On Some Motifs in Baudelaire," in *SW*, IV, 338.

26. According to von Balthasar, "*charis* refers to the attractive 'charm' of the beautiful, but it also means 'grace.' . . . We believe that what is beautiful in this world—being spirit as it makes its appearance—possesses a total dimension that also calls for moral decision"; *Glory of the Lord*, 34.

27. In a rich essay on the writing of the body in Hopkins's canon, Lesley Higgins offers a fine account of the interpretive difficulties raised by the sermon's provocative invocation of the body of Christ: "What consternates if not divides readers today . . . is the issue of how we should interpret the speaker's gaze, how to read Christ's body as the object of Hopkins's desire"; see Higgins, "'Bone-House' and 'Lovescape': Writing the Body in Hopkins's Canon," in *Rereading Hopkins: Selected New Essays*, ed. Francis L. Fennell (Victoria: University of Victoria, 1996), 23. This "consternation" becomes genuine division if we compare the role "Christ Our Hero" plays in Richard Dellamora's important account of the homoerotic dimensions of Hopkins's "spousal love"; Dellamora, *Masculine Desire: The Sexual Politics of Victorian Aestheticism* (Chapel Hill: Univer-

sity of North Carolina Press, 1990), 42–57, with, for instance, Bishop Richard Harries's characterization of Hopkins's description as verging on *"kitsch"*: "in his description of the physical build of Christ, Gerard Manley Hopkins is in grave danger of slipping into *kitsch*. *Kitsch* is the enemy of all that is true, good, and beautiful. . . . In art *kitsch* takes the form of the pretty, the sentimental and fashionable. . . . [K]*itsch*, in whatever form, is an enemy of Christian faith and must be exposed as such. . . . [K]*itsch* reveals to us that the aesthetic, the moral and the spiritual realms are inseparably connected"; Harries, *Art and the Beauty of God, A Christian Understanding* (London: Mowbray, 1993), 58, 60. Kierkegaard in his own journals muses upon the "real problem" of Christ's beauty: "Christianity does not at all emphasize the idea of earthly beauty, which was every thing to the Greeks. . . . It is a real problem: to what extent should Christ be portrayed as an ideal of human beauty—and strangely enough, although many other kinds of similarities have been discerned between Christ and Socrates, no one has thought at all about this aspect, for Socrates was, as is well known, uglier than original sin"; Kierkegaard, *Journals*, no. 797, 368.

28. In Elizabeth Schneider's distinguished reading of the poem, the "cry" is the event; see Schneider, *The Dragon in the Gate: Studies in the Poetry of G. M. Hopkins* (Berkeley: University of California Press, 1968), 20–41; see also Sprinker, *Counterpoint*, 102–5. But Miller's account of the relationship between the event and its "re-experiencing" demands to be quoted in full: "The narrative doubling, the memory of his own experience doubling his vivid picture of the shipwreck, causes a redoubling in a new experience of God's presence to the poet. This new experience of grace occurs within the poem itself and is identical with the writing of it"; *Linguistic Moment*, 255.

29. Isobel Armstrong, *Victorian Poetry: Poetry, Poetics, and Politics* (London: Routledge, 1993), 433.

30. Paul Felstiner reports that Celan wrote his first draft of "In Memoriam Paul Eluard" in his copy of Hopkins's poems; see Felstiner, *Paul Celan: Poet, Survivor, Jew* (New Haven: Yale University Press, 1995), 67. I want to thank Max Novick for alerting me to the presence of Hopkins in Celan and, more importantly, for our discussions of Hopkins's poetics.

31. Adorno, *Aesthetic Theory*, trans. Robert Hullot-Kentor (Minneapolis: University of Minnesota Press, 1997), 322.

32. The poem confirms von Balthasar's judgment of Hopkins as the poet who, along with Hölderlin, "show[s] us a Christ who 'inherits' the gods of paganism: that is to say 'inherits' the splendour of the theophanies which now passes over to Him, who is the sole Heir and Wholly other. Hopkins can see a primeval landscape in a 'christophanic' manner"; von Balthasar, *Glory of the Lord*, 501.

33. Hopkins's writings are punctuated by the "witnessing" of many such events, what one might call an aesthetic illumination and its "reckoning." His remarkable early journal entry [Sept. 24, 1870] recording his first encounter with the Northern Lights is worth quoting at length:

My eye was caught by beams of light and dark very like the crown of horny rays the sun makes behind a cloud. At first I thought of silvery cloud until I saw that these were more luminous and did not dim the clearness of the stars in the Bear. They rose slightly radiating thrown out from the earthline. Then I saw soft pulses of light one after another rise and pass upwards arched in shape but waveringly and with the arch broken. They seemed to float. . . . This busy working of nature wholly independent of the earth and seeming to go on in a strain of time not reckoned by our reckoning of days and years but simpler and as if correcting the preoccupation of the world being preoccupied with and appealing to and dated to the day of judgment was like a new witness to God and filled me with delightful fear. (*J* 200)

I am interested in the form of this aesthetic encounter—the eye is "caught by beams of light and dark"—and the "reckoning" that is opened by this illumination, a "reckoning" beyond the "reckoning of days and years." Here, of course, the crisis of this "delightful fear" results in something "like a new witness to God." But such an aesthetic experience of "pulses of light" "floating" beyond the "arch" and arc of vision is precisely that which can also result in something other than a "delightful fear," something whose telling is "a billion / Times told lovelier" *and* "more dangerous," something that courts a radical aestheticism.

34. J. R. Watson, *The Poetry of Gerard Manley Hopkins* (Harmondsworth: Penguin, 1987), 85.

35. Agamben, *The Idea of Prose*, trans. Michael Sullivan and Sam Whitsitt (Albany: State University of New York Press, 1995), 40.

36. See Sprinker's account of the interpretive problems posed by the "buckle" of these lines, an account that develops into a generous engagement with both Gardner and Empson; Sprinker, *Counterpoint*, 12–15.

37. William Empson, *Seven Types of Ambiguity*, 3rd ed. (Harmondsworth: Penguin, 1961), 192.

5. SUPERFICIALITY: WHAT IS LOVING AND WHAT IS DEAD IN DANTE GABRIEL ROSSETTI

1. This fact makes those few brilliant readings seem all the more precious. John Dixon Hunt's *The Pre-Raphaelite Imagination, 1848–1900* (Lincoln: University of Nebraska Press, 1968) remains the most careful and acute study of the movement. All readers of Rossetti are indebted to the scholarship of David Riede; see in particular *Dante Gabriel Rossetti and the Limits of Victorian Vision* (Ithaca: Cornell University Press, 1983). Richard L. Stein's chapters on Pre-Raphaelite literature, especially his treatment of the relationship between "painting and poetic form" in Rossetti, are unsurpassed; see *The Ritual of Interpretation: The Fine Arts as Literature in Ruskin, Rossetti, and Pater* (Cambridge, Mass.: Harvard University Press, 1975). Jonathan Freedman's *Professions of Taste: Henry James, British Aestheticism, and Commodity Culture* (Stanford: Stanford University Press, 1990) is as important a contribution to our critical understanding of Brit-

ish aestheticism as it is to the interpretation of James. Jerome McGann's *Dante Gabriel Rossetti and the Game That Must Be Lost* (New Haven: Yale University Press, 2000) is certain to be this generation's most provocative contribution to the understanding of Rossetti. Elizabeth K. Helsinger's magisterial *Poetry and the Pre-Raphaelite Arts* (New Haven: Yale University Press, 2008) is now our richest scholarly resource of the relationship between the arts in the Pre-Raphaelite movement. Among Rossetti's contemporaries, Walter Pater's "appreciation" of Rossetti is not only the most illuminating and genuine *reading* of the poet, but one of the most important contributions to British aestheticism; see *Appreciations* (New York: Macmillan, 1922), 205–18. Regarding *The House of Life*, Paull Franklin Baum's annotations and introduction remain an indispensable guide with a fascinating and contentious interlocutor; see Rossetti, *The House of Life*, ed. Paull Franklin Baum (Cambridge, Mass.: Harvard University Press, 1928).

2. Jerome Hamilton Buckley, "The Fear of Art," reprinted in *Pre-Raphaelitism*, ed. James Sambrook (Chicago: University of Chicago Press, 1974), 187. I will argue that an aestheticism emerges in Rossetti in spite of his fears and suspicions; but it is certainly the case that the term "poet-painter" is as pertinent for Rossetti as it was for Blake, not merely because he practiced both arts, but because he engaged the nature of their relationships as thoroughly as the romantic poet-painter he so admired. Indeed, the crossings between poetry and painting are prominent as those between love and death—and not unrelated to them. If Buckley is justified in his assessment that Rossetti "feared the autonomy of art," he did not fear the potentially mutual *heteronomy* between poetry and painting.

3. Quotations of Rossetti's poems and prose are from *Collected Writings of Dante Gabriel Rossetti*, ed. Jan Marsh (Chicago: New Amsterdam, 2000).

4. Lisa Freinkel's account of the migration of the concept of the fetish in Freud concludes with a fine and relevant reading of Shakespeare's "catachrestic love" in Sonnet 20 ("A woman's face with nature's own hand"): "The fetish as Freud finally comes to define it, is memorial instead of relic, and further, it is a memorial that commemorates quite literally nothing. It erects itself as *Denkmal* (both memorial and monument) to an event that cannot be remembered (e.g., the traumatic sight of castration), and to a loss that we can never lose (e.g., the missing maternal penis)"; Freinkel, "The Shakespearean Fetish," in *Spiritual Shakespeares*, ed. Ewan Fernie (London: Routledge, 2005), 119.

5. Elizabeth Bronfen, *Over Her Dead Body: Death, Femininity, and the Aesthetic* (Manchester: Manchester University Press, 1992).

6. Jan Marsh, *Dante Gabriel Rossetti: Painter and Poet* (London: Routledge, 2005), 17.

7. Not only is Benjamin anticipated in Rossetti's linkage between translation and critical commentary, but other important works in the Benjaminian legacy are certain to resonate, especially Gayatri Spivak's account of "The Politics of Translation": "The translator must surrender to the text," Spivak declares. "No amount of tough talk can get around the fact that translation is the most inti-

mate act of reading. . . . To surrender in translation is more erotic than ethical";
Spivak, *Outside in Teaching Machine* (New York: Routledge, 1993), 183.

8. Agamben, *Stanzas: Word and Phantasm in Western Culture* (Minneapolis: University of Minnesota Press, 1993), 129.

9. Agamben's study of the "pneumo-phantastic doctrine" and its formative role in the development of the love lyric delivers him to a famous tercet in Dante's *Purgatorio*, which our later Dante knew well:

> And I to him: "I am one who, when
>
> Love inspires me, takes note, and in the manner
>
> That he dictates within I go signifying."
>
> (XXIV, 52–54)

According to Agamben, "inspiration" is to be understood here in terms of the breath: "Love 'breathes' (*spira*) because it is essentially and properly a 'spiritual motion' (to use Dante's own expression)" (*Stanzas*, 125). Love is breathing, living: love, this "spiritual motion," is the very thing that distinguishes the quick from the dead. This "(in)spiration of love" is, according to Agamben, the basis of Dante's "theory of the linguistic sign: indeed he defines his own making of poetry as the notation and signification of inspiring love" (*Stanzas*, 125). When Dante "characterized poetic expression precisely as the dictation of an inspiring love," asserts Agamben, he "reinserted the theory of language into the pneumo-phantastic doctrine that we have seen play such an essential part in the love lyric" (*Stanzas*, 127). It certainly plays an essential part in the love lyrics of Dante Gabriel Rossetti. To cite but three examples from *The House of Life*: in "Youth's Antiphony," "Love breathed in sighs and silences / Through two blent souls one rapturous undersong"(ll.13–14); in "Genius in Beauty," the "sovereign face" of this beauty "whose love-spell breathes / Even from its shadowed contour on the wall" (ll.7–8); and in "Love's Testament," the "breath" of the speaker's beloved is "felt" "to be / The inmost incense of his sanctuary. "Love's Testament" is the third of the sonnets in *The House of Life*: preceding "lovesight," it could as well have been called "Lovebreath." Following Agamben, we can say that for Rossetti as for Dante "poetry is then properly *joi d'amour* because it is the *stantia* (chamber) in which the beatitude of love is celebrated. Dante expressed the singular mutual implication of Eros and poetic language with his usual clarity when he affirmed, in a fundamental passage of the *Vita Nuova*, that the goal and beatitude of his love are to be found in 'those words which praise my Lady' (XVIII, 6)" (*Stanzas*, 128–29).

10. Barbara Gates, *Victorian Suicides* (Princeton: Princeton University Press, 1988), 149.

11. Griselda Pollock, *Vision and Difference: Feminism, Femininity, and the Histories of Art* (London: Routledge, 1988), 94.

12. Bronfen is far from the only critic to regard the paintings as iterations of a single structure or pattern. Referring to a series of pictures Rossetti painted

in the late 1850s and 1860s, David G. Riede says that "the paintings all have such great stylistic affinities that a description of any one of them seems to do for them all" (*DGR and Limits*, 69). Moreover, these "affinities" have to do with the repetition in painting after painting of a profusion of details on the surface: lacking background, the pictures seem to be given over to the play of surface-patterns.

13. In other words, it is not merely the form and content of this artistic relationship that is deplorable, but the fact that the relationship refuses to remain in the space of representation. But such a critique amounts to a tacit acknowledgment of the power of the mechanisms it condemns. And in condemning the promiscuity of these images or semblances as they pass into reality, Bronfen's critique presumes that the permeability between life and art is derived from the permeability between the literal and the figural. This dilemma becomes even more disorienting when we recognize that Bronfen's critique relies on the very figures—the chiasmic nature of the mirrored crossings between art and life, the abstracting personifications of love—that Rossetti deploys in his poetry with a high degree of rhetorical self-awareness.

14. Quoted in William Gault, *The Pre-Raphaelite Dream* (New York: Schocken, 1966), 68.

15. Clement Greenberg, *Collected Essays and Criticism*, vol. 4, *Modernism with a Vengeance 1957–1969* (Chicago: University of Chicago Press), 242.

16. These are not Greenberg's only remarks on the Pre-Raphaelites. Indeed, references to and discussions of the Pre-Raphaelites are scattered throughout Greenberg's writings; and it is worth noting that they do not offer a seamlessly consistent assessment. Greenberg's references to British poetry also serve as a reminder of his own sense of the fluidity between the media. Fredric Jameson offers a fascinating account of "the complex phenomenon of the transfer of a theory of painting to the other arts and media" that characterizes Greenberg's project. Predicated on what Jameson calls "an idea of aesthetic autonomy" and what Greenberg calls "the idea of art," this conception of the work of art is the basis for Greenberg's appropriation of the notion of the *avant-garde*; see Jameson, *A Singular Modernity* (London: Verso, 2002), 170–73.

17. Michael Fried, *Manet's Modernism* (Chicago: University of Chicago Press, 1996), 404, 405. And see the earlier forms the argument takes in Fried, *Courbet's Realism* (Chicago: University of Chicago Press, 1990).

18. This issue of evaluation is the vein of Fried's thought explored in Pippin's provocative essay, "Authenticity in Painting: Remarks on Michael Fried's Art History," *Critical Inquiry* 31, no. 3 (2005). Pippin links the anti-theatrical impulse to what he calls a "general ontological condition, brought to a crisis starting in Enlightenment modernity" and best articulated by Diderot's critique of a "theatrical mode of social existence" (581, 590). Pippin's discussion extends this motif to various twentieth-century philosophical efforts to reckon with the crisis-ridden "ontological condition" of modernity, most notably Heidegger's

notion of "inauthenticity." According to Pippen, Fried's discernment of theatricality appears to ascribe to certain forms of painterly composition a fundamentally *inauthentic* mode of being:

> Mannered painting is objectionable not so much just because theatricality insures aesthetic failure (breaking the arresting spell great painting can create) or because of Cartesian or representationalist distortions of our being-in-the-world but because a painting's theatricality should be counted a failure in the same way that a theatrical mode of social existence should be counted a failure. (590)

19. Robert Buchanan, "The Fleshly School of Poetry: Mr. D. G. Rossetti" (1871), reprinted in *Critical Essays on Dante Gabriel Rossetti*, ed. David G. Riede (New York: Macmillan, 1992), 24–39.

20. Harold Wetherby, "Problems of Form and Content in the Poetry of Dante Gabriel Rossetti," *Victorian Poetry* 2 (1964): 14–15.

21. C. M. Bowra, *The Romantic Imagination* (Cambridge, Mass.: Harvard University Press, 1949), 197–220.

22. Jerome J. McGann, "Rossetti's Significant Details," *Victorian Poetry* 7 (1969): 44.

23. Jan Marsh chronicles Rossetti's personal and artistic relationships with what Fried calls "The Generation of 1863"—Whistler, Fantin, Legros, and above all, Manet. Marsh describes Rossetti's vituperative attack on all that he saw in Paris generally and in Manet's studio especially—"the whole of French art at present is a beastly slop and really makes one sick," "simple putrescence and decomposition"—and notes Rossetti's defensive reaction to "the new French aesthetic": "Visiting the studios and salons as well as the galleries, he perceived plainly how this was an avant-garde of new departures and new challenges. Finding himself so much more in tune with Delacroix than with Manet, his own preferences and aims suddenly seemed traditional rather innovative. British artists had been overtaken, and his negative reaction was defensively competitive"; Marsh, *Rossetti: Painter and Poet*, 285.

24. McGann sees the relationship differently, identifying—inexplicably and unconvincingly—in Rossetti's canvases a "social critique of his world, as devastating as Courbet's or Manet's, slipped between the conscious innocence of the one and the uncertain cynicism of the other" (*DGR and the Game*, 7). McGann also notes the relationship between Manet and Rossetti, invoking *Fazio's Mistress*, *Monna Vanna*, and *Lady Lilith* as comparators for *Olympia*: "Whereas Manet's treatment of the Venetian style is ironical and self-consciously 'modern,' there is no irony at all in Rossetti's pictures, whose self-awareness is of another order. As polemical as Manet's, a painting like *Fazio's Mistress* is more an artifice of absorption—almost an act of magic, like a Joseph Cornell collage—than a bold play of conscious wit. Such pictures operate as machines of desire" (*DGR and the Game*, 20–21). For McGann, Rossetti's work not only calls to mind Joseph Cornell; indeed, Rossetti is "like Duchamp," "primarily a conceptual artist" (*DGR and the Game*, 7). I confess that I cannot see the basis for McGann's comparisons

to modernist (or postmodernist) artists such as Cornell or Duchamp. More apparent to my "superficial" view is the way in which Rossetti's art can be at once highly allegorical and, simultaneously, appear to undo of the opposition between figuration and abstraction. This is most evident in the watercolors such as "Roman de la Rose" (1864), "How Sir Galahad" (1864), and even "The Wedding of Saint George and the Princess Sabra" (1857), where the representation of allegorical scenes appear to have emerged from abstract patterns of design.

25. And thus is Lynn Pearce forced to ask herself in the context of Rossetti's paintings whether it is "ethically legitimate to deconstruct/reconstruct a text in which the dominant ideology is blatantly sexist/misogynistic and make it 'work for feminism'"? Pearce, *Woman/Image/Text: Readings in Pre-Raphaelite Art and Literature* (Toronto: University of Toronto Press, 1991), 2. If Manet's canvas offers us a revolutionary example in which "the dominant ideology" of the gendered gaze is deconstructed and "made to 'work for feminism," in the case of Rossetti, the weight of ethical obligation falls upon the feminist viewer who must do what Rossetti's paintings seem to disallow.

This is also the crux of my disagreement with McGann's discussion. McGann sees what it is that Rossetti is doing; and his discussions of Rossetti's earliest paintings are particularly acute. McGann is certainly correct to say that Rossetti avoids "Manet's ironical treatment of his subject" and that "instead of distance Rossetti cultivates involvement" (*DGR and the Game*, 103). But throughout his book McGann also insists on Rossetti's *critical* activity, a critique undertaken by the poems as well as the paintings. And yet such an artistic critique, one that McGann explicitly links to Marxist theory, relies on the same critical distance that Rossetti's own work undoes, *just as McGann has demonstrated*. McGann wants it both ways; and this desire leads the critic into a fundamental contradiction that is never addressed, much less resolved. McGann's two allegiances—to Rossetti's artistic practice and to the critical function of art—are irreconcilable and responsible for the occasional incoherence of an otherwise valuable work of scholarship.

This tension is a recurrent problem for even the finest readers of Rossetti. Isobel Armstrong, for instance, declares that the sonnets of *The House of Life* "are built on the despair of separation. . . . They become a critique of the consequences of idealism in sexual relations and in language even as they long for it, disclosing a concurrent language of the body and the soul, two languages which are always either diverging or collapsing into one-sidedness or dissolving away" (*Victorian Poetry*, 453).

26. I am taking the terms of this difference between love and ethics from Gayatri Spivak's "*The Politics of Translation*," in *Outside in the Teaching Machine* (New York: Routledge, 1993), 179–200). And by this light Rossetti's painted emblems of love pose an interesting challenge to the Diderotian terms of Fried's analysis: if few things could be more "absorptive" than the actions of lovers, actions that in coupling tend to blur the very boundaries of being, few things appear more "theatrical" than the representations of love, even in the depic-

tion of a single figure "in love." Rossetti's *Beata Beatrix* is a case in point. The inevitability with which love's most absorptive aspect spills into theatricality may well account for the relative absence of amorous representations in Fried's own analysis and in the body of paintings with which he is concerned.

27. Slavoj Žižek, *The Metastases of Enjoyment* (London: Verso, 1994), 90. Žižek's account of the critical fortunes of Pre-Raphaelite painting are worth quoting in detail, given the way in which they "respond" to Greenberg's evaluations. "In art history," Žižek observes, "the Pre-Raphaelites offer a paradoxical borderline case of the avant-garde overlapping with *kitsch*: they were first perceived as the bearers of an anti-traditionalist revolution in painting, breaking with the entire traditions from the Renaissance onwards; but only a short time later—with the rise of Impressionism in France—they were devalued as the epitome of damp Victorian pseudo-romantic *kitsch*" (113). Žižek goes on to note the persistence of this devaluation: "This scornful evaluation persisted until the 1960's, that is to say, until the emergence of postmodernism, when the Pre-Raphaelites suddenly staged a critical comeback. How was it," Žižek asks, "that the Pre-Raphaelites became 'readable' only retroactively, through the postmodernist paradigm?" (113). This anticipates McGann's argument that "a Postmodern vantage has restored our access to the power of artists like Gustave Moreau and Rossetti, where abstraction comes erotically charged in fetishized forms" (*DGR and the Game*, 3). My argument is that the work of the Pre-Raphaelite we are considering here has been "readable" from the beginning: the difference is the shift in the critical positions assigned to that reading.

28. Jacques Lacan, *The Seminar of Jacques Lacan*, book XX, *On Feminine Sexuality, the Limits of Love and Knowledge*, ed. J.-A. Miller, trans. Bruce Fink (New York: Norton, 1999), 69.

29. Lacan, *The Seminar of Jacques Lacan*, book VII, *The Ethics of Psychoanalysis (1959–1960)*, ed. J.-A. Miller, trans. Dennis Porter (New York: Norton, 1992), 151.

30. This points to another way to reopen the Lacanian analysis. For the fact that the Dantean structure of idealization and deanimation is repeated in Rossetti addresses something more significant than the Victorian invocation and translation of duecento models of courtly love. It is, in other words, something more than an artistic decision, because the nature of courtly love as "a scholastics of unhappy love" is for Lacan inseparable from the very nature of art as such. It is the structure of courtly love, after all, that provides Lacan with the point of departure for his famous accounts of painting as *anamorphosis*. Indeed, much of Lacan's 1959–1960 seminar on the *ethics* of psychoanalysis is in fact devoted to questions of *aesthetics*, to the third Critique and the status of the beautiful. It is as if aesthetics is itself the *anamorphosis* around which the Lacanian ethics of psychoanalysis is organized. Throughout the seminar Lacan seems to acknowledge at least implicitly what we've called the *imposition* or *insistence* of the aesthetic. Moreover, Lacan makes the "aesthetic register" into the very

template for his model of the analytical experience, precisely in the eruptive and interruptive force of aesthetic experience:

> It is at the very moment when a thought is clearly about to appear in a subject, as in the narration of a dream for example, a thought that one recognizes as aggressive relative to one of the fundamental terms of his subjective constellation, that, . . . he will make some reference to a passage from the Bible, to an author, whether a classic or not, or to some piece of music. (*Ethics of Psychoanalysis*, 239)

This aesthetic eruption—which can be discerned or "picked up," Lacan asserts, "with the precision of a Geiger counter"—"belongs to the register of a destructive drive" (*Ethics of Psychoanalysis*, 238). The instance and the insistence of the aesthetic in the subject is not, in other words, the occurrence of a creative impulse, but the force of a negation that Lacan links to the destructive drive. For Lacan this is *inherently* the case, because "a work of art always involves encircling the Thing (*das Ding*)" (*Ethics of Psychoanalysis*, 141), that which is not available as such, which marks the intrusion of the Real into the fabric of the Symbolic, and whose sensory manifestation is registered as an experience of undoing. Thus for Lacan the poetry of courtly love not only articulates the fundamental structure of love and desire, but does so by way of "a form of sublimation specific to art":

> The poetry of courtly love, in effect, tends to locate in the place of the Thing certain discontents of the culture. . . . By means of a form of sublimation specific to art, poetic creation consists in positing an object I can only describe as terrifying, an inhuman partner. (*Ethics of Psychoanalysis*, 150)

31. See also the use of the hand in Schiller's account of semblance at the end of ninth letter, where "the play of your semblance" requires that "you can try your shaping hand [*bildende Hand*]." This fundamentally Romantic motif finds its most famous British version in Wordsworth's account in *The Prelude* of "this forming hand" and, as we have seen, undergoes its most extraordinary crisis in Keats's "This living hand." For Rossetti it is more apt to characterize his version of this motif as "this loving hand." Rossetti returns to this motif time and again, explicitly in "Hand and Soul" and by the persistent metonymical connection with "draw" in so many of the sonnets.

32. The ambiguities inscribed in the history of the term "semblance" identify a fundamental feature of Rossetti's project as well as the critical ambivalence it evokes. If the definition of semblance has, according to the *OED*, more or less settled on "the appearance or outward aspect of a person or thing," an early and now obsolete definition of semblance is "the fact of appearing to view," a definition that highlights the *mechanism* of semblance, the means by which "the outward aspect" of something or someone can be beheld as such. With the obsolescence of this definition, the mechanism fades, leaving semblance *as an ostensible property* of the person or thing.

33. *The Promises of Glass* is the title of a book of selected poems published by Michael Palmer (New York: New Directions, 2000). Though Palmer's poems do not, as far as I can discern, engage in Rossetti's poetic legacy, the title seems the best way to capture the work of Rossetti's poetic superficiality. However, in his preface to the 2002 New York Review Books edition of Rossetti's translation of the *Vita Nuova*, Palmer quotes at length from Rossetti's theory of translation and concludes that no other English translation of the poems "bears the historical and poetic resonance of Rossetti's, which must qualify, in itself, as a significant literary document of its time"; *Dante: The New Life*, trans. Dante Gabriel Rossetti, preface Michael Palmer (New York: NYRB, 2000), xiii.

34. Moreover, the relationship between literary symbol and allegory discerned by de Man is closely related to the fundamentally Diderotian models of absorption and theatricality in painting developed by Fried. Thus aestheticism's "authenticity," to invoke Pippin's version of this problem, is constituted precisely by its refusal of authenticity, its self-conscious awareness of the inherent impossibility of successfully defeating theatricality.

35. It is worth repeating in this context the dubious claim Freedman makes regarding the potential aestheticist origins—"well-heads," perhaps—of deconstruction: "Aestheticism itself might . . . represent a moment within the very tradition of thought from which deconstructive praxis springs, and to which deconstructive theory then naturally refers" (*Professions*, 30).

36. It is, for instance, worth comparing Freedman's claim for deconstruction's "aestheticist" origins with de Man's derision of "pictorial, Pre-Raphaelite writing" in "Image and Emblem in Yeats," the Yeats chapter of de Man's Harvard dissertation. The Pre-Raphaelites are invoked there to describe the immature and superficial visuality of Yeats's *The Wanderings of Oisin*: "This is pictorial, picture-book writing," writes de Man about a particularly lush passage, "with a picture-book delight in colors that exist merely for the color's sake" (*Rhetoric of Romanticism*, 152).

37. Joel Fineman's reading of Shakespeare's sonnet sequence not only offers a new critical paradigm for the reading of the sonnets—the invention of Western subjectivity—it sheds light on why Rossetti, an avid reader of Shakespeare and a compulsive sonneteer, might turn instead to Dante for his model of a sonnet sequence. We might in fact say that Rossetti's sonnets are "pre-Shakespearean" in the same form that his paintings are "pre-Raphaelite": not only because the poems of *The House of Life* assume an early Italianate form with their embrace of Dante and his circle, but because the rhetorically ornate poetics of beatitude in Rossetti's sonnets *points* to Dante, *points* to a time and poetry before "the invention of subjectivity" in Shakespeare. If Fineman relies on the discourse of novelty to describe the epistemological—or at least ontological—break ushered into existence by Shakespeare, we can say that the Rossetti's poetics of subjectivity is neither novel nor revolutionary, but old, remote, thoroughly obsolete, *dead* and, therefore, both allegorical (in the de Manian sense) and superficial; see

Fineman, *Shakespeare's Perjured Eye: The Invention of Poetic Subjectivity in the Sonnets* (Berkeley: University of California Press, 1986).

38. The historical debates regarding the classifications of figures extend to chiasmus as much as they do to any of the other principal tropes. I follow the *OED* in defining chiasmus as a "grammatical figure in which the order of words in one of two parallel clauses is inverted in the second"; and I would thus identify both *epanados* and *antimetabole* as versions of the chiasmus, insofar as they produce the spatial arrangement organized in the form of an *x*.

39. Though "Love's Testament" may well be a coerced desacralization of the 1870 version of the sonnet known as "Love's Redemption," one in which the sacramental references—"The body and blood of Love in sacrament"—are abandoned, the effect of this desacralization under duress is, paradoxically, to foreground the rhetorical machinations that were always at work in the sacramental relationship.

40. Lacan, *The Four Fundamental Concepts of Psychoanalyis*, trans. Alan Sheridan (New York: Norton, 1978), 89.

6. "RINGS, PEARLS, AND ALL": WILDE'S EXTRAVAGANCE

1. Of the authors assembled in this study, none has undergone over the past two decades the fundamental critical reevaluation enjoyed by Oscar Wilde. Given the breadth, quality, and innovation of the scholarship, it is fair to call our own moment the golden age of Wilde criticism. This is the case in part because the facts of Wilde's life and times, his trials and tribulations, as well as his critical and creative work, have come to occupy a decisive place, not only in a wide range of contemporary cultural studies, but in our own social and cultural imaginary. The pioneering contributions of critics such as Regina Gagnier, (*Idylls of the Marketplace: Oscar Wilde and the Victorian Public* [Stanford: Stanford University Press, 1986]); Wayne Koestenbaum ("Wilde's Hard Labor and the Birth of Gay Reading," in *Engendering Men*, ed. Joseph Boone and Michael Cadden [New York: Routledge, 1990]); Jonathan Dollimore (*Sexual Dissidence: Augustine to Wilde, Freud to Foucault* [Oxford: Clarendon, 1991]); Ed Cohen (*Talk on the Wilde Side: Toward a Genealogy of a Discourse on Male Sexualities* [New York: Routledge, 1993]); Alan Sinfield (*The Wilde Century: Effeminacy, Oscar Wilde, and the Queer Moment* [London: Cassell, 1994]), Joseph Bristow (*Effeminate England: Homoerotic Writing after 1885* [New York: Columbia University Press, 1995]); Jeff Nunokawa (*The Tame Passions of Wilde: The Styles of Manageable Desire* [Princeton: Princeton University Press, 2003]); and the inimitable Neil Bartlett (*Who Was That Man? A Present for Mr. Oscar Wilde* [London: Serpent's Tail, 1988]) are touchstones for my own evolving understanding of Wilde's project, his practice, and its implications. This critical renaissance—to invoke a term dear to Wilde's thinking—has made us aware of a theoretical sophistication that seems to anticipate certain strains in "postmodern" thought,

his critical explorations and subversions of the forms and practices of sexual and social identity, his proto-Brechtian theatrical innovations, his manipulations of generic expectations in each of the many literary modes he employs, and even his analysis of the withering of the soul under the economic rule of commodity relations.

This constitutes a welcome and genuine critical rehabilitation of an author whose work and reputation languished for most of the century in a state of condescension and neglect, if not outright contempt and disregard. And yet this critical rehabilitation has taken place without a corresponding revaluation of Wilde's aestheticism. Indeed, I would argue that Wilde has come to be valued—and valued greatly—at the *expense* of his aestheticist project. This is not to say that critics have ignored Wilde's aestheticism, but—to extend the economic metaphor—his aestheticism most often serves as the currency through which Wilde's critics purchase what they conceive to be his primary contribution, usually one with more contemporary value: identity, politics, even ethics.

2. "The English Renaissance of Art," in *The Collected Works of Oscar Wilde*, ed. Robert Ross (Boston: John W. Luce, 1908), 14:248. All other quotations of Wilde's texts are from *Complete Works of Oscar Wilde*, 5th rev. ed. (London: Harper Collins, 2003), hereafter indicated by page number. "The English Renaissance of Art" is one of the four lectures in rotation during Wilde's 1882 tour ("The Decorative Arts," "The House Beautiful," and "Irish Poets and Poetry of the Nineteenth Century," each less formal, were the others). Paul K. Saint-Amour has demonstrated how here and elsewhere Wilde adopts freely and often without acknowledgment from his mentors; see Saint-Amour, "Oscar Wilde: Orality, Literary Property, and Crimes of Writing," *Nineteenth-Century Literature* 55 (June 2000): 59–91. Ruskin, Morris, and Pater are the authors "reconstellated" in this lecture. "Of course, I plagiarize," Wilde acknowledged: "it is the privilege of the appreciative man."

3. *New York Evening Post*, 4 January 1882; collected in *Oscar Wilde in America: The Interviews*, ed. Matthew Hofer and Gary Scharnhorst (Urbana: University of Illinois Press, 2010), 15.

4. At the outset of *The Tame Passions of Wilde*, to my mind the most compelling search for the shape and meaning of this "wild longing," Jeff Nunokawa quotes in its entirety this compelling passage from *The Picture of Dorian Gray*: "Out of the unreal shadows of the night comes back the real life that we had known. We have to resume it where we left off, and there steals over us a terrible sense of the necessity for the continuous of energy in the same wearisome round of stereotyped habits, or a wild longing, it may be, that our eyelids might open some morning upon a world that had been refashioned anew in the darkness for our pleasure" (1).

5. The decisive essay is "The Notion of Expenditure," collected along with other important early essays in Georges Bataille, *Visions of Excess: Selected Writings*, ed. and trans. Allan Stoekl (Minneapolis: University of Minnesota Press, 1985), 116–29.

6. Regina Gagnier's groundbreaking book on the political intervention of Wilde's plays and his aestheticism makes this point in a different economic register: "aestheticism came to mean the irrational in both productive (art) and reproductive (sexuality) realms: an indication of the art world's divorce from middle-class life" (*Idylls*, 139).

7. "The criminal classes," writes Wilde in "A Few Maxims," "are so far away from us that only the poet can understand them" (1242).

8. Of course, this Wildean "constellation" is but a later iteration of an eremetic asceticism that, as Geoffrey Galt Harpham puts it, can be traced back to St. Anthony's "flight from the world," one that "placed him in a chain of succession that originated with Christ . . . and ran through Paul, John the Baptist, and, in other ways, the martyrs"; Harpham, *The Ascetic Imperative in Culture and Criticism* (Chicago: University of Chicago Press, 1992), 42. On the relationship between British aestheticism and Victorian asceticism, see James Eli Adams, *Dandies and Desert Saints* (Ithaca: Cornell University Press, 1995).

9. And what a tour it turned out to be. Not only did Wilde travel to and lecture in the cosmopolitan centers of New York, Boston, and San Francisco, where he might well have expected disciples of "our romantic movement," but the aesthetic wilderness of Topeka, Dubuque, Leadville, Galveston, Ogden. Wilde's tour was scheduled to correspond with the traveling production of Gilbert and Sullivan's *Patience* and its aesthete protagonist, Bunthorne, whom audiences took to be a parody of the tall, young Irish preacher of art and beauty. The irony of this coordinated campaign is that Wilde made the parody work to his own ends: Wilde's tour and the journalistic "buzz" that accompanied it effectively *posited* the aestheticist perspective above the parody. For the entire journalistic record, see *Oscar Wilde in America*.

10. "What Is Enlightenment?" in *The Essential Works of Foucault, 1954–1984*, vol. 1, *Ethics*, ed. Paul Rabinow, trans. Robert Hurley, et al (New York: The New Press, 1997), 303–19; hereafter referred to in the text as *Foucault Ethics*. See also Foucault's essays on and inspired by Bataille, especially "Preface to Transgression" and "The Thought of the Outside," in *The Essential Works of Foucault, 1954–1982*, vol. 2, *Aesthetics, Method, and Epistemology*, ed. Paul Rabinow, trans. Robert Hurley, et al (New York: The New Press, 1998), 69–88, 147–70; hereafter referred to in the text as *AME*.

11. And thus does Foucault seem to reassert another version of what we have come to describe, via de Man, as the "Schillerization of Kant": de Man dismisses the legitimacy of "any lineage that is supposed to lead from Kant, by ways of Schiller and Coleridge, to decadent formalism and aestheticism," by declaring that "the juxtaposition of Kant and Oscar Wilde" "borders on caricature"; de Man, *Aesthetic Ideology*, 119.

12. "Then had come Lord Henry Wotton," says Dorian to himself, "with his strange panegyric on youth, his terrible warning of his brevity. That had stirred him at the time, and now, as he stood gazing at the shadow of his own loveliness, the full reality of the description flashed across him" (33).

13. For Foucault this means that "Enlightenment" is not a synonym for humanism: "Humanism is something entirely different [from Enlightenment]. . . . [A]t least since the seventeenth century, what is called 'humanism' has always been obliged to lean on certain conceptions of man borrowed form religion, science, or politics. . . . [Humanism] can be opposed by the principle of a critique and a permanent creation of ourselves in our autonomy. . . . I am inclined to see Enlightenment and humanism in a state of tension rather than identity" (*Foucault Ethics*, 314).

14. Wayne Koestenbaum argues that this letter and "The Ballad of Reading Gaol" establish a new mode of cultural signification, one predicated on a new "communal" mode of address: "Wilde gestured toward . . . a gay male reader and suggested that 'gay identity' is constructed through reading, although once it has been located on the page, it glows like an essence that already existed *before* a reader's glance brought it to life"; "Wilde's Hard Labor," 177.

15. Terry Eagleton's characterization of Wilde's tragic "persona" in *De Profundis* is as "bumptious" and "self-satisfied" as his description of Shaw's own dismissal of the Wilde "affair": "the spiritually chastened Wilde of the prison writings was among other things just another assiduously cultivated persona. Having sported a number of masks in his time, Oscar was now trying on Jesus Christ for size"; Eagleton, *Sweet Violence: The Idea of the Tragic* (London: Blackwell, 2003), 196.

16. If Wilde were committed more to the dialectic than the chiasmus, our own Hegelian impulses might be tempt us to call Wilde's artistic "fulfillment" of Christ's project a sublation or *Aufhebung*.

17. Kerry Powell argues that it was Wilde's need to elevate himself as a "poet" from the melodramatists and farce writers who dominated the popular stage in the 1890s that prompted him to "overestimate the merit of a 'poetic' drama like *Salomé*" and to be "so comparatively modest, even deprecatory about *The Importance of Being Earnest*"; Powell, *Oscar Wilde and the Theatre of the 1890's* (Cambridge: Cambridge University Press, 1990), 5.

18. See pages 16–19 of my introduction for a discussion of Frye's account of this "lyricization." The critical tradition is far from convinced by Wilde's claim for the originality of this process in the context of *Salomé*: Mario Praz was one of the first critics who, despite expectations, found little in Wilde's play that was original; Praz, *Romantic Agony*, trans. Angus Davidson (Oxford: Oxford University Press, 1933), 298–306. It has long been something of a sport to locate the sources of the many allusions in *Salomé*, in no small part in order to demonstrate its lack of originality.

19. Neil Bartlett demonstrates how mobile this lyrical vantage point can be, how Wilde makes the personal perspective *historically* transferable, and how his plays enact this substitutability. One of Bartlett's most compelling examples of this Wildean transfer is his treatment of *Salomé*, in which Bartlett both alludes to and demonstrates the porous nature of time and subjectivity for Wilde. Bartlett's personal interpretation of *Salomé* is compelling for its beautifully queered

and dehistoricized image of the "princess" and for the illuminating reading of the play prompted by this image in the chapter of his book called "Flowers." There Bartlett presents us with another drama being played out in the shadows of *Salomé*, one that manifests this transferability: "When the Princess orders the young Syrian captain to bring forth the Baptist so that she may look at him, she sweetens her demand with a little tease: 'You will do this thing for me . . . and to-morrow when I pass in my litter beneath the gateway of the idol-sellers, I will let fall for you a little flower, a little green flower'" (588). "With all her great wealth," Bartlett muses, "what the Princess offers him, the morning after, is a little green flower" (*Who Was That Man?*, 44). The promise of the "little green flower" is for Bartlett a secret metonymy deposited in the play, one that opens itself to a "hothouse of homosexual desire": "The Princess reveals, when she promises her young man a little green flower, that she is part of an elaborate imagery and system of beliefs associated with homosexuality" (48). For Bartlett the artifice of the "little green flower"—the "heraldic device" that is a signal to its co-conspirators—reveals a secret economy of homosexual desires. If for Bartlett the extravagance of "unnatural" flowers is the gift that can be redeemed from the particular coded vantage point of homosexual desire, in my more modest project "the little green flower"—like the "green carnation," that "magnificent flower," that "work of art" Wilde claims to have "invented"—demonstrates how *any* vantage point in this play is an unstable, mobile aestheticist effect, open to substitutions and transfers. The best way I know to describe *Salomé*'s spectacular theater of the specular gaze is to turn to Bersani and Dutoit's account of the theatrics of Caravaggio's pictures: "Not only are there all the looks, poses, and expressions that enigmatically solicit our attention, depriving us of the spectatorial luxury of a space outside the painting occupied only by an undisturbed, contemplative viewer (*Caravaggio's Secrets*, 46).

20. Mary Anne Doane, "Introduction" to *Revision: Essays in Feminist Film Criticism*, ed. Doane, et al (Los Angeles: American Film Institute, 1984), 14.

21. Joan Copjec, *Read My Desire: Lacan Against the Historicists* (Cambridge, Mass.: MIT Press, 1996), 17.

22. Rosalind Krauss, "Cindy Sherman: Untitled," in *Cindy Sherman: 1976–1993* (New York: Rizzoli, 1993), 91.

23. *Tame Passions of Wilde*, 125. Nunokawa's chapter on Wilde's "Passions of the Eye" takes *Salomé*'s theater of the gaze as the starting point for his reading of sight and spectacle, city and subjectivity in *The Picture of Dorian Gray*.

24. Michael Patrick Gillespie's informative account of the relationship between Beardsley's drawings and the text of *Salomé* offers more evidence for this multiplicity of perspectives; see Gillespie, *Oscar Wilde and the Poetics of Ambiguity* (Gainesville: University Press of Florida, 1996), 133–54.

25. Bataille, *Inner Experience*, trans. Leslie Ann Boldt (Albany: SUNY Press, 1988), 53.

26. Laura Mulvey, *Visual and Other Pleasures* (Bloomington: Indiana University Press, 1989). One of the earliest entries in this feminist debate is Kate

Millet's denunciation of *Salomé* as "a drama of homosexual guilt and rejection" that reaches its climax in "a death of crushing and penetration under an army of males." For Millet, Wilde's Princess is not the incarnation of Ibsen's "New Woman" for British theater, but an "archaic slanderous . . . accusation against women"; Millet, *Sexual Politics* (Garden City, N.Y.: Doubleday, 1970), 153–55. Compare Millet's characterization with Regina Gagnier, who argues that the Princess pursues "sex for sex's sake, without purpose or production" and thus "subverts the laws and authority of the Tetrarch and the Kingdom"; Gagnier, *Idylls*, 165. More recently, Erin Williams Hyman has historicized this subversive version of the play's sexual politics. Hyman argues that the first French "production of *Salomé* in Paris at the time of Wilde's imprisonment" "was a representation of the open expression of sexual desire as an anarchic force capable of destabilizing a regime of power. Within the French context, the play and the polemic around it made the defense of homosexuality part of the anarchist struggle, placing erotic liberty squarely under the banner of libertarian politics"; Hyman, "*Salomé* as Bombshell, or How Oscar Wilde Became an Anarchist," in *Oscar Wilde and Modern Culture*, ed. Joseph Bristow (Athens: Ohio University Press, 2008), 99.

27. Foucault's account of Bataille's "eye" is worth quoting at some length for its illumination of Bataille's thought and for its resonance with the "zone" in which the theatrical experience of *Salomé* is played out: "The enucleated or rolled-back eye marks the zone of Bataille's philosophical language, the void into which it pours and loses itself, but in which it never stops talking—somewhat like the interior, diaphanous, and illuminated eye of mystics and spiritualists that marks the point at which the secret language of prayer is embedded and choked by a marvelous communication that silences it. Similarly, but in an inverted manner, the eye in Bataille delineates the zone shared by language and death, the place where language discovers its being in the crossing of its limits—the non-dialectical form of philosophical language"; Foucault, *AME*, 83–84.

28. Steven Shaviro, *Doom Patrols: A Theoretical Fiction About Postmodernism* (London: Serpent's Tail, 1996), 80.

29. Reading Bataille, Foucault poses a question already posed by *Salomé*: "Profanation in a world that no longer recognizes any positive meaning in the sacred—is this not more or less what we may call transgression?"; *AME*, 70. Is this not "more or less" what we encounter on the stage of *Salomé*? Some of the characters may well believe there is "positive meaning in the sacred," but I would argue that the *play* does not.

30. On Wilde's conception and composition of *Salomé* as a "symbolist" drama and the pressures this places on its staging, see William Tydeman and Steven Price, *Wilde: Salomé* (Cambridge: Cambridge University Press, 1996), 3–11.

31. See, in particular, Jakobson, "Two Aspects of Language and Two Types of Aphasiac Disturbances" and "Linguistics and Poetics," in *Language in Litera-*

ture, ed. Krystyna Pomorska and Stephen Rudy (Cambridge, Mass.: Harvard University Press, 1987), 62–114.

32. *Salomé* is as much a rhetorical laboratory as it is a theatrical experiment. In that volatile "rhet-lab," we are likely to find our received understanding and classification of figures put severely to the test. Jakobson's radical reorientation of the workings of rhetorical figures opened a new vista on the vital figurative dimensions of the realist novel. It also prompted some of the most compelling theoretical investigations of the twentieth century into not only the operations, but the effects and implications of figuration. The rigors and provocations of Barthes, Genette, and de Man, to name but three of the most important directions in this strain of rhetorical investigation, are made possible by Jakobson's work. That work has also served as the authorization for what de Man recognized as a critical reversal: the valorization of metonymy (as the figure that refuses transcendence, verticality, identity in favor of contingency, detail, horizontality, history) has resulted not only in the demotion of metaphor, but in a new metonymic "orthodoxy." I will invoke one of the most important and illuminating recent works of criticism to demonstrate how this enabling reversal relies on a questionable characterization of metaphor. *The Ideas in Things*, Elaine Freedgood's nimble and nuanced practice of a "strong metonymic reading," is predicated on the assumption of the "stability of metaphors" and "the unpredictability of metonyms"; Freedgood, *The Ideas in Things: Fugitive Meaning in the Victorian Novel* (Chicago: University of Chicago Press, 2006), 7. I refer to Freedgood's characterization because I want to return to her illuminating account of the Victorian adventures of the metonymy; and I want to challenge her claim that the critical study of "the potential power" of metonymy "has long been neglected" (11).

33. In his account of "the displaced body of Jesus Christ," Graham Ward describes "the transfiguration" in terms of an exorbitant economy: it "sets Jesus outside any economy of exchange, any economy where the value of an object can be known and its exchange negotiated. . . . [The figure of Jesus] breaks upon them as one situated within another economy, an economy of loving and beloved"; Ward, *Radical Orthodoxy*, ed. John Millbank, Catherine Pickstock, and Graham Ward (London: Routledge, 1999), 166. If with Salomé's descriptions of Jokanaan, Wilde is alluding to those remarkable accounts of the transfiguration in Matthew and Luke, the play inverts and ironizes them: unlike Christ, the face of this "holyman" is not divine and, with eyes like "black holes," does not "shine like the sun." In *Salomé* we are confronted with an exorbitant economy that may well partake in the sacred; but is certainly not the gift of divine love.

34. The theatre of Herod's "metonymic imagination" results in a parody of what Freedgood calls "a strong metonymic reading": like Magwitch's "Negro head tobacco" in *Great Expectations*, Herod presents us with precious objects whose acquisitions by the Tetrarch can be traced through the various historical archives and whose possession tells us something about the material culture of

the Roman empire in the time of John the Baptist. But Herod both begins and forecloses such "strong metonymic reading," telling us on the one hand not only about the value or beauty of these objects, but their provenance and their power relations, "mantles," for instance, "that have been brought from the land of the Seres, and bracelets decked about with carbuncles and with jade that come from the city of Euphrates" (603). And yet if Herod's metonyms begin to spell out the forms of "disavowed historical narratives," they do not function as Freedgood seems to believe that they must, as "conventional, obvious, literal," as that which "conjures up the real so successfully that its status as a trope seems to disappear"; *Ideas*, 12. They are metonyms that immediately open not onto a real material world, but onto other metonyms: they all add up to a dizzying pleasuredome of metonymic relations that are as dazzling and as exuberant as any metaphor. In other words, Herod's (and Wilde's) "metonymic imagination" ironizes any such "strong metonymic reading" and leaves us weak in the face of its rhetorical powers.

35. This is also what Foucault claims for Bataille's explorations of transgression: "transgression contains nothing negative, but affirms limited being—affirms the limitlessness into which it leaps as it opens this zone to existence for the first time" ("Preface to Transgression," 74).

36. In "Seeing Is Reading," Rei Terada offers a rigorous reading of the metaphorical and literal meanings of the word "seeing" and, in the process, proffers a relevant definition of aestheticism. "'Seeing' does not always function as an aesthetic figure for the phenomenalization of thought; still less does that figure represent what seeing may actually be. The word 'seeing,' in all its ambiguity, encompasses both perceptual and cognitive, literal and figurative, meanings, and *only our own interpretive decision* to collapse its inner difference can unify, and hence aestheticize it" (163–64, emphasis added). I disagree only with the phrase I have highlighted: indeed, one of the principal objectives of this book has been to demonstrate where certain texts themselves "collapse this inner difference" and produce a fused if not "unified" experience that does indeed "aestheticize it."

37. The status of the "Baptist" is fascinating in the Gospels and in subsequent accounts: Are his testimonies prefigurative of Christ's teachings or, as von Balthasar puts it, "only homages to the One who is unique" (*Glory of the Lord*, 614) or, as in Matthew 3:11, "He who is coming"?

38. Kerry Powell is the first critic I know of to press on some of the more obvious questions that surround *Salomé*'s composition and attempted production: "Why did Wilde write the play in French? How could he have gone into the third week of rehearsal when the subject matter appeared certain to arouse the censor and make performance impossible?" (*Wilde and the Theatre of the 1890's*, 33). Powell goes on to argue that Wilde had every reason to believe that by writing the play in French, he could smuggle it into production: "*Salomé*'s being written in French was from the first, or at some point became, an elaborate joke on the censorship of the stage" (37).

39. From the theatrical perspective, when Wilde places the action of the play in the period reported in the Gospels and prior to the institution of the church and its history of restrictions on theatrical representations and after the classical dramatic tradition, he allows *Salomé* to stage an expansive and lateral pre-Christian tragic-comic theatre *retrospectively in advance* of the assertion of Christian verticality; see von Balthasar, *Theo-Drama*, 135–257.

40. Rebecca Comay, "Gift Without Presents: Economics of Experience in Bataille and Heidegger," *Yale French Studies: On Bataille* 78 (1990): 83.

41. Nunokawa looks at this economy of promises with a different optic, "the shadow" of the "commodity form": "the commodity aspect of the items that make up this gorgeous catalogue shows up not only in their spectacular specificities, but no less in the difficulty we have preserving a view of them. . . . By the time we get to the king's ransom, who can avoid the sense that once we've seen one gorgeous thing" (*Tame Passions*, 126).

42. "Bataille, Hegel, Death, and Sacrifice," trans. Jonathan Strauss, *Yale French Studies: On Bataille* 78 (1990): 21. This passage is taken from Bataille's 1955 essay on Kojeve's reading of Hegel. Bataille is particularly drawn to the lectures of 1805–06, in which we encounter the Hegel who insists on the violence of Negation, this "disconcerting world" in which "Spirit attains its truth only by finding itself in absolute dismemberment" (10, 14). Indeed, the essay is in one sense a gloss and elaboration of the passage he cites from Hegel: "It is not that (prodigious) power by being the Positive that *turns away* from the Negative, as when we say of something: this is nothing or (this is) false and, having (thus) disposed of it, pass from there to something else; no, Spirit is that power only to the degree in which it contemplates the Negative face to face (and) dwells with it. This prolonged sojourn is the magical force that transposes the negative into given-Being" (14). In terms of *Salomé*, I take *"absolute* dismemberment" not to be the beheading itself, but that moonlit moment in which the princess comes face to face with that head, "dwells with it," and by *kissing* it, transposes it. Thus, does *Salomé* give us Hegel's "night on all sides" or "night of the world," the "phantasmagorical representation" in which "here suddenly surges up a blood-spattered head."

43. Though the institution of Christianity may have enshrined and "sanctified" the killing of the Baptist, in Wilde's play the "holyman" remains Jokanaan and thus opens the space of this transgression. If, as Bataille claims, "misunderstanding the sanctity of transgression is one of the foundations of Christianity" (*E*, 90), Wilde's play eludes that foundation.

44. Bataille, *Theory of Religion*, trans. Robert Hurley (New York: Zone Books, 1989), 36.

45. Gagnier argues that when the Princess pursues "sex for sex's sake, without purpose or production," she thus "subverts the laws and authority of the Tetrarch and the Kingdom" (*Idylls*, 165).

46. Quoted in Tydeman and Price, *Wilde: Salomé*, 178. This review of *Salomé* makes von Balthasar's account of Paul's reservations about the tragic spectacle

particularly pertinent: "how dangerous it is to sit in the auditorium and receive so passively what is being won by someone else's suffering!" (*Theo-Drama*, 154).

47. "A violent death disrupts the creature's discontinuity," writes Bataille about the "sacramental element." "What remains, what the tense onlookers experience in the succeeding silence," and thus what *Salomé's* own "tense onlookers experience," "is the continuity of all existence with which the victim is now one" (*E*, 82). "The continuity of all existence": this is Bataille's version of Benjamin's "aura," an "oceanic" saturation of sensual experience that overcomes the "discontinuity of you and I." It is also Bataille's understanding of the *experience* of transgression: "in the hushed silence of that one moment, that moment of death, the unity of being is revealed through the intensity of those experiences in which truth stands clear of life and its objects" (*E*, 270).

48. *New York Evening Post*, 4 January 1882, reprinted in *Oscar Wilde in America*, 14. The same might be said for a radical aestheticism. And if the notion of radical aestheticism possesses conceptual validity, there are likely to be many instances of the literary radicalization of aesthetic experience after Wilde; and in my introduction I pointed at some twentieth-century candidates for a radical aestheticism. But to demonstrate this, one must undertake another round of historical interpretation. One must first demonstrate how, for instance, the Modernist or postmodern text in question does indeed still participate in this elongated version of the Romantic problematic and in a sense reconstruct the mode and idiom in which it is produced and the discourses through which it is received.

49. Richard A. Kaye, "Oscar Wilde and the Politics of Posthumous Sainthood: Hofmannsthal, Mirabeau, Proust," in *Oscar Wilde and Modern Culture*, 113. On Wilde's constitutive "after-life," see Shelton Waldrop, *The Aesthetics of Self-Invention: Oscar Wilde to David Bowie* (Minneapolis: University of Minnesota Press, 2004).

absence: Dickinson and, 113–16; Rossetti and, 194. *See also* vacancy

absorption: and Manet, 282n23; and theatricality, 89, 182–83, 186, 194

abstraction: in painting, 289n24; in poetry, 108, 122, 195, 197

"A Charm invests a face" (Dickinson), 127–28

Adonais (Shelley), 47, 71

Adorno, Theodor, 8, 45, 51, 53, 65, 163, 249n15, 264n33

aestheticism: crisis and, 19; espousal of, 2–3; Foucault and, 216–17; Hopkins and, 148–49; Keats and, 70; rejection of, 6–7, 249n15, 250n16, 269n20; Rossetti and, 171, 173, 196–97, 202; term, 1; Wilde and, 209–43, 293n1, 295n6. *See also* radical aestheticism

aesthetics, 6–11, 118; Barthes and, 80–81; cinema and, 187; Dickinson and, 117, 121, 123–42; Hopkins and, 146–47, 152–53, 157, 160; Keats and, 67–70, 78, 93, 95–99, 101; Lacan and, 290n30; machine and, 118; Rossetti and, 192, 201; Shelley and, 33

Agamben, Giorgio, 110, 113, 121, 154, 168; and Benjamin, 261n19; on enjambment, 166–67; on event, 20, 160; on inspiration, 286n9; on lyric, 178; on pronouns, 136

allegory: de Man on, 196; Rossetti and, 201

Althusser, Louis, 251n21

The Ambassadors (Holbein), 204

ambiguity: Hopkins and, 167–68; Wilde and, 228–29

anamorphosis, 204, 290n30

Anderson, Charles, 107

Angelus Novus (Klee), 41, 64–65

antinomy, 10, 118; Wilde and, 223–24

Apollo, 92–95

aporia: Dickinson and, 107, 116–18, 120–21, 126

apostrophe: Keats and, 86–87, 90; Shelley and, 47–48

The Apparition (Moreau), xii

Armstrong, Isobel, 161, 194, 289n25

Arnold, Matthew, 38

art: Bataille and, 220; catastrophe and, 24; ideology and, 51; Keats and 89–91; reflections on, 2–4; Rossetti and, 173–74; Wilde and, 217

"Artists wrestled here!" (Dickinson), 134–36

"As kingfishers catch fire" (Hopkins), 147, 153–54, 157, 166

"A something in a summer's Day" (Dickinson), 127–29

Atemwende. See breathturn

aura: Benjamin and, 42–44, 154–55, 262n23, 282n23, 302n47; Dickinson and, 124–28; Hopkins and, 154–56, 163, 169; Keats and, 77–79; Rossetti and, 175, 186, 192, 205–6; Shelley and, 43–44, 48, 59; Wilde and, 230, 237

Austin, J. L., 269n21, 280n9

avant-garde, 182, 214, 259n15, 262n26

Aveling, Edward, 38, 41, 259n15

"A Word dropped careless on a Page" (Dickinson), 112–13, 274n15, 275n16

"A word made Flesh is seldom" (Dickinson), 111

Badiou, Alain, 7, 248n13, 253n28, 257n5, 259n15, 275n18

Bahti, Timothy, 21, 267n7, 271n29

Barnes, Julian, 24

Barthes, Roland, 74–76, 78, 83–5, 87–90, 98; on aestheticism, 80–81, 268n19; on author, 270n24; and Benveniste, 269n22; on binarism, 267n8; on cinema, 230–31, 254n36; and de Man, 270n26; on indolence, 20, 267n7; on threat, 96; on Twombly, 267n11, 268n19; on ungluing, 21, 96

Bartlett, Neil, 296n19

Bataille, Georges, 24–25, 298n27, 300n35, 301n42, 302n47; on expenditure, 20, 213–14, 256n43; and Foucault, 216: on gaze, 229, 231; on sacred, 221, 238–39, 301n42, 302n47; and Wilde, 213–14, 219–20

Baudelaire, Charles, 216–17

Baum, Paull Franklin, 184, 189, 197, 200, 203–4

beauty: Badiou and, 257n5; Benjamin and, 127; Dickinson and, 125–27; Hart and, 257n4, 282n22; Hopkins and, 153, 155–56; Nebel and, 280n7; Shelley and, 29–35; Wilde and, 229, 242

"Beauty - be not caused - It is -" (Dickinson), 126, 277n28

"Before I got my eye put out -" (Dickinson), 130–31

beholding: Dickinson and, 137–38; Keats and, 90–91; Rossetti and, 204–5; Wilde and, 225–31

The Beloved (The Bride) (Rossetti), 185–86, 207f

Benjamin, Walter, 8, 43–44; and aura, 20, 154–55, 237, 262n23, 282n23, 302n47; and constellation, 44, 260n18, 260n19; and history, 57, 63–65; and Shelley, 41–42, 46, 261n20; and veiling, 126–27

Benveniste, Emile, 109, 136, 223, 269n22

Berger, John, 253n28

Bersani, Leo, 91–92, 272n35, 297n19

Bible, 79, 212, 222, 299n33, 300n37

Blake, William, 13, 119, 254n30

Blanchot, Maurice, 247n11

"The Blessed Damozel" (Rossetti), 174, 176

Blue Velvet (Lynch), 187

blindness, Dickinson and, 130–31

body: Hopkins and, 149; Rossetti and, 183–84

Bourdieu, Pierre, 5, 7, 247n10

Bowles, Paul, 15, 215

Bowra, C. M., 184

Brawne, Fanny, 71, 82, 88–89

breathturn (*Atemwende*): Hopkins and, 149–58; term, 152

Brecht, Bertolt, 38, 230–31, 260n17

Bronfen, Elisabeth, 176, 179–80, 185, 203, 287n13

Brontë, Emily, 14–15

Brown, Ford Maddox, 180

Brown, Marshall, 100, 273n42

Browning, Robert, 195

Brunner, Emil, 7

Bruns, Gerald, 159, 247n11, 253n26, 281n11

Bryson, Norman, 255n38

Buchanan, Robert, 182–84, 192

Buckley, Jerome, 173

Burger, Peter, 247n10

Butler, Judith, 264n36, 280n9

Byron, George Gordon, Lord, 14, 39, 73; Napoleon and, 259n16; Wilde on, 258n11

Cameron, Sharon, 107, 109, 113, 116–17, 120–21, 123, 138–39, 274n9, 278n34

Caravaggio, Michelangelo, 91–92, 103f, 255n38, 272n35, 297n19

"Carrion Comfort" (Hopkins), 163

catachresis, 83, 140, 265n42, 270n23

catastrophe, 24–25, 98

Celan, Paul, 5, 117, 152, 163, 275n18, 281n15; and Hopkins, 162, 283n30

censorship, Wilde and, 236, 240

Chandler, James, 71, 263n26, 264n29

chiasmus: Rossetti and, 197–200, 206, 292n38; Wilde and, 242

Christ, 212; Dickinson and, 111; Hopkins and, 156, 169, 282n27; Shelley on, 60; Wilde and, 215–23, 299n33

cinema: Barthes on, 230–31; and Pre-Raphaelite painting, 187

Cohen, Leonard, 270n16

Coleridge, Samuel Taylor, 14, 114, 257n6

Comay, Rebecca, 237

conscience, Keats and, 85–86, 88

constellation: Benjamin and, 44, 260n19

Cornell, Joseph, 25–26, 27f

Courbet, Gustav, 183, 186

courtly love, 189; term, 188

crisis, 18–21, 254n34; Dickinson and, 110; Hopkins and, 162; Rossetti and, 178; Shelley and, 56–57; term, 19

Culler, Jonathan, 86–87, 280n9

dandyism, Foucault and, 216–17, 295n11; Wilde and, 215–17

Dante Alighieri, 170f, 177–78, 189, 195–96, 286n9

dashes, Dickinson and, 116–17

Davidson, Michael, 38

David with the Head of Goliath (Caravaggio), 91–92, 103f

da Vinci, Leonardo, xii, 28f, 47–57

death: Keats and, 71, 76, 83–84, 86, 88; Rossetti and, 173–74, 178, 201, 203

"The Death of the Author" (Barthes), 83–84

de Bolla, Peter, 10, 78

Debussy, Claude, 242

deconstruction: and aestheticism, 8–9; and Barthes, 80–81; and de Man, 8, 85, 196; and Derrida, 248n11, 267n8; and threat, 85

A Defence of Poetry (Shelley), 3, 31, 42, 110, 222, 259n15

deixis: Dickinson and, 132, 134–36; Keats and, 81, 90; Rossetti and, 202

Le Dejeuner sur l'herbe (Manet), 186

Delacroix, Eugene, 23

"Delight - becomes pictorial -" (Dickinson), 129–30

Dellamora, Richard, 282n27

de Man, Paul, 60, 246n7, 265n42; and aestheticism, 6, 8–9, 250n18, 250n19,

295n11; and Barthes, 85, 270n26; and catachresis, 270n23; and crisis, 20, 254n34; and hermeneutics, 121–22; and Keats, 72, 271n28; and Pre-Raphaelites, 292n36; and reading, 254n37, 270n27; and Romanticism, 10, 13–14, 196; and Shelley, 16, 63, 265n41; and threat, 85; and turning away, 20–21

dépense, 213

De Profundis (Wilde), 16, 211, 218, 220–22, 232

Derrida, Jacques, 35, 56, 83, 106; on Barthes, 267n8; on event-machine, 20, 117–19; Levinas and, 247n11; on monstrosity, 118–19, 273n3, 275n20; on skepticism, 265n38

Dickinson, Emily, 26, 104f, 105–42, 143f, 243; and radical aestheticism, 12–13; and Romanticism, 13, 108–10, 254n30, 254n31

dismemberment, Caravaggio and, 91–92; Keats and, 87–88, 92; Moreau and, xxi; Wilde, and, 238–39, 301n42

Du Bois, W. E. B., 38

Duns Scotus, John, 152–54, 156–57, 159, 280n8

Dutoit, Ulysse, 91–92, 272n35, 297n19

Eagleton, Terry, 9, 296n15

Early Italian Poets (Rossetti), 177–78

echo, Hopkins and, 155

ecstasy: Dickinson and, 111, 125–26, 129; Hopkins and, 146, 151, 166; Shelley and, 34

ekphrasis, 255n40; Dickinson and, 134–35; Hopkins and, 166; Keats and, 268n18, 272n33; and radical aestheticism, 3; Rossetti and, 180, 199; Shelley and, 41, 51, 53–54

Eliot, T. S., 38, 40, 57

Empson, William, 167–68

Endymion (Keats), 72

Engels, Friedrich, 38–39

"England in 1819" (Shelley), 35, 45–46

"The English Renaissance of Art" (Wilde), 2–3, 11–12, 38, 40, 70, 210–12, 223

enjambment, Hopkins and, 166–67

Enlightenment, 216–17, 296n13

epigrams, Wilde and, 217–18
Epipsychidion (Shelley), 32
ethics: Keats and, 67–102; and painting, 183, 187; Rossetti and, 203
event: aesthetic, 134; Agamben and, 160; Derrida and, 106, 117; Dickinson and, 105–42; Hopkins and, 159–60; Shelley and, 46–47, 64
excess, Hopkins and, 153–54
expenditure: Bataille on, 24–25, 213–14, 219–20, 256n43
extravagance: term, 212–13; Wilde and, 209–43
eyes: Bataille and, 298n27; Rossetti and, 185; Wilde and, 228. *See also* gaze

face: Levinas and, 264n36; Manet and, 186; Rossetti and, 175; Shelley and, 54–55
"The Fall of Hyperion" (Keats), 16, 86, 95–102
Fantin-Latour, Henri, 185
Farr, Judith, 113, 278n31
Felstiner, Paul, 283n30
feminist analysis: and Rossetti, 176–77, 179–81, 185, 189–90; and Wilde, 225, 297n26
Ferris, David, 155, 269n20
"A Few Maxims for the Instruction of the Overeducated" (Wilde), 213, 218
Fineman, Joel, 292n37
finger-pointing, 269n20; Keats and, 81–92
fire: Dickinson and, 105; Hopkins and, 158–65. *See also* kindling
first lines, Dickinson and, 107–10
"Five English Poets" (Rossetti), 171
flash, Benjamin and, 42, 44
"Flowers - Well - if anybody" (Dickinson), 124–26
Ford, Karen Jackson, 107, 128, 140, 274n7
Foucault, Michel, 216–17, 231, 269n19, 295n10, 296n13, 298n27, 298n29, 300n35
Francois, Anne-Lise, 106, 254n31, 273n2
Frankenstein (Mary Shelley), 14, 82–83
Freedgood, Elaine, 299n32, 299n34

Freedman, Jonathan, 176, 196, 292n35
Freinkel, Lisa, 177, 285n4
Freudian psychoanalysis, 50, 180–81, 225, 285n4
Fried, Michael, 20, 22, 182–83, 186, 194, 272n32, 287n17–18, 292n34
Frye, Northrop, 16–17, 232, 245n4, 255n40
Fussell, Paul, 151

Gagnier, Regina, 295n6, 298n26, 301n45
Gates, Barbara, 179
gaze: feminist analysis on, 177; Manet and, 185–86; Rossetti and, 185; Shelley and, 54–56, 63; Wilde and, 223, 225–29
genre, and radical aestheticism, 15–17
Géricault, Theodor, xvif, 21–25, 140–41
Giotto Painting Dante's Portrait (Rossetti), 170f, 172–73
"God's Grandeur" (Hopkins), 152–53
grace, 127, 282n26; and beauty, 133; Hopkins and, 147, 155, 158; and theology, 147–48
Graham, Jorie, 273n2
Greenberg, Clement, 181–82, 185, 287n16
Guillory, John, 7, 247n10, 249n14

"Hand and Soul" (Rossetti), 192
hands, Keats and, 71, 81–92
Harpham, Geoffrey Galt, 295n8
Hartman, Geoffrey, 258n8
Harries, Richard, 283n27
Hart, David Bentley, 153, 252n25, 257n4, 282n22
heart, Keats and, 87–88
"Heart's Haven" (Rossetti), 195
Hegel, G. W. F., 9, 172, 301n42
Heidegger, Martin, 57, 93, 113, 249n13
Hellas (Shelley), 46
"Henry Purcell" (Hopkins), 145
hermeneutics: de Man on, 121–22; Dickinson and, 124; Hopkins and, 161; Oberhaus and, 122–23
Hertz, Neil, 50, 164n31
Higgins, Lesley, 282n27
Higginson, Thomas, 13, 119, 254n30

history: Benjamin and, 41–42, 44, 57, 63–65; criticism and, 251n22; Keats on, 94; machine and, 118; Shelley and, 45–48, 57–65

Hogle, Jerrold, 12, 38, 253n27, 258n8, 258n9, 265n42

Holbein, Hans, 204

Hölderlin, Friedrich, 57, 283n32

Hollier, Denis, 24–25

Hopkins, Gerard Manley, 144*f*, 145–69, 243, 257n4; on Keats, 70–72; and radical aesthetics, 5, 12–13, 284n30

The House of Life (Rossetti), 174–75, 179, 192–206

Howard, Richard, 84–85

How They Saw Themselves (Rossetti), 199

Hunt, William Holman, 182, 187

Huysmans, J.-K., xii

Hyman, Erin Williams, 298n26

"Hymn to Intellectual Beauty" (Shelley), 10, 16, 30–34, 36–37, 43, 47, 257n4

"Hyperion" (Keats), 72, 80, 92–102, 243

hypotyposis, 6

ideology: Adorno on, 8; aesthetics and, 54; Althusser on, 251n21; de Man on, 6; Marxism and, 41; Shelley and, 31, 60

"I died for Beauty" (Dickinson), 126

indolence: Barthes on, 74–75; Keats and, 75–77, 101–2

inspiration, 286n9; Hopkins and, 147, 151, 159

interjections, Hopkins and, 150–51

"In the Artist's Studio" (Christina Rossetti), 180

"I saw no Way - The Heavens were stitched -" (Dickinson), 120–21, 130

"It might be easier" (Dickinson), 26

"I would not paint - a picture -" (Dickinson), 136–38, 278n34

Jackson, Virginia, 274n8, 274n9

Jacobs, Carol, 33–34, 52–53, 55

Jacobson, Eric, 263n27

Jakobson, Roman, 85, 232, 298n31

Jameson, Fredric, 250n19, 287n16

John the Baptist/Jokanaan, 214, 224, 226–28, 236, 300n37

Kant, Immanuel, 2, 6, 8, 216–17

Kaufman, Robert, 42, 261n22

Kaye, Richard A., 243

Keach, William, 251n22

Keats, John, 3, 66*f*, 67–102, 124, 126, 129, 137, 211, 243; and aesthetics, 10; and genre, 16; and radical aesthetics, 5; Wilde on, 12, 70, 214;

Kelly, Teresa, 268n18

kindling, 4–5, 29, 44; Keats and, 98, 101; Shelley and, 47–57, 264n28

Kirkland, Caroline, 119

kitsch, Hopkins and, 283n27

Klee, Paul, 41, 64–65

Koestenbaum, Wayne, 296n14

Krauss, Rosalind, 225–26

Krieger, Murray, 128–29, 135, 255n40, 276n30

"Kubla Khan" (Coleridge), 14

Lacan, Jacques, 20, 187–90, 192, 204–5, 225–26, 228, 231, 290n30

Laclau, Ernesto, 245n4

"The Lamp's Shrine" (Rossetti), 189

language: Coleridge on, 114; Dickinson and, 112–13; Hopkins and, 157; Keats and, 96–97; poetry and, 110; Wilde and, 231–37

"The Leaden Echo and the Golden Echo" (Hopkins), 155

Leavis, F. R., 38

Levinas, Emmanuel, 7, 247n11, 264n36

Levinson, Marjorie, 79, 268n17

"Like Eyes that looked on Wastes" (Dickinson), 104*f*, 108, 130, 143*f*, 278n31

"Lines on Seeing a Lock of Milton's Hair" (Keats), 268n16

literalism, Wilde and, 235

love: courtly, 188–89; Dickinson and, 141; Hopkins and, 169; Keats and, 76, 88–89; Lacan on, 188–90; Rossetti and, 171–206; Wilde and, 239, 242

"The Love-Letter" (Rossetti), 193, 197

"The Lovers' Walk" (Rossetti), 193–94, 197

"Lovesight" (Rossetti), 189, 191

"Love's Lovers" (Rossetti), 198

"Love's Testament" (Rossetti), 199, 201

Luke, 222
Lynch, David, 187
lyric, 255n40; Agamben on, 110, 178;
    Culler on, 87; Dickinson and, 107–8,
    114, 122–23; and lyricization, 15–16;
    Rossetti and, 177; Shelley and, 38;
    Wilde and, 223, 232

machine: Derrida and, 106; Dickinson
    and, 111–23, 133; term, 114–15; Wil-
    liams and, 114
Mallarmé, Stéphane, 254n34, 268n19
Manet, Édouard, 181–87, 288n23–24
Marsh, Jan, 177, 185, 288n23
Marx Aveling, Eleanor, 38, 41, 259n15
Marx, Karl, 8, 38; on aestheticism, 250n16
Marxism, 29; and aestheticism, 8; Benja-
    min and, 43; Shelley and, 35, 38–39
Matthew, 299n33, 300n37
McCole, John, 42–43
McDonagh, Enda, 281n18
McGann, Jerome, 177, 184, 201–2,
    288n24, 289n25
Medusa, 99; da Vinci and, 28f; Géricault
    and, xvif, 21–25; Shelley and, 47–57
melos, 232
metalepsis, 2, 114, 133
metaphors: Dickinson and, 114–15; Hop-
    kins and, 161; Wilde and, 234
metonymy, 228, 277n26, 297n19, 299n32
Meurent, Victorine, 186
"Mid-Rapture" (Rossetti), 194–95
Millais, John Everett, 182
Miller, J. Hillis, 147, 150–51
Millet, Kate, 297n26
Milton, John, 42, 215, 268n16
mirrors, 188; Rossetti and, 173, 180,
    192–94, 198, 205–6; Wilde and, 229
Mitchell, W. J. T., 52–53
Mnemosyne, 92–93, 95
modernity, Baudelaire and, 216
Moneta, 96–101
"The Monochord" (Rossetti), 199–202
monstrosity: Derrida on, 118–19, 275n20;
    Rossetti and, 196
"Mont Blanc" (Shelley), 32, 36–37, 129
Moreau, Gustave, xii, 208f

Mouffe, Chantal, 245n4
Moulton, Louise Chandler, 119
Mulvey, Laura, 177, 230
music: Bataille and, 220; Dickinson and,
    137–38; Frye and, 16; Hopkins and,
    145–46; Rossetti and, 199–202; Shelley
    and, 62–63; Wilde and, 236
"My Sister's Sleep" (Rossetti), 184

narcissism, 188; Rossetti and, 173, 198,
    203; Wilde and, 229
Nebel, Gerhard, 280n7
Nunokawa, Jeff, 228, 301n41
"Nuptial Sleep" (Rossetti), 183

Oberhaus, Dorothy Huff, 122–23,
    276n25, 277n26–27
"Ode: Intimations of Immortality from
    Recollections of Early Childhood"
    (Wordsworth), 191
"Ode on a Grecian Urn" (Keats), 3, 126,
    129
"Ode on Indolence" (Keats), 76–77
"Ode on Melancholy" (Keats), 72, 271n28
"Ode to a Nightingale" (Keats), 76
"Ode to the West Wind" (Shelley),
    47–48, 50
Olympia (Manet), 185–86
"On Life" (Shelley), 31, 36
"On Seeing the Elgin Marbles" (Keats),
    77–79, 89–90
"On Sitting Down to Read *King Lear*
    Once Again" (Keats), 67–69
"On the Grave of Keats" (Wilde), 70
"On the Medusa of Leonardo da Vinci
    in the Florentine Gallery" (Shelley),
    47–57, 129
Ovid, 173–74
"Ozymandias" (Shelley), 3, 51

P.A. (reviewer), 21–23
painting: *The Apparition*, xii; *The Beloved*,
    185–86, 207f; Bersani and, 91–92;
    David with the Head of Goliath, 91–92,
    103f; Dickinson and, 134–39; Fried
    and, 182–83, 186; *Giotto Painting
    Dante*, 170f, 172–73; Greenberg and,

181–87; Hopkins and, 146–47; Keats and, 89–92; Manet and, 181–87; *The Medusa*, 28f; *Olympia*, 185–86; Pre-Raphaelite, criticism of, 181–82, 187–92; *The Raft of the Medusa*, xvif, 21–25; Rossetti and, 170f, 172–75, 185–86, 198, 207f; *Salome dansant*, 208f; Shelley and, 48–56; *Toward the Blue Peninsula (For Emily Dickinson)*, 25–26, 27f; Zizek and, 189–92

Palmer, Michael, 39–41, 260n17, 292n33

Pater, Walter, 1–2, 15, 148–49; and Hopkins, 279n6; and Rossetti, 178, 193, 195–98; and Wilde, 211

Pearce, Lynn, 289n25

performativity, 280n9; Hopkins and, 150, 159; Rossetti and, 204; Wilde and, 217

Perseus, 52–53

personification: Dante and, 196; Rossetti and, 195–97

Petrarch, 177–78

Pfau, Thomas, 17, 251n20

phenomenality, 2, 255n37, 300n36; as auratic, 43

"Phrases and Philosophies for the Use of the Young" (Wilde), 217

The Picture of Dorian Gray (Wilde), 211–13, 215, 217–18, 294n4, 295n12

"Pied Beauty" (Hopkins), 153, 281n18

Pippen, Robert, 183, 287n18

Plant, Robert, 234

Poe, Edgar Allan, 12

poetics: de Man on, 121–22; Dickinson and, 106, 108, 114–18, 120–21, 124; Hopkins and, 145; Rossetti and, 178; Williams and, 114

poetry: Bataille and, 220; Dickinson and, 106, 139–42; Keats and, 90, 95–97; and language, 110; and radical aestheticism, 15, 17; Rossetti and, 183–84, 198

pointing, 269n20; Keats and, 81–92

politics: Shelley and, 29, 35–47, 57–65

Pollock, Griselda, 179

polyptoton, 195

Porter, David, 106, 115, 140

"The Portrait" (Rossetti), 180, 191–92

Pound, Ezra, 40

Powell, Kerry, 296n17, 300n38

Pre-Raphaelite Brotherhood, 12, 172, 185; criticism of, 181, 187–92, 290n27; and women, 176–81, 187–89

Prettejohn, Elizabeth, 182

project, 209–10; definition of, 17–19; Dickinson and, 106, 209; Hopkins and, 146; Keats and, 68–69, 72, 209; Rossetti and, 174, 186, 192; Shelley and, 29, 35–47, 63; Wilde and, 209–14

Prometheus Unbound (Shelley), 35

pronouns, Dickinson and, 109, 132, 136

prosopopoeia, 37, 83, 270n23, 271n27

psychoanalysis, 50, 180–81, 225, 285n4; Lacanian, 187–92

Purcell, Henry, 145–46

"Quantum Mutata" (Wilde), 215

Raab, Josef, 112–13, 274n15

radical, term, xi

radical aestheticism, 302n48; conditions for, 3–4; Dickinson and, 106–7, 139–42; Hopkins and, 148, 157–58, 162–69; Keats and, 70, 92–102; nature of, 1–6, 210; Rossetti and, 171–72, 193, 202–6; Shelley and, 47–57, 63–65; term, xi–xii, 1, 11; Wilde and, 223, 230, 239–40, 302n48

The Raft of the Medusa (Géricault), xvif, 21–25

Rajan, Balachandra, 272n40

Rancière, Jacques, 259n15, 262n26, on the aesthetic regime, 252n26

reading, 21, 81; de Man and, 254n37, 270n27; Keats on, 67–70, 94–95; Stewart and, 157; Terada and, 300n36; Wilde and, 240

Redfield, Marc, 2, 251n20, 262n24

religion. *See* theology

rhetorical figures: allegory, 196, 201; analogies, 137; apostrophe, 86–87, 90; caesuras, 164; catachresis, 83, 140, 265n42, 270n23; chiasmus, 197–200, 202, 206, 242, 287n13, 293n38; hypotyposis, 6; metalepsis, 2, 114, 133; metaphors, 114–15, 161, 234; metonymy, 228,

rhetorical figures (*continued*)
  233, 277n26, 297n19, 299n32, 299n34;
  personification, 194–97; polyptoton,
  195; prosopopoeia, 37, 83, 270n23,
  271n27; similes, 33–34, 195, 232–34;
  Wilde and, 299n32
Richards, I. A., 157
Ricks, Christopher, 268n15, 272n39
Ricoeur, Paul, 279n4
Riede, David, 173, 287n12
Romanticism, 10–21, 171; aura and, 42;
  Dickinson and, 110; politics and, 35;
  Wilde and, 210, 222, 243
Rossetti, Christina, 180, 187
Rossetti, Dante Gabriel, 107, 170*f*,
  171–206, 207*f*, *243*; criticism of, 172,
  181–87; Wilde on, 12
Rossetti, William Michael, 199, 202–3
Rousseau, Jean-Jacques, 60–63

sacred, sacrifice: Bataille on, 238–39;
  Keats and, 88, 90; Wilde and, 221,
  235–39, 242, 299n33
La Sainte Courtisane (Wilde), 241–43
*Salomé dansant (Salomé Dancing Before
  Herod)* (Moreau), 208*f*
Salomé (Wilde), 15–17, 223–40
*Say Goodbye, Catullus, to the Shores of Asia
  Minor* (Twombly), 75
Schelling, F. W. J., 2
Schiller, Friedrich, 1–2, 6, 190–91,
  291n31
semblance: Lacan on, 190; Rossetti and,
  177–78, 191–92, 198; term, 291n32
Severn, Joseph, 66*f*
Shakespeare, William, 67–68, 281n14,
  285n4, 292n37
Shaviro, Steven, 231
Shelley, Mary, 14
Shelley, Percy Bysshe, xi, 3, 29–65, 129,
  243; and aestheticism, 10; Benjamin
  and, 261n20; and genre, 15–16; and
  radical aestheticism, 4–5; and trou-
  badours, 110; Wilde and, 12, 28, 214,
  258n11
Sherman, Cindy, 225
Shoptaw, John, 274n14

Siddal, Elizabeth, 176, 179–80, 203
sighs: Hopkins and, 145–58, 160, 163;
  Shakespeare and, 281n14
skepticism: Derrida on, 265n38; Dickinson and, 111
Sleep and Poetry (Keats), 68–69, 72–73, 90
Socrates, 60
sonnets: Dickinson and, 125; Hopkins
  and, 150, 162–63, 165–69; Keats
  and, 79; Rossetti and, 172, 174–75,
  192–206; Shakespeare and, 292n37;
  Shelley and, 46
"The Soul of Man Under Socialism"
  (Wilde), 211
spelling, Shelley and, 29–35, 44, 47,
  57–65; Dickinson and, 124–25; Hopkins and, 157; and politics, 39; Rossetti
  and, 175; Wilde and, 236
"Spelt from Sybil's Leaves" (Hopkins),
  150, 158
Sperry, Stuart, 76, 78, 90
Spivak, Gayatri, 285n7, 289n26
Sprinker, Michael, 157, 162, 251n21,
  279n3
sprung rhythm, Hopkins and, 150–51,
  166
"St. Alphonsus Rodriguez" (Hopkins), 149
Stein, Richard, 198, 200–201
Stewart, Garrett, 153, 157
Stoddard, Richard Henry, 119
Stoekl, Allan, 256n43
Stonum, Gary Lee, 13, 110, 115–16,
  121–22
"The Stream's Secret" (Rossetti), 195
strength: Dickinson and, 140; Keats and,
  71–73, 90–94, 99
stress, Hopkins and, 158–65
structuralism, 118
sublime: Dickinson and, 120–21; Rossetti
  and, 194; Shelley and, 37
superficiality: Barthes and, 85; Pre-
  Raphaelites and, 181–82; Rossetti and,
  171–206; term, 172–73
"A Superscription" (Rossetti), 202–6
Swann, Karen, 266n5, 268n16
Swinburne, Algernon, 183
Symons, Arthur, 240

synaesthesia: and aesthetic experience, 255n37; and auratic experience, 154–55; Dickinson and, 128; Shelley and, 62–63; Wilde and, 232

taste, Hopkins and, 147
Terada, Rei, 246n7, 272n37, 300n36
"That Nature is a Heraclitean Fire and of the comfort of the Resurrection" (Hopkins), 149, 163–65
theatricality: Barthes and, 78; Fried on, 182–83; Hopkins and, 168; Keats and, 89; Rossetti and, 183–84, 194–95; Wilde and, 217, 223–40
theology: Dickinson and, 111, 122–23; Hopkins and, 145–69; Rossetti and, 184; Scotist, 152–54, 156–57, 159, 280n8; Shelley and, 58; von Balthasar on, 248n12, 279n2; Wilde and, 215–23, 236–39, 241–42
"The thought beneath so slight a film -" (Dickinson), 128
"The Zeroes taught Us - Phosphorus -" (Dickinson), 105
"This living hand" (Keats), 81–92, 271n28
"This was a Poet" (Dickinson), 132–34
Thomas Aquinas, 280n8
Thompson, Maurice, 119
threats: Keats and, 81–92, 96; nature of, 83
titles, absence of, Dickinson and, 113–14
"To Haydon" (Keats), 78–79
"To pile like Thunder to it's close" (Dickinson), 139–42
"To tell the Beauty would decrease" (Dickinson), 124
"To the Reader of The House of Life" (Rossetti), 174
Toward the Blue Peninsula (For Emily Dickinson) (Cornell), 25–26, 27f
"To what serves mortal beauty?" (Hopkins), 155
"To Wordsworth" (Shelley), 215
tragedy, Wilde and, 223
"Transfigured Life" (Rossetti), 199
translation, 285n7; Rossetti and, 177–78
The Triumph of Life (Shelley), xi, 10, 15–16, 31, 42–43, 57–65, 106, 265n42

troubadours, 110, 113
turning away, 19–22; Hopkins and, 146–48, 162; Keats and, 97; Wilde and, 240–43
Twombly, Cy, 74–75, 267n11, 268n19

utmost, Rossetti and, 193–94, 197

vacancy, vacating: Shelley and, 31–32, 45–46
vantage point, Wilde and, 211, 215, 218, 223, 235, 240
veiling, Dickinson and, 126–28, 131; Shelley and, 59
verse, term, 168–69
Vickers, Nancy, 177
vitality, vital tendency, 15, 252n26; Keats and, 70; Shelley and, 29, 36–37; Wilde on, 11, 29, 210, 214–15
La Vita Nuova (Dante Alighieri), 177, 195
von Balthasar, Hans Urs, 7, 20, 153, 248n12, 279n2, 282n26, 283n32

Wang, Orrin N.C., 265n41
Ward, Graham, 299n33
Warminski, Andrzej, 250n18, 254n37
Wasserman, Earl, 36
Watson, J. R., 166
weakness: Dickinson and, 139; Keats and, 70–81, 91–92, 101–2; Shelley and, 71
Weisbuch, Robert, 110
Wetherby, Harold, 184
White, Deborah Elise, 264n28
Wilde, Oscar, 209–43; and aestheticism, xii, 2–3, 9; and genre, 16; and Keats, 12, 70, 214–15; and Romanticism, 11–13; and Pater, 211; and Shelley, 12, 28–29, 38, 40, 214–15, 221–22, 258n11
Williams, William Carlos, 114
"The Windhover" (Hopkins), 165–69
The Witch of Atlas (Shelley), 256n2
Wolfson, Susan, 84, 89, 271n28
women: Lacanian analysis and, 187–89; Rossetti and, 176–81
Wordsworth, William, 10, 13–14, 191, 215, 291n31

The Wreck of the Deutschland (Hopkins),
146, 148, 158–62
Wuthering Heights (Brontë), 14–15

Yeats, William Butler, 151
"Youth's Antiphony" (Rossetti), 192

zeroes, zeroing: Dickinson and, 105–6,
108, 113–17, 121, 123, 132, 136, 139,
142
Žižek, Slavoj, 20, 187–89, 192, 205,
290n27